Political Thought in the United States

Edited by Lyman Tower Sargent

Political Thought in the United States

✳ ✳ ✳

A Documentary History

New York University Press

New York and London

Every effort was made to reach the copyright holders of the documents included herein.
Any oversights will be corrected in subsequent reprints.

NEW YORK UNIVERSITY PRESS
New York and London

Copyright © 1997 by New York University
All rights reserved

Library of Congress Cataloging-in-Publication Data
Political thought in the United States : a documentary history /
edited by Lyman Tower Sargent.
p. cm.
Includes index.
ISBN 0-8147-8047-4 (cloth : alk. pap.).—ISBN 0-8147-8048-2
(pbk. : alk. pap.)
1. Political science—United States—History—Sources.
2. Minorities—United States—Political activity—History—Sources.
I. Sargent, Lyman Tower, 1940–   .
JA84.U5P624 1997
320.5'0973—dc21   97-4664
                   CIP

New York University Press books are printed on acid-free paper,
and their binding materials are chosen for strength and durability.

Manufactured in the United States of America

10 9 8 7 6 5 4 3 2 1

To
Evan, Jennifer, Ian, and Kieran

Contents

5. The New Nation, 1790–1840

Preface

American political thought has a rich and varied history, but that history is not readily available to the contemporary reader. Rather than writing treatises, American political thinkers have written newspaper articles, laws, legal decisions, novels, short stories, and songs, given speeches, and developed constitutions. As a result, no set of books reflects their thought. There is a relatively familiar mainstream that most educated people could recite. It consists of the basic documents of the American Revolution and the constitutional period—leaving out the opponents of the Constitution; a few legal cases such as *Brown* v. *Board of Education of Topeka;* a few classic essays such as Henry David Thoreau's "Civil Disobedience"; documents such as the Emancipation Proclamation; a few critiques of industrialism (probably Edward Bellamy's *Looking Backward*); and a few twentieth-century items, mostly centering around the New Deal and its opponents. The reader will find all of that here, but there is much more. This book samples the wide range of the reality of American political thought. Previous compilations have tended to ignore North American Indians, African Americans, women, ethnic and religious minorities, and radical and reactionary thought, all of which have contributed to the richness of the American experience. Therefore, I have included minority as well as mainstream thought as it unfolded chronologically.

It is important for us to recognize that all the components of the rich mosaic that is American thought have never been and are not now given equal weight by thinkers, politicians, or the citizenry. Most people are now aware that there have always been minorities who have been excluded from the political process in the United States. It is also essential for us to learn that these peoples have expressed their views throughout American history. It is equally important that we not pretend that the so-called "melting pot" actually melted the components into any whole. If one is to use a metaphor, "tossed salad" is a much better one than "melting pot" because it recognizes that the component parts remain as distinguishable elements in the whole.

The voices of African Americans, Indians, women, the poor, and other excluded groups were treated as "problems" rather than contributors. They were rarely listened to outside of their own groups, except perhaps by a few forward-looking supporters. We falsify our own history and their voices if we forget the context of prejudice and suppression within which they spoke and wrote. As

America gradually includes the previously excluded, it is important that their voices are heard in their own context rather than just in the dominant culture's.

In my brief notes and connecting narratives I provide a context to help the reader understand why certain issues were particularly important when they were. Where I think that a text can stand on its own, I have allowed it to do so. Therefore, on the whole, my comments are more extensive in the earlier period and less so as the present is approached. The first chapter sets the stage and provides excerpts from some texts that were influential later.

I have included enough of each selection so that the reader can see both the conclusions drawn and how the arguments were made. Different time periods produced different modes of argumentation. The material from Puritan New England reads very differently even from the material of the late eighteenth century, let alone the nineteenth or twentieth centuries.

Many aspects of American political thought are currently controversial. I have not consciously favored any side in these disputes. My main concern has been to provide documentation that shows the richness of political thought in the United States at any given time in its history.

Along with the subsidiary themes that develop from time to time, two main themes emerge in this book: the relationship between the included and the excluded and, sometimes part of the same theme, the location of power in the American system. From the earliest times to the present, these two themes have appeared in American political discourse. The locus of power has long been recognized as central to the history of political thought, but I have enriched the normal presentation by including those who go beyond the normal federal government-state governments dichotomy to include those who insist that power should be in the hands of the citizens rather than in the hands of elected officials, or, what is a different way of putting the same point, that elected officials should be kept on a very short leash indeed.

The issue of the included and the excluded—or, as it is more traditionally put, majority versus minority rights—has been a primary concern of democratic theory from the seventeenth century to the present, and American contributions to this debate are among the most important in the history of political thought.

Both of these items are part of contemporary political debate in the United States and much of the rest of the world. Hence, a text like this one that allows us to see the arguments as they occurred throughout the U.S. history can enrich our understanding of contemporary politics and improve our ability, as citizens, to participate in the decisions that are currently being made about our own futures and those of our children and grandchildren.

Acknowledgments

I have had a great deal of help in compiling this book, and I wish to thank a number of research assistants, particularly Ellen Braverman, Carla Cox, Jennifer Horan, Stacy Tipp, and Lisa A. Raskas. In addition, James A. Clifton suggested some of the selections regarding American Indians and, early in the process of developing the book, Mary T. Weiler suggested some of the selections regarding the history of the various women's movements in American history. The office staff of the Department of Political Science at the University of Missouri-St. Louis were continuously helpful, and I particularly wish to thank Jan Frantzen and Lana Vierdag. The reference librarians at the University of Missouri-St. Louis Thomas Jefferson Library came to my rescue with some last-minute information, for which they and e-mail have my heartfelt thanks. Praise Wong typed the manuscript on a very tight schedule.

CHAPTER I

The Intellectual and Cultural Background

✳ ✳ ✳

The Perceptions of the Explorers and Early Settlers

The seventeenth-century English settlers in North America were quickly followed by people from the European continent and those from Africa, who generally did not come by choice.[1] The settlers brought with them political and religious beliefs and a set of expectations about what they would find. Previous explorers had written extensively about both the land and the inhabitants of the Americas, and these descriptions helped shape the settlers' understanding of the New World. For example, the early explorers regularly referred to the New World as an earthly paradise or Eden. A letter traditionally attributed to Amerigo Vespucci (1451–1512) says, "Sometimes I was so wonderstruck by the fragrant smells of the herbs and flowers and the savor of the fruits and the roots that I fancied myself near the Terrestrial Paradise."[2] Christopher Columbus (1451–1506) believed he was near the earthly paradise, and Peter Martyr (1457–1526) directly compared Hispaniola (the island that today contains the countries of the Dominican Republic and Haiti) to the earthly paradise.

Similar imagery was used in North America. As one scholar put it, during colonization "people believed that the time had come to renew the Christian world, and the true renewal was the return to the earthly paradise."[3] One of the most widely quoted statements, taken from a report on a trip to Virginia in 1584–85, said the land was "so full of grapes as the very beating and surge of the sea overflowed them, of which we found such plenty, as well there as in all places else, both on the sand and on the green soils on the hills as in the plains, as well on every little shrub as also climbing towards the tops of the high cedars, that I think in all the world the like abundance is not to be found."[4]

The images regarding the indigenous inhabitants of the Americas were much more varied and controversial, and the debates they aroused among Europeans included broad questions such as the nature of the human race and civilization and narrower questions such as the appropriateness of slavery. If the indigenous peoples could be defined as animals rather than humans, the question of slavery did not arise. In addition, an earthly paradise populated by Indians living without Christianity proved a serious problem for Christians. How could these beings be good without Christianity? This became an even more fundamental problem as it became apparent that contact with the *conquistadores* was corrupting the Indian.

The treatment of Indians by the *conquistadores*, and by many of the priests, was based on the assumption that their humanity was borderline at best. About 1517 Francisco Ruiz, bishop of Avila, had written, "Indians are malicious people who are able to think up ways to harm Christians, but they are not capable of natural judgment or of receiving the faith, nor do they have the other virtues required for their conversion and salvation . . . and they need just as a horse or beast does, to be directed and governed by Christians who treat them well and not cruelly."[5]

The complex of attitudes involved and the difficulty Europe had integrating the New World into the Old have been examined by a number of scholars, and the general outlines of the experience are fairly well known. The first problem was technically settled in 1537, when Pope Paul III declared the Indian was human. In *Sublimus Deus*, he wrote,

> We . . . consider . . . that the Indians are truly men and that they are not only capable of understanding the catholic faith but, according to our information, they desire exceedingly to receive it. Desiring to provide ample remedy for these evils, We define and declare . . . that, notwithstanding whatever may have been or may be said to the contrary, the said Indians and all other people who may later be discovered by Christians, are by no means to be deprived of their liberty or the possession of their property, even though they be outside the faith of Jesus Christ; and that they may and should, freely and legitimately, enjoy their liberty and the possession of their property; nor should they be in any way enslaved; should the contrary happen it shall be null and of no effect.[6]

But this declaration did little to affect the behavior of those intent on exploitation. A description of the indigenous peoples, attributed to Vespucci, illustrates the problems: "Having no laws and no religious faith, they live according to nature. They understand nothing of the immortality of the soul. There is no possession of private property among them, for everything is in common. They have no boundaries of kingdom or province. They have no king, nor do they obey anyone. Each one is his own master. There is no administration of justice, which is unnecessary to them, because in their code no one rules."[7] In 1502 this violated every canon of what it meant to be civilized. Gold and land provided what little justification was needed for the slaughter that followed, but the papal definition of the Indians as human meant that in South America they were accorded a legal status that they were never given in North America.

However, for many it was not that simple. In the first place, further contact and more accurate information dispelled much of the early image. As J. H. Elliott notes, "By living in polities and regulating their lives in accordance with fixed rules and regulations—however defective these may have been from a Christian standpoint—large numbers of North American Indians had satisfied the Aristotelian criteria for acceptance as political and social beings."[8] Also, the morals of the *conquistadores* did not stand up in comparison with the morals of the indigenous peoples. The *conquistadores* had the supposed advantage of being Christian, but it was obvious that the Indians were being corrupted by their contacts with their conquerors. This was not an acceptable interpretation for the time; Christian had to be better than non-Christian, white better than colored, conqueror better than conquered, even if evidence pointed the other way. In fact, the debate did not stop but was continued among the North American settlers.

This debate also paralleled the growth of Reformation theology, which, with its emphasis on human depravity, gave further credence to the position of those who wished to think of the Indians as less than human. Roy Harvey Pearce has argued that "American Indians were everywhere found to be, simply enough, men who were not men, who were religiously and politically incomplete."[9] In 1609, Richard Johnson noted that Virginia "is inhabited with wild and savage people, that live and lie up and downe in troupes like heards of Deare in a Forrest: they have no law but nature, their apparell skinnes of beasts, but most go naked: the better sort have houses, but poore ones, they have no Arts or Sciences, yet they live under superior command such as it is, they are generally very loving and gentle and doe entertaine and relieue our people with great kindness."[10] The potential settler was being told the native peoples were like animals and therefore were no impediment to settlement. After all, it was also important that the Indians not be seen as too fierce; no one wishes certain death as a result of his or her good works.

The Puritans rejoiced at God's showing them His favor by killing off the Indians with smallpox and were more than ready to help Him along. The land was intended by God for the Puritans; the Indians were simply in the way. On the other hand, Roger Williams reported an Indian saying, "We wearne no Clothes, have many gods, And yet our sinnes are lesse: You are Barbarians, Pagans wild, *Your* Land's the Wilderness."[11] And there were others, most notably John Eliot, the "Apostle to the Indians," who saw in them something much more than mere animals. The infamous Thomas Morton of Merry Mount also had a more positive view of the native peoples. He wrote, "They love not to bee cumbered with many utensilles, and although every proprietor knowes his owne, yet all things (so long as they will last), are used in common amongest them: A bisket cake given to one; that one breakes it equally into so many parts, as there be persons in his company, and distributes it. Platoes Commonwealth is so much practised by these people." [12] But the dominant position was that the Indians were less than human. As their numbers decreased, the Indians became more noble until they were virtually eliminated. Then, hardly a threat, the process of romanticizing them could begin.

The Political Thought of the Indigenous Peoples

The indigenous peoples had their own political ideas. Indigenous peoples are rarely mentioned in treatments of American political thought because it has been believed that their thought and practice had no influence on the dominant culture. A blend of racism and the difficulty of understanding the political thought of cultures that left few written records meant that indigenous peoples have simply been ignored. In addition, the rigid borders between academic disciplines meant that relevant information from anthropology was not known by political theorists. Today, inspired by our growing concern to understand minorities and scholarship suggesting that they influenced the dominant culture, we know that indigenous peoples had coherent political cultures based on sets of ideas that, while presented differently, included many concepts congruent with those of the dominant culture.

Still, problems remain. First, although there are similarities among them, the many indigenous peoples inhabiting the area now known as the United States differed in their political ideas and practices. Scholarship has not advanced far enough to allow these differences to be treated adequately. Therefore, in this section, I emphasize the League of Five Nations. The practices of the League influenced Benjamin Franklin (1706–90), who may, in turn, have been instrumental in bringing some of those practices—such as federalism—into the U.S. political system.

The selections that follow serve as an introduction to texts found throughout the rest of the book from Native American Indians from various times and places that, together, demonstrate a coherent world view. Some chapters also include items that reflect the dominant culture's treatment of indigenous peoples.

The selections in this section include parts of "The Great Law of Peace" and "The Formation of the Ho-de-no-sau-ne or League of the Five Nations." These two excerpts show the traditional political system of the indigenous peoples of the northeastern United States as interpreted by contemporary Mohawks. The basic points that emerge are that the political leaders were elected through a federal system and kept their power through continued acceptance by the people.

Aren Akweks

The Formation of the Ho-de-no-sau-ne
or League of the Five Nations

Deganahwideh said, "In every nation there are wise and pure men. These men should be appointed to become chiefs of their people. They will be the advisers of their people and will make any new laws that will be needful. They are to be selected by the Clan mothers but must have the good will of the entire clan."

"When these chiefs are selected they will be crowned with deer antlers, emblems of friendship," said Deganahwideh.

The Clan Mothers of the People of Flint (Mohawks) brought forward

nine chiefs and

one war-chief

They, the chiefs, were of the clans, Bear, Wolf and Turtle.

The Clan Mothers of the People of the Upright Stone (Oneidas) brought forward

Nine chiefs and

One war-chief.

They, the chiefs, were of the clans, Bear, Wolf and Turtle.

The Clan Mothers of the People of the Hills (Onondagas) brought forward

Fourteen chiefs and

One war-chief.

They were of the clans, Turtle, Snipe, Bear, Deer, Wolf and Ball.

The Clan Mothers of the People of the Great Pipe or the People of the Mucklands (Cayugas) brought forward

Ten chiefs and

one war-chief.

They were of the Clans, Heron, Deer, Turtle, Bear and Snipe.

The Clan Mothers of the People of the Great Hill (Senecas) brought forward

Eight chiefs and

one war-chief.

They were of the Clans, Bear, Snipe, Turtle, Wolf and Eagle.

Deganahwideh then said to the chiefs, "I place upon your heads, deer antlers as emblems of your power. Your old names are taken away and new names, which have more power, are given to you. Your old clothes are removed and new robes are given to you. Your patience must be very great, seven thumbs thick. You must walk and work in unity. Never think of your own interests but work to benefit the people and those yet unborn. All of your power comes from the Great Peace and you must pledge yourselves to it."

The fifty chiefs of the Mohawks, Oneidas, Onondagas, Cayugas and Senecas, each gave to Deganahwideh a string of lake-shell wampum as a pledge of truth and loyalty to the Laws of the Great Peace.

Deganahwideh said that a chief must always speak the truth, that his tongue must be straight.

He, a chief, must have a big heart (kind, considerate, generous) and must always consider the welfare of his people. He must give freely of what he owns to his people, especially the poor and less fortunate.

He must always be ready to help those of his people who are in want or need. His aid must be given willingly and he must receive no pay or reward for his services.

He must even be willing to give away his own personal belongings, even skins and meat, if it will better his people by doing so.

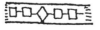

A Chief must never forget the Creator of Mankind. He must ever ask God for help and assistance.

He must always remember the Laws of the Great Peace. They must come before every other thought.

The chiefs of the Five Nations must council and work together. They must work in unity and not try to do things separately, less their nation become divided. Any great move, step or act must have the consent of all of the Five Nations.

A chief must be very wise, very patient. He must never let his temper get the best of him, less he not be able to cast good judgment. His skin must be seven thumbs thick.

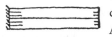

Always must he remember that the Great Confederacy was organized for peace. Peace and friendship among all people was the main aim of the Great Law.

The Mohawks, Oneidas, Onondagas, Cayugas and Senecas are as one nation or people. They are bound together. As one people they must work together. Only in unity will there be strength.

The Head Men must always remember that other nations are to be invited to take shelter beneath the Tree of Long Leaves. The eagle on the top of the Tree will guard and watch all peoples who wish to rest under the Tree.

Source: Akwesasne Counselor Organization, St. Regis Mohawk Reservation, Hogansburg, New York.

The Great Law of Peace

8

The Firekeepers shall formally open and close all councils of the statesmen of the League, they shall pass upon all matters deliberated upon by the two sides, and render their decision.

Every Onondaga statesmen (or his deputy) must be present at every Council of the League, and must agree with the majority without unwarrantable dissent, so that a unanimous decision may be rendered.

If Atotarho or any of his cousin statesmen are absent from a Council of the League, any other Firekeeper may open and close the Council, but the Firekeepers present may not give any decisions, unless the matter is of small importance. . . .

10

In all cases, the procedure must be as follows: when the Mohawk and Seneca statesmen have unanimously agreed upon a question, they shall report their decision to the Cayuga and Oneida statesmen, who shall deliberate upon the question and report a unanimous decision to the Mohawk statesmen. The Mohawk statesmen will then report the standing of the case to the Firekeepers, who shall render a decision as they see fit in case of a disagreement by the two bodies, or confirm the decisions of the two bodies if they are identical. The Firekeepers shall then report their decision to the Mohawk statesmen who shall announce it to the open Council. . . .

13

No chief shall ask a question of the body of chiefs of the League when they are discussing a case, question, or proposition. He may only deliberate in a low tone with the separate body of which he is a member. . . .

RIGHTS,
DUTIES,
QUALIFICATIONS
OF THE STATESMEN

17

A bunch of certain shell (wampum) strings each two spans in length shall be given to each of the female families in which the chieftain titles are vested. The right of bestowing the titles shall be hereditary of the family of females legally possessing the bunch of shell strings, and the strings shall be the token that the females of the family have the ownership to the Chieftainship title for all time to come, subject to certain restrictions mentioned here.

18

If any chief of the League neglects or refuses to attend the Council of the League, the other chiefs of the nation of which he is a member shall require their War Chief to request the female sponsors of the chief so guilty of neglecting his duties to demand his attendance at the Council. If he refuses, the women holding the title shall immediately select another candidate for the title.

No chief shall be asked more than once to attend the Council of the League.

19

If at any time it shall be apparent that a chief of the League has not in mind the welfare of the people, or disobeys the rules of the Great Law, the men or the women of the League, or both jointly, shall come to the Council and scold the erring chief through his war chief. If the complaint of the people through the war chief is not heeded, on the first occasion, it shall be uttered again, and then if no attention is given, a third complaint and a warning shall be given. If the chief is still disobedient, the matter shall go to the Council of War Chiefs. The War Chiefs shall then take away the title of the erring chief by order of the women in whom the title is vested. When the chief is deposed, the women shall notify the chiefs of the League through their war chief and the chiefs of the League shall sanction the act. The women will then select another of their sons as a candidate and the chiefs shall elect him. . . .

25

If a chief of the League should seek to establish any authority independent of the jurisdiction of the League of the Great Peace, which is the Five Nations, he shall be warned three times in open Council, first by the women relatives, second by the men relatives, and finally by the chiefs of the Nation to which he belongs.

If the offending chief is still persistent, he shall be dismissed by the war chief of his nation for refusing to conform to the laws of the Great Peace. His Nation shall then install the candidate nominated by the female name holders of his family. . . .

44

The lineal descent of the people of the Five Nations shall run in the female line. Women shall be considered the progenitors of the Nation. They shall own the land, and the soil. Men and women shall follow the status of their mothers.

Source: The Great Law of Peace of the People of the Longhouse. Roosevelt, N.Y.: White Roots of Peace, n.d.

The Religious Background

American mythology has it that the first European settlers came for freedom of religion. A more accurate formulation would be that one of the motivations for many of the early settlers was the freedom to practice their particular religious beliefs. There was little notion of toleration of other beliefs.

The early settlers were mostly Protestants (Maryland was first settled by Roman Catholics, as were Florida and California) and within Protestantism, mostly Calvinists, meaning that they had been strongly influenced by the teachings of John Calvin (1509–64). Calvin taught that the kingdoms of grace and power should be combined with the latter in a subordinate position. This means that religious and political authority should be unified, not separate, and that the religion should predominate. This form of government is known as the-

ocracy (theo = God; cracy = rule by) in which the religious authorities are the representatives of God.

Other settlers came from a religious background that is sometimes called Pietist or Separatist or, more generally, Heterodox Protestant. These people, the most important representatives in the colonies being the Quakers or Society of Friends in Pennsylvania, derived from the Anabaptist movements of central Europe. Anabaptists (the name reflects their rejection of infant baptism) believe in a rigid separation of church and state, stress the importance of the individual conscience, and conceive of the church as a voluntary association of believers. Groups with Anabaptist roots, many of them practicing community of goods, flourished in North America in the late eighteenth century and throughout the nineteenth century, with some still in existence today.

New England was the center of Puritan thought "in that it was founded largely for the purpose of trying an experiment in Christian living," [13] and Puritan theology had a social dimension. "For the English Puritans, the basic core of this new revelation was that God wanted men to live in a simple relationship with Him. God wanted man to form autonomous congregations as the basic theological and social unit for the purpose of worshipping Him." [14] The Puritans were convinced "that the final drama of moral regeneration and universal salvation was to begin here, with them." [15] This image of themselves and the New World is basic to an understanding of the ambivalent attitude the Puritans, as Calvinists, express regarding the development of social order. On the one hand, Cotton Mather could write, "There are many Arguments to persuade us, That our Glorious Lord, will have an Holy City in America; A City, the Streets whereof will be Pure Gold." [16] And Charles Sanford can say, "The most popular doctrine in the colonies was that America had been singled out, from all the nations of the earth, as the site of the Second Coming; and that the millennium of the saints, while essentially spiritual in nature, would be accompanied by a paradisiac transformation of the earth as the outward symbol of their inward state." [17] The evidence is compelling that the Puritans believed, and many later colonists continued to believe, they were part of the founding of a Holy Commonwealth by God's will and under His direction. On the other hand, the Puritans believed in the sinful nature of the human race. As H. Richard Niebuhr notes, seventeenth-century Protestants "were for the most part thoroughly convinced that mankind had somehow been corrupted; they knew that the order of glory had not yet been established; they were pilgrims all who did not expect to be satisfied in the time of their pilgrimage." [18]

The Puritans had a fairly thoroughly and consistently worked out social theory based in part on Calvin's ideal, developed in Geneva, of a theocracy in which the church leaders effectively established public policy, in part on their experiences in England and Holland, and in part on the settlers' responses to the specific problems of wilderness America. All these ideas and events were filtered through minds imbued with debates on the proper role of the state, particularly with regard to religion.

But the Puritans' social theory had to incorporate the obdurate material of the sinful human being. It was this attitude that marked a new departure in the ambivalence to utopia. If God chooses, He may give us utopia; but God has chosen to give us struggle against an at best recalcitrant, at worst overtly hostile environment. Still, God gave the Puritans a New World to tame, with which to create what they could. And they believed God had given them a truth that had been hidden from humankind until it was revealed to them. They could, thus, live better, more godly lives if they could find somewhere to live.

The Puritans of Plymouth and Massachusetts Bay contributed to American thought a fundamental ambivalence regarding the possibilities of life in this world. The human race, being sinful, could not escape the wrath of God, but the Puritans, chosen by God, could hope for salvation both individually and collectively. Sacvan Bercovitch, writing about the American jeremiad (sermons of exhortation), said, "The purpose of their jeremiads was to direct an imperiled people of God toward the fulfillment of their destiny, to guide them individually toward salvation, and collectively toward the American city of God." [19]

The Philosophic Background

Later settlers were also influenced by secular beliefs about society. A number of streams of thought converged in the intellectual development of the colonies in the period prior to the American Revolution. Five particular traditions contributed to the ways of thought of the colonists, namely, the classics, particularly Roman literature, enlightenment rationalism, the English common law tradition, covenant theology, and the radical social and political thought of the English Civil War and the Commonwealth.

The classics were widely but not deeply known in early America. The English common or customary law provided forms of adjudication and sets of legal principles such as trial by jury, a system of courts, and freedom from arbitrary imprisonment. Most importantly, it included the idea of the supremacy of the law, thereby limiting the arbitrary power of political authority. In the United States this ultimately led to the power of the courts to declare legislation unconstitutional.

From these sources Americans came to focus on the problem of the potential conflict between power and liberty. As it developed, this conflict emphasized the possibility of creating virtuous citizens in light of the known ability of power to corrupt. Put this way, this is a problem that the New England Puritans could easily understand, and in this issue a number of strands of colonial thought came together.

From the Civil War and Commonwealth came some lesser-known but even more influential figures. James Harrington (1611–77) was frequently cited during the Constitutional Convention. Harrington was important for his sense that a stable government must represent the varied interests of a society.

James Harrington
The Commonwealth of Oceana

By what hath been shown in reason and experience it may appear that though commonwealths in general be governments of the senate proposing, the people resolving, and the magistracy executing, yet some are not so good at these orders as others, through some impediment or defect in the frame, balance, or capacity of them, according unto which they are of divers kinds.

The first division of them is into such as are single . . . and such as are by leagues. . . .

The second . . . is into such as are for preservation, . . . and such as are for increase . . . in which I can see no more than that the former taketh in no more citizens than are necessary for defence, and the latter so many as are capable of increase.

The third division (unseen hitherto) is into equal and unequal, and this is the main point especially as to domestic peace and tranquillity; for to make a commonwealth unequal is to divide it into parties, which setteth them at perpetual variance, the one party endeavouring to preserve their eminence and inequality, and the other to attain unto equality, whence the people of Rome derived their perpetual strife with the nobility or senate: but in an equal commonwealth, there can be no more strife than there can be over-balance in equal weights. . . .

An equal commonwealth is such an one as is equal both in the balance or foundation and in the superstructures, that is to say in her agrarian law and in her rotation.

An equal agrarian is a perpetual law establishing and preserving the balance of dominion, by such a distribution that no one man or number of men within the compass of the few or aristocracy can come to overpower the whole people by their possessions in lands.

As the agrarian answereth unto the foundation, so doth rotation unto the superstructures.

Equal rotation is equal vicissitude in government, or succession unto magistracy conferred for such convenient terms, enjoying equal vacations, as take in the whole body by parts, succeeding others through the free election or suffrage of the people.

The contrary whereunto is prolongation of magistracy which, trashing the wheel of rotation, destroys the life or natural motion of a commonwealth.

The election or suffrage of the people is freest where it is made or given in such a manner that it can neither oblige . . . nor disoblige another, or through fear of an enemy, or bashfuless towards a friend, impair a man's liberty. . . .

An equal commonwealth (by that which hath been said) is a government established upon an equal agrarian, arising into the superstructures or three orders, the senate debating and proposing, the people resolving, and the magistracy executing by an equal rotation through the suffrage of the people given by the ballot. For though rotation may be without the ballot, and the ballot without rotation, yet the ballot not only as to the ensuing model includeth both, but is by far the most equal way. . . .

Source: The Common-wealth of Oceana. By James Harrington. London: Printed by J. Streater for Livewell Chapman, 1656.

James Harrington (1611–77) was an English political theorist.

*   *   *

John Locke (1632–1704) has traditionally been ascribed the most important role in providing the philosophic foundation for American political thought. The influence of his thought can clearly be seen in the Declaration of Independence. The following selection from Locke shows the form of argument used by social contract thinkers, which influenced many Americans. Locke argues that society and government originated through consent as a mechanism for the protection of property (which Locke defined to include a person's life). Since consent can be given it can also be withdrawn, an argument the colonists used to justify their break from Britain.

An important part of Locke's argument, from the point of view of American thinkers, was his discussion of natural law or "the higher law," as it was often called. Natural law governed the state of nature, but there was no way of enforcing it and, as a result, the peaceful state of nature degenerated into a state of war. Therefore, human beings formed societies and governments to avoid the dangers of the state of war. (Chapter 2 of Locke's *Second Treatise* is entitled "Of the State of Nature"; Chapter 3 is "Of the State of War.") American thinkers generally insisted that as they did so they brought the natural law with them and enshrined it in civil law.

John Locke
Second Treatise of Government
Of the State of Nature.

4. To understand political power right, and derive it from its original, we must consider, what state all men are naturally in, and that is, *a state of perfect freedom* to order their actions, and dispose of their possessions and persons, as they think fit, within the bounds of the law of nature, without asking leave, or depending upon the will of any other man.

A *state* also of *equality,* wherein all the power and jurisdiction is reciprocal, no one having more than another; there being nothing more evident, than that creatures of the same species and rank, promiscuously born to all the same advantages of nature, and the use of the same faculties, should also be equal one amongst another without subordination or subjection, unless the lord and master of them all should, by any manifest declaration of his will, set one above another, and confer on him, by an evident and clear appointment, an undoubted right to dominion and sovereignty. . . .

13. I easily grant, that *civil government* is the proper remedy for the inconveniences of the state of nature, which must certainly be great, where men may be judges of their own case, since it is easy to be imagined, that he who was so unjust as to do his brother an injury, will scarce be so just as to condemn himself for it: but I shall desire those who make this objection, to remember, that *absolute monarchs* are but men; and if government is to be the remedy of those evils, which necessarily follow from men's being judges in their own cases, and the state of nature is therefore not to be endured, I desire to know what kind of government that is, and how much better it is than the state of nature, where one man, commanding a multitude, has the liberty to be judge of his own case, and may do to all his subjects whatever he pleases, without the least liberty to any one to question or control those who execute his pleasure? and in whatsoever he doth, whether led by reason, mistake or passion, must be submitted to? much better it is in the state of nature, wherein men are not bound to submit to the unjust will of another: and if he that judges, judges amiss in his own, or any other case, he is answerable for it to the rest of mankind.

14. It is often asked as a mighty objection, *where are,* or ever were there any *men in such a state of nature?* To which it may suffice as an answer at present, that since all princes and rulers of *independent* governments all through the world, are in a state of nature, it is plain the world never was, nor ever will be, without numbers of men in that state. I have named all governors of *independent communities,* whether they are, or are not, in league with others: for it is not every compact that puts an end to the state of nature between men, but only this one of agreeing to-

gether mutually to enter into one community, and make one body politic; other promises, and compacts, men may make one with another, and yet still be in the state of nature. The promises and bargains for truck, &c. between the two men in the desert island . . . or between a *Swiss* and an *Indian,* in the woods of *America,* are binding to them, though they are perfectly in a state of nature, in reference to one another: for truth and keeping of faith belongs to men, as men, and not as members of society. . . .

Of PROPERTY

25. Whether we consider natural *reason,* which tells us, that men, being once born, have a right to their preservation, and consequently to meat and drink, and such other things as nature affords for their subsistence: or *revelation,* which gives us an account of those grants God made of the world to *Adam,* and to *Noah,* and his sons, it is very clear, that God, as king *David* says, *Psal.* cxv. 16. *has given the earth to the children of men;* given it to mankind in common. But this being supposed, it seems to some a very great difficulty, how any one should ever come to have a *property* in any thing: I will not content myself to answer, that if it be difficult to make out *property,* upon a supposition that God gave the world to *Adam,* and his posterity in common, it is impossible that any man, but one universal monarch, should have any *property* upon a supposition, that God gave the world to *Adam,* and his heirs in succession, exclusive of all the rest of his posterity. But I shall endeavour to shew, how men might come to have a *property* in several parts of that which God gave to mankind in common, and that without any express compact of all the commoners.

26. God, who hath given the world to men in common, hath also given them reason to make use of it to the best advantage of life, and convenience. The earth, and all that is therein, is given to men for the support and comfort of their being. And tho' all the fruits it naturally produces, and beasts it feeds, belong to mankind in common, as they are produced by the spontaneous hand of nature; and no body has originally a private dominion, exclusive of the rest of mankind, in any of them, as they are thus in their natural state: yet being given for the use of men, there must of necessity be *a means to appropriate* them some way or other, before they can be of any use, or at all beneficial to any particular man. The fruit, or venison, which nourishes the wild *Indian,* who knows no inclosure, and is still a tenant in common, must be his, and so his, *i. e.* a part of him, that another can no longer have any right to it, before it can do him any good for the support of his life.

27. Though the earth, and all inferior creatures, be common to all men, yet every man has a *property* in his own *person:* this no body has any right to but himself. The *labour* of his body, and the *work* of his hands, we may say, are properly

his. Whatsoever then he removes out of the state that nature hath provided, and left it in, he hath mixed his *labour* with, and joined to it something that is his own, and thereby makes it his *property*. It being by him removed from the common state nature hath placed it in, it hath by this *labour* something annexed to it, that excludes the common right of other men; for this *labour* being the unquestionable property of the labourer, no man but he can have a right to what that is once joined to, at least where there is enough, and as good, left in common for others. . . .

Of the Beginning of Political Societies.

95. MEN being, as has been said, by nature, all free, equal, and independent, no one can be put out of this estate, and subjected to the political power of another, without his own consent. The only way whereby any one divests himself of his natural liberty, and puts on the *bonds of civil society*, is by agreeing with other men to join and unite into a community for their comfortable, safe, and peaceable living one amongst another, in a secure enjoyment of their properties, and a greater security against any, that are not of it. This any number of men may do, because it injures not the freedom of the rest; they are left as they were in the liberty of the state of nature. When any number of men have so *consented to make one community or government,* they are thereby presently incorporated, and make *one body politic*, wherein the *majority* have a right to act and conclude the rest.

96. For when any number of men have, by the consent of every individual, made a *community,* they have thereby made that community one body, with a power to act as one body, which is only by the will and determination of the *majority:* for that which acts any community, being only the consent of the individuals of it, and it being necessary to that which is one body to move one way; it is necessary the body should move that way whither the greater force carries it, which is the *consent of the majority:* or else it is impossible it should act or continue one body, *one community,* which the consent of every individual that united into it, agreed that it should; and so every one is bound by that consent to be concluded by the *majority.* And therefore we see, that in assemblies, impowered to act by positive laws, where no number is set by that positive law which impowers them, the *act of the majority* passes for the act of the whole, and of course determines, as having, by the law of nature and reason, the power of the whole.

97. And thus every man, by consenting with others to make one body politic under one government, puts himself under an obligation, to every one of that society, to submit to the determination of the *majority,* and to be concluded by it; or else this *original compact,* whereby he with others incorporates into *one society,* would signify nothing, and be no compact, if he be left free, and under no other ties than he was in before in the state of nature. For what appearance would there

be of any compact? what new engagement if he were no farther tied by any decrees of the society, than he himself thought fit, and did actually consent to? This would be still as great a liberty, as he himself had before his compact, or any one else in the state of nature hath, who may submit himself, and consent to any acts of it if he thinks fit. . . .

99. Whosoever . . . out of a state of nature unite into a *community*, must be understood to give up all the power, necessary to the ends of which they unite into society, to the *majority* of the community, unless they expressly agreed in any number greater than the majority. And this is done by barely agreeing to *unite into one political society*, which is *all the compact* that is, or needs be, between the individuals, that enter into, or make up a *common-wealth*. And thus that, which begins and actually *constitutes any political society*, is nothing but the consent of any number of freemen capable of a majority to unite and incorporate into such a society. And this is that, and that only, which did, or could give beginning to any *lawful government* in the world.

Source: Two Treatises of Government. By John Locke. London: Printed by A. Millar et al., 1764.

John Locke (1632–1704) was an English philosopher and political theorist.

* * *

Among the other figures from the English Civil War and Commonwealth periods who were influential on the colonies were John Trenchard (1622–1723) and Thomas Gordon (?-1751). A central issue for Americans, which goes all the way back to Niccolò Machiavelli (1469–1527), is the question of a standing or professional army versus a citizen's militia. The American position was fairly consistently opposed to a standing army. This position was taken by Trenchard in his *An Argument, Shewing that a Standing Army Is Inconsistent with a Free Government* (1697) and later in *Cato's Letters* (1722), numbers 94–95.

In other numbers of *Cato's Letters*, which were originally published as a series of newspaper articles, Trenchard and Gordon discussed other issues of central importance to the colonists, including the problem of corruption (no. 18), the right of the people to judge government (no. 38), and, in perhaps the most read letter in the colonies, the nature of colonies (no. 106). In the section included here, they discuss the North American colonies; earlier in the essay they had dismissed the possibility of holding colonies by force and noted that the South American colonies posed totally different problems because they did not produce goods that directly competed with British goods, whereas the North American ones did.

Thomas Gordon
John Trenchard

Cato's Letters

Saturday, *December* 8, 1722. No. 106.

Of Plantations and Colonies.

I intend, in this Letter, to give my Opinion about Plantations; a Subject which seems to me to be understood but by few, and little Use is made of it where it is. It is most certain, that the Riches of a Nation consist in the Number of its Inhabitants, when those Inhabitants are usefully employed, and no more of them live upon the Industry of others (like Drones in a Hive) than are necessary to preserve the Economy of the Whole. . . .

Colonies are for Trade, and intended to increase the Wealth and Power of the native Kingdom; which they will abundantly do, if managed prudently, and put and kept under a proper Regulation. No Nation has, or ever had, all the Materials of Commerce within itself: No Climate produces all Commodities; and yet it is the Interest, Pleasure, or Convenience of every People, to use or trade in most or all of them; and rather to raise them themselves, than to purchase them from others, unless in some Instances, when they change their own Commodities for them, and employ as many or more People at Home in that Exchange, such as would lose their Employment by purchasing them from Abroad. Now Colonies planted in proper Climates, and kept to their proper Business, undoubtedly do this; and particularly many of our own Colonies in the *West Indies* employ ten Times their own Number in *Old England,* by sending them from hence Provisions, Manufactures, Utensils for themselves and their Slaves, by Navigation, working up the Commodities that they send us, by retaining and exporting them afterwards, and in returning again to us Silver and Gold, and Materials for new Manufactures; and our Northern Colonies do, or may if encouraged, supply us with Timber, Hemp, Iron and other Metals, and indeed with most or all the Materials of Navigation, and our Neighbours too, through our Hands; and by that Means settle a solid Naval Power in *Great Britain,* not precarious and subject to Disappointments, and the Caprices of our Neighbours; which Management would make us soon Masters of most of the Trade of the World.

I would not suggest so distant a Thought, as that any of our Colonies, when they grow stronger, should ever attempt to wean themselves from us; however, I think too much Care cannot be taken to prevent it, and to preserve their Dependencies upon their Mother-Country. It is not to be hoped in the corrupt State of human Nature, that any Nation will be subject to another any longer than it finds its own Account in it, and cannot help itself. Every Man's first Thought will be for himself and his own Interest, and he will not be long to seek for Arguments to justify his being so when he knows how to attain what he proposes. Men will think it hard to work, toil, and run Hazards, for the Advantage of others, any longer than they find their own Interest in it, and especially for those who use them ill: All Nature points out that Course: No Creatures suck the Teats of their Dams longer than they can draw Milk from thence, or can provide themselves with better Food: Nor will any Country continue their Subjection to another, only because their Great-Grandmothers were acquainted.

This is the Course of Human Affairs; and all wise States will always have it before their Eyes. They will well consider therefore how to preserve the Advantages arising from Colonies, and avoid the Evils. And I conceive that there can be but two Ways in Nature to hinder them from throwing off their Dependence; one to keep it out of their Power, and the other out of their Will. The first must be by Force; and the latter by using them well, and keeping them employed in such Productions, and making such Manufactures, as will support themselves and Families comfortably, and procure them Wealth too, or at least not prejudice their Mother-Country.

Force can never be used effectually to answer the End, without destroying the Colonies themselves. Liberty and Encouragement are necessary to carry People thither, and to keep them together when they are there; and Violence will hinder both. Any Body of Troops considerable enough to awe them, and keep them in Subjection, under the Direction too of a needy Governor, often sent thither to make his Fortune, and at such a Distance from any Application for Redress, will soon put an End to all Planting, and leave the Country to the Soldiers alone; and if it did not, would eat up all the Profit of the Colony. For this Reason, Arbitrary Countries have not been equally successful in planting Colonies, with free ones; and what they have done in that kind, has either been by Force, at a vast Expense, or by departing from the Nature of their Government, and giving such Privileges to Planters as were denied to their other Subjects. And I dare say, that a few prudent Laws, and a little prudent Conduct, would soon give us far the greatest Share of the Riches of all *America,* perhaps drive many of other Nations out of it, or into our Colonies for Shelter.

If Violence, or Methods tending to Violence, be not used to prevent it, our Northern Colonies must constantly increase in People, Wealth, and Power. Men living in healthy Climates, paying easy or no Taxes, not molested with Wars, must vastly increase by natural Generation; besides that vast Numbers every Day flow thither from our own Dominions, and from other Parts of *Europe,* because they have their ready Employment, and Lands given to them for Tilling; insomuch, that I am told they have doubled their Inhabitants since the Revolution, and in less than a Century must become powerful States; and the more powerful they grow, still the more People will flock thither. And there are so many Exigencies in all States, so many foreign Wars and domestic Disturbances, that these Colonies can never want Opportunities, if they watch for them to do what they shall find their Interest to do; and therefore we ought to take all the Precautions in our Power, that it shall never be their Interest to act against that of their native Country; an Evil which can no otherwise be averted than by keeping them fully employed in such Trades as will increase their own, as well as our Wealth: for it is much to be feared, if we do not find Employment for them, they may find it for us.

No two Nations, no two Bodies of Men, or scarce two single Men, can long continue in Friendship, without having some Cement of their Union; and where Relation, Acquaintance, or mutual Pleasures are wanting, mutual Interests alone can bind it: But when these Interests separate, each Side must assuredly pursue their own. The Interest of Colonies is often to gain Independency; and is always so when they no longer want Protection, and when they can employ themselves more advantageously, than in supplying Materials of Traffick to others; And the Interest of the Mother-Country is always to keep them dependent, and so employed; and it requires all their Address to do it; and it is certainly more easily and effectually done by gentle and insensible Methods, than by Power alone.

Men will always think that they have a Right to Air, Earth, and Water, a Right to employ themselves for their own Support, to live by their own Labours, to apply the Gifts of God to their own Benefit; and in order to it, to make the best of their Soil, and to work up their own Product: And when this cannot be done without Detriment to their Mother-Country, there can be but one fair, honest, and indeed effectual Way to prevent it, which is, to divert them upon other Employments as advantageous to themselves, and more so to their Employers; that is in raising such Growth, and making such Manufactures as will not prejudice their own, or at least in no Degree equal to the Advantage which they bring: And when such Commodities are raised or made, they ought to be taken off their Hands, and the People ought not to be forced to find out other Markets by stealth, or to throw themselves upon new Protectors. Whilst People have full Employment, and can maintain themselves comfortably in a Way which they have been used to, they will never seek after a new one, especially when they meet Encouragement in one, and are discountenanced in the other.

As without this Conduct, Colonies must be mischievous to their Mother-Country for the Reasons before given, so with it the greatest Part of the Wealth which they acquire centers there; for all their Productions are so many Augmentations of our Power and Riches, as they are Returns of the People's Labour, the Rewards of Merchants, or Increase of Navigation; without which, all who are sent Abroad are a dead Loss to their Country, and as useless as if really dead; and worse than so, if they become Enemies; for we can send no Commodities to them, unless they have others to exchange for them, and such as we find our Interest in taking.

Source: Cato's Letters; or, Essays on Liberty, Civil and Religious, and other Important Subjects. By Thomas Gordon and John Trenchard. 3rd edition. 4 volumes. London: W. Wilkins, 1733.

Thomas Gordon (?-1751) and John Trenchard (1622–1723) coauthored various works that were very influential in colonial America.

* * *

One of the central principles of the U.S. Constitution, separation of powers, was summarized most effectively by Charles de Secondat, Baron de La Brède et de Montesquieu (1689–1755), better known as Montesquieu, whose *Esprit de Lois (Spirit of the Laws)* used an erroneous description of the government of England as the basis for his argument that power should not be unified.

Montesquieu
Spirit of the Laws

In every government there are three sorts of power; the legislative, the executive in respect to things dependent on the law of nations; and the executive in regard to matters that depend on the civil law.

By virtue of the first, the prince or magistrate enacts temporary or perpetual laws, and amends or abrogates those that have been already enacted. By the second, he makes peace or war, sends or received embassies, establishes the public security, and provides against invasions. By the third, he punishes criminals, or determines the disputes that arise between individuals. The latter we shall call the judiciary power, and the other simply the executive power of the state.

The political liberty of the subject is a tranquility of mind arising from the opinion each person has of his safety. In order to have this liberty, it is requisite the government be so constituted as one man need not be afraid of another.

When the legislative and executive powers are united in the same person, or in the same body of magistrates, there can be no liberty; because apprehensions may arise, lest the same monarch or senate should enact tyrannical laws, to execute them in a tyrannical manner.

Again, there is no liberty, if the judiciary power be not separated from the legislative and executive. Were it joined with the legislative, the life and liberty of the subject would be exposed to arbitrary control; for the judge would be then the legislator. Were it joined to the executive power, the judge might behave with violence and oppression.

There would be an end of everything, were the same man or the same body, whether of the nobles or of the people, to exercise those three powers, that of enacting laws, that of executing the public resolutions, and of trying the causes of individuals. . . .

The judiciary power ought not to be given to a standing senate; it should be exercised by persons taken from the body of the people at certain times of the year, and consistently with a form and manner prescribed by law, in order to erect a tribunal that should last only so long as necessity requires.

By this method the judicial power, so terrible to mankind, not being annexed to any particular state or profession, becomes, as it were, invisible. People have not then the judges continually present to their view; they fear the office, but not the magistrate.

In accusations of a deep and criminal nature, it is proper the person accused should have the privilege of choosing, in some measure, his judges, in concurrence with the law; or at least he should have a right to except against so great a number that the remaining part may be deemed his own choice.

The other two powers may be given rather to magistrates or permanent bodies, because they are not exercised on any private subject; one being no more than the general will of the state, and the other the execution of that general will.

But though the tribunals ought not to be fixed, the judgments ought; and to such a degree as to be ever conformable to the letter of the law. Were they to be the private opinion of the judge, people would then live in society, without exactly knowing the nature of their obligations.

The judges ought likewise to be of the same rank as the accused, or, in other words, his peers; to the end that he may not imagine he is fallen into the hands of persons inclined to treat him with rigor.

If the legislature leaves the executive power in possession of a right to imprison those subjects who can give security for their good behavior, there is an end of liberty; unless they are taken up, in order to answer without delay to a capital crime, in which case they are really free, being subject only to the power of the law.

But should the legislature think itself in danger by some secret conspiracy against the state, or by a correspondence with a foreign enemy, it might authorize the executive power, for a short and limited time, to imprison suspected persons, who in that case would lose their liberty only for a while, to preserve it forever. . . .

As in a country of liberty, every man who is supposed a free agent ought to be his own governor; the legislative power should reside in the whole body of the people. But since this is impossible in large states, and in small ones is subject to many inconveniences, it is fit the people should transact by their representatives what they cannot transact by themselves.

The inhabitants of a particular town are much better acquainted with its wants and interests than with those of other places; and are better judges of the capacity of their neighbors than of that of the rest of their countrymen. The members, therefore, of the legislature should not be chosen from the general body of the nation; but it is proper that in every considerable place a representative should be elected by the inhabitants.

The great advantage of representatives is, their capacity of discussing public affairs. For this the people collectively are extremely unfit, which is one of the chief inconveniences of a democracy. . . .

All the inhabitants of the several districts ought to have a right of voting at the election of a representative, except such as are in so mean a situation as to be deemed to have no will of their own.

One great fault there was in most of the ancient republics, that the people had a right to active resolutions, such as require some execution, a thing of which they are absolutely incapable. They ought to have no share in the government but for the choosing of representatives, which is within their reach. For though few can tell the exact degree of men's capacities, yet there are none but are capable of knowing in general whether the person they choose is better qualified than most of his neighbors.

Neither ought the representative body to be chosen for the executive part of government, for which it is not so fit; but for the enacting of laws, or to see whether the laws in being are duly executed, a thing suited to their abilities, and which none indeed but themselves can properly perform.

In such a state there are always persons distinguished by their birth, riches, or honors; but were they to be confounded with the common people, and to have only the weight of a single vote like the rest, the common liberty would be their slavery, and they would have no interest in supporting it, as most of the popular resolutions would be against them. The share they have, therefore, in the legislature ought to be proportioned to their other advantages in the state; which happens only when they form a body that has a right to check the licentiousness of the people, as the people have a right to oppose any encroachment of theirs.

The legislative power is therefore committed to the body of the nobles, and to that which represents the people, each having their assemblies and deliberations apart, each their separate views and interests. . . .

The executive power ought to be in the hands of a monarch, because this branch of government, having need of despatch, is better administered by one than by many: on the other hand, whatever depends on the legislative power is oftentimes better regulated by many than by a single person.

But if there were no monarch, and the executive power should be committed to a certain number of persons selected from the legislative body, there would be an end then of liberty; by reason the two powers would be united, as the same persons would sometimes possess, and would be always able to possess, a share in both.

Were the legislative body to be a considerable time without meeting, this would likewise put an end to liberty. For of two things one would naturally follow: either that there would be no longer any legislative resolutions, and then the state would fall into anarchy; or that these resolutions would be taken by the executive power, which would render it absolute.

It would be needless for the legislative body to continue always assembled. This would be troublesome to the representatives, and, moreover, would cut out too much work for the executive power, so as to take off its attention to its office, and oblige it to think only of defending its own prerogatives, and the right it has to execute.

Again, were the legislative body to be always assembled, it might happen to be kept up only by filling the places of the deceased members with new representatives; and in that case, if the legislative body were once corrupted, the evil would be past all remedy. When different legislative bodies succeed one another, the people who have a bad opinion of that which is actually sitting may reasonably entertain some hopes of the next: but were it to be always the same body, the people upon seeing it once corrupted would no longer expect any good from its laws; and of course they would either become desperate or fall into a state of indolence.

The legislative body should not meet of itself. For a body is supposed to have no will but when it is met; and besides, were it not to meet unanimously, it would be impossible to determine which was really the legislative body; the part assembled, or the other. And if it had a right to prorogue itself, it might happen never to be prorogued; which would be extremely dangerous, in case it should ever attempt to encroach on the executive power. Besides, there are seasons, some more proper than others, for assembling the legislative body: it is fit, therefore, that the executive power should regulate the time of meeting, as well as the duration of those assemblies, according to the circumstances and exigencies of a state known to itself.

Were the executive power not to have a right of restraining the encroachments of the legislative body, the latter would become despotic; for as it might arrogate to itself what authority it pleased, it would soon destroy all the other powers.

But it is not proper, on the other hand, that the legislative power should have a right to stay the executive. For as the execution has its natural limits, it is useless to confine it; besides, the executive power is generally employed in momentary operations. The power, therefore, of the Roman tribunes was faulty, as it put a stop not only to the legislation, but likewise to the executive part of government; which was attended with infinite mischief.

But if the legislative power in a free state has no right to stay the executive, it has a right and ought to have the means of examining in what manner its laws have been executed. . . .

But whatever may be the issue of that examination, the legislative body ought not to have a power of arraigning the person, nor, of course, the conduct, of him who is intrusted with the executive power. His person should be sacred, because as it is necessary for the good of the state to prevent the legislative body from rendering themselves arbitrary, the moment he is accused or tried there is an end of liberty.

In this case the state would be no longer a monarchy, but a kind of republic, though not a free government. But as the person intrusted with the executive power cannot abuse it without bad counsellors, and such as have the laws as ministers, though the laws protect them as subjects, these men may be examined and punished. . . .

Though, in general, the judiciary power ought not to be united with any part of the legislative, yet this is liable to three exceptions, founded on the particular interest of the party accused.

The great are always obnoxious to popular envy; and were they to be judged by the people, they might be in danger from their judges, and would, moreover, be deprived of the privilege which the meanest subject is possessed of in a free state, of being tried by his peers. The nobility, for this reason, ought not to be cited before the ordinary courts of judicature, but before that part of the legislature which is composed of their own body. . . .

The executive power, pursuant of what has been already said, ought to have a share in the legislature by the power of rejecting; otherwise it would soon be stripped of its prerogative. But should the legislative power usurp a share of the executive, the latter would be equally undone.

If the prince were to have a part in the legislature by the power of resolving, liberty would be lost. But as it is necessary he should have a share in the legislature for the support of his own prerogative, this share must consist in the power of rejecting. . . .

Here, then, is the fundamental constitution of the government we are treating of. The legislative body being composed of two parts, they check one another by the mutual privilege of rejecting. They are both restrained by the executive power, as the executive is by the legislative.

These three powers should naturally form a state of repose or inaction. But as there is a necessity for movement in the course of human affairs, they are forced to move, but still in concert.

As the executive power has no other part in the legislative than the privilege of rejecting, it can have no share in the public debates. It is not even necessary that it should propose, because as it may always disapprove of the resolutions that shall be taken, it may likewise reject the decisions on those proposals which were made against its will.

In some ancient commonwealths, where public debates were carried on by the people in a body, it was natural for the executive power to propose and debate in conjunction with the people, otherwise their resolutions must have been attended with a strange confusion.

Were the executive power to determine the raising of public money, otherwise than by giving its consent, liberty would be at an end; because it would become legislative in the most important point of legislation.

If the legislative power was to settle the subsidies, not from year to year, but forever, it would run the risk of losing its liberty, because the executive power would be no longer dependent; and when once it was possessed of such a perpetual right, it would be a matter of indifference whether it held it of itself or of another. The same may be said if it should come to a resolution of intrusting, not an annual, but a perpetual command of the fleets and armies to the executive power.

To prevent the executive power from being able to oppress, it is requisite that the armies with which it is intrusted should consist of the people, and have the same spirit as the people, as was the case at Rome till the time of Marius. To obtain this end, there are only two ways, either that the persons employed in the army should have sufficient property to answer for their conduct to their fellow-subjects, and be enlisted only for a year, as was customary at Rome; or if there should be a standing army, composed chiefly of the most despicable part of the nation, the legislative power should have a right to disband them as soon as it pleased; the soldiers should live in common with the rest of the people; and no separate camp, barracks, or fortress should be suffered.

When once an army is established, it ought not to depend immediately on the legislative, but on the executive power; and this from the very nature of the thing, its business consisting more in action than in deliberation.

It is natural for mankind to set a higher value upon courage than timidity, on activity than prudence, on strength than counsel. Hence the army will ever despise a senate, and respect their own officers. They will naturally slight the orders sent them by a body of men whom they look upon as cowards, and therefore unworthy to command them. So that as soon as the troops depend entirely on the legislative body, it becomes a military government; and if the contrary has ever happened, it has been owing to some extraordinary circumstances. It is because the army was always kept divided; it is because it was composed of several bodies that depended each on a particular province: it is because the capital towns were strong places, defended by their natural situation, and not garrisoned with regular troops.

Source: The Spirit of the Laws. By Montesquieu. Translated by Thomas Nugent. London: Nourse, 1750.

Montesquieu (Charles de Secondat, Baron de La Brède et de Montesquieu) (1689–1755) was a French lawyer and political theorist.

*   *   *

Many other thinkers were influential, but these are the thinkers who are generally considered to have had the greatest impact on early American thought. They were not slavishly imitated, and the classic documents of American political thought are not simple recreations in the American context of particular European thinkers. As we have seen, many different streams of thought converged in America, and American political thought reflects that convergence.

Notes

1. Parts of this chapter are reprinted from Lyman Tower Sargent, "Utopianism in Colonial America," *History of Political Thought* 4, no. 3 (Winter 1983): 483–522.

2. Vespucci's "Letter from Lisbon," 1502. Quoted in *The European Reconnaissance: Selected Documents,* edited by J. H. Parry (New York: Harper & Row, 1968), 187.

3. Mircea Eliade, "Paradise and Utopia: Mythical Geography and Eschatology," in *Utopias and Utopian Thought,* edited by Frank E. Manuel (Boston: Beacon Press, 1967), 262–63.

4. *The first voyage made to the coasts of America, with two barks, where in were Captains M. Philip Amadas, and M. Arthur Barlowe, who discovered part of the Countrey now called Virginia, Anno 1584. Written by one of the said Captaines, and sent to Sir Walter Raleigh knight, at whose charge and direction, the said voyage was set forth.* In Richard Hakluyt, *The Principle Navigations Voyages Traffiques & Discoveries of the English Nation made by Sea or Overland to the Remote Farthest Distant Quarters of the Earth at any time within the compasse of these 1,000 yeares,* 8 volumes (London: E. P. Dutton, n.d.), 6:128.

5. Quoted in Lewis Hanke, *All Mankind Is One: A Study of the Disputation between Bartolome de Las Casas and Juan de Sepulveda in 1550 on the Intellectual and Religious Capacity of the American Indians* (DeKalb: Northern Illinois University Press, 1974), 11.

6. Quoted in ibid., 21. Translated by Mariano Cuevas, S.J., from *Documentos ineditos de siglo XVI para la historia de Mexico* (Mexico, 1914), 84–86.

7. Vespucci, "Letter from Lisbon," 187.

8. Elliott, *The Discovery of America and the Discovery of Man* (London: Oxford University Press for the British Academy, 1972), 8.

9. Roy Harvey Pearce, *The Savages of America: A Study of the Indian and the Idea of Civilization*, revised edition (Baltimore: Johns Hopkins University Press, 1965), 6.

10. [Richard Johnson,] *Nova Brittania: offering most excellent fruites by planting in Virginia—Exciting all such as be well affected to further the same* (London, 1609), 8. Reprinted in *Tracts and Other Papers, relating principally to the origin, Settlement and Progress of the Colonies in North America, from the Discovery of the Country to the Year 1776*, compiled by Peter Force, 4 volumes (New York: Peter Smith, 1947), vol. 1. Each tract is separately paged.

11. Roger Williams, *Key into the Language of America* (1643). Quoted in George H. Williams, *Wilderness and Paradise in Christian Thought: The Biblical Experience in the History of Christianity & the Paradise Theme in the Theological Idea of the University* (New York: Harper & Row, 1962), 103.

12. Thomas Morton, *New English Canaan: or New Canaan, Containing an Abstract of New England* (1632), 39. Reprinted in Force, *Tracts*, vol. 2, tract 5.

13. Samuel Eliot Morison, *The Intellectual Life of Colonial New England*, 2d edition (Ithaca, N.Y.: Cornell University Press, 1956), 6–7.

14. David W. Noble, *Historians against History: The Frontier Thesis and the National Covenant in American Historical Writing since 1830* (Minneapolis: University of Minnesota Press, 1965), 5–6.

15. Charles L. Sanford, *The Quest for Paradise: Europe and the American Moral Imagination* (Urbana: University of Illinois Press, 1961), 55.

16. [Cotton Mather,] *Theopolis Americana: an Essay on the Golden Street of the Holy City: Publishing, a Testimony against the Corruptions of the Market Place. With. Some Good Hopes of Better Things to be yet seen in the American World* (Boston: Printed by B. Green, 1710), 42.

17. Sanford, *Quest for Paradise*, 82.

18. H. Richard Niebuhr, *The Kingdom of God in America* (New York: Harper & Brothers, 1937), 49.

19. Sacvan Bercovitch, *The American Jeremiad* (Madison: University of Wisconsin Press, 1978), 9.

CHAPTER 2

The Colonial Period,
1620–1760

✳ ✳ ✳

The American colonies were much more complex than traditional history used to pretend. The image of the American as a new Adam (Eve seems to have been left behind) created when he stepped on Plymouth Rock forgets the previous attempts at colonization and, more importantly, the continuous series of contacts between North America and Europe going back to the early 1500s.

Shortly after landing in 1620, the Puritans were put into contact with an English-speaking Indian who had earlier been taken to Europe and returned. Although such travel by Indians was not common, it was far from unknown. A substantial number of North and South American Indians had been taken to Europe, learned languages spoken there, and, in some cases, returned. Thus, neither North America nor its indigenous inhabitants were entirely unknown to the settlers, nor were the settlers a totally new experience for the inhabitants. In fact, previous contact had spread disease among the Indians—a situation in which the Puritans saw the hand of God clearing the land for them.

Puritan Political Thought

The New England Puritans saw themselves as establishing a Holy Commonwealth or theocracy. They would be, as they put it, "a citty on a hill" that would provide an example to the world of a truly Christian commonwealth.

The fundamental propositions of Puritan political thought are hierarchy, as expressed in the notion of calling; covenant theology; and a theory of church-state relations that emphasizes the unification of church and state and rejects any notion of religious freedom or toleration. In the early seventeenth century the idea of tolerating opposing beliefs was not viewed positively. It was a good thing to be intolerant and a bad thing to be tolerant. Although today tolerating differences is generally thought of favorably, the old attitude is still easy to find.

The selections in this section show how Puritan political thought played out in the New World. The Mayflower Compact is the first agreement among the Puritans before they landed. Roger Williams's (1603?-83) "The Bloudy Tenent" shows his opposition to theocracy. Cotton Mather's (1663–1728) "A Platform of Church Discipline" and speeches on government from John Winthrop (1588–1649) and John Cotton (1584–1652) illustrate the range of orthodox Puritan political beliefs, particularly as they relate to the church-state question. Divisions over the relations of church and state and the question of religious freedom grew in importance, symbolized by Williams's flight from Massachusetts to establish the Commonwealth of Rhode Island.

The Mayflower Compact demonstrates one of the effects of covenant theology. This document is not a social contract; that concept did not yet exist. Covenant theology holds that a series of covenants have existed between God and individuals or groups of people. There were covenants between God and Adam, God and Abraham, and God and the nation of Israel. The Puritans believed they had a new covenant with God in which they would be granted peace and prosperity in exchange for their obedience to scriptural law. Thus, the Puritans saw themselves as a new "chosen people" predestined by God to lead the world back to God through their example.

"Calling" was the belief that God had chosen or called each individual to particular activities and a particular station in life. Each person called is provided by God with the skills needed to fulfill that station. Thus, everyone is in a position of trust or stewardship; God will judge the use each person makes of the skills provided, and God does not call anyone to anything that is not of benefit to both the individual and the community.

The selections included here present perspectives on all these issues. Winthrop's speech stresses the potential for conflict between the authority of the magistrate and the liberty of the people. It is important to recognize, however, that for Winthrop liberty is only possible under authority. His statement of the position of women should be noted. Cotton argues for liberty under authority in a similar manner by emphasizing the sinful nature of humanity. Human corruption, which in the middle ages had been used as a justification for strong government, is here used to justify limited government. Mather stresses the independence of the congregation. The congregational form of governance puts power in the hands of each group of church members. This is again seen as a mechanism for limiting authority. At this time, however, the minister had immense personal authority. Although he could be removed by the congregation, such an action was not taken lightly.

The Mayflower Compact

In the Name of God, Amen.

We whose names are underwritten, the loyal subjects of our dread Sovereign Lord King James, by the Grace of God of Great Britain, France, and Ireland King Defender of the Faith, etc.

Having undertaken, for the Glory of God and advancement of the Christian Faith and Honour of our King and Country, a Voyage to plant the First Colony in the Northern Parts of Virginia, do by these presents solemnly and mutually in the presence of God and one of another, Covenant and Combine ourselves together into a Civil Body Politic, for our better ordering and preservation and furtherance of the ends aforesaid; and by virtue hereof to enact, constitute and frame such just and equal Laws, Ordinances, Acts, Constitutions and Offices, from time to time, as shall be thought most meet and convenient for the general good of the Colony, unto which we promise all due submission and obedience. In witness whereof we have hereunder subscribed our names at Cape Cod, the 11th of November, in the year of the reign of our Sovereign Lord King James, of England, France and Ireland the eighteenth, and of Scotland the fifty-fourth. Anno Domini 1620.

Source: The Federal and State Constitutions, Colonial Charters, and Other Organic Laws of the U.—S.—. Part I. Compiled by Ben. Perley Poore. 2nd edition. Washington, D.C.: Government Printing Office, 1878.

Roger Williams

The Bloudy Tenent

Whether the Kings of Israel and Judah were not types of Civill Magistrate? now I suppose by what hath been already spoken, these things will be evident.

First, that those former *types* of the *Land*, of the *People*, of their *Worships* were *types* and *figures* of a *Spirituall Land*, *Spirituall People* and *Spirituall Worship* under *Christ*. Therefore consequently, their *Saviours, Redeemers, Deliverers, Judges, Kings*, must also have their *Spirituall Antitypes*, and so consequently not *civill* but *Spirituall Governours* and *Rulers;* lest the very *essential* nature of *Types, Figures* and Shadowes be overthrowue.

Secondly, although the Magistrate by a Civill sword might well compell that Nationall Church to the externall exercise of their Naturall Worship: yet it is not possible (according to the rule of the New Testament) to compell whole Nations to true Repentance and Regeneration, without which (so farre as may be discerned true) the Worship and holy Name of God is prophaned and blasphemed.

An Arme of Flesh, and Sword of Steele cannot reach to cut the darknesse of the Mind, the hardnesse and unbeleefe of the Heart, and kindely operate upon the Soules affections to forsake a long continued Fathers worship, and to imbrace a new, though the best and truest. This worke performes alone that sword out of the mouth of Christ, with two edges, *Rev.* 1. & 3.

Thirdly, we have not one tittle in the New Testament of *Christ Jesus* concerning such a *parallel,* neither from *Himselfe,* nor from his *Ministers,* with whom he conversed fourty dayes after his *Resurrection,* instructing them in the matters of his *Kingdome, Acts* 1.

Neither find we any such *commission* or *direction* given to the *Civill Magistrate* to this purpose, nor to the *Saints* for their *submission* in matters spirituall, but the contrary *Acts* 4. & 5. 1 *Cor.* 7. 23. *Coloss.* 2. 18.

Fourthly, we have formerly viewed the very nature and essence of a *Civill Magistrate,* and find it the same in all parts of the *World,* where ever people live upon the face of the *Earth,* agreeing together in *Townes, Cities, Provinces, Kingdomes* : I say the same essentially Civill, both from, 1. the *rise* and *fountaine* whence it springs, to wit, the *peoples* choice and free consent. 2. The Object of it, viz. the *common-weale* or *safety* of such a *people* in their *bodies* and *goods,* as the *Authours* of this *Modell* have themselves confessed.

This *civill* Nature of the *Magistrate* we have proved to receive no *addition* of *power* from the Magistrates being a *Christian,* no more then it receives *diminution* from his not being a *Christian:* even as the *Common-weale* is a true *Common-weale,* although it have not heard of *Christianitie,* and *Christianitie* professed in it (as in *Pergamus, Ephesus,* &c.) makes it ne're no more a Commonweale, and *Christianitie* taken away, and the *candlestick* removed, makes it ne're the lesse a Commonweale.

Fifthly, the *Spirit* of *God* expresly related the worke of the *civill Magistrate* under the *Gospel,* Rom. 13. expresly mentioning (as the *Magistrates* object) the duties of the *second Table,* concerning the *bodies* and *goods* of the *subject.*

2. The *reward* or *wages* which people owe for such a worke, to wit, (not the *contribution* of the *Church* for any *spirituall* work, but) *tribute, toll, custome* which are *wages* payable by all sorts of men, *Natives* and *Forreigners,* who enjoy the same benefit of *publick peace* and *commerce* in the *Nation.*

Sixthly, Since the *civill Magistrate,* whether *Kings* or *Parliaments, States* and *Governours,* can receive no more in *justice* then what the People give, and are therefore but the *eyes* and *hands* and *instruments* of the people (simply considered, without respect to this or that *Religion*) it must inevitably follow . . . that if *Magistrates* have received their power from the *people,* then the greatest number of the people of every Land have received from *Christ Jesus* a power to *establish, correct, reforme* his *Saints* and *servants,* his *wife* and *spowse,* the *Church* : And she that by the expresse *word* of the *Lord* (*Psal.* 149.) binds *Kings* in *chaines,* and *Nobles* in *links* of *iron,* must her selfe be subject to the changeable pleasures of the people of the World (which lies in *wickednesse,* 1 *John* 5.) even in matters of Heavenly and *Spirituall* Nature.

Hence therefore in all controversies concerning the Church, Ministrie and worship, the last Appeale must come to the Bar of the People or Commonweal, where all may personally meet, as in some Commonweales of small number or in greater by their Representatives. . . .

No person cast forth and excommunicated, but as the Commonweale and people please, and in conclusion, no Church of Christ in this Land or World, and consequently no visibly Christ the Head of it. Yea yet higher, consequently no God in the World worshipped according to the institutions of Christ Jesus, except the severall peoples of the Nations of the World shall give allowance.

Source: The Bloudy Tenent of Persecution. By Roger Williams. London, 1644.

Roger Williams (1603?-83) was an American minister and the founder of Rhode Island.

John Winthrop
Little Speech on Liberty

The great questions that have troubled the country are about the authority of the magistrates and the liberty of the people. It is yourselves who have called us to this office, and being called by you, we have our authority from God, in way of an ordinance, such as hath the image of God eminently stamped upon it, the contempt and violation whereof hath been vindicated with examples of divine vengeance. I entreat you to consider that, when you choose magistrates, you take them from among yourselves, men subject to like passions as you are. Therefore, when you see infirmities in us, you should reflect upon your own, and that would make you bear the more with us, and not be severe censurers of the failings of your magistrates, when you have continual experience of the like infirmities in yourselves and others. We account him a good servant who breaks not his covenant. The covenant between you and us is the oath you have taken of us, which is to this purpose, that we shall govern you and judge your causes by the rules of God's laws and our own, according to our best skill. When you agree with a workman to build you a ship or house, etc., he undertakes as well for his skill for his faithfulness; for it is his profession, and you pay him for both. But, when you call one to be a magistrate, he doth not profess nor undertake to have sufficient skill for that office, nor can you furnish him with gifts, etc., therefore you must run the hazard of his skill and ability. But if he fail in faithfulness, which by his oath he is bound unto, that he must answer for. If it fall out that the case be clear to common apprehension, and the rule clear also, if he transgress here, the error is not in the skill, but in the evil of the will: it must be required of him. But if the case be doubtful, or the rule doubtful, to men of such understanding and parts as your magistrates are, if your magistrates should err here, yourselves must bear it.

For the other point concerning liberty, I observe a great mistake in the country about that. There is a twofold liberty, natural (I mean as our nature is now corrupt) and civil or federal. The first is common to man with beasts and other creatures. By this, man as he stands in relation to man simply, hath liberty to do what he lists: it is a liberty to evil as well as to good. This liberty is incompatible and inconsistent with authority, and cannot endure the least restraint of the most just authority. The exercise and maintaining of this liberty makes men grow more evil, and in time to be worse than brute beasts. . . . This is that great enemy of truth and peace, that wild beast, which all the ordinances of God are bent against, to restrain and subdue it. The other kind of liberty I call civil or federal; it may also be termed moral, in reference to the covenant between God and man, in the moral law, and the politic covenants and constitutions, amongst men themselves. This liberty is the proper end and object of authority, and cannot subsist without it; and it is a liberty to that only which is good, just, and honest. This liberty you are to stand for, with the hazard (not only of your goods, but) of your lives, if need be. Whatsoever crosseth this is not authority, but a distemper thereof. This liberty is maintained and exercised in a way of subjection to authority; it is of the same kind of liberty wherewith Christ hath made us free. The woman's own choice makes such a man her husband; yet, being so chosen, he is her lord, and she is to be subject to him, yet in a way of liberty, not of bondage; and a true wife accounts her subjection her honor and freedom, and would not think her condition safe and free but in her subjection to her husband's authority. Such is the liberty of the church under the authority of Christ, her king and husband; his yoke is so easy and sweet to her as a bride's ornaments; and if through forwardness or wantonness, etc., she shake it off, at any time, she is at no rest in her spirit until she take it up again; and whether her lord smiles upon her, and embraceth her in his arms, or whether he frowns, or rebukes, or smites her, she apprehends the sweetness of his love in all, and is refreshed, supported, and instructed by every such dispensation of his authority over her. On the other side, ye know who they are that complain of this yoke and say, let us break their bands, etc., we will not have this man to rule over us. Even so, brethren, it will be between you and your magistrates. If you stand for your natural corrupt liberties, and will do what is good in your own eyes, you will not endure the least weight of authority, but will murmur, and oppose, and be always striving to shake off that yoke; but if you will be satisfied to enjoy such civil and lawful liberties, such as Christ allows you, then will you quietly and cheerfully submit unto that authority which is set over you, in all the administrations of it, for your good. Wherein, if we fail at any time, we hope we shall be willing (by God's assistance) to hearken to good advice from any of you, or in any other way of God; so shall your liberties be preserved, in upholding the honor and power of authority amongst you.

Source: Old South Leaflets, vol. 3, no. 66 (n.d.).

John Winthrop (1588–1649) was the first governor of Massachusetts Bay Colony.

John Cotton
Limitation of Government

Let all the world learn to give mortall men no greater power then they are content they shall use, for use it they will: and unlesse they be better taught of God, they will use it ever and anon, it may be make it the passage of their proceeding to speake what they will: And they that have liberty to speak great things, you will finde it to be true, they will speak great blasphemies. No man would think what desperate deceit and wickednesse there is in the hearts of men: And that was the reason why the Beast did speak such great things, hee might speak, and no body might controll him: What, saith the Lord in *Jer.* 3: 5. *Though hast spoken and done evill things as thou couldst.* If a Church or head of a Church could have done worse, he would have done it: This is one of the straines of nature, it affects boundlesse liberty, and to runne to the utmost extent: What ever power he hath received, he hath a corrupt nature that will improve it in one thing or other; if he have liberty, he will think why may he not use it. Set up the Pope as Lord Paramount over Kings and Princes, and they shall know that he hath power over them, he will take liberty to depose one, and set up another. Give him power to make Laws, and he will approve, and disprove as he list; what he approves is canonicall, what hee disproves is rejected: Give him that power, and he will so order it at length, he will make such a State of Religion, that he that so lives and dyes shall never be saved, and all this springs from the vast power that is given to him, and from the deep depravation of nature. Hee will open his mouth, *His tongue is his owne, who is Lord over him,* Psal. 12: 3, 4. It is therefore most wholesome for Magistrates and Officers in Church and Commonwealth, never to affect more liberty and authority then will do them good, and the People good; for whatever transcendant power is given, will certainly over-run those that give it, and those that receive it: There is a straine in a mans heart that will sometime or other runne out to excesse, unless the Lord restraine it, but it is not good to venture it:

It is necessary therefore, that all power that is on earth be limited, Church-power or other: If there be power given to speak great things, then look for great blasphemies, look for a licentious abuse of it. It is counted a matter of danger to the State to limit Prerogatives; but it is a further danger, not to have them limited: They will be like a Tempest, if they be not limited: A Prince himselfe cannot tell where he will confine himselfe, nor can the people tell: But if he have liberty to speak great things, then he will make and unmake, say and unsay, and undertake such things as are neither for his owne honour, nor for the safety of the State. It is therefore fit for every man to be studious of the bounds which the Lord hath set: and for the People, in whom fundamentally all power lyes, to give as much power as God in his word gives to men: And it is meet that Magistrates in the Commonwealth, and so Officers in Churches should desire to know the utmost bounds of their own power, and it is safe for both: All intrenchment upon the bounds which God hath not given, they are not enlargements, but burdens and snares; They will certainly lead the spirit of a man out of his way sooner or later. It is wholsome and safe to be dealt withall as God deales with the vast Sea; *Hitherto shalt thou come, but there shalt thou stay thy proud waves:* and therefore if they be but banks of simple sand, they will be good enough to check the vast roaring Sea. And so for Imperiall Monarchies, it is safe to know how far their power extends; and then if it be but banks of sand, which is most slippery, it will serve, as well as any brazen wall. If you pinch the Sea of its liberty, though it be walls of stone or brasse, it will beate them downe: So it is with Magistrates, stint them where God hath not stinted them, and if they were walls of brasse, they would beate them downe, and it is meet they should: but give them the liberty God allows, and if it be but a wall of sand it will keep them: As this liquid Ayre in which we breath, God hath set it for the waters of the Clouds to the Earth; It is a Firmament, it is the Clouds, yet it stand firme enough, because it keeps the Climate where they are, it shall stand like walls of brasse: So let there be due bounds sct, and I may apply it to Families; it is good for the Wife to acknowledge all power and authority to the Husband, and for the Husband to acknowledge honour to the Wife, but still give them that which God hath given them, and no more nor lesse: Give them the full latitude that God hath given, else you will finde you dig pits, and lay snares, and cumber their spirits, if you give them lesse: there is never peace where full liberty is not given, nor never stable peace where more then full liberty is granted: Let them be duely observed, and give men no more liberty then God doth, nor women, for they will abuse it: The Devill will draw them, and Gods providence leade them thereunto, therefore give them no more then God gives. And so for children; and servants, or any others you are to deale with, give them the liberty and authority you would have them use, and beyond that stretch not the tether, it will not tend to their good nor yours: And also from hence gather, and goe home with this meditation; That certainly here is this distemper in our natures, that we cannot tell how to use liberty, but wee shall very readily corrupt our selves: Oh the bottomlesse depth of sandy earth! of a corrupt spirit, that breaks over all bounds, and loves inordinate vastnesse; that is it we ought to be carefull of.

Source: An Exposition upon the Thirteenth Chapter of the Revelation. By John Cotton. London: Printed for Livewel Chapman, 1655.

John Cotton (1584–1652) was the main leader of Congregationalism in America and was known as the "Patriarch of New England."

Cotton Mather
A Platform of Church Discipline, Gathered Out of the Word of God, And Agreed Upon By the Elders and Messengers of the Churches Assembled in the Synod, at Cambridge, in New-England. To Be Presented to the Churches and General Court for Their Consideration and Acceptance in the Lord, the 8th Month, Anno 1649.

Chapter I.
Of the Form of Church-Government; And That It Is One, Immutable, and Prescribed In the Word.

3. The parts of church-government are all of them exactly described in the word of God, being parts or means of instituted worship according to the second commandment, and therefore to continue one and the same unto the appearing of our Lord Jesus Christ, as a kingdom that cannot be shaken, until he shall deliver it up unto God, even to the Father. So that it is not left in the power of men, officers, churches, or any state in the world, to add, or diminish, or alter any thing in the least measure therein.

4. The necessary circumstances, as time and place, &c., belonging unto order and decency, are not so left unto men, as that, under pretence of them, they may thrust their own inventions upon the churches, being circumscribed in the word with many general limitations, where they are determined with respect to the matter to be neither worship it self, nor circumstances separable from worship. In respect of their end, they must be done unto edification; in respect of the manner, decently and in order, according to the nature of the things themselves, and civil and church custom. . . .

Chapter III.
Of the Matter of the Visible Church, Both in Respect of Quality and Quantity.

1. The matter of the visible church are saints by calling.

2. By saints, we understand—1, Such as have not only attained the knowledge of the principles of religion, and are free from gross and open scandals, but also do, together with the profession of their faith and repentance, walk in blameless obedience to the word, so as that in charitable discretion they may be accounted saints by calling, (tho' perhaps some or more of them be unsound and hypocrites inwardly) because the members of such particular churches are commonly by the Holy Ghost called "saints and faithful brethren in Christ;" and sundry churches have been reproved for receiving, and suffering such persons to continue in fellowship among them, as have been offensive and scandalous; the name of God also, by this means, is blasphemed, and the holy things of God defiled and profaned, the hearts of the godly grieved, and the wicked themselves hardened and holpen forward to damnation. The example of such doth endanger the sanctity of others, a little leaven leaveneth the whole lump. 2, The children of such who are also holy. . . .

4. The matter of the church, in respect of its *quantity*, ought not to be of greater number than may ordinarily meet together conveniently in one place; nor ordinarily fewer than may conveniently carry on church-work. . . .

5. Nor can it with reason be thought but that every church appointed and ordained by Christ, had a ministry appointed and ordained for the same, and yet plain it is that there were no ordinary officers appointed by Christ for any other than congregational churches; elders being appointed to feed not all flocks, but the particular flock of God, over which the Holy Ghost had made them over seers, and that flock they must attend, even the whole flock: and one congregation being as much as any ordinary elders can attend, therefore there is no greater church than a congregation which may ordinarily meet in one place.

Chapter IV.
Of the Form of the Visible Church, and of Church Covenant.

2. Particular churches cannot be distinguished one from another but by their forms. . . . [E]ach one [is] a distinct society of itself, having officers of their own, which had not the charge of others; virtues of their own, for which others are not praised; corruptions of their own, for which others are not blamed.

3. This form is the *visible covenant*, agreement or consent, whereby they give up themselves unto the Lord, to the observing of the ordinances of Christ together in the same society, which is usually call'd the "church covenant." . . . The

covenant, as it was that which made the family of Abraham and children of Israel to be a church and people unto God, so is it that which now makes the several societies of Gentile believers to be churches in these days.

4. This voluntary agreement, consent or covenant—for all these are here taken for the same—altho' the more express and plain it is, the more fully it puts us in mind of our mutual duty; and stirreth us up to it, and leaveth less room for the questioning of the truth of the church-estate of a company of professors, and the truth of membership of particular persons; yet we conceive the substance of it is kept where there is real agreement and consent of a company of faithful persons to meet constantly together in one congregation, for the publick worship of God, and their mutual edification: which real agreement and consent they do express by their constant practice in coming together for the publick worship of God and by their religious subjection unto the ordinances of God there. . . .

5. This form being by mutual covenant, it followeth, it is not faith in the heart, nor the profession of that faith, nor cohabitation, nor baptism. 1, Not *faith in the heart,* because that is invisible. 2, Not *a bare profession,* because that declareth them no more to be members of one church than another. 3, Not *cohabitation:* Atheists or Infidels may dwell together with believers. 4, Not *Baptism,* because it presupposeth a church-estate, as circumcision in the Old Testament, which gave no being to the church, the church being before it, and in the wilderness without it. Seals presuppose a covenant already in being. One person is a compleat subject of baptism, but one person is uncapable of being a church. . . .

Chapter VIII.
Of the Election of Church Officers.

1. No man may take the honour of a church-officer unto himself but he that was called of God, as was Aaron. .

2. Calling unto office is either *immediate,* by Christ himself—such was the *call* of the apostles and prophets; this manner of calling ended with them, as hath been said—or *mediate,* by the church.

3. It is meet that, before any be ordained or chosen officers, they should first be tried and proved, because hands are not suddenly to be laid upon any, and both elders and deacons must be of both honest and good report.

4. The things in respect of which they are to be tried, are those gifts and vertues which the Scripture requireth in men that are to be elected unto such places. . . .

5. Officers are to be called by such churches whereunto they are to minister. Of such moment is the preservation of this power, that the churches exercised it in the presence of apostles.

6. A church being free, cannot become subject to any but by a free election; yet when such a people do chuse any to be over them in the Lord, then do they be-

come subject, and most willingly submit to their ministry in the Lord, whom they have chosen.

7. And if the church have power to chuse their officers and ministers, then, in case of manifest unworthiness and delinquency, they have power also to depose them: for to open and shut, to chuse and refuse, to constitute in office, and to remove from office, are acts belonging to the same power.

8. We judge it much conducing to the well-being and communion of the churches, that, where it may conveniently be done, neighbour churches be advised withal, and their help be made use of in trial of church-officers, in order to their choice.

9. The choice of such church-officers belongeth not to the civil magistrate as such, or diocesan bishops, or patrons: for of these, or any such like, the Scripture is wholly silent, as having any power therein.

Chapter IX.
Of Ordination and Imposition of Hands.

1. CHURCH-OFFICERS are not only to be chosen by the church, but also to be ordained by imposition of hands and prayer, with which at the ordination of elders, fasting also is to be joined.

2. This ordination we account nothing else but the solemn putting a man into his place and office in the church, whereunto he had right before by election; being like the installing of a magistrate in the common-wealth. Ordination therefore is not to go before, but to follow election. The essence and substance of the outward calling of an ordinary officer in the church does not consist in his ordination, but in his voluntary and free election by the church, and his accepting of that election; whereupon is founded that relation between pastor and flock, between such a minister and such a people. Ordination does not constitute an officer, nor give him the essentials of his office. . . .

Chapter XVII.
Of the Civil Magistrate's Power in Matters Ecclesiastical.

1. It is lawful, profitable and necessary for Christians to gather themselves together into church estate, and therein to exercise all the ordinances of Christ, according unto the word, although the consent of the magistrate could not be had thereunto; because the apostles and Christians in their time did frequently thus practise, when the magistrates, being all of them Jewish and Pagan, and most persecuting enemies, would give no countenance or consent to such matters.

2. Church-government stands in no opposition to civil government of commonwealths, nor any way intrencheth upon the authority of civil magistrates in

their jurisdictions; nor any whit weakeneth their hands in governing but rather strengtheneth them, and furthereth the people in yielding more hearty and conscionable obedience to them, whatsoever some ill affected persons to the ways of Christ have suggested, to alienate the affections of kings and princes from the ordinances of Christ; as if the kingdom of Christ in his church could not rise and stand, without the falling and weakening of their government, which is also of Christ, whereas the contrary is most true, that they may both stand together and flourish, the one being helpful unto the other, in their distinct and due administrations.

3. The power and authority of magistrates is not for the restraining of churches or any other good works, but for helping in and furthering thereof; and therefore the consent and countenances of magistrates, when it may be had, is not to be slighted, or lightly esteemed; but, on the contrary, it is part of that honor due to Christian magistrates to desire and crave their consent and approbation therein; which being obtained, the churches may then proceed in their way with much more encouragement and comfort.

4. It is not in the power of magistrates to compel their subjects to become church-members, and to partake of the Lord's Supper; . . . those whom the church is to cast out, if they were in, the magistrate ought not to thrust them into the church, nor to hold them therein.

5. As it is unlawful for church-officers to meddle with the sword of the magistrate, so it is unlawful for the magistrate to meddle with the work proper to church-officers. . . .

6. The end of the magistrate's office is not only the quiet and peaceable life of the subject in matters of righteousness and honesty, but also in matters of godliness; yea, of all godliness. . . .

7. The objects of the power of the magistrate are not things meerly inward, and so not subject to his cognizance and views: as unbelief, hardness of heart, erroneous opinions not vented, but only such things as are acted by the outward man; neither their power to be exercised in commanding such acts of the outward man, and punishing the neglect thereof, as are but meer inventions and devices of men, but about such acts as are commanded and forbidden in the word: yea, such as the word doth clearly determine, tho' not always clearly to the judgment of the magistrate or others, yet clearly in its self. In these he, of right, ought to put forth his authority, tho' oft-times actually he doth it not.

8. Idolatry, blasphemy, heresie, venting corrupt and pernicious opinions, that destroy the foundation, open contempt of the word preached, prophanation of the Lord's Day, disturbing the peaceable administration and exercise of the worship and holy things of God, and the like, are to be restrained and punished by civil authority.

9. If any church, one or more, shall grow schismatical, rending itself from the

communion of other churches, or shall walk incorrigibly and obstinately in any corrupt way of their own, contrary to the rule of the word, in such case, the magistrate is to put forth his coercive power, as the matter shall require.

Source: Magnalia Christi Americana; or, The Ecclesiastical History of New-England, From Its First Planting, In the Year 1620, Unto the Year of Our Lord 1698. In Seven Books. By Cotton Mather. 2 volumes. New York: Russell & Russell, 1967. Reprint of 1852 edition.

Cotton Mather (1663–1728) was an American Congregationalist minister.

Freedom of the Press

An issue that appeared in the colonies as early as the 1730s was press freedom. An early statement of the position is found in the following speech by Andrew Hamilton (1676–1741) in defense of the printer John Peter Zenger (1697–1746), who was on trial for libel. Zenger's paper, the New York *Weekly Journal*, had consistently attacked the policies of the governor of New York, who sued Zenger for libel. After the governor had prohibited any New York lawyer from acting for Zenger, Andrew Hamilton came from Pennsylvania, where he had been attorney general, to take on Zenger's defense. Hamilton established the truth of the material Zenger had printed and, as a result, the jury found Zenger innocent. This case established that truth was a defense against a charge of libel.

Andrew Hamilton
Speech at the Trial of Peter Zenger

There is heresy in law as well as in religion, and both have changed very much; and we well know that it is not two centuries ago that a man would have been burnt as an heretic for owning such opinions in matters of religion as are publicly wrote and printed at this day. They were fallible men, it seems, and we take the liberty not only to differ from them in religious opinions, but to condemn them and their opinions too; and I must presume that in taking these freedoms in thinking and speaking about matters of faith or religion, we are in the right: For, though it is said there are very great liberties of this kind taken in New York, yet I have heard of no information preferred by Mr. Attorney for any offenses of this sort. From which I think it is pretty clear that in New York a man may make very free with his God, but he must take special care what he says of his governor. It is agreed upon by all men that this is a reign of liberty, and while men keep within the bounds of truth, I hope they may with safety both speak and write their sentiments of the conduct of men in power. I mean of that part of their conduct only which affects the liberty or property of the people under their administration; were this to be denied, then the next step may make them slaves: For what notions can be entertained of slavery beyond that of suffering the greatest injuries and oppressions without the liberty of complaining; or if they do, to be destroyed, body and estate, for so doing?

It is said and insisted on by Mr. Attorney *that government is a sacred thing; that it is to be supported and reverenced; it is government that protects our persons and estates; that prevents treasons, murders, robberies, riots, and all the train of evils that overturns kingdoms and states and ruins particular persons; and if those in the administration, especially the supreme magistrate, must have all their conduct censured by private men, government cannot subsist.* This is called *a licentiousness not to be tolerated.* It is said *that it brings the rulers of the people into contempt, and their authority not to be regarded, and so in the end the laws cannot be put in execution.* These I say, and such as these, are the general topics insisted upon by men in power and their advocates. But I wish it might be considered at the same time how often it has happened that the abuse of power has been the primary cause of these evils, and that it was the injustice and oppression of these great men which has commonly brought them into contempt with the people. The craft and art of such men is great, and who that is the least acquainted with history or law can be ignorant of the specious pretenses which have often been made use of by men in power to introduce arbitrary rule and destroy the liberties of a free people.

Power may justly be compared to a great river, while kept within its due bounds, is both beautiful and useful; but when it overflows its banks, it is then too impetuous to be stemmed, it bears down all before it and brings destruction and desolation wherever it comes. If then this is the nature of power, let us at least do our duty, and like wise men (who value freedom) use our utmost care to support liberty, the only bulwark against lawless power, which in all ages has sacrificed to its wild lust and boundless ambition the blood of the best men that ever lived. . . .

I am truly very unequal to such an undertaking on many accounts. And you see I labor under the weight of many years, and am borne down with great infirmities of body; yet old and weak as I am, I should think it my duty, if required, to go to the utmost part of the land where my service could be of any use in assisting to quench the flame of prosecutions upon informations set on foot by the government to deprive a people of the right of remonstrating (and complaining too) of the arbitrary attempts of men in power. Men who injure and oppress the people under their administration provoke them to cry out and complain; and then make that very complaint the foundation for new oppressions and prosecutions. I wish I could say there were no instances of this kind. But to conclude; the question before the Court and you gentlemen of the jury is not of small nor private concern, it is not the cause of a poor printer, nor of New York alone, which you are now trying: No! It may in its consequence affect every freeman that lives under a British government on the main of America. It is the best cause. It is the cause of liberty; and I make no doubt but your upright conduct this day will not only entitle you to the love and esteem of your fellow citizens; but every man who prefers freedom to a life of slavery will bless and honor you as men who have baffled the attempt of tyranny; and by an impartial and uncorrupt verdict, have laid a noble foundation for securing to ourselves, our posterity, and our neighbors that to which nature and the laws of our country have given us a right—the liberty—both of exposing and opposing arbitrary power (in these parts of the world, at least) by speaking and writing truth.

Source: A Brief Narrative of the Case and Trial of John Peter Zenger, Printer of the New York Weekly Journal. By James Alexander. Edited by Stanley Nider Katz. Cambridge, Mass.: Belknap Press of Harvard University Press, 1963.

Andrew Hamilton (1676–1741) was an American lawyer.

Minorities

A constant theme throughout American political thought is the question of minority rights. The definition of minorities changes and the responses of the dominant groups vary, but the issue remains. The first selection is a Maryland law regarding slavery. Following this are two selections regarding the treatment of Indians. One is a famous letter from William Penn (1644–1718) to the Indians in which he expresses friendship and indicates that relations should progress on the basis of negotiations. Penn developed generally positive relations with Indians in Pennsylvania. The other is more typical of relations with the Indians; it is a law from Connecticut proposing means of controlling them.

AFRICAN AMERICANS

An act concerning Negroes and other slaves

Be it enacted by the Right Honorable the Lord Proprietary by the advise and consent of the upper and lower house of this present Generall Assembly, that all Negroes or other slaves already within the province, and all Negroes and other slaves to be hereafter imported into the province, shall serve *durante vita* [hard labor for life]. And all children born of any Negro or other slave shall be slaves as their fathers were, for the term of their lives. And forasmuch as divers freeborn English women, forgetful of their free condition and to the disgrace of our nation, marry Negro slaves, by which also divers suits may arise touching the issue

of such women, and a great damage befalls the masters of such Negroes for prevention whereof, for deterring such freeborn women from such shameful
matches. Be it further enacted by the authority, advise, and consent aforesaid,
that whatsoever freeborn woman shall marry any slave from and after the last day
of this present Assembly shall serve the master of such slave during the life of her
husband. And that all the issue of such freeborn women so married shall be slaves
as their fathers were. And be it further enacted, that all the issues of English or
other freeborn women that have already married Negroes shall serve the masters
of their parents till they be thirty years of age and no longer.

Source: Proceedings and Acts of the General Assembly of Maryland (September 1664).

INDIANS

William Penn
Letter to the Indians

My Freinds

There is one great God and Power that hath made the world and all things
therein, to whom you and I and all People owe their being and wellbeing, and to
whom you and I must one Day give an account, for all that we do in this world:
this great God hath written his law in our hearts, by which we are taught and
commanded to love and help and do good to one an other, and not to do harme
and mischeif one unto one another: Now this great God hath been pleased to
make me concerned in y^r parts of the World, and the king of the Countrey where
I live, hath given unto me a great Province therein, but I desire to enjoy it with
your Love and Consent, that we may always live together as neighbours and
freinds, else what would the great God say to us, who have made us not to de-
voure and destroy one an other but live Soberly and kindly together in the
World. Now I would have you well to observe, that I am very Sensible of the unkindness and Injustice that hath been too much exercised toward you by the People of thes Parts off the world, who have sought themselves, and to make great
Advantages by you, rather then be examples of Justice and Goodness unto you,
which I hear, hath been matter of trouble to you, and caused great Grudgeings
and Animosities, sometimes to the shedding of blood, which hath made the great
God Angry, but I am not such a Man, as is well known in my own Country: I
have great love and regard towards you, and I desire to Winn and gain your
Love & Freindship by a kind, just and peaceable life; and the People I send are of
the same mind, & shall in all things behave themselves accordingly; and if in any
thing any shall offend you or your People, you shall have a full and Speedy Satis-

faction for the same by an equall number of honest men on both sides that by no means you may have just Occasion of being offended against them; I shall shortly come to you my selfe.

At what time we may more largely and freely confer & discourse of thes matters; in the mean time, I have sent my Commissioners to treat with you about land & a firm league of peace. Lett me desire you to be kind to them and the People, and receive thes Presents and Tokens which I have sent to you, as a Testimony of my Good will to you, and my resolution to live Justly peaceably and friendly with you, I am your Freind.

Source: The Papers of William Penn. Volume 2, 1680–1684. Edited by Richard S. Dunn and Mary Maples Dunn. Philadelphia: University of Pennsylvania Press, 1982.

William Penn (1644–1718) was the Quaker founder of Pennsylvania.

An Act for the more effectual well ordering of the Indians, and for the bringing of them to the knowledge of the gospel.

Whereas, pursuant to an act of the Assembly, holden in Hartford in the present year one thousand seven hundred and seventeen: The Governor and Council have laid before this Assembly several measures for bringing the Indians in this Colony to the knowledge of the gospel, which was the avowed design of those that obtained the patent for this corporation, to hold the land and government of the Colony:

Upon consideration of which measures, the Governor and Company of this, his Majestie's colony, in General Court assembled, desirous of pursuing in the best manner the solemn professions of our predecessors, have enacted,

And it is hereby enacted by the Governor, Council, and Representatives, in General Court assembled, and by the authority of the same, That care be taken annually by the authority of each town, to convene the Indians inhabiting in each town, and acquaint them with the laws of the Government for punishing such immoralities as they shall be guilty of, and make them sensible that no exemption from the penalties of such laws lies for them, any more than for other his Majesty's subjects. . . .

And forasmuch as idleness appears to be a great obstruction to the Indians receiving the gospel of truth, and it might very much conduce to their reformation, in that particular, if they were, by easy and agreeable methods, brought off from their pagan manner of living and encouraged to make settlements in convenient places, in villages, after the English manner:

It is hereby resolved, That measures shall be used to form villages of the natives, wherein the several families of them should have suitable portions of land appropriated to them, so that the said portions shall descend from the father to his children, the more to encourage them to apply themselves to husbandry, and good diligence therein, for their support.

Source: Laws of the Colonial and State Governments, Relating to Indians and Indian Affairs, 1663–1831 Inclusive. With an Appendix Containing the Proceedings of the Congress of the Confederation and the Laws of Congress from 1800 to 1830. On the same Subject. Washington City: Thompson and Homans, 1832.

CHAPTER 3

The Revolution, 1763–1780

✳ ✳ ✳

The period of the American Revolution was a time of great creativity in American political thought. The thought of the time is dominated by those arguing for a break from Britain, but the American Loyalists or Tories who opposed such a break should not be forgotten. It is also important to recognize that the American revolutionists saw themselves as part of a process to change American culture. The First Continental Congress discussed a number of issues in addition to relations with Britain. For instance, the Congress banned cockfighting, horse-racing, and the theater and modified the funeral ceremony.[1] From the middle of the eighteenth century through the first part of the nineteenth, a real revolution in American life and culture took place.[2]

Statements on Relations with Britain

Although the actual revolution took place in the mid to late 1770s, the process began long before. No event like the American Revolution occurs without substantial intellectual and political preparation, and the debates over separation from Britain have a history that significantly pre-dates the violent confrontations. Two examples will suffice to express the early sentiment regarding Britain — "Instructions of the Town of Braintree" of 1765, written by John Adams (1735–1826) of Massachusetts, and the "Anson County Petition" of 1769 from North Carolina.

Adams was one of the most important early American political theorists. Generally labeled a conservative, he often disagreed with his close friend

Thomas Jefferson (1743–1826), but on many things the two agreed. Adams believed that aristocracy (defined as the rule of the few) was inevitable, and he argued for a system in which rule would be by a natural aristocracy—that is, an aristocracy of influence, not of birth.

He recognized as a central problem of political practice the issue of how to balance the moral right to equal treatment against the fact of differential influence. In later writings, he saw the American Constitution as a mechanism for doing this. Free government would control rivalries; separation of powers would allow the executive branch to mediate between the rich and the poor, represented by the Senate and the House of Representatives. Federalism and the checks-and-balances system would also help limit influence.

"Instructions" is an early statement of the "no taxation without representation" argument that became one of the most important themes for the colonies. Adams also argues for the jury system, which ultimately became part of the Bill of Rights, and he says that judges have too much power, an argument that opponents of the Constitution later made. The "Anson County Petition" emphasizes the poverty that English policy has produced. Thus, these statements reflect arguments about both institutional arrangements and social conditions.

John Adams
Instructions of the Town of Braintree to Their Representative, 1765

In all the calamities which have ever befallen this country, we have never felt so great a concern, or such alarming apprehensions, as on this occasion. Such is our loyalty to the King, our veneration for both houses of Parliament, and our affection for all our fellow-subjects in Britain, that measures which discover any unkindness in that country towards us are the more sensibly and intimately felt. And we can no longer forbear complaining, that many of the measures of the late ministry, and some of the late acts of Parliament, have a tendency, in our apprehension, to divest us of our most essential rights and liberties. We shall confine ourselves, however, chiefly to the act of Parliament, commonly called the Stamp Act, by which a very burthensome, and, in our opinion, unconstitutional tax, is to be laid upon us all; and we subjected to numerous and enormous penalties, to be prosecuted, sued for, and recovered, at the option of an informer, in a court of admiralty, without a jury.

We have called this a burthensome tax, because the duties are so numerous and so high, and the embarrassments to business in this in fact, sparsely-settled country so great, that it would be totally impossible for the people to subsist under it, if we had no controversy at all about the right and authority of imposing it. Considering the present scarcity of money, we have reason to think, the execution of that act for a short space of time would drain the country of its cash, strip multitudes of all their property, and reduce them to absolute beggary. And what the consequence would be to the peace of the province, from so sudden a shock and such a convulsive change in the whole course of our business and subsistence, we tremble to consider. We further apprehend this tax to be unconstitutional. We have always understood it to be a grand and fundamental principle of the constitution, that no freeman should be subject to any tax to which he has not given his own consent, in person or by proxy. And the maxims of the law, as we have constantly received them, are to the same effect, that no freeman can be separated from his property but by his own act or fault. We take it clearly, therefore, to be inconsistent with the spirit of the common law, and of the essential fundamental principles of the British constitution, that we should be subject to any tax imposed by the British Parliament; because we are not represented in that assembly in any sense, unless it be by a fiction of law, as insensible in theory as it would be injurious in practice, if such a taxation should be grounded on it.

But the most grievous innovation of all, is the alarming extension of the power of courts of admiralty. In these courts, one judge presides alone! No juries have any concern there! The law and the fact are both to be decided by the same single judge, whose commission is only during pleasure, and with whom, as we are told, the most mischievous of all customs has become established, that of taking commissions on all condemnations; so that he is under a pecuniary temptation always against the subject. . . . We cannot help asserting, therefore, that this part of the act will make an essential change in the constitution of juries, and it is repugnant to the Great Charter [Magna Carta] itself. . . .

As these, sir, are our sentiments of this act, we, the freeholders and other inhabitants, legally assembled for this purpose, must enjoin it upon you, to comply with no measures or proposals for countenancing the same, or assisting in the execution of it, but by all lawful means, consistent with our allegiance to the King, and relation to Great Britain, to oppose the execution of it, till we can hear the success of the cries and petitions of America for relief.

We further recommend the most clear and explicit assertion and vindication of our rights and liberties to be entered on the public records, that the world may know, in the present and all future generations, that we have a clear knowledge and a just sense of them, and, with submission to Divine Providence, that we never can be slaves.

Source: *The Works of John Adams, Second President of the United States: With a Life of the Author, Notes and Illustrations by His Grandson Charles Francis Adams.* Volume 3. Freeport, N.Y.: Books for the Libraries Press, 1969. Reprint of the 1850–56 edition.

John Adams (1735–1826) was the second president of the United States.

Anson County Petition

The Petition of the Inhabitants of Anson County, being part of the Remonstrance of the Province of North Carolina.
Humbly Sheweth

That the Province in general labour under general grievances, and the Western part thereof under particular ones; which we not only see, but very sensibly feel, being crouch'd beneath our sufferings: and notwithstanding our sacred priviledges, have too long yielded ourselves slaves to remorseless oppression. — Permit us to conceive it to be our inviolable right to make known our grievances, and to petition for redress; as appears in the Bill of Rights pass'd in the reign of King Charles the first, as well as the act of Settlement of the Crown of the Revolution. We therefore beg leave to lay before you a specimen thereof that your compassionate endeavours may tend to the relief of your injured Constituents, whose distressed condition calls aloud for aid. The alarming cries of the oppressed possibly may reach your Ears; but without your zeal how shall they ascend the throne — how relentless is the breast without sympathy, the heart that cannot bleed on a View of our calamity; to see tenderness removed, cruelty stepping in: and all our liberties and priviledges invaded and abridg'd (by as it were) domesticks: who are, conscious of their guilt and void of remorse. — O how daring! how relentless! whilst impending Judgments loudly threaten and gaze upon them with every emblem of merited destruction.

A few of the many grievances are as follows, (Viz')

1. That the poor Inhabitants in general are much oppress'd by reason of disproportionate Taxes, and those of the western Counties in particular; as they are generally in mean circumstances.

2. That no method is prescribed by Law for the payment of the Taxes of the Western Counties in produce (in lieu of a Currency) as is in other Counties within this Province; to the Peoples great oppression.

3. That Lawyers, Clerks, and other pentioners; in place of being obsequious Servants for the Country's use, are become a nuisance, as the business of the people is often transacted without the least degree of fairness, the intention of the law evaded, exorbitant fees extorted, and the sufferers left to mourn under their oppressions.

4. That an Attorney should have it in his power, either for the sake of ease or interest, or to gratify their malevolence and spite, to commence suits to what Courts he pleases, however inconvenient it may be to the Defendant: is a very great oppression.

5. That all unlawful fees taken on Indictment, where the Defendant is acquitted by his Country (however customary it may be) is an oppression.

6. That Lawyers, Clerks, and others, extorting more fees than is intended by law; is also an oppression.

7. That the violation of the King's Instructions to his delegates, their artfulness in concealing the same from him; and the great Injury the People thereby sustains: is a manifest oppression.

And for remedy whereof, we take the freedom to recommend the following mode of redress, not doubting audience and acceptance; which will not only tend to our relief, but command prayers as a duty from your humble Petitioners.

1. That at all elections each suffrage be given by Ticket & Ballot.

2. That the mode of Taxation be altered, and each person to pay in proportion to the profits arising from his Estate.

3. That no future tax be laid in Money, untill a currency is made.

4. That there may be established a Western as well as a Northern and Southern District, and a Treasurer for the same.

5. That when a currency is made it may be let out by a Loan office (on Land security) and not to be call'd in by a Tax.

6. That all debts above 40s. and under £10 be tried and determined without Lawyers, by a jury of six freeholders, impanneled by a Justice, and that their verdict be enter'd by the said Justice, and be a final judgment.

7. That the Chief Justice have no perquisites, but a Sallary only.

8. That Clerks be restricted in respect to fees, costs, and other things within the course of their office.

9. That Lawyers be effectually Barr'd from exacting and extorting fees.

10. That all doubts may be removed in respect to the payment of fees and costs on Indictments where the Defendant is not found guilty by the jury, and therefore acquitted.

11. That the Assembly make known by Remonstrance to the King, the conduct of the cruel and oppressive Receiver of the Quit Rents, for omitting the customary easie and effectual method of collecting by distress, and pursuing the expensive mode of commencing suits in the most distant Courts.

12. That the Assembly in like manner make known that the governor and Council do frequently grant Lands to as many as they think proper without regard to Head Rights, not withstanding the contrariety of His Majesties Instructions; by which means immense sums has been collected, and numerous Patents

granted, for much of the most fertile lands in this Province, that is yet uninhab-
ited and uncultivated, environed by great number of poor people who are neces-
sitated to toil in the cultivation of bad Lands whereon they hardly can subsist,
who are thereby deprived of His Majesties liberality and Bounty: nor is there the
least regard paid to the cultivation clause in said Patent mentioned, as many of
the said Council as well as their friends and favorites enjoy large Quantities of
Lands under the above-mentioned circumstances.

13. That the Assembly communicates in like manner the Violation of His Majesties Instructions respecting the Land Office by the Governor and Council, and
of their own rules, customs and orders, if it be sufficiently proved, that after they
had granted Warrants for many Tracts of Land, and that the same was in due
time survey'd and return'd, and the Patent fees timely paid into the said office;
and that if a private Council was called on purpose to avoid spectators, and pe-
remptory orders made that Patents should not be granted: and Warrants by their
orders arbitrarily to have Issued in the names of other Persons for the same
Lands, and if when intreated by a solicitor they refus'd to render so much as a reason for their so doing, or to refund any part of the money by them extorted.

14. That some method may be pointed out that every improvement on Lands
in any of the Proprietors part be proved when begun, by whom, and every sale
made, that the eldest may have the preference of at least 300 Acres.

15. That all Taxes . . . be paid as in other Counties in the Province (i.e.) in the
produce of the Country and that ware Houses be erected. . . .

16. That every denomination of People may marry according to their respective Mode Ceremony and custom after due publication or Licence.—

17. That Doct͏ʳ Benjamin Franklin or some other known patriot be appointed
Agent, to represent the unhappy state of this Province to his Majesty, and to so-
licit the several Boards in England.

Source: The Colonial Records of North Carolina. Volume 8, *1769 to 1779.* Edited by William
L. Saunders. Raleigh, N.C.: Josephus Daniels, 1890.

* * *

**As the revolution approached, stronger statements were made regarding separa-
tion from Britain. One of the most important was the "Declaration of Rights"
of 1774. Note resolution 6 of the declaration, which says that the colonies
should get to choose the laws that apply to them. No government could accept
such a position.**

Declaration of Rights

In Congress, at Philadelphia, October 14, 1774

Whereas, since the close of the last war, the British Parliament, claiming a power of right to bind the people of America, by statute, in all cases whatsoever, hath in some acts expressly imposed taxes on them, and in others, under various pretenses, but in fact for the purpose of raising a revenue, hath imposed rates and duties payable in these colonies established a board of commissioners, with unconstitutional powers, and extended the jurisdiction of courts of admiralty, not only for collecting the said duties, but for the trial of causes merely arising within the body of a county.

And whereas, in consequence of other statutes, judges, who before held only estates at will in their offices, have been made dependent on the Crown alone for their salaries, and standing armies kept in times of peace:

And whereas, it has lately been resolved in Parliament, that by force of a statute, made in the thirty-fifth year of the reign of King Henry the Eighth, colonists may be transported to England, and tried there upon accusations for treasons, and misprisions, or concealments of treasons committed in the colonies, and by a late statute, such trials have been directed in cases therein mentioned.

And whereas in the last session of Parliament, three statutes were made. . . . All which statutes are impolitic, unjust and cruel, as well as unconstitutional, and most dangerous and destructive of American rights.

The good people of the several colonies of New Hampshire, Massachusetts Bay, Rhode Island and Providence Plantations, Connecticut, New York, New Jersey, Pennsylvania, New Castle, Kent and Sussex on Delaware, Maryland, Virginia, North Carolina, and South Carolina, justly alarmed at these arbitrary proceedings of Parliament and administration, have severally elected, constituted, and appointed deputies to meet and sit in general congress, in the city of Philadelphia, in order to obtain such establishment, as that their religion, laws, and liberties may not be subverted:

Whereupon the deputies so appointed being now assembled, in a full and free representation of these colonies, taking into their most serious consideration, the best means of attaining the ends aforesaid, do in the first place, as Englishmen, their ancestors in like cases have usually done, for asserting and vindicating their rights and liberties, declare,

That the inhabitants of the English colonies in North America, by the immutable laws of nature, the principles of the English Constitution, and the several charters or compacts, have the following rights:

Resolved, N. C. D. 1. That they are entitled to life, liberty, and property, and they have never ceded to any sovereign power whatever, a right to dispose of either without their consent.

Resolved, N. C. D. 2. That our ancestors, who first settled these colonies, were at the time of their emigration from the mother country, entitled to all the rights, liberties, and immunities of free and natural born subjects, within the realm of England.

Resolved, N. C. D. 3. That by such emigration they by no means forfeited, surrendered, or lost any of those rights, but that they were, and their descendants now are, entitled to the exercise and enjoyment of all such of them, as their local and other circumstances enable them to exercise and enjoy.

Resolved, 4. That the foundation of English liberty, and of all free government, is a right in the people to participate in their legislative council: and as the English colonists are not represented, and from their local and other circumstances, can not properly be represented in the British Parliament, they are entitled to a free and exclusive power of legislation in their several provincial legislatures, where their right of representation can alone be preserved, in all cases of taxation and internal polity, subject only to the negative of their sovereign, in such manner as has been heretofore used and accustomed. But, from the necessity of the case, and a regard to the mutual interest of both countries, we cheerfully consent to the operation of such acts of the British Parliament, as are bona fide, restrained to the regulation of our external commerce, for the purpose of securing the commercial advantages of the whole empire to the mother country, and the commercial benefits of its respective members; excluding every idea of taxation, internal or external, for raising a revenue on the subjects in America, without their consent.

Resolved, N. C. D. 5. That the respective colonies are entitled to the common law of England, and more especially to the great and inestimable privilege of being tried by their peers of the vicinage, according to the course of that law.

Resolved, N. C. D. 6. That they are entitled to the benefit of such of the English statutes as existed at the time of their colonization; and which they have, by experience, respectively found to be applicable to their several local and other circumstances.

Resolved, N. C. D. 7. That these, His Majesty's colonies, are likewise entitled to all the immunities and privileges granted and confirmed to them by royal charters, or secured by their several codes of provincial laws.

Resolved, N. C. D. 8. That they have a right peaceably to assemble, consider of their grievances, and petition the King; and that all prosecutions, prohibitory proclamations, and commitments for the same, are illegal.

Resolved, N. C. D. 9. That the keeping a standing army in these colonies, in times of peace, without the consent of the legislature of that colony, in which such army is kept, is against law.

Resolved, N. C. D. 10. It is indispensably necessary to good government, and rendered essential by the English constitution, that the constituent branches of the legislature be independent of each other; that, therefore, the exercise of legislative power in several colonies, by a council appointed, during pleasure by the Crown, is unconstitutional, dangerous, and destructive to the freedom of American legislation.

All and each of which the aforesaid deputies, in behalf of themselves and their constituents, do claim, demand, and insist on, as their indubitable rights and liberties; which can not be legally taken from them, altered or abridged by any power whatever, without their own consent, by their representatives in their several provincial legislatures.

In the course of our inquiry, we find many infringements and violations of the foregoing rights, which, from an ardent desire, that harmony and mutual intercourse of affection and interest may be restored, we pass over for the present, and proceed to state such acts and measures as have been adopted since the last war, which demonstrate a system formed to enslave America.

Source: Journal of the Continental Congress of 1774–1789. Edited by Worthington Chauncey Ford. Washington, D.C.: Government Printing Office, 1904.

Loyalists

At the same time, there was opposition to separation from Britain. This is reflected in the following selection from Jonathan Boucher (1738–1804). Boucher very strongly opposes most of the positions taken by those advocating independence. He rejects consent theory, equality, revolution, and democracy. It is important to recognize that such opponents of the revolution and supporters of Britain also existed in the colonies.

Jonathan Boucher
Passive Obedience and Non-Resistance

[The] popular notion, that government was originally formed by the consent or by a compact of the people, rests on, and is supported by, another similar notion, not less popular, nor better founded. This other notion is, that the whole human race is born equal; and that no man is naturally inferior, or, in any respect, subjected to another; and that he can be made subject to another only by his own consent. The position is equally ill-founded and false both in it's premises and conclusions. In hardly any sense that can be imagined is the position strictly true; but, as applied to the case under consideration, it is demonstrably not true. Man differs from man in everything that can be supposed to lead to supremacy and subjection, *as one star differs from another star in glory.* It was the purpose of the Creator, that man should be social: but, without government, there can be no society; nor, without some relative inferiority and superiority, can there be any government. A musical instrument composed of chords, keys, or pipes, all perfectly equal in size and power, might as well be expected to produce harmony, as a society composed of members all perfectly equal to be productive of order and peace. If (according to the idea of the advocates of this chimerical scheme of equality) no man could rightfully *be compelled to come in* and be a member even of a government to be formed by a regular compact, but by his own individual consent; it clearly follows, from the same principles, that neither could he rightfully be made or compelled to submit to the ordinances of any government already formed, to which he has not individually or actually consented. On the principle of equality, neither his parents, nor even the vote of a majority of the society, (however virtuously and honourably that vote might be obtained,) can have any such authority over any man. Neither can it be maintained that acquiescence implies consent; because acquiescence may have been extorted from impotence or incapacity. Even an explicit consent can bind a man no longer than he chooses to be bound. The same principle of equality that exempts him from being governed without his own consent clearly entitles him to recall and resume that consent whenever he sees fit; and he alone has a right to judge when and for what reasons it may be resumed.

Any attempt, therefore, to introduce this fantastic system into practice, would reduce the whole business of social life to the wearisome, confused, and useless talk of mankind's first expressing, and then withdrawing, their consent to an endless succession of schemes of government. Governments, though always forming, would never be completely formed: for, the majority to-day, might be the minority tomorrow; and, of course, that which is now fixed might and would be soon unfixed. . . .

Government being assumed to be a mere human ordinance, it is thence inferred, that "rulers are the servants of the public:" and, if they be, no doubt it necessarily follows, that they may (in the coarse phrase of the times) be *cashiered* or continued in pay, be reverenced or resisted, according to the mere whim or caprice of those over whom they are appointed to rule. Hence the author of this sermon also takes occasion to enter his protest against "passive obedience and non-resistance".

All government, whether lodged in one or in many, is, in it's nature, absolute and irresistible. It is not within the competency even of the supreme power to limit itself; because such limitation can emanate only from a superior. For any government to make itself irresistible, and to cease to be absolute, it must cease to be supreme; which is but saying, in other words, that it must dissolve itself, or be destroyed. If, then, to resist government be to destroy it, every man who is a subject must necessarily owe to the government under which he lives an obedience either active or passive: active, where the duty enjoined may be performed without offending God; and passive, (that is to say, patiently to submit to the penalties annexed to disobedience), where that which is commanded by man is forbidden by God. No government upon earth can rightfully compel any one of it's subjects to an active compliance with any thing that is, or that appears to his conscience to be, inconsistent with, or contradictory to, the known laws of God: because every man is under a prior and superior obligation to *obey God in all things.* When such cases of incompatible demands of duty occur, every well-informed person knows what he is to do; and every well-principled person will do what he ought, viz. he will submit to the ordinances of God, rather than comply with the commandments of men. In this acting he cannot err: and this alone is "passive obedience;" which I entreat you to observe is so far from being "un-limited obedience," (as it's enemies wilfully persist to miscall it,) that it is the direct contrary. Resolute not to disobey God, a man of good principles determines, in case of competition, as the lesser evil, to disobey man: but he knows that he should also disobey God, were he not, at the same time, patiently to submit to any penalties incurred by his disobedience to man. . . .

Source: *A View of the Causes and Consequences of the American Revolution; In Thirteen Discourses, Preached in North America between 1763 and 1775: With an Historical Preface.* By Jonathan Boucher. New York: Russell & Russell, 1967. Originally published 1797.

Jonathan Boucher (1738–1804) was an Anglican clergyman.

Thomas Paine

Thomas Paine (1737–1809) had only recently arrived from Britain, but he quickly became embroiled in the controversy. *Common Sense* **(1776), his pamphlet calling for a break with Britain and attacking the institution of the monarchy, was Paine's first major foray into political debate. He was never far from such debate throughout the rest of his life, much of it spent outside the United States involved in revolutionary activity in France and Great Britain. It is a bit difficult to know how to treat Paine, since much of his work was written outside the United States and directed to European issues. In America he is clearly most important for** *Common Sense,* **but his attacks on religion in** *The Age of Reason* **(1793, 1795), his defense of human rights in** *The Rights of Man* **(1791–92), and his arguments for economic justice in the second part of** *The Rights of Man* **and in** *Agrarian Justice* **(1796) have remained both important and controversial.**

Thomas Paine

Common Sense

Of the Origin and Design of Government General.
With Concise Remarks on the English Constitution.

Some writers have so confounded society with government, as to leave little or no distinction between them; whereas they are not only different, but have different origins. Society is produced by our wants, and government by our wickedness; the former promotes our happiness *positively* by uniting our affections, the latter *negatively* by restraining our vices. The one encourages intercourse, the other creates distinctions. The first is a patron, the last a punisher.

Society in every state is a blessing, but government even in its best state is but a necessary evil; in its worst state an intolerable one; for when we suffer, or are exposed to the same miseries *by a government,* which we might expect in a country *without government,* our calamities is heightened by reflecting that we furnish the means by which we suffer. Government, like dress, is the badge of lost innocence; the palaces of kings are built on the ruins of the bowers of paradise. For were the impulses of conscience clear, uniform, and irresistibly obeyed, man would need no other lawgiver; but that not being the case, he finds it necessary to surrender up a part of his property to furnish means for the protection of the rest; and this he is induced to do by the same prudence which in every other case advises him out of two evils to choose the least. *Wherefore,* security being the true design and end of government, it unanswerably follows that whatever *form* thereof appears most likely to ensure it to us, with the least expense and greatest benefit, is preferable to all others.

In order to gain a clear and just idea of the design and end of government, let us suppose a small number of persons settled in some sequestered part of the earth, unconnected with the rest, they will then represent the first peopling of any country, or of the world. In this state of natural liberty, society will be their first thought. A thousand motives will excite them thereto, the strength of one man is so unequal to his wants, and his mind so unfitted for perpetual solitude, that he is soon obliged to seek assistance and relief of another, who in his turn requires the same. Four or five united would be able to raise a tolerable dwelling in the midst of a wilderness, but *one* man might labour out the common period of life without accomplishing any thing; when he had felled his timber he could not remove it, nor erect it after it was removed; hunger in the mean time would urge him from his work, and every different want call him a different way. Disease, nay even misfortune would be death, for though neither might be mortal, yet either would disable him from living, and reduce him to a state in which he might rather be said to perish than to die.

Thus necessity, like gravitating power, would soon form our newly arrived emigrants into society, the reciprocal blessings of which, would supercede, and render the obligations of law and government unnecessary while they remained perfectly just to each other; but as nothing but heaven is impregnable to vice, it will unavoidably happen, that in proportion as they surmount the first difficulties of emigration, which bound them together in a common cause, they will begin to relax in their duty and attachment to each other; and this remissness, will point out the necessity, of establishing some form of government to supply the defect of moral virtue.

Some convenient tree will afford them a State-House, under the branches of which, the whole colony may assemble to deliberate on public matters. It is more than probable that their first laws will have the title only of REGULATIONS, and be enforced by no other penalty than public disesteem. In this first parliament every man, by natural right will have a seat.

But as the colony increases, the public concerns will increase likewise, and the distance at which the members may be separated, will render it too inconvenient for all of them to meet on every occasion as at first, when their number was small, their habitations near, and the public concerns few and trifling. This will point out the convenience of their consenting to leave the legislative part to be managed by a select number chosen from the whole body, who are supposed to have the same concerns at stake which those have who appointed them, and who will act in the same manner as the whole body would act were they present. If the colony continue increasing, it will become necessary to augment the number of the representatives, and that the interest of every part of the colony may be attended to, it will be found best to divide the whole into convenient parts, each part sending its proper number; and that the *elected* might never form to themselves an interest separate from the *electors*, prudence will point out the propriety of having elections often; because as the *elected* might by that means return and mix again with the general body of the *electors* in a few months, their fidelity to the public will be secured by the prudent reflexion of not making a rod for themselves. And as this frequent interchange will establish a common interest with every part of the community, they will mutually and naturally support each other, and on this (not on the unmeaning name of king) depends the *strength of government, and the happiness of the governed.*

Here then is the origin and rise of government; namely, a mode rendered necessary by the inability of moral virtue to govern the world; here too is the design and end of government, viz. freedom and security. And however our eyes may be dazzled with snow, or our ears deceived by sound; however prejudice may warp our wills, or interest darken our understanding, the simple voice of nature and of reason will say, it is right.

I draw my idea of the form of government from a principle in nature, which no art can overturn, viz. that the more simple any thing is, the less liable it is to be disordered, and the easier repaired when disordered; and with this maxim in view, I offer a few remarks on the so much boasted constitution of England. That it was noble for the dark and slavish times in which it was erected is granted. When the world was over-run with tyranny the least remove therefrom was a glorious rescue. But that it is imperfect, subject to convulsions, and incapable of producing what it seems to promise, is easily demonstrated. . . .

Source: *Common Sense; addressed to the inhabitants of America.* By Thomas Paine. Philadelphia, 1776.

Thomas Paine (1737–1809) was a political agitator, revolutionist, and political theorist.

The Declaration of Independence

The Declaration of Independence, one of the classics of American political thought, was clearly influenced by John Locke (1632–1704) and was written by Thomas Jefferson in consultation with others. The Declaration, although a strong statement of political independence, was the result of political compromise. Jefferson wanted to include a statement condemning slavery, but it was deleted in order to keep Southern support. Note the structure of the argument. The beginning is a statement of general principles. This is followed by the bulk of the Declaration, which consists of examples of ways in which the British government has violated those principles.

Declaration of Independence

The unanimous Declaration of the thirteen united States of America

When in the course of human events, it becomes necessary for one people to dissolve the political bands which have connected them with another, and to assume among the Powers of the earth, the separate and equal station to which the laws of Nature and of Nature's God entitle them, a decent respect to the opinions of mankind requires that they should declare the causes which impel them to the separation.

We hold these truths to be self-evident, that all men are created equal, that they are endowed by their Creator with certain unalienable Rights, that among these are Life, Liberty, and the pursuit of Happiness. That to secure these rights, Governments are instituted among Men, deriving their just powers from the consent of the governed; That whenever any Form of Government becomes destructive of these ends, it is the Right of the People to alter or to abolish it, and to institute new Government, laying its foundation on such principles and organizing its powers in such form, as to them shall seem most likely to effect their Safety and Happiness. Prudence, indeed, will dictate that Governments long established should not be changed for light and transient causes; and accordingly all experience hath shown, that mankind are more disposed to suffer, while evils are sufferable, than to right themselves by abolishing the forms to which they are accustomed. But when a long train of abuses and usurpations, pursuing invariably the same Object evinces a design to reduce them under absolute Despotism, it is their right, it is their duty, to throw off such Government, and to provide new Guards for their future security. — Such has been the patient sufferance of these Colonies; and such is now the necessity which constrains them to alter their former Systems of Government. The history of the present King of Great Britain is a history of repeated injuries and usurpations, all having in direct object the establishment of an absolute Tyranny over these States. To prove this, let Facts be submitted to a candid world.

He has refused his Assent to Laws, the most wholesome and necessary for the public good.

He has forbidden his Governors to pass Laws of immediate and pressing importance, unless suspended in their operation till his Assent should be obtained; and when so suspended, he has utterly neglected to attend to them.

He has refused to pass other Laws for the accommodation of large districts of people, unless those people would relinquish the right of Representation in the Legislature, a right inestimable to them and formidable to tyrants only.

He has called together legislative bodies at places unusual, uncomfortable, and distant from the depository of their Public Records, for the sole purpose of fatiguing them into compliance with his measures.

He has dissolved Representative Houses repeatedly, for opposing with manly firmness his invasions on the rights of the people.

He has refused for a long time, after such dissolutions, to cause others to be elected; whereby the Legislative Powers, incapable of Annihilation, have returned to the People at large for their exercise; the State remaining in the meantime exposed to all the dangers of invasion from without, and convulsions within.

He has endeavoured to prevent the population of these States; for that purposed obstructing the Laws of Naturalization of Foreigners; refusing to pass others to encourage their migration hither, and raising the conditions of new Appropriations of Lands.

He has obstructed the Administration of Justice, by refusing his Assent to Laws for establishing Judiciary Powers.

He has made Judges dependent on his Will alone, for the tenure of their offices, and the amount and payment of their salaries.

He has erected a multitude of New Offices, and sent hither swarms of Officers to harass our People, and eat out their substance.

He has kept among us, in times of peace, Standing Armies without the Consent of our legislature.

He has affected to render the Military independent of and superior to the Civil Power.

He has combined with others to subject us to a jurisdiction foreign to our constitution, and unacknowledged by our laws; giving his Assent to their acts of pretended legislation:

For quartering large bodies of armed troops among us:

For protecting them, by a mock Trial, from Punishment of any Murders which they should commit on the inhabitants of these States:

For cutting off our Trade with all parts of the world:

For imposing taxes on us without our Consent:

For depriving us in many cases, of the benefits of Trial by Jury:

For transporting us beyond Seas to be tried for pretended offences:

For abolishing the free System of English Laws in a neighbouring Province, establishing therein an Arbitrary government, and enlarging its Boundaries so as the render it at once an example and fit instrument for introducing the same absolute rule into these Colonies:

For taking away our Charters, abolishing our most valuable Laws, and altering fundamentally the Forms of our Governments:

For suspending our own Legislature, and declaring themselves invested with Power to legislate for us in all cases whatsoever.

He has abdicated Government here, by declaring us out of his Protection and waging War against us.

He has plundered our seas, ravaged our Coasts, burnt our towns, and destroyed the lives of our people.

He is at this time transporting large armies of foreign mercenaries to complete the works of death, desolation and tyranny, already begun with circumstances of Cruelty & perfidy scarcely paralleled in the most barbarous ages, and totally unworthy the Head of a civilized nation.

He has constrained our fellow Citizens taken Captive on the high Seas to bear Arms against their Country, to become the executioners of their friends and Brethren, or to fall themselves by their Hands.

He has excited domestic insurrections amongst us, and has endeavoured to bring on the inhabitants of our frontiers, the merciless Indian Savages, whose known rule of warfare, is an undistinguished destruction of all ages, sexes and conditions.

In every stage of these Oppressions We have Petitioned for Redress in the most humble terms: Our repeated Petitions have been answered only by repeated injury. A Prince, whose character is thus marked by every act which may define a Tyrant, is unfit to be the ruler of a free People.

Nor have We been wanting in attention to our British brethren. We have warned them from time to time of attempts by their legislature to extend an unwarrantable jurisdiction over us. We have reminded them of the circumstances of our emigration and settlement here. We have appealed to their native justice and magnanimity, and we have conjured them by the ties of our common kindred to disavow these usurpations, which would inevitably interrupt our connections and correspondence. They too have been deaf to the voice of justice and of consanguinity. We must, therefore, acquiesce in the necessity, which denounces our Separation, and hold them, as we hold the rest of mankind, Enemies in War, in Peace Friends.

We, therefore, the Representatives of the United States of America, in General Congress, Assembled, appealing to the Supreme Judge of the world for the rectitude of our intentions do, in the Name, and by Authority of the good People of these Colonies, solemnly publish and declare, That these United Colonies are, and of Right ought to be Free and Independent States; that they are Absolved from all Allegiance to the British Crown, and that all political connection between them and the State of Great Britain, is and ought to be totally dissolved; and that as Free and Independent States, they have full Power to levy War, conclude Peace, contract Alliances, establish Commerce, and to do all other Acts and Things which Independent States may of right do. And for the support of this Declaration, with a firm reliance on the Protection of Divine Providence, we mutually pledge to each other our Lives, our Fortunes and our sacred Honor.

Source: The Federal and State Constitutions, Colonial Charters, and Other Organic Laws of the U.—S.—. Part I. Compiled by Ben. Perley Poore. 2nd edition. Washington, D.C.: Government Printing Office, 1878.

Women's Rights

Abigail Adams (1744–1818) suggested to her husband John Adams that some statement be included in the Declaration of Independence regarding women's rights. He rejected this suggestion in no uncertain terms.

Abigail Adams to John Adams

Braintree   March 31 1776

I long to hear that you have declared an independancy—and by the way in the new Code of Laws which I suppose it will be necessary for you to make I desire you would Remember the Ladies, and be more generous and favourable to them than your ancestors. Do not put such unlimited power into the hands of the Husbands. Remember all Men would be tyrants if they could. If perticuliar care and attention is not paid to the Laidies we are determined to foment a Rebelion, and will not hold ourselves bound by any Laws in which we have no voice, or Representation.

That your Sex are Naturally Tyrannical is a Truth so thoroughly established as to admit of no dispute, but such of you as wish to be happy willingly give up the harsh title of Master for the more tender and endearing one of Friend. Why then, not put it out of the power of the vicious and the Lawless to use us with cruelty and indignity with impunity. Men of Sense in all Ages abhor those customs which treat us only as the vassals of your Sex. Regard us then as Beings placed by providence under your protection and in immitation of the Supreem Being make use of that power only for our happiness.

John Adams to Abigail Adams

Ap. 14. 1776

As to your extraordinary Code of Laws, I cannot but laugh. We have been told that our Struggle has loosened the bands of Government every where. That Children and Apprentices were disobedient—that schools and Colledges were grown turbulent—that Indians slighted their Guardians and Negroes grew insolent to their Masters. But your Letter was the first Intimation that another Tribe more numerous and powerfull than all the rest were grown discontented.—This is rather too coarse a Compliment but you are so saucy, I wont blot it out.

Depend upon it, We know better than to repeal our Masculine systems. Altho they are in full Force, you know they are little more than Theory. We dare not exert our Power in its full Latitude. We are obliged to go fair, and softly, and in Practice you know We are the subjects. We have only the Name of Masters, and rather than give up this, which would compleatly subject Us to the Despotism of the Peticoat, I hope General Washington, and all our brave Heroes would fight.

Abigail Adams to John Adams

B[raintre]e   May 7 1776

I can not say that I think you very generous to the Ladies, for whilst you are proclaiming peace and good will to Men, Emancipating all Nations, you insist upon retaining an absolute power over Wives. But you must remember that Arbitary power is like most other things which are very hard, very liable to be broken—and notwithstanding all your wise Laws and Maxims we have it in our power not only to free ourselves but to subdue our Masters, and without voilence throw both your natural and legal authority at our feet.

Abigail Adams to Mercy Otis Warren

Braintree   April 27 1776

He is very sausy to me in return for a List of Female Grievances which I transmitted to him. I think I will get you to join me in a petition to Congress. I thought it was very probable our wise Statesmen would erect a New Goverment and form a new code of Laws. I ventured to speak a word in behalf of our Sex, who are rather hardly dealt with by the Laws of England which gives such unlimitted power to the Husband to use his wife Ill.

I requested that our Legislators would consider our case and as all Men of Delicacy and Sentiment are averse to Excercising the power they possess, yet as there is a natural propensity in Humane Nature to domination, I thought the most generous plan was to put it out of the power of the Arbitary and tyranick to injure us with impunity by Establishing some laws in our favour upon just and Liberal principals.

I believe I even threatned fomenting a Rebellion in case we were not considerd, and assured him we would not hold ourselves bound by any Laws in which we had neither a voice, nor representation.

In return he tells me he cannot but Laugh at My Extrodonary Code of Laws. That he had heard their Struggle had loosned the bands of Government, that children and apprentices were dissabedient, that Schools and Colledges were grown turbulant, that Indians slighted their Guardians, and Negroes grew insolent to their Masters. But my Letter was the first intimation that another Tribe more numerous and powerfull than all the rest were grown discontented. This is rather too coarse a complement, he adds, but that I am so sausy he wont blot it out.

So I have help'd the Sex abundantly, but I will tell him I have only been making trial of the Disintresstedness of his Virtue, and when weigh'd in the balance have found it wanting.

It would be bad policy to grant us greater power say they since under all the disadvantages we Labour we have the assendancy over their Hearts.

And charm by accepting, by submitting sway.

Source: Adams Family Correspondence. Volume 1. Edited by L. H. Butterfield. Cambridge, Mass.: Belknap Press of Harvard University Press, 1963.

Abigail Adams (1744–1818) was the wife of John Adams.
John Adams (1735–1826) was the second president of the United States.

Thomas Jefferson

Thomas Jefferson, generally labelled a liberal, believed in a natural aristocracy as much as his friend John Adams, but he wanted to ensure that it was an aristocracy of talent. As a result, he stressed education. He believed that democracy requires universal, free education and agrarianism. He argued for majority rule and against the power of the judiciary. He also believed that no society should blindly follow the past, and, as a remedy, he argued for the elimination of all laws and constitutions every twenty years. At the same time he wanted as little government as possible at any time. He distrusted political power and suggested that regular violent revolutions were healthy.

His tombstone records that he was the author of the Declaration of Independence, the Act for Establishing Religious Freedom, and the founder of the University of Virginia; he did not consider being the president of the United States as important as these other accomplishments. The Act for Establishing Religious Freedom was drafted as early as 1777 but was not adopted until 1786.

Thomas Jefferson
An Act for Establishing Religious Freedom

Well aware that Almighty God hath created the mind free; that all attempts to influence it by temporal punishments or burdens, or by civil incapacitations, tend only to beget habits of hypocrisy and meanness, and are a departure from the plan of the Holy Author of our religion, who being Lord both of body and mind, yet chose not to propagate it by coercions on either, as was in his Almighty power to do; that the impious presumption of legislators and rulers, civil as well as ecclesiastical, who, being themselves but fallible and uninspired men have assumed dominion over the faith of others, setting up their own opinions and modes of thinking as the only true and infallible, and as such endeavoring to impose them on others, hath established and maintained false religions over the greatest part of the world, and through all time; that to compel a man to furnish contributions of money for the propagation of opinions which he disbelieves, is sinful and tyrannical; that even the forcing him to support this or that teacher of his own religious persuasion, is depriving him of the comfortable liberty of giving his contributions to the particular pastor whose morals he would make his pattern, and whose powers he feels most persuasive to righteousness, and is withdrawing from the ministry those temporal rewards, which proceeding from an approbation of their personal conduct, are an additional incitement to earnest and unremitting labors for the instruction of mankind that our civil rights have no dependence on our religious opinions, more than our opinions in physics or geometry; that, therefore, the proscribing any citizen as unworthy the public confidence by laying upon him an incapacity of being called to the offices of trust and emolument, unless he profess or renounce this or that religious opinion, is depriving him injuriously of those privileges and advantages to which in common with his fellow citizens he has a natural right; that it tends also to corrupt the principles of that very religion it is meant to encourage, by bribing, with a monopoly of worldly honors and emoluments, those who will externally profess and conform to it; that though indeed these are criminal who do not withstand such temptation, yet neither are those innocent who lay the bait in their way; that to suffer the civil magistrate to intrude his powers into the field of opinion and to restrain the profession or propagation of principles, on the supposition of their ill tendency, is a dangerous fallacy, which at once destroys all religious liberty, because he being of course judge of that tendency, will make his opinions the rule of judgment, and approve or condemn the sentiments of others only as they shall square with or differ from his own; that it is time enough for the rightful purposes of civil government, for its offices to interfere when principles break out into overt acts against peace and good order; and finally, that truth is great and will prevail if left to herself, that she is the proper and sufficient antagonist to error, and has nothing to fear from the conflict, unless by human interposition disarmed of her natural weapon, free argument and debate, errors ceasing to be dangerous when it is permitted freely to contradict them.

Be it therefore enacted by the General Assembly, That no man shall be compelled to frequent or support any religious worship, place or ministry whatsoever, nor shall be enforced, restrained, molested, or burthened in his body or goods, nor shall otherwise suffer on account of his religious opinions of belief; but that all men shall be free to profess, and by argument to maintain, their opinions in matters of religion, and that the same shall in nowise diminish, enlarge, or affect their civil capacities.

And though we well know this Assembly, elected by the people for the ordinary purposes of legislation only, have no power to restrain the acts of succeeding assemblies, constituted with the powers equal to our own, and that therefore to declare this act irrevocable, would be of no effect in law, yet we are free to declare, and do declare, that the rights hereby asserted are of the natural rights of mankind, and that if any act shall be hereafter passed to repeal the present or to narrow its operation, such act will be an infringement of natural right.

Source: Report of the Committee of Revisors Appointed by the General Assembly in MDCCLXXVI. Richmond, 1784.

Thomas Jefferson (1743–1826) was the third president of the United States.

African Americans

The Revolution produced further concern with the treatment of minorities in America. As we have seen, the Declaration of Independence caused debate over the position of women, and Jefferson wanted to use it to denounce slavery. In addition, both free African Americans and slaves took the opportunity to speak out.

Slaves Petition for Freedom During Revolutionary War

To his Excellency Thomas Gage Esq. Captain General and governor in Chief in and over this Province.

To the Honourable his Majestys Council and the Honourable House of Representatives in General Court assembled May 25, 1774.

The Petition of a Grate Number of Blacks of this Province who by divine permission are held in a state of Slavery within the bowels of a free and Christian Country

Humbly Shewing

That your Petitioners apprehind we have in common with all other men a naturel right to our freedoms without Being depriv'd of them by our fellow men as we are a freeborn Pepel and have never forfeited this Blessing by aney compact or agreement whatever. But we were unjustly dragged by the cruel hand of power from our dearest frinds and sum of us stolen from the bosoms of our tender Parents and from a Populous Pleasant and plentiful country and Brought hither to be made slaves for Life in a Christian land. Thus we are deprived of every thing that hath a tendency to make life even tolerable, the endearing ties of husband and wife we are strangers to for we are no longer man and wife than our masters or mistresses thinkes proper marred or onmarred. Our children are also taken from us by force and sent maney miles from us wear we seldom or ever see them again there to be made slaves of for Life which sumtimes is vere short by Reson of Being dragged from their mothers Breest Thus our Lives are imbittered to us on these accounts By our deplorable situation we are rendered incapable of shewing our obedience to Almighty God how can a slave perform the duties of a husband to a wife or parent to his child How can a husband leave master to work and cleave to his wife How can the wife submit themselves to there husbands in all things How can the child obey their parents in all things. There is a great number of us sencear . . . members of the Church of Christ how can the master and the slave be said to fulfil that command Live in love let Brotherly Love contuner and abound Beare yea onenothers Bordenes How can the master be said to Beare my Borden when he Beares me down whith the Have chanes of slavery and operson against my will and how can we fulfill our parte of duty to him whilst in this condition and as we cannot searve our God as we ought whilst in this situation. Nither can we reap an equal benefet from the laws of the Land which doth not justifi but condemns Slavery or if there had bin aney Law to hold us in Bondage we are Humbely of the Opinion the never was aney to inslave our children for life when Born in a free Countrey. We therfor Bage your Excellency and Honours will give this its deer weight and consideration and that you will accordingly cause an act of the legislative to be pessed that we may obtain our Natural right our freedoms and our children be set at lebety at the yeare of twentyone for whoues sekes more petequeley your Petitioners is in Duty ever to pray.

Source: Massachusetts Historical Society, *Collections,* 5th series, vol. 3 (1877)

Preamble of the Free African Society

Philadelphia [12th, 4th mo., 1778].—WHEREAS, Absalom Jones and Richard Allen, two men of the African race, who, for their religious life and conversation have obtained a good report among men, these persons, from a love to the people of their complexion whom they beheld with sorrow, because of their irreligious and uncivilized state, often communed together upon this painful and important subject in order to form some kind of religious society, but there being too few to be found under the like concern, and those who were, differed in their religious sentiments; with these circumstances they labored for some time, till it was proposed, after a serious communication of sentiments, that a society should be formed, without regard to religious tenets, provided, the persons lived an orderly and sober life, in other to support one another in sickness, and for the benefit of their widows and fatherless children.

ARTICLES.

[17th, 5th mo., 1787.] — We, the free Africans and their descendants, of the City of Philadelphia, in the State of Pennsylvania, or elsewhere, do unanimously agree, for the benefit of each other, to advance one shilling in silver Pennsylvania currency a month; and after one year's subscription from the date hereof, then to hand forth to the needy of this Society, if any should require, the sum of three shillings and nine pence per week of the said money: provided, this necessity is not brought on them by their own imprudence.

And it is further agreed, that no drunkard nor disorderly person be admitted as a member, and if any should prove disorderly after having been received, the said disorderly person shall be disjointed from us if there is not an amendment, by being informed by two of the members, without having any of his subscription money returned.

And if any should neglect paying his monthly subscription for three months, and after having been informed of the same by two of the members, and no sufficient reason appearing for such neglect, if he do not pay the whole the next ensuing meeting, he shall be disjointed from us, by being informed by two of the members as an offender, without having any of his subscription money returned.

Also, if any person neglect meeting every month, for every omission he shall pay three pence, except in case of sickness or any other complaint that should require the assistance of the Society, then, and in such a case, he shall be exempt from the fines and subscription during the said sickness.

Also, we apprehend it to be just and reasonable, that the surviving widow of a deceased member should enjoy the benefit of this Society as long as she remains his widow, complying with the rules thereof, excepting the subscriptions.

And we apprehend it to be necessary, that the children of our deceased members be under the care of the Society, so far as to pay for the education of their children, if they cannot attend the free school; also to put them out apprentices to suitable trades or places, if required.

Source: Annals of the First African Church in the United States of America — now styled the African Episcopal Church of St. Thomas, Philadelphia. By Rev. William Douglass. Philadelphia: King and Baird, 1862.

Notes

1. See Ann Fairfax Withington, *Toward a More Perfect Union: Virtue and the Formation of the American Republics* (New York: Oxford University Press, 1991).

2. See Gordon S. Wood, *The Radicalism of the American Revolution* (New York: Alfred A. Knopf, 1992).

CHAPTER 4

The Constitutional Debates, 1780–1789

✴ ✴ ✴

Becoming American

An important aspect of the post-Revolutionary period was the development of the sense of what it means to be an American. The classic statement comes from a Frenchman, J. Hector St. John de Crèvecoeur (1735–1813).

J. Hector St. John de Crèvecoeur
What Is an American?

I wish I could be acquainted with the feelings and thoughts which must agitate the heart and present themselves to the mind of an enlightened Englishman when he first lands on this continent. He must greatly rejoice that he lived at a time to see this fair country discovered and settled; he must necessarily feel a share of national pride when he views the chain of settlements which embellish these extended shores. When he says to himself, "This is the work of my countrymen, who, when convulsed by factions, afflicted by a variety of miseries and wants, restless and impatient, took refuge here. They brought along with them their national genius, to which they principally owe what liberty they enjoy and what substance they possess." Here he sees the industry of his native country displayed in a new manner and traces in their works the embryos of all the arts, sciences, and ingenuity which flourish in Europe. Here he beholds fair cities, substantial villages, extensive fields, an immense country filled with decent houses, good roads, orchards, meadows, and bridges where an hundred years ago all was wild, woody, and uncultivated! What a train of pleasing ideas this fair spectacle must suggest; it is a prospect which must inspire a good citizen with the most heart-felt pleasure. The difficulty consists in the manner of viewing so extensive a scene. He is arrived on a new continent; a modern society offers itself to his contemplation, different from what he had hitherto seen. It is not composed, as in Europe, of great lords who possess everything and of a herd of people who have nothing. Here are no aristocratical families, no courts, no kings, no bishops, no ecclesiastical dominion, no invisible power giving to a few a very visible one, no great manufactures employing thousands, no great refinements of luxury. The rich and the poor are not so far removed from each other as they are in Europe. Some few towns excepted, we are all tillers of the earth, from Nova Scotia to West Florida. We are a people of cultivators scattered over an immense territory, communicating with each other by means of good roads and navigable rivers, united by the silken bands of mild government, all respecting the laws without dreading their power, because they are equitable. We are all animated with the spirit of an industry which is unfettered and unrestrained, because each person works for himself. If he travels through our rural districts, he views not the hostile castle and the haughty mansion, contrasted with the clay-built hut and miserable cabin, where cattle and men help to keep each other warm and dwell in meanness, smoke, and indigence. A pleasing uniformity of decent competence appears throughout our habitations. The meanest of our log-houses is a dry and comfortable habitation. Lawyer or merchant are the fairest titles our towns afford; that of a farmer is the only appellation of the rural inhabitants of our country. It must take some time ere he can reconcile himself to our dictionary, which is but short in words of dignity and names of honour. There, on a Sunday, he sees a congregation of respectable farmers and their wives, all clad in neat homespun, well mounted, or riding in their own humble waggons. There is not among them an esquire, saving the unlettered magistrate. There he sees a parson as simple as his flock, a farmer who does not riot on the labour of others. We have no princes for whom we toil, starve, and bleed; we are the most perfect society now existing in the world. Here man is free as he ought to be, nor is this pleasing equality so transitory as many others are. Many ages will not see the shores of our great lakes replenished with inland nations, nor the unknown bounds of North America entirely peopled. Who can tell how far it extends? Who can tell the millions of men whom it will feed and contain? For no European foot has as yet travelled half the extent of this mighty continent!

The next wish of this traveller will be to know whence came all these people. They are a mixture of English, Scotch, Irish, French, Dutch, Germans, and Swedes. From this promiscuous breed, that race now called Americans have arisen. The eastern provinces must indeed be excepted as being the unmixed descendants of Englishmen. I have heard many wish that they had been more intermixed also; for my part, I am no wisher and think it much better as it has happened. They exhibit a most conspicuous figure in this great and variegated picture; they too enter for a great share in the pleasing perspective displayed in these thirteen provinces. I know it is fashionable to reflect on them, but I respect them for what they have done; for the accuracy and wisdom with which they have settled their territory; for the decency of their manners; for their early love of letters; their ancient college, the first in this hemisphere; for their industry, which to me who am but a farmer is the criterion of everything. There never was a people, situated as they are, who with so ungrateful a soil have done more in so short a time. Do you think that the monarchical ingredients which are more prevalent in other governments have purged them from all foul stains? Their histories assert the contrary.

In this great American asylum, the poor of Europe have by some means met together, and in consequence of various causes; to what purpose should they ask one another what countrymen they are? Alas, two thirds of them had no country. Can a wretch who wanders about, who works and starves, whose life is a continual scene of sore affliction or pinching penury—can that man call England or any other kingdom his country? A country that had no bread for him, whose fields procured him no harvest, who met with nothing but the frowns of the rich, the severity of the laws, with jails and punishments, who owned not a single foot of the extensive surface of this planet? No! Urged by a variety of motives, here they came. Everything has tended to regenerate them: new laws, a new mode of living, a new social system; here they are become men: in Europe they were as so many useless plants, wanting vegetative mould and refreshing showers; they withered, and were mowed down by want, hunger, and war; but now, by the power of transplantation, like all other plants they have taken root and flourished! Formerly they were not numbered in any civil lists of their country, except in those of the poor; here they rank as citizens. By what invisible power hath this surprising metamorphosis been performed? By that of the laws and that of their industry. The laws, the indulgent laws, protect them as they arrive, stamping on them the symbol of adoption; they receive ample rewards for their labours; these accumulated rewards procure them lands; those lands confer on them the title of freemen, and to that title every benefit is affixed which men can possibly require. This is the great operation daily performed by our laws. Whence proceed these laws? From our government. Whence that government? It is derived from the original genius and strong desire of the people ratified and confirmed by the crown. This is the great chain which links us all, this is the picture which every province exhibits. . . .

What, then, is the American, this new man? He is neither an European nor the descendant of an European; hence that strange mixture of blood, which you will find in no other country. I could point out to you a family whose grandfather was an Englishman, whose wife was Dutch, whose son married a French women, and whose present four sons have now four wives of different nations. He is an American, who, leaving behind him all his ancient prejudices and manners, receives new ones from the new mode of life he has embraced, the new government he obeys, and the new rank he holds. He becomes an American by being received in the broad lap of our great Alma Mater. Here individuals of all nations are melted into a new race of men, whose labours and posterity will one day cause great changes in the world. Americans are the western pilgrims who are carrying along with them that great mass of arts, sciences, vigour, and industry which began long since in the East; they will finish the great circle. The Americans were once scattered all over Europe; here they are incorporated into one of the finest systems of population which has ever appeared, and which will hereafter become distinct by the power of the different climates they inhabit. The American ought therefore to love this country much better than that wherein either he or his forefathers were born. Here the rewards of his industry follow with equal steps the progress of his labour; his labour is founded on the basis of nature, self-interest; can it want a stronger allurement? Wives and children, who before in vain demanded of him a morsel of bread, now, fat and frolicsome, gladly help their father to clear those fields whence exuberant crops are to arise to feed and to clothe them all, without any part being claimed, either by a despotic prince, a rich abbot, or a mighty lord. Here religion demands but little of him: a small voluntary salary to the minister and gratitude to God; can he refuse these? The American is a new man, who acts upon new principles; he must therefore entertain new ideas and form new opinions. From involuntary idleness, servile dependence, penury, and useless labour, he has passed to toils of a very different nature, rewarded by ample subsistence. This is an American.

Source: Letters from an American Farmer. By J. Hector St. John de Crèvecoeur. New York: Driffied, 1904.

J. Hector St. John de Crèvecoeur was the pseudonym of Michel Guillaume Jean de Crèvecoeur (1735–1813), who emigrated to the United States in 1759 and became a naturalized citizen in 1765.

Central versus State versus Local Authority

The most important issue in the debates that arose after the Revolution was the locus of power, and it boiled into armed conflict in Shays's Rebellion. The documents of this period are among the most fundamental in American history and political thought—the Articles of Confederation, the Northwest Ordinance, the Constitution, and the Federalist Papers—and they all focus to some degree on this issue.

During the Revolution the colonies faced the problem of establishing a government for themselves. This ultimately took about ten years and produced considerable conflict, a number of important documents, and some of the most interesting and important political thinking in American history.

The Articles of Confederation is the most neglected of the fundamental documents of American constitutionalism and rests uneasily between the two best known, the Declaration of Independence and the Constitution. The Articles should be remembered at least for the fact that under them the United States of America first became a reality. The Articles were a product of an agreement among thirteen entities that saw themselves as independent nations that needed to cooperate. Therefore, they drew up a document in which power resided in the states rather than in a national government. The Articles reflect one of the longest running controversies in American political thought and practice—that is, the locus of sovereignty. Should power reside with a central government, the people, the states, or divided among these in some way?

Most people have labeled the Articles of Confederation an abject failure, but others (both at the time and since) have argued that under the Articles the United States successfully fought a war and negotiated a workable peace, established a diplomatic corps, gained credit, created a bureaucracy, and established a national domain.

Articles of Confederation

November 15, 1777

To all to whom these Presents shall come, we the undersigned Delegates of the States affixed to our names send greeting.

Whereas The Delegates of the United States of America in Congress Assembled did on the fifteenth day of November in the year of our Lord One Thousand Seven Hundred and Seventy-seven, and in the Second Year of the Independence of America agree to certain articles of Confederation and perpetual Union between the States of Newhampshire, Massachusetts-bay, Rhodeisland and Providence Plantations, Connecticut, New York, New Jersey, Pennsylvania, Delaware, Virginia, North-Carolina, South-Carolina and Georgia in the Words following, viz.

"ARTICLES OF CONFEDERATION AND PERPETUAL UNION BETWEEN THE STATES OF NEWHAMPSHIRE, MASSACHUSETTS-BAY, RHODEISLAND AND PROVIDENCE PLANTATIONS, CONNECTICUT, NEW YORK, NEW JERSEY, PENN-

SYLVANIA, DELAWARE, MARYLAND, VIRGINIA, NORTH-CAROLINA, SOUTH-CAROLINA AND GEORGIA."

ARTICLE I. The stile of this confederacy shall be "The United States of America."

ARTICLE II. Each State retains its sovereignty, freedom and independence, and every power, jurisdiction and right, which is not by this confederation expressly delegated to the United States, in Congress assembled.

ARTICLE III. The said States hereby severally enter into a firm league of friendship with each other, for their common defence, the security of their liberties, and their mutual and general welfare, binding themselves to assist each other, against all force offered to, or attacks made upon them, or any of them, on account of religion, sovereignty, trade or any other pretence whatever.

ARTICLE IV. The better to secure and perpetuate mutual friendship and intercourse among the people of the different States in this Union, the free inhabitants of each of these States, paupers, vagabonds and fugitives from justice excepted, shall be entitled to all privileges and immunities of free citizens in the several States; and the people of each State shall have free ingress and regress to and from any other State, and shall enjoy therein all the privileges of trade and commerce, subject to the same duties, impositions and restrictions as the inhabitants whereof respectively, provided that such restrictions shall not extend so far as to prevent the removal of property imported into any State, to any other State of which the owner is an inhabitant; provided also that no imposition, duties or restriction shall be laid by any State, on the property of the United States, or either of them.

If any Person guilty of, or charged with treason, felony, or other high misdemeanor in any State, shall flee from justice, and be found in any of the United States, he shall upon demand of the Governor or Executive power, of the State from which he fled, be delivered up and removed to the State having jurisdiction of his offence.

Full faith and credit shall be given in each of these States to the records, acts and judicial proceedings of the courts and magistrates of every other State.

ARTICLE V. For the more convenient management of the general interest of the United States, delegates shall be annually appointed in such manner as the legislature of each State shall direct, to meet in Congress on the first Monday in November, in every year, with a power reserved to each State, to recall its delegates, or any of them, at any time within the year, and to send others in their stead, for the remainder of the year.

No State shall be represented in Congress by less than two, nor by more than seven members; and no person shall be capable of being a delegate for more than three years in any term of six years; nor shall any person, being a delegate, be capable of holding any office under the United States, for which he, or another for his benefit receives any salary, fees or emolument of any kind.

Each State shall maintain its own delegates in a meeting of the States, and while they act as members of the committee of the States.

In determining questions in the United States, in Congress assembled, each State shall have one vote.

Freedom of speech and debate in Congress shall not be impeached or questioned in any court, or place out of Congress, and the members of Congress shall be protected in their persons from arrests and imprisonments, during the time of their going to and from, and attendance on Congress, except for treason, felony, or breach of the peace.

ARTICLE VI. No State without the consent of the United States in Congress assembled, shall send any embassy to, or receive any embassy from, or enter into any conference, agreement, alliance or treaty with any king, prince or state; nor shall any person holding any office of profit or trust under the United States, or any of them, accept of any present, emolument, office or title of any kind whatever from any king, prince or foreign state; nor shall the United States in Congress assembled, or any of them, grant any title of nobility.

No two or more States shall enter into any treaty, confederation or alliance whatever between them, without the consent of the United States in Congress assembled, specifying accurately the purposes for which the same is to be entered into, and how long it shall continue.

No State shall lay any imposts or duties, which may interfere with any stipulations in treaties, entered into by the United States in Congress assembled, with any king, prince or state, in pursuance of any treaties already proposed by Congress, to the courts of France and Spain.

No vessels of war shall be kept up in time of peace by any State, except such number only, as shall be deemed necessary by the United States in Congress assembled, for the defence of such State, or its trade; nor shall any body of forces be kept up by any State, in time of peace, except such number only, as shall be deemed requisite to garrison the forts necessary for the defence of such State; but every State shall always keep up a well regulated and disciplined militia, sufficiently armed and accoutered, and shall provide and constantly have ready for use, in public stores, a due number of field pieces and tents, and a proper quantity of arms, ammunition and camp equipage.

No State shall engage in any war without the consent of the United States in Congress assembled, unless such State be actually invaded by enemies, or shall have received certain advice of a resolution being formed by some nation of Indians to invade such State, and the danger is so imminent as not to admit of a delay, till the United States in Congress assembled can be consulted: nor shall any State grant commissions to any ships or vessels of war, nor letters of marque or reprisal, except it be after a declaration of war by the United States in Congress assembled, and then only against the kingdom or state and the subjects thereof, against which war has been so declared, and under such regulations as shall be established by the United States in Congress assembled, unless such State be infested by pirates, in which case vessels of war may be fitted out for that occasion, and kept so long as the danger shall continue, or until the United States in Congress assembled shall determine otherwise.

ARTICLE VII. When land-forces are raised by any State for the common defence, all officers of or under the rank of colonel, shall be appointed by the Legislature of each State respectively by whom such forces shall be raised, or in such manner as such State shall direct, and all vacancies shall be filled up by the State which first made the appointment.

ARTICLE VIII. All charges of war, and all other expenses that shall be incurred for the common defence or general welfare, and allowed by the United States in Congress assembled, shall be defrayed out of a common treasury, which shall be supplied by the several States, in proportion to the value of all land within each State, granted to or surveyed for any person, as such land and the buildings and improvements thereon shall be estimated according to such mode as the United States in Congress assembled, shall from time to time direct and appoint.

The taxes for paying that proportion shall be laid and levied by the authority and direction of the Legislatures of the several States within the time agreed upon by the United States in Congress assembled.

ARTICLE IX. The United States in Congress assembled, shall have the sole and exclusive right and power of determining on peace and war, except in the cases mentioned in the sixth article — of sending and receiving ambassadors — entering into treaties and alliances, provided that no treaty of commerce shall be restrained from imposing such imposts and duties on foreigners, as their own people are subjected to, or from prohibiting the exportation or importation of any species of goods or commodities whatsoever — of establishing rules for deciding in all cases, what captures on land or water shall be legal, and in what manner prizes taken by land or naval forces in the service of the United States shall be divided or appropriate — of granting letters of marque and reprisal in times of peace — appointing courts for the trial of piracies and felonies committed on the high seas and establishing courts for receiving and determining finally appeals in all cases of captures, provided that no member of Congress shall be appointed a judge of any of the said courts.

The United States in Congress assembled shall also be the last resort on appeal in all disputes and differences now subsisting or that hereafter may arise between two or more States concerning boundary, jurisdiction or any other cause whatever; which authority shall always be exercised in the manner following. Wherever the legislative or executive authority or lawful agent of any State in controversy with another shall present a petition to Congress, stating the matter in question and praying for a hearing, motive thereof shall be given by order of Congress to the legislative or executive authority of the other State in controversy, and a day assigned for the appearance of the parties by their lawful agents, who then be directed to appoint by joint consent, commissioners or judges to constitute a court for hearing and determining the matter in question: but if they cannot agree, Congress shall name three persons out of each of the United States, and from the list of such persons each party shall alternately strike out one, the petitioners beginning, until the number shall be reduced to thirteen; and from that number not less than seven, or more than nine names as Congress shall direct in the presence of Congress be drawn out by lot, and the persons whose names shall be so drawn or any five of them, shall be commissioners or judges, to hear and finally determine the controversy, so always as a major part of the judges who shall hear the cause shall agree in the determination: and if either party shall neglect to attend at the day appointed, without showing reasons, which Congress shall judge sufficient, or being present shall refuse to strike, the Congress shall proceed to nominate three persons out of each State, and the Secretary of Congress shall strike in behalf of such party absent or refusing; and the judgment and sentence of the court to be appointed, in the manner before prescribed, shall be final and conclusive, and if any of the parties shall refuse to submit to the authority of such court, or to appear or defend their claim or cause, the court shall nevertheless proceed to pronounce sentence, or judgement, which shall in like manner be final and decisive, the judgment or sentence and other proceedings being in either case transmitted to Congress, and lodged among the acts of Congress for the security of the parties concerned: provided that every commissioner, before he sits in judgment, shall take an oath to be administered by one of the judges of the supreme or superior court of the State; where the cause shall be tried, "well and truly to hear and determine the matter in question, according to the best of his judgment, without favour, affection or hope of reward:" provided also that no State shall be deprived of territory for the benefit of the United States.

All controversies concerning the private right of soil claimed under the different grants of two or more States, whose jurisdiction as they may respect such lands, and the States which passed such grants are adjusted, the said grants or either of them being at the same time claimed to have originated antecedent to such settlement of jurisdiction, shall on the petition of either party to the Congress of the United States, be finally determined as near as may be in the same manner as is before prescribed for deciding disputes respecting territorial jurisdiction between different States.

The United States in Congress assembled shall also have the sole and exclusive right and power of regulating the alloy and value of coin struck by their own authority, or by that of the respective States—fixing the standard of weights and measures throughout the United States—regulating the trade and managing affairs with the Indians, not members of any of the States, provided that the legislative right of any State within its own limits be not infringed or violated—establishing and regulating post-offices from one State to another, throughout all the United States, and exacting such postage on the papers passing thro' the same as may be requisite to defray the expenses of the said office—appointing all officers of the land forces, in the service of the United States, excepting regimental officers—appointing all the officers of the naval forces, and commissioning all officers whatever in the service of the United States, excepting regimental officers—making rules for the government and regulation of the said land and naval forces, and directing their operations.

The United States in Congress assembled shall have authority to appoint a committee, to sit in the recess of Congress, to be denominated "a Committee of the States," and to consist of one delegate from each State; and to appoint such other committees and civil officers as may be necessary for managing the general affairs of the United States under their direction—to appoint one of their number to preside, provided that no person be allowed to serve in the office of president more than one year in any term of three years; to ascertain the necessary sums of money to be raised for the service of the United States, and to appropriate and apply the same for defraying the public expenses—to borrow money, or emit bills on the credit of the United States, transmitting every half year to the respective States an account of the sums of money so borrowed or emitted,—to build and equip a navy—to agree upon the number of land forces, and to make requisitions from each State for its quota, in proportion to the number of white inhabitants in such State; which requisition shall be binding, and thereupon the Legislature of each State shall appoint the regimental officers, raise the men and cloath, arm and equip them in a soldier like manner, at the expense of the United States; and the officers and men so cloathed, armed and equipped shall march to the place appointed, and within the time agreed on by the United States in Congress assembled: but if the United States in Congress assembled shall, on consideration of circumstances judge proper that any State should not raise men, or should raise a greater number of men than the quota thereof, such extra number shall be raised, officered, cloathed, armed and equipped in the same as the quota of such State, unless the Legislature of such State shall judge that such extra number cannot be safely spared outside of the same, in which case they shall raise, officer, cloath, arm and equip as many of such extra number as they judge can be safely spared. And the officers and men so cloathed, armed and equipped, shall march to the place appointed, and within the time agreed on by the United States in Congress assembled.

The United States in Congress assembled shall never engage in a war, nor grant letters of marque and reprisal in time of peace, nor enter into any treaties of alliances, nor coin money, nor regulate the value thereof, nor ascertain the sums and expenses necessary for the defence and welfare of the United States, or any of them, nor emit bills, nor borrow money on the credit of the United States, nor appropriate money, nor agree upon the number of vessels of war, to be built or purchased, or the number of land or sea forces to be raised, nor appoint a commander in chief of the army or navy, unless nine States assent to the same: nor shall a question on any other point, except for adjourning from day to day be determined, unless by the votes of a majority of the United States in Congress assembled.

The Congress of the United States shall have power to adjourn to any time within the year, and to any place within the United States, so that no period of adjournment be for a longer duration that the space of six months, and shall publish the journal of their proceedings monthly, except such parts thereof relating to treaties, alliances or military operations, as in their judgment require secrecy; and the yeas and nays of the delegates of each State on any question shall be entered on the journal, when it is desired by any delegate; and the delegates of a State, or any of them, at his or their request shall be furnished with a transcript of the said journal, except such parts as are above excepted, to lay before the Legislatures of the several States.

ARTICLE X. The committee of the States, or any nine of them, shall be authorized to execute, in the recess of Congress, such of the powers of Congress as the United States in Congress assembled, by the consent of nine States, shall from time to time think expedient to vest them with; provided that no power be delegated to the said committee, for the exercise of which, by the articles of confederation, the voice of nine States in the Congress of the United States assembled is requisite.

ARTICLE XI. Canada acceding to this confederation, and joining in the measures of the United States, shall be admitted into, and entitled to all the advantages of this Union: but no other colony shall be admitted into the same, unless such admission be agreed to by nine States.

ARTICLES XII. All bills of credit emitted, monies borrowed and debts contracted by, or under the authority of Congress, before the assembling of the United States, in pursuance of the present confederation, shall be deemed and considered as a charge against the United States, for payment and satisfaction whereof the said United States, and the public faith are hereby solemnly pledged.

ARTICLE XIII. Every state shall abide by the determinations of the United States in Congress assembled, on all questions which by this confederation are submitted to them. And the articles of this confederation shall be inviolably observed by every State, and the Union shall be perpetual; nor shall any alteration at any time hereafter be made in any of them; unless such alteration be agreed to in a Congress of United States, and be afterwards confirmed by the Legislatures of every State.

And Whereas it hath pleased the Great Governor of the World to incline the hearts of the Legislatures we respectively represent in Congress, to approve of, and to authorize us to ratify the said articles of confederation and perpetual union, Know ye that we the undersigned delegates, by virtue of the power and authority to us given for that purpose, do by these presents, in the name and in behalf of our respective constituents, fully and entirely ratify and confirm each and every of the said articles of confederation and perpetual union, and all and singular the matters and things therein contained: and we do further solemnly plight and engage the faith of our respective constituents, that they shall abide by the determinations of the United States in Congress assembled, on all questions, which by the said confederation are submitted to them. And that the articles thereof shall be inviolably observed by the States we respectively represent, and that the Union shall be perpetual.

In witness whereof we have hereunto set our hands in Congress. Done at Philadelphia in the State of Pennsylvania the ninth of July in the year of our Lord one thousand seven hundred and seventy-eight, and in the third year of the independence of America.

Source: The Federal and State Constitutions, Colonial Charters, and Other Organic Laws of the U.—S.—. Part I. Compiled by Ben. Perley Poore. 2nd edition. Washington, D.C.: Government Printing Office, 1878.

* * *

Thomas Jefferson expressed one of the concerns of those worried about the concentration of power in the following letter to James Madison (1751–1836). Jefferson was most worried by the concentration of wealth and the related radical inequality that he found in France, one of the factors that contributed to the French Revolution a few years later. But Jefferson did not propose equality as the solution to the problem. In common with most thinkers of the time, he believed that "the earth is given as a common stock for man to labour on" but that commercial activity required unequal holdings. Therefore, Jefferson argued for some form of economic security but did not define the form.

Thomas Jefferson
Letter to James Madison

Fontainebleau Oct. 28. 1785.

Dear Sir

Seven o'clock, and retired to my fireside, I have determined to enter into conversation with you; this is a village of about 5,000 inhabitants when the court is not here and 20,000 when they are, occupying a valley thro' which runs a brook, and on each side of it a ridge of small mountains most of which are naked rock. The king comes here in the fall always, to hunt. His court attend him, as do also the foreign diplomatic corps. But as this is not indispensably required, and my finances do not admit the expence of a continued residence here, I propose to come occasionally to attend the king's levees, returning again to Paris, distant 40 miles. This being the first trip, I set out yesterday morning to take a view of the place. For this purpose I shaped my course towards the highest of the mountains in sight, to the top of which was about a league. As soon as I had got clear of the town I fell in with a poor woman walking at the same rate with myself and going the same course. Wishing to know the condition of the labouring poor I entered into conversation with her, which I began by enquiries for the path which would lead me into the mountain: and thence proceeded to enquiries into her vocation, condition and circumstance. She told me she was a day labourer, at 8. sous or 4 d. sterling the day [about 80 cents]; that she had two children to maintain, and to pay a rent of 30 livres [about $75.00] for her house (which would consume the hire of 75 days), that often she could get no emploiment, and of course was without bread. As we had walked together near a mile and she had so far served me as a guide, I gave her, on parting 24 sous. She burst into tears of a gratitude which I could perceive was unfeigned, because she was unable to utter a word. She had probably never before received so great an aid. This little attendrissement, with the solitude of my walk led me into a train of reflections on that unequal division of property which occasions the numberless instances of wretchedness which I had observed in this country and is to be observed all over Europe. The property of this country is absolutely concentered in a very few hands, having revenues of from half a million of guineas a year downwards. These employ the flower of the country as servants, some of them having as many as 200 domestics, not labouring. They employ also a great number of manufacturers, and tradesmen, and lastly the class of labouring husbandmen. But after all these comes the most numerous of all the classes, that is, the poor who cannot find work. I asked myself what could be the reason that so many should be permitted to beg who are willing to work, in a country where there is a very considerable proportion of uncultivated lands? These lands are kept idle mostly for the sake of game. It should seem then that it must be because of the enormous wealth of the proprietors which places them above attention to the increase of their revenues by permitting these lands to be laboured. I am conscious that an equal division of property is impracticable. But the consequences of this enormous inequality producing so much misery to the bulk of mankind, legislators cannot invent too many devices for subdividing property, only taking care to let their subdivisions go hand in hand with the natural affections of the human mind. The descent of property of every kind therefore to all the children, or to all the brothers and sisters, or other relations in equal degree is a politic measure, and a practicable one. Another means of silently lessening the inequality of property is to exempt all from taxation below a certain point, and to tax the higher portions of property in geometrical progression as they rise. Whenever there is in any country, uncultivated lands and unemployed poor, it is clear that the laws of property have been so far extended as to violate natural right. The earth is given as a common stock for man to labour and live on. If, for the encouragement of industry we allow it to be appropriated, we must take care that other employment be furnished to those excluded from the appropriation. If we do not the fundamental right to labour the earth returns to the unemployed. It is too soon yet in our country to say that every man who cannot find employment but who can find uncultivated land, shall be at liberty to cultivate it, paying a moderate rent. But it is not too soon to provide by every possible means that as few as possible shall be without a little portion of land. The small landholders are the most precious part of a state.

Source: *The Papers of James Madison.* Edited by James T. Hutchinson and William M. E. Rachal (Chicago: University of Chicago Press, 1973), 8:385–87.

Thomas Jefferson (1743–1826) was the third president of the United States.

SHAYS'S REBELLION

The same sentiment concerning the importance of small landholders was expressed in Shays's Rebellion and in one of Jefferson's letters regarding it. Shays's Rebellion was an armed revolt in Western Massachusetts in 1786–87. Debt-ridden farmers appealed to the state legislature for relief and were rebuffed. Daniel Shays (1747?-1825) and others forcibly prevented county courts from meeting to make judgments for debt. Although suppressed, the rebellion gained considerable support and realized some of its goals. Since Shays and others argued that the state legislature, and particularly the state senate, was in the hands of the upper classes and was being used for their benefit, the rebellion worried many in the upper classes in other states.

Shays's Rebellion

An Address to the People of the several towns in the county of Hampshire, now at arms.

"GENTLEMEN,

"We have thought proper to inform you of some of the principal causes of the late risings of the people, and also of their present movement, viz.

"1st. The present expensive mode of collecting debts, which, by reason of the great scarcity of cash, will of necessity fill our gaols with unhappy debtors, and thereby a reputable body of people rendered incapable of being serviceable either to themselves or the community.

"2nd. The monies raised by impost and excise being appropriated to discharge the interest of governmental securities, and not the foreign debt, when these securities are not subject to taxation.

"3rd. A suspension of the writ of Habeas Corpus, by which those persons who have stepped forth to assert and maintain the rights of the people, are liable to be taken and conveyed even to the most distant part of the Commonwealth, and thereby subjected to an unjust punishment.

"4th. The unlimited power granted to Justices of the Peace and Sheriffs, Deputy Sheriffs, and Constables, by the Riot Act, indemnifying them to the prosecution thereof; when perhaps, wholly actuated from a principle of revenge, hatred, and envy.

Furthermore, Be assured, that this body, now at arms, despise the idea of being instigated by British emissaries, which is so strenuously propagated by the enemies of our liberties: And also wish the most proper and speedy measures may be taken, to discharge both our foreign and domestick debt

Per Order,
DANIEL GRAY, *Chairman of the Committee, for the above purpose.*

At the same time appeared another publication, signed by a leader of the insurgents, and purporting to come from the same authority. If it was the act of the people then assembled in arms, it shews their further sense of publick grievances; if it was only founded on the authority of the subscriber, it serves to evince the confidence, with which the unhappy tumults of the times inspired an obscure individual to become a reformer, and to assume the sovereign right of contending for his object by the sword.

This publication was as follows, viz.

"To the Printer of the Hampshire Herald

"SIR,

"It has some how or other fallen to my lot to be employed in a more conspicuous manner than some others of my fellow citizens, in stepping forth in defence of the rights and privileges of the people, more especially of the county of Hampshire.

"Therefore, upon the desire of the people now at arms, I take this method to publish to the world of mankind in general, particularly the people of this Commonwealth, some of the principal grievances we complain of, and of which we are now seeking redress, and mean to contend for, until a redress can be obtained, which we hope, will soon take place; and if so, our brethren in this Commonwealth, that do not see with us as yet, shall find we shall be as peaceable as they be.

"In the first place, I must refer you to a draught of grievances drawn up by a committee of the people, now at arms, under the signature of Daniel Gray, chairman, which is heartily approved of; some others also are here added, viz.

"1st. The General Court, for certain obvious reasons, must be removed out of the town of Boston.

"2d. A revision of the constitution is absolutely necessary.

"3d. All kinds of governmental securities, now on interest, that have been bought of the original owners for two shillings, three shillings, four shillings, and the highest for six shillings and eight pence on the pound, and have received more interest than the principal cost the speculator who purchased them—that if justice was done, we verily believe, nay positively know, it would save this Commonwealth thousands of pounds.

"4th. Let the lands belonging to this Commonwealth, at the eastward, be sold at the best advantage, to pay the remainder of our domestick debt.

"5th. Let the monies arising from impost and excise be appropriated to discharge the foreign debt.

"6th. Let that act, passed by the General Court last June, by a small majority of only seven, called the Supplementary Aid, for twenty five years to come, be repealed.

"7th. The total abolition of the Inferiour Court of Common Pleas and General Sessions of the Peace.

"8th. Deputy Sheriffs totally set aside, as a useless set of officers in the community; and Constables who are really necessary, be empowered to do the duty, by which means a large swarm of lawyers will be banished from their wonted haunts, who have been more damage to the people at large, especially the common farmers, than the savage beasts of prey.

"To this I boldly sign my proper name, as a hearty wellwisher to the real rights of the people.

"THOMAS GROVER.

Worcester, Dec. 7, 1786.

Source: The History of the Insurrections in Massachusetts. In the Year Seventeen Hundred and Eighty Six and the Rebellion Consequent Thereon. By George Richards Minot. 2nd edition. Freeport, N.Y.: Books for Libraries Press, 1970. Originally published 1810.

Letter from Thomas Jefferson to James Madison

Paris Jan. 30. 1787

Dear Sir

My last to you was of the 16th. of Dec. since which I have received yours of Nov. 25. & Dec. 4. which afforded me, as your letters always do, a treat on matters public, individual & oeconomical. I am impatient to learn your sentiments on the late troubles in the Eastern states [Shays's Rebellion]. So far as I have yet seen, they do not appear to threaten serious consequences. Those states have suffered by the stoppage of the channels of their commerce, which have not yet found other issues. This must render money scarce, and make the people uneasy. This uneasiness has produced acts absolutely unjustifiable: but I hope they will provoke no severities from the governments. A consciousness of those in power that their administration of the public affairs has been honest, may produce too great a degree of indignation; and those characters wherein fear predominates over hope may apprehend too much from these instances of irregularity. They may conclude too hastily that nature has formed man insusceptible of any other government but that of force, a conclusion not founded in truth, nor experience. Societies exist under three forms sufficiently distinguishable. 1. Without government, as among our Indians. 2. Under governments wherein the will of every one has a just influence, as in the case in England in a slight degree and in our states, in a great one. 3. Under governments of force: as in the case in all other monarchies & in most of the other republics. To have an idea of the curse of existence under these last, they must be seen. It is a government of wolves over sheep. It is a problem, not clear in my mind, that the 1st. condition is not the best, but I believe it to be inconsistent with any degree of population. The second state has a great deal of good in it. The mass of mankind under that enjoys a precious degree of liberty & happiness. It has it's evils too: the principal of which is the turbulence to which it is subject. But weigh this against the oppressions of monarchy, and it becomes nothing. . . . Even this evil is productive of good. It prevents the degeneracy of government, and nourishes a general attention to the public affairs. I hold it that a little rebellion now and then is a good thing, and as necessary in the political world as storms in the physical. Unsuccessful rebellions indeed generally establish the incroachments on the rights of the people which have produced them. An observation of this truth should render honest republican governors so mild in their punishment of rebellions, as not to discourage them too much. It is a medicine necessary for the sound health of government.

Source: The Papers of Thomas Jefferson. Volume 11, 1 January to 6 August 1787. Edited by Julian Boyd. Princeton: Princeton University Press, 1955.

Thomas Jefferson (1743–1826) was the third president of the United States.

THE NORTHWEST ORDINANCE

Probably the most successful act under the Articles of Confederation was the passage of the Northwest Ordinance, which added significant territory to the United States and established rules for governing the territories and adding states to the United States. The most interesting part of the Northwest Ordinance was the recognition of the need for education as a basis for democracy.

An Ordinance for the Government of the Territory of the United States north-west of the river Ohio.

Be it ordained by the United States in Congress assembled, That the said territory, for the purposes of temporary government, be one district; subject, however, to be divided into two districts, as future circumstances may, in the opinion of Congress, make it expedient.

Be it ordained by the authority aforesaid, That the estates both of resident and non-resident proprietors in the said territory, dying intestate, shall descend to, and be distributed among their children, and the descendants of a deceased child in equal parts; the descendants of a deceased child or grandchild, to take the share of their deceased parent in equal parts among them: And where there shall be no children or descendants, then in equal parts to the next of kin, in equal degree; and among collaterals, the children of a deceased brother or sister of the intestate, shall have in equal parts among them their deceased parents' share; and there shall in no case be a distinction between kindred of the whole and half blood; saving in all cases to the widow of the intestate, her third part of the real estate for life, and one third part of the personal estate; and this law relative to descents and dower, shall remain in full force until altered by the legislature of the district.—And until the governor and judges shall adopt laws as hereinafter mentioned, estates in the said territory may be devised or bequeathed by wills in writing, signed and sealed by him or her, in whom the estate may be (being of full age) and attested by three witnesses;—and real estates may be conveyed by lease and release, or bargain and sale, signed, sealed and delivered by the person, being of full age, in whom the estate may be, and attested by two witnesses, provided such wills be duly proved, and such conveyances be acknowledged, or the execution thereof duly proved, and be recorded within one year after proper magistrates, courts and registers shall be appointed for that purpose; and personal property may be transferred by delivery; saving, however, to the French and Canadian inhabitants, and other settlers of the Kaskaskies, St. Vincent's, and the neighbouring villages, who have heretofore professed themselves citizens of Virginia, their laws and customs now in force among them, relative to the descent and conveyance of property.

Be it ordained by the authority aforesaid, That there shall be appointed from time to time, by Congress, a governor, whose commission shall continue in force for the term of three years, unless sooner revoked by Congress: he shall reside in the district, and have a freehold estate therein, in one thousand acres of land, while in the exercise of his office.

There shall be appointed from time to time by Congress, a secretary, whose commission shall continue in force for four years, unless sooner revoked; he shall reside in the district, and have a freehold estate therein, in five hundred acres of land, while in the exercise of his office: it shall be his duty to keep and preserve the acts and laws passed by the legislature, and the public records of the district, and the proceedings of the governor in his executive department; and transmit authentic copies of such acts and proceedings, every six months, to the secretary of Congress: There shall also be appointed a court to consist of three judges, any two of whom to form a court, who shall have a common law jurisdiction, and reside in the district, and have each therein a freehold estate in five hundred acres of land, while in the exercise of their offices; and their commissions shall continue in force during good behaviour.

The governor and judges, or a majority of them, shall adopt and publish in the district, such laws of the original States, criminal and civil, as may be necessary, and best suited to the circumstances of the district, and report them to Congress, from time to time; which laws shall be in force in the district until the organization of the general assembly therein, unless disapproved of by Congress; but afterwards the legislature shall have authority to alter them as they shall think fit. The governor for the time being, shall be commander-in-chief of the militia, appoint and commission all officers in the same, below the rank of general officers; all general officers shall be appointed and commissioned by Congress.

Previous to the organization of the general assembly, the governor shall appoint such magistrates and other civil officers, in each county or township, as he shall find necessary for the preservation of the peace and good order in the same: After the general assembly shall be organized, the powers and duties of magistrates and other civil officers shall be regulated and defined by the said assembly; but all magistrates and other civil officers, not herein otherwise directed, shall during the continuance of this temporary government, be appointed by the governor.

For the prevention of crimes and injuries, the laws to be adopted or made shall have force in all parts of the district, and for the execution of process, criminal and civil, the governor shall make proper divisions thereof—and he shall proceed from time to time, as circumstances may require, to lay out the parts of the district in which the Indian titles shall have been extinguished, into counties and townships, subject, however, to such alterations as may thereafter be made by the legislature.

So soon as there shall be five thousand free male inhabitants, of full age, in the district, upon giving proof thereof to the governor, they shall receive authority, with time and place, to elect representatives from their counties or townships, to represent them in the general assembly; provided that for every five hundred free male inhabitants, there shall be one representative, and so on progressively with the number of free male inhabitants shall the right of representation increase, until the number of representatives shall amount to twenty-five; after which the number and proportion of representatives shall be regulated by the legislature: provided that no person be eligible or qualified to act as a representative, unless he shall have been a citizen of one of the United States three years, and be a resident in the district, or unless he shall have resided in the district three years; and in either case, shall likewise hold in his own right, in fee simple, two hundred acres of land within the same: provided also, that a freehold in fifty acres of land in the district, having been a citizen of one of the States, and being resident in the district, or the like freehold and two years residence in the district shall be necessary to qualify a man as an elector of a representative.

The representatives thus elected, shall serve for the term of two years; and in case of the death of a representative, or removal from office, the governor shall issue a writ to the county or township, for which he was a member, to elect another in his stead, to serve for the residue of the term.

The general assembly, or legislature, shall consist of the governor, legislative council, and a house of representatives. The legislative council shall consist of five members, to continue in office five years, unless sooner removed by Congress; any three of whom to be a quorum: and the members of the council shall be nominated and appointed in the following manner, to wit: As soon as representatives shall be elected, the governor shall appoint a time and place for them to meet together, and, when met, they shall nominate ten persons, residents in the district, and each possessed of a freehold in five hundred acres of land, and return their names to Congress; five of whom Congress shall appoint and commission to serve as aforesaid; and whenever a vacancy shall happen in the council, by death or removal from office, the house of representatives shall nominate two persons, qualified as aforesaid, for each vacancy, and return their names to Congress; one of whom Congress shall appoint and commission for the residue of the term. And every five years, four months at least before the expiration of the time of service of the members of council, the said house shall nominate ten persons, qualified as aforesaid, and return their names to Congress; five of whom Congress shall appoint and commission to serve as members of the council five years, unless sooner removed. And the governor, legislative council, and house of representatives, shall have authority to make laws, in all cases, for the good government of the district, not repugnant to the principles and articles in this ordinance established and declared. And all bills having passed by a majority in the house, and by a majority in the council, shall be referred to the governor for his assent; but no bill or legislative act whatever, shall be of any force without his assent. The governor shall have power to convene, prorogue and dissolve the general assembly, when in his opinion it shall be expedient.

The governor, judges, legislative council, secretary, and such other officers as Congress shall appoint in the district, shall take an oath or affirmation of fidelity, and of office; the governor before the president of Congress, and all other officers before the governor. As soon as a legislature shall be formed in the district, the council and house assembled, in one room, shall have authority, by joint ballot, to elect a delegate to Congress, who shall have a seat in Congress, with a right of debating, but not of voting during this temporary government.

And for extending the fundamental principles of civil and religious liberty, which form the basis whereon these republics, their laws and constitutions are erected; to fix and establish those principles as the basis of all laws, constitutions, and governments, which forever hereafter shall be formed in the said territory: to provide also for the establishment of States, and permanent government therein, and for their admission to a share in the federal councils on an equal footing with the original States, at as early periods as may be consistent with the general interest:

It is hereby ordained and declared, by the authority aforesaid, That the following articles shall be considered as articles of compact between the original States, and the people and States in the said territory, and forever remain unalterable, unless by common consent, to wit:

ART. I. No person, demeaning himself in a peaceable and orderly manner, shall ever be molested on account of his mode of worship or religious sentiments, in the said territory.

ART. II. The inhabitants of the said territory, shall always be entitled to the benefits of the writ of habeas corpus, and of the trial by jury; of a proportionate representation of the people in the legislature, and of judicial proceedings according to the course of the common law. All persons shall be bailable, unless for capital offences, where the proof shall be evident, or the presumption great. All fines shall be moderate; and no cruel or unusual punishments shall be inflicted. No man shall be deprived of his liberty or property, but by the judgment of his peers, or the law of the land, and should the public exigencies make it necessary, for the common preservation, to take any person's property, or to demand his particular services, full compensation shall be made for the same. And in the just preservation of rights and property, it is understood and declared, that no law ought ever to be made, or have force in the said territory, that shall in any manner whatever interfere with, or affect private contracts or engagements, bona fide, and without fraud previously formed.

ART. III. Religion, morality, and knowledge, being necessary to good government and the happiness of mankind, schools and the means of education shall forever be encouraged. The utmost good faith shall always be observed towards the Indians; their land and property shall never be taken from them without their consent; and in their property, rights and liberty, they never shall be invaded or disturbed, unless in just and lawful wars authorized by Congress; but laws founded in justice and humanity shall from time to time be made, for preventing wrongs being done to them, and for preserving peace and friendship with them.

ART. IV. The said territory, and States which may be formed therein, shall forever remain a part of this confederacy of the United States of America, subject to the articles of confederation, and to such alterations therein, as shall be constitutionally made; and to all the acts and ordinances of the United States in Congress assembled, conformable thereto. The inhabitants and settlers in the said territory, shall be subject to pay a part of the federal debts, contracted or to be contracted, and a proportional part of the expenses of government, to be apportioned on them by Congress, according to the same common rule and measure, by which apportionments thereof shall be made on the other States; and the taxes for paying their proportion, shall be laid and levied by the authority and direction of the legislatures of the district or districts or new States, as in the original States, within the time agreed upon by the United States in Congress assembled. The legislatures of those districts or new States, shall never interfere with the primary disposal of the soil by the United States in Congress assembled, nor with any regulations Congress may find necessary for securing the title in such soil to the bona fide purchasers. No tax shall be imposed on land the property of the United States; and in no case shall non-resident proprietors be taxed higher than residents. The navigable waters leading into the Mississippi and St. Lawrence, and the carrying places between the same, shall be common highways, and forever free, as well to the inhabitants of the said territory, as to the citizens of the United States, and those of any other States that may be admitted into the confederacy, without any tax, impost, or duty therefor.

ART. V. There shall be formed in the said territory, not less than three, nor more than five States. . . . And whenever any of the said States shall have sixty thousand free inhabitants therein, such State shall be admitted, by its delegates, into the Congress of the United States, on an equal footing with the original States, in all respects whatever; and shall be at liberty to form a permanent constitution and State government: Provided the constitution and government so to be formed, shall be republican and in conformity to the principles contained in these articles; and so far as it can be consistent with the general interest of the confederacy, such admission shall be allowed at an earlier period, and when there may be a less number of free inhabitants in the State than sixty thousand.

ART. VI. There shall be neither slavery nor involuntary servitude in the said territory, otherwise than in punishment of crimes, whereof the party shall have been duly convicted: Provided always, that any person escaping into the same, from whom labour or service is lawfully claimed in any one of the original States, such fugitive may be lawfully reclaimed, and conveyed to the person claiming his or her labour or service as aforesaid.

Done by the United States in Congress assembled, the thirteenth day of July, in the year of our Lord one thousand seven hundred and eighty-seven, and of their sovereignty and independence the twelfth.

WILLIAM GRAYSON, Chairman.

Source: *Journals of the Continental Congress 1774–1789.* Edited by Worthington Chauncey Ford. Washington, D.C.: Government Printing Office, 1904.

THE CONSTITUTION

The Articles of Confederation were ultimately rejected, and the Constitution was adopted by the convention in Philadelphia and recommended to the states for ratification. The major reasons for rejecting the Articles and adopting the Constitution were the perceived failures (somewhat inflated) of the Articles, particularly to facilitate internal economic development, and the oft-repeated statement that the Articles were "too democratic." The Constitution was designed to provide a better balance between the states and the national government (federalism), to establish a system of separation of powers, and to legitimize policy by the consent of the governed.

The particular institutions adopted were often the result of complex compromises among positions. For example, the Constitution establishes two houses of Congress elected on different principles (territory and population) to satisfy

both small states (equally represented in the Senate) and large states (more seats in the House of Representatives). Most provisions of the Constitution were based on similar compromises.

The limitations on popular control are best seen in the fact that neither the Senate nor the president and vice president are directly elected by the people in the original Constitution. The president and vice president still are not directly elected; the procedures for electing the Senate were changed in the Seventeenth Amendment, which was passed in 1913.

The Constitution was not immediately accorded the status it now has, and there were heated debates throughout the country over its ratification. The most famous materials published in support of ratification were the so-called Federalist Papers.

The Constitution of the United States

WE THE PEOPLE OF THE UNITED STATES, IN ORDER TO FORM A MORE PERFECT UNION, ESTABLISH JUSTICE, INSURE DOMESTIC TRANQUILITY, PROVIDE FOR THE COMMON DEFENCE, PROMOTE THE GENERAL WELFARE, AND SECURE THE BLESSINGS OF LIBERTY TO OURSELVES AND OUR POSTERITY, DO ORDAIN AND ESTABLISH THIS CONSTITUTION FOR THE UNITED STATES OF AMERICA.

Article I

SECTION 1. All legislative Powers herein granted shall be vested in a Congress of the United States, which shall consist of a Senate and House of Representatives.

SECTION 2. (1) The House of Representatives shall be composed of Members chosen every second Year by the People of the several States, and the Electors in each State shall have the Qualifications requisite for Electors of the most numerous Branch of the State Legislature.

(2) No person shall be a Representative who shall not have attained to the Age of Twenty-five years, and been seven Years a Citizen of the United States, and who shall not, when elected, be an inhabitant of that State in which he shall be chosen.

(3) Representatives and direct Taxes shall be apportioned among the several States which may be included within this Union, according to their respective Numbers, which shall be determined by adding to the whole Number of free Persons, including those bound to Service for a Term of Years, and excluding Indians not taxed, three fifths of all other Persons. The actual Enumeration shall be

made within three Years after the first Meeting of the Congress of the United States, and within every subsequent Term of ten Years, in such Manner as they shall by Law direct. The Number of Representatives shall not exceed one for every thirty Thousand, but each State shall have at Least one Representative; and until such enumeration shall be made, the State of New Hampshire shall be entitled to chuse three, Massachusetts eight, Rhode Island and Providence Plantations one, Connecticut five, New York six, New Jersey four, Pennsylvania eight, Delaware one, Maryland six, Virginia ten, North Carolina five, South Carolina five, and Georgia three.

(4) When vacancies happen in the Representation from any State, the Executive Authority thereof shall issue Writs of Election to fill such Vacancies.

(5) The House of Representatives shall chuse their Speaker and other Officers; and shall have the sole Power of Impeachment.

SECTION 3. (1) The Senate of the United States shall be composed of two Senators from each State, chosen by the Legislature thereof, for six Years; and each Senator shall have one vote.

(2) Immediately after they shall be assembled in Consequence of the first Election, they shall be divided as equally as may be into three Classes. The Seats of the Senators of the first Class shall be vacated at the Expiration of the second year, of the second Class at the Expiration of the fourth Year, and of the third Class at the Expiration of the sixth Year, so that one third may be chosen every second Year; and if Vacancies happen by Resignation, or otherwise, during the Recess of the Legislature of any State, the Executive thereof may make temporary Appointments until the next meeting of the Legislature, which shall then fill such Vacancies.

(3) No person shall be a Senator who shall not have attained to the Age of thirty Years, and been nine Years a Citizen of the United States, and who shall not, when elected, be an Inhabitant of that State for which he shall be chosen.

(4) The Vice President of the United States shall be President of the Senate, but shall have no Vote, unless they be equally divided.

(5) The Senate shall chuse their other Officers, and also a President pro tempore, in the Absence of the Vice President, or when he shall exercise the Office of President of the United States.

(6) The Senate shall have the sole Power to try all Impeachments. When sitting for that Purpose, they shall be on Oath or Affirmation. When the President of the United States is tried, the Chief Justice shall preside: And no Person shall be convicted without the Concurrence of two thirds of the Members present.

(7) Judgment in Cases of Impeachment shall not extend further than to removal from Office, and disqualification to hold and enjoy any Office of honor, Trust or Profit under the United States: but the Party convicted shall nevertheless

be liable and subject to Indictment, Trial, Judgment and Punishment, according to Law.

SECTION 4. (1) The Times, Places and Manner of holding Elections for Senators and Representatives, shall be prescribed in each State by the Legislature thereof; but the Congress may at any time by Law make or alter such Regulations, except as to the Places of chusing Senators.

(2) The Congress shall assemble at least once in every Year, and such Meeting shall be on the first Monday in December, unless they shall by Law appoint a different Day.

SECTION 5. (1) Each House shall be the Judge of the Elections, Returns and Qualifications of its own Members, and a Majority of each shall constitute a Quorum to do Business; but a smaller Number may adjourn from day to day, and may be authorized to compel the Attendance of absent Members, in such Manner, and under such Penalties as each house may provide.

(2) Each House may determine the Rules of its Proceedings, punish its members for disorderly Behaviour, and, with the Concurrence of two thirds, expel a Member.

(3) Each House shall keep a Journal of its Proceedings, and from time to time publish the same, excepting such Parts as may in their Judgment require Secrecy; and the Yeas and Nays of the Members of either House on any question shall, at the Desire of one fifth of those Present, be entered on the Journal.

(4) Neither House, during the Session of Congress, shall, without the Consent of the other, adjourn for more than three days, nor to any other Place than that in which the two Houses shall be sitting.

SECTION 6. (1) The Senators and Representatives shall receive a Compensation for their Services, to be ascertained by Law, and paid out of the Treasury of the United States. They shall in all Cases, except Treason, Felony and Breach of the Peace be privileged from Arrest during their Attendance at the Session of their respective Houses, and in going to and returning from the same; and for any Speech or Debate in either House, they shall not be questioned in any other Place.

(2) No Senator or Representative shall, during the Time for which he was elected, be appointed to any civil Office under the authority of the United States, which shall have been created, or the Emoluments whereof shall have been increased during such time; and no Person holding any Office under the United States, shall be a Member of either House during his Continuance in Office.

SECTION 7. (1) All Bills for raising Revenue shall originate in the House of Representatives; but the Senate may propose or concur with Amendments as on other Bills.

(2) Every bill which shall have passed the House of Representatives and the

Senate, shall, before it become a Law, be presented to the President of the United States; If he approve he shall sign it, but if not he shall return it, with his Objections to that House in which it shall have originated, who shall enter the Objections at large on their Journal, and proceed to reconsider it. If after such Reconsideration two thirds of that House shall agree to pass the Bill, it shall be sent, together with the Objections, to the other House, by which it shall likewise be reconsidered, and if approved by two thirds of that House, it shall become a Law. But in all such Cases the Votes of both Houses shall be determined by Yeas and Nays, and the Names of the Persons voting for and against the Bill shall be entered on the Journal of each House respectively. If any Bill shall not be returned by the President within ten Days (Sundays excepted) after it shall have been presented to him, the Same shall be a law, in like Manner as if he had signed it, unless the Congress by their Adjournment prevent its Return, in which Case it shall not be a Law.

(3) Every Order, Resolution, or Vote to which the Concurrence of the Senate and House of Representatives may be necessary (except on a question of Adjournment) shall be presented to the President of the United States; and before the Same shall take Effect, shall be approved by him, or being disapproved by him shall be repassed by two thirds of the Senate and House of Representatives, according to the Rules and Limitations prescribed in the Case of a Bill.

SECTION 8. (1) The Congress shall have Power To lay and collect Taxes, Duties, Imposts and Excises, to pay the Debts and provide for the common Defence and general Welfare of the United States; but all Duties, Imposts and Excises shall be uniform throughout the United States;

(2) To borrow money on the Credit of the United States.

(3) To regulate Commerce with foreign Nations, and among the several States, and with the Indian Tribes;

(4) To establish an uniform Rule of Naturalization, and uniform Laws on the subject of Bankruptcies throughout the United States;

(5) To coin Money, regulate the Value thereof, and of foreign Coin, and to fix the Standard of Weights and Measures;

(6) To provide for the Punishment of counterfeiting the Securities and current Coin of the United States;

(7) To establish Post Offices and post Roads;

(8) To promote the Progress of Science and useful Arts, by securing for limited Times to Authors and Inventors the exclusive Right to their respective Writings and Discoveries;

(9) To constitute Tribunals inferior to the Supreme Court;

(10) To define and Punish Piracies and Felonies committed on the high Seas, and Offences against the Law of Nations;

(11) To declare War, grant Letters of Marque and Reprisal, and make Rules concerning Captures on Land and Water;

(12) To raise and support Armies, but no Appropriation of Money to that Use shall be for a longer Term than two Years;

(13) To provide and maintain a Navy;

(14) To make Rules for the Government and Regulation of the land and naval Forces;

(15) To provide for calling forth the Militia to execute the Laws of the Union, suppress Insurrections and repel Invasions;

(16) To provide for organizing, arming, and disciplining, the Militia, and for governing such Part of them as may be employed in the Service of the United States, reserving to the States respectively, the Appointment of the Officers, and the Authority of training the Militia according to the discipline prescribed by Congress;

(17) To exercise exclusive Legislation in all Cases whatsoever, over such District (not exceeding ten Miles square) as may, by Cession of particular States, and the Acceptance of Congress, become the Seat of the Government of the United States, and to exercise like Authority over all Places purchased by the Consent of the Legislature of the State in which the Same shall be, for the Erection of Forts, Magazines, Arsenals, dock-Yards, and other needful Buildings; — And

(18) To make all Laws which shall be necessary and proper for carrying into Execution the foregoing Powers, and all other Powers, vested by this Constitution in the Government of the United States, or in any Department or Officer thereof.

SECTION 9. (1) The Migration or Importation of such Persons as any of the States now existing shall think proper to admit, shall not be prohibited by the Congress prior to the Year one thousand eight hundred and eight, but a Tax or Duty may be imposed on such Importation, not exceeding ten dollars for each Person.

(2) The Privilege of the Writ of Habeas Corpus shall not be suspended unless when in Cases of Rebellion or Invasion the public Safety may require it.

(3) No Bill of Attainder or ex post facto Law shall be passed.

(4) No Capitation, or other direct, tax shall be laid, unless in Proportion to the Census or Enumeration herein before directed to be taken.

(5) No Tax or Duty shall be laid on Articles exported from any State.

(6) No preference shall be given by any Regulation of Commerce or Revenue to the Ports of one State over those of another; nor shall Vessels bound to, or from, one State, be obliged to enter, clear, or pay Duties in another.

(7) No Money shall be drawn from the Treasury, but in Consequence of Appropriations made by Law; and a regular Statement and Account of the Receipts and Expenditures of all public Money shall be published from time to time.

(8) No Title of Nobility shall be granted by the United States: And no Person holding any Office of Profit or Trust under them, shall, without the Consent of the Congress, accept of any present, Emolument, Office, or Title, of any kind whatever, from any King, Prince, or foreign State.

SECTION 10. (1) No State shall enter into any Treaty, Alliance, or Confederation; grant Letters of Marque and Reprisal; coin Money; emit Bills of Credit; make any Thing but gold and silver Coin a Tender in Payment of Debts; pass any Bill of Attainder, ex post facto Law, or Law impairing the Obligation of Contracts, or grant any Title of Nobility.

(2) No State shall, without the Consent of the Congress, lay any Imposts or Duties on Imports or Exports, except what may be absolutely necessary for executing its inspection Laws: and the net Produce of all Duties and Imposts, laid by any State on Imports or Exports, shall be for the Use of the Treasury of the United States; and all such Laws shall be subject to the Revision and control of the Congress.

(3) No State shall, without the Consent of Congress, lay any Duty of Tonnage, keep Troops, or Ships of War in time of Peace, enter into any Agreement or Compact with another State, or with a foreign Power, or engage in War, unless actually invaded, or in such imminent Danger as will not admit of Delay.

Article II

SECTION 1. (1) The executive Power shall be vested in a President of the United States of America. He shall hold his Office during the Term of four Years, and, together with the Vice President, chosen for the same Term, be elected, as follows:

(2) Each State shall appoint, in such Manner as the Legislature thereof may direct, a Number of Electors, equal to the whole Number of Senators and Representatives to which the State may be entitled in the Congress: but no Senator or Representative or Person holding an Office of Trust or Profit under the United States, shall be appointed an Elector.

The Electors shall meet in their respective States, and vote by ballot for two Persons, of whom one at least shall not be an Inhabitant of the same State with themselves. And they shall make a List of all the Persons voted for, and of the Number of Votes for each; which List they shall sign and certify, and transmit sealed to the Seat of Government of the United States, directed to the President of the Senate. The President of the Senate shall, in the Presence of the Senate and House of Representatives, open all the Certificates, and the Votes shall then be counted. The Person having the greatest Number of Votes shall be the President, if such Number be a Majority of the whole Number of Electors appointed; and if there be more than one who have such Majority and have an equal Number of

Votes, then the House of Representatives shall immediately chuse by Ballot one of them for President; and if no person have a Majority, then from the five highest on the List the said House shall in like Manner chuse the President. But in chusing the President, the Votes shall be taken by States, the Representation from each State having one Vote; A quorum for this Purpose shall consist of a Member or Members from two-thirds of the States, and a Majority of all the States shall be necessary to a Choice. In every Case, after the Choice of the President, the person having the greatest Number of Votes of the Electors shall be the Vice President. But if there should remain two or more who have equal votes, the Senate shall chuse from them by Ballot the Vice-President.

(3) The Congress may determine the Time of chusing the Electors, and the Day on which they shall give their Votes; which Day shall be the same throughout the United States.

(4) No Person except a natural born Citizen, or a Citizen of the United States, at the time of the Adoption of this Constitution, shall be eligible to the Office of President; neither shall any Person be eligible to that Office who shall not have attained to the Age of thirty five Years, and been fourteen Years a Resident within the United States.

(5) In Case of the Removal of the President from Office or of his Death, Resignation, or Inability to discharge the Powers and Duties of the said Office, the same shall devolve on the Vice President, and the Congress may by Law provide for the Case of Removal, Death, Resignation, or Inability, both of the President and Vice President, declaring what Officer shall then act as President, and such Officer shall act accordingly, until the Disability be removed, or a President shall be elected.

(6) The President shall, at stated Times, receive for his Services a Compensation, which shall neither be increased nor diminished during the Period for which he shall have been elected, and he shall not receive within that Period any other Emolument from the United States, or any of them.

(7) Before he enter on the Execution of his Office, he shall take the following Oath or Affirmation: — "I do solemnly swear (or affirm) that I will faithfully execute the Office of President of the United States, and will to the best of my Ability, preserve, protect and defend the Constitution of the United States."

SECTION 2. (1) The President shall be Commander in Chief of the Army and Navy of the United States, and of the Militia of the several States, when called into actual Service of the United States; he may require the Opinion, in writing, of the principal Officer in each of the executive Departments, upon any subject relating to the Duties of their respective Offices, and he shall have Power to grant Reprieves and Pardons for Offences against the United States, except in Cases of Impeachment.

(2) He shall have Power, by and with the Advice and Consent of the Senate, to

make Treaties, provided two thirds of the Senators present concur; and he shall nominate, and by and with the Advice and Consent of the Senate, shall appoint Ambassadors, other public Ministers and Councils, Judges of the supreme Court, and all other Officers of the United States, whose Appointments are not herein otherwise provided for, and which shall be established by Law: but the Congress may by Law vest the Appointment of such inferior Officers as they think proper, in the President alone, in the Courts of Law, or in the Heads of Departments.

(3) The President shall have power to fill up all Vacancies that may happen during the Recess of the Senate, by granting Commissions which shall expire at the End of their next Session.

SECTION 3. He shall from time to time give to the Congress Information of the State of the Union, and recommend to their Consideration such Measures as he shall judge necessary and expedient; he may, on extraordinary Occasions, convene both Houses, or either of them, and in Case of Disagreement between them, with Respect to the Time of Adjournment, he may adjourn them to such Time as he shall think proper; he shall receive Ambassadors and other public Ministers; he shall take Care that the Laws be faithfully executed, and shall Commission all the Officers of the United States.

SECTION 4. The President, Vice President and all civil Officers of the United States, shall be removed from Office on Impeachment for, and Conviction of, Treason, Bribery, or other high Crimes and Misdemeanors.

Article III

SECTION 1. The judicial Power of the United States, shall be vested in one supreme Court, and in such inferior Courts as the Congress may from time to time ordain and establish. The Judges, both of the supreme and inferior Courts, shall hold their Offices during good Behaviour, and shall, at stated Times, receive for their Services, a Compensation, which shall not be diminished during their Continuance in Office.

SECTION 2. (1) The judicial Power shall extend to all Cases, in Law and Equity, arising under this Constitution, the Laws of the United States, and Treaties made, or which shall be made, under their Authority; — to all Cases affecting Ambassadors, other public Ministers and Consuls; — to all Cases of admiralty and maritime Jurisdiction; — to Controversies to which the United States shall be a party; — to Controversies between two or more States; — between a State and Citizens of another State; — between Citizens of different States; — between Citizens of the same State claiming Lands under Grants of different States, and between a State, or the Citizens thereof, and foreign States, Citizens or subjects.

(2) In all Cases affecting Ambassadors, other public Ministers and Consuls,

and those in which a State shall be a Party, the Supreme Court shall have original Jurisdiction. In all the other Cases before mentioned, the supreme Court shall have appellate Jurisdiction, both as to Law and Fact, with such Exceptions, and under such Regulations as the Congress shall make.

(3) The Trial of all Crimes, except in Cases of Impeachment, shall be by Jury; and such Trial shall be held in the State where the said Crimes shall have been committed; but when not committed within any State, the Trial shall be at such Place or Places as the Congress may by Law have directed.

SECTION 3. (1) Treason against the United States, shall consist only in levying War against them, or in adhering to their Enemies, giving them Aid and Comfort. No person shall be convicted of Treason unless on the Testimony of two Witnesses to the same overt Act, or on Confession in open Court.

(2) The Congress shall have Power to declare the Punishment of Treason, but no Attainder of Treason shall work Corruption of Blood, or Forfeiture except during the Life of the Person attainted.

Article IV

SECTION 1. Full Faith and Credit shall be given in each State to the public Acts, Records, and judicial Proceedings of every other State. And the Congress may by general Laws prescribe the Manner in which such Acts, Records and Proceedings shall be proved, and the Effect thereof.

SECTION 2. (1) The Citizens of each State shall be entitled to all Privileges and Immunities of Citizens in the several States.

(2) A person charged in any State with Treason, Felony, or other Crime, who shall flee from Justice, and be found in another State, shall on Demand of the executive Authority of the State from which he fled, be delivered up to be removed to the State having Jurisdiction of the Crime.

(3) No person held to Service or Labour in one State, under the Laws thereof, escaping into another, shall, in Consequence of any Law or Regulation therein, be discharged from such Service or Labour, but shall be delivered up on Claim of the Party to whom such service or Labour may be due.

SECTION 3. (1) New States may be admitted by the Congress into this Union; but no new State shall be formed or erected within the Jurisdiction of any other State; nor any State be formed by the Junction of two or more States, or Parts of States, without the Consent of the Legislatures of the States concerned as well as of the Congress.

(2) The Congress shall have Power to dispose of and make all needful Rules and Regulations respecting the Territory or other Property belonging to the United States; and nothing in this Constitution shall be so construed as to Prejudice any Claims of the United States, or of any particular State.

SECTION 4. The United States shall guarantee to every State in this Union a Republican Form of Government, and shall protect each of them against Invasion; and on Application of the Legislature, or of the Executive (when the Legislature cannot be convened) against domestic Violence.

Article V

The Congress, whenever two thirds of both Houses shall deem it necessary, shall propose Amendments to this Constitution, or, on the Application of the Legislatures of two thirds of the several States, shall call a Convention for proposing Amendments, which, in either Case, shall be valid to all Intents and Purposes, as Part of this Constitution, when ratified by the Legislatures of three fourths thereof, as the one or the other Mode of Ratification may be proposed by the Congress; Provided that no Amendment which may be made prior to the Year One thousand eight hundred and eight shall in any Manner affect the first and fourth Clauses in the Ninth Section of the first Article; and that no State, without its Consent, shall be deprived of its equal Suffrage in the Senate.

Article VI

(1) All Debts contracted and Engagements entered into, before the Adoption of this Constitution, shall be as valid against the United States under this Constitution, as under the Confederation.

(2) This Constitution, and the Laws of the United States which shall be made in pursuance thereof; and all Treaties made, or which shall be made, under the Authority of the United States, shall be the supreme Law of the Land; and the Judges in every State shall be bound thereby, any Thing in the Constitution or Laws of any State to the Contrary notwithstanding.

(3) The Senators and Representatives before mentioned, and the Members of the several State Legislatures, and all executive and judicial Officers, both of the United States and of the several States, shall be bound by Oath or Affirmation, to support this Constitution; but no religious Test shall ever be required as a Qualification to any Office or public Trust under the United States.

Article VII

The Ratification of the Conventions of nine States, shall be sufficient for the Establishment of this Constitution between the States so ratifying the Same.

DONE In Convention by the Unanimous Consent of the States present the Seventeenth Day of September in the Year of our Lord one thousand seven hundred and Eighty seven and of the Independence of the United States of America the Twelfth. *In Witness* whereof We have hereunto subscribed our Names.

Source: *The Federal and State Constitutions, Colonial Charters, and Other Organic Laws of the U.—S.—. Part I.* Compiled by Ben. Perley Poore. 2nd edition. Washington, D.C.: Government Printing Office, 1878.

The Federalist Papers

In the debates following the adoption of the Constitution by the convention in Philadelphia, the Federalist Papers by James Madison (1751–1836), Alexander Hamilton (1757–1804), and John Jay (1745–1829) were the most important documents on the side of ratification. Originally published as newspaper articles during the debate over ratification in New York, the Federalist Papers are now considered among the most important contributions to American political thought.

The papers were originally written under the pseudonym Publius, but the individual authors have been identified. All the papers reprinted here are by Hamilton and Madison. Jay wrote only a few papers, which were fairly limited in scope. There are fundamental differences between Hamilton and Madison. The former favored a centralized government with a strong executive, perhaps even a monarch. Hamilton argued in his famous Federalist No. 23 on implied powers that the Constitution provided for such a strong executive. Madison favored the complex set of checks and balances found in the separation of powers and the federal system. He argued that these systems would keep any part of government from becoming too powerful. The most famous of the Federalist Papers is No. 10, where Madison makes a sustained argument that the system of government under the Constitution can avoid the evil of faction or the dominance of the political process by group interest. Madison even argues that a "majority faction" will be constrained by the system. But Madison lived in an era without modern political parties or interest groups.

James Madison
The Federalist No. 10

Among the numerous advantages promised by a well-constructed Union, none deserves to be more accurately developed than its tendency to break and control the violence of faction. The friend of popular governments never finds himself so much alarmed for their character and fate, as when he contemplates their propensity to this dangerous vice. He will not fail, therefore, to set a due value on any plan which, without violating the principles to which he is attached, provides a proper cure for it. The instability, injustice, and confusion introduced into the public councils, have, in truth, been the mortal diseases under which popular governments have everywhere perished; as they continue to be the favorite and fruitful topics from which the adversaries to liberty derive their most specious declamations. The valuable improvements made by the American constitutions on the popular models, both ancient and modern, cannot certainly be too much admired; but it would be an unwarrantable partiality, to contend that they have as effectually obviated the danger on this side, as was wished and expected. Complaints are everywhere heard from our most considerate and virtuous citizens, equally the friends of public and private faith, and of public and personal liberty, that our governments are too unstable, that the public good is disregarded in the conflicts of rival parties, and that measures are too often decided, not according to the rules of justice and the rights of the minor party, but by the superior force of an interested and overbearing majority. However anxiously we may wish that these complaints have no foundation, the evidence of known facts will not permit us to deny that they are in some degree true. It will be found, indeed, on a candid review of our situation, that some of the distresses under which we labor have been erroneously charged on the operation of our governments; but it will be found, at the same time, that other causes will not alone account for many of our heaviest misfortunes; and, particularly, for that prevailing and increasing distrust of public engagements, and alarm for private rights, which are echoed from one end of the continent to the other. These must be chiefly, if not wholly, effects of the unsteadiness and injustice with which a factious spirit has tainted our public administrations.

By a faction, I understand a number of citizens, whether amounting to a majority or minority of the whole, who are united and actuated by some common impulse of passion, or of interest, adverse to the rights of other citizens, or to the permanent and aggregate interests of the community.

There are two methods of curing the mischiefs of faction: the one, by removing its causes; the other, by controlling its effects.

There are again two methods of removing the causes of faction: the one, by destroying the liberty which is essential to its existence; the other, by giving to every citizen the same opinions, the same passions, and the same interests.

It could never be more truly said than of the first remedy, that it was worse than the disease. Liberty is to faction what air is to fire, an aliment without which it instantly expires. But it could not be less folly to abolish liberty, which is essential to political life, because it nourishes faction, than it would be to wish the annihilation of air, which is essential to animal life, because it imparts to fire its destructive agency.

The second expedient is as impracticable as the first would be unwise. As long as the reason of man continue fallible, and he is at liberty to exercise it, different opinions will be formed. As long as the connection subsists between his reason and his self-love, his opinions and his passions will have a reciprocal influence on each other; and the former will be objects to which the latter will attach themselves. The diversity in the faculties of men, from which the rights of property originate, is not less an insuperable obstacle to a uniformity of interests. The protection of these faculties is the first object of government. From the protection of different and unequal faculties of acquiring property, the possession of different degrees and kinds of property immediately results; and from the influence of these on the sentiments and views of the respective proprietors, ensues a division of the society into different interests and parties.

The latent causes of faction are thus sown in the nature of man; and we see them everywhere brought into different degrees of activity, according to the different circumstances of civil society. A zeal for different opinions concerning religion, concerning government, and many other points, as well of speculation as of practice; an attachment to different leaders ambitiously contending for pre-eminence and power; or to persons of other descriptions whose fortunes have been interesting to the human passions, have, in turn, divided mankind into parties, inflamed them with mutual animosity, and rendered them much more disposed to vex and oppress each other than to co-operate for their common good. So strong is this propensity of mankind to fall into mutual animosities, that where no substantial occasion presents itself, the most frivolous and fanciful distinctions have been sufficient to kindle their unfriendly passions and excite their most violent conflicts. But the most common and durable source of factions has been the various and unequal distribution of property. Those who hold and those who are without property have ever formed distinct interests in society. Those who are creditors, and those who are debtors, fall under a like discrimination. A landed interest, a manufacturing interest, a mercantile interest, a moneyed interest, with many lesser interests, grow up of necessity in civilized nations, and divide them into different classes, actuated by different sentiments and views. The regulation of these various and interfering interests forms the principal task of modern legislation, and involves the spirit of party and faction in the necessary and ordinary operations of the government.

No man is allowed to be a judge in his own cause, because his interest would certainly bias his judgment, and, not improbably, corrupt his integrity. With equal, nay with greater reason, a body of men are unfit to be both judges and parties at the same time; yet what are many of the most important acts of legislation, but so many judicial determinations, not indeed concerning the rights of single persons, but concerning the rights of large bodies of citizens? And what are the different classes of legislators but advocates and parties to the causes which they determine? Is a law proposed concerning private debts? It is a question to which the creditors are parties on one side and the debtors on the other. Justice ought to hold the balance between them. Yet the parties are, and must be, themselves the judges; and the most numerous party, or, in other words, the most powerful faction must be expected to prevail. Shall domestic manufactures be encouraged, and in what degree, by restrictions on foreign manufacturers? are questions which would be differently decided by the landed and the manufacturing classes, and probably by neither with a sole regard to justice and the public good. The apportionment of taxes on the various descriptions of property is an act which seems to require the most exact impartiality; yet there is, perhaps, no legislative act in which greater opportunity and temptation are given to a predominant party to trample on the rules of justice. Every shilling with which they overburden the inferior number, is a shilling saved to their own pockets.

It is in vain to say that enlightened statesmen will be able to adjust these clashing interests, and render them all subservient to the public good. Enlightened statesmen will not always be at the helm. Nor, in many cases, can such an adjustment be made at all without taking into view indirect and remote considerations, which will rarely prevail over the immediate interest which one party may find in disregarding the rights of another or the good of the whole.

The inference to which we are brought is, that the *causes* of faction cannot be removed, and that relief is only to be sought in the means of controlling its *effects*.

If a faction consists of less than a majority, relief is supplied by the republican principle, which enables the majority to defeat its sinister views by regular vote. It may clog the administration, it may convulse the society; but it will be unable to execute and mask its violence under the forms of the Constitution. When a majority is included in a faction, the form of popular government, on the other hand, enables it to sacrifice to its ruling passion or interest both the public good and the rights of other citizens. To secure the public good and private rights against the danger of such a faction, and at the same time to preserve the spirit and the form of popular government, is then the great object to which our inquiries are directed. Let me add that it is the great desideratum by which this form of government can be rescued from the opprobrium under which it has so long labored, and be recommended to the esteem and adoption of mankind.

By what means is this object attainable? Evidently by one of two only. Either the existence of the same passion or interest in a majority at the same time must be prevented, or the majority, having such coexistent passion or interest, must be rendered, by their number and local situation, unable to concert and carry into effect schemes of oppression. If the impulse and the opportunity be suffered to coincide, we well know that neither moral nor religious motives can be relied on as an adequate control. They are not found to be such on the injustice and violence of individuals, and lose their efficacy in proportion to the number combined together, that is, in proportion as their efficacy becomes needful.

From this view of the subject it may be concluded that a pure democracy, by which I mean a society consisting of a small number of citizens, who assemble and administer the government in person, can admit of no cure for the mischiefs of faction. A common passion or interest will, in almost every case, be felt by a majority of the whole; a communication and concert result from the form of government itself; and there is nothing to check the inducements to sacrifice the weaker party or an obnoxious individual. Hence it is that such democracies have ever been spectacles of turbulence and contention; have ever been found incompatible with personal security or the rights of property; and have in general been as short in their lives as they have been violent in their deaths. Theoretic politicians, who have patronized this species of government, have erroneously supposed that by reducing mankind to a perfect equality in their political rights, they would, at the same time, be perfectly equalized and assimilated to their possessions, their opinions, and their passions.

A republic, by which I mean a government in which the scheme of representation takes place, opens a different prospect, and promises the cure for which we are seeking. Let us examine the points in which it varies from pure democracy, and we shall comprehend both the nature of the cure and the efficacy which it must derive from the Union.

The two great points of difference between a democracy and a republic are: first, the delegation of the government, in the latter, to a small number of citizens elected by the rest; secondly, the greater number of citizens, and greater sphere of country, over which the latter may be extended.

The effect of the first difference is, on the one hand, to refine and enlarge the public views, by passing them through the medium of a chosen body of citizens, whose wisdom may best discern the true interest of their country, and whose patriotism and love of justice will be least likely to sacrifice it to temporary or partial considerations. Under such a regulation, it may well happen that the public voice, pronounced by the representatives of the people, will be more consonant to the public good than if pronounced by the people themselves, convened for the purpose. On the other hand, the effect may be inverted. Men of factious tempers, of local prejudices, or of sinister designs, may, by intrigue, by corruption, or by other means, first obtain the suffrages, and then betray the interests, of the people. The question resulting is, whether small or extensive republics are more favorable to the election of proper guardians of the public weal; and it is clearly decided in favor of the latter by two obvious considerations:

In the first place, it is to be remarked that however small the republic may be, the representatives must be raised to a certain number, in order to guard against the cabals of a few; and that, however large it may be, they must be limited to a certain number, in order to guard against the confusion of a multitude. Hence, the number of representatives in the two cases not being in proportion to that of the two constituents, and being proportionally greater in the small republic, it follows that, if the proportion of fit characters be not less in the large than in the small republic, the former will present a greater opinion, and consequently a greater probability of a fit choice.

In the next place, as each representative will be chosen by a greater number of citizens in the large than in the small republic, it will be more difficult for unworthy candidates to practise with success the vicious arts by which elections are too often carried; and the suffrages of the people being more free, will be more likely to centre in men who possess the most attractive merit and the most diffusive and established characters.

It must be confessed that in this, as in most other cases, there is a mean, on both sides of which inconveniences will be found to lie. By enlarging too much the number of electors, you render the representatives too little acquainted with all their local circumstances and lesser interests; as by reducing it too much, you render him unduly attached to these, and too little fit to comprehend and pursue great and national objects. The federal Constitution forms a happy combination in this respect; the great and aggregate interests being referred to the national, the local and particular to the State legislatures.

The other point of difference is, the greater number of citizens and extent of territory which may be brought within the compass of republican than of democratic government; and it is this circumstance principally which renders factious combinations less to be dreaded in the former than in the latter. The smaller the society, the fewer probably will be the distinct parties and interests composing it; the fewer the distinct parties and interests, the more frequently will a majority be found of the same party; and the smaller the number of individuals composing a majority, and the smaller the compass within which they are placed, the more easily will they concert and execute their plans of oppression. Extend the sphere, and you take in a greater variety of parties and interests; you make it less probable that a majority of the whole will have a common motive to invade the rights of other citizens; or if such a common motive exists, it will be more difficult for all who feel it to discover their own strength, and to act in unison with each other. Besides other impediments, it may be remarked that, where there is a consciousness of unjust or dishonorable purposes, communication is always checked by distrust in proportion to the number whose concurrence is necessary.

Hence, it clearly appears, that the same advantage which a republic has over a democracy, in controlling the effects of faction, is enjoyed by a large over a small republic, — is enjoyed by the Union over the States composing it. Does the advantage consist in the substitution of representatives whose enlightened views and virtuous sentiments render them superior to local prejudices and to schemes of injustice? It will not be denied that the representation of the Union will be most likely to possess these requisite endowments. Does it consist in the greater security afforded by a greater variety of parties, against the event of any one party being able to outnumber and oppress the rest? In an equal degree does the increased variety of parties comprised within the Union, increase this security. Does it, in fine, consist in the greater obstacles opposed to the concert and accomplishment of the secret wishes of a unjust and interested majority? Here, again, the extent of the Union gives it the most palpable advantage.

The influence of factious leaders may kindle a flame within their particular States, but will be unable to spread a general conflagration through the other States. A religious sect may degenerate into a political faction in a part of the Confederacy; but the variety of sects dispersed over the entire face of it must secure the national councils against any danger from that course. A rage for paper money, for an abolition of debts, for an equal division of property, or for any other improper or wicked project, will be less apt to pervade the whole body of the Union than a particular member of it; in the same proportion as such a malady is more likely to taint a particular country or district, than an entire State.

In the extent and proper structure of the Union, therefore, we behold a republican remedy for the disease most incident to republican government. And according to the degree of pleasure and pride we feel in being republicans, ought to be our zeal in cherishing the spirit and supporting the character of Federalists.

*　*　*

In Federalist No. 14 Madison argues further that the enumeration of the subjects to which central government activity is limited and the existence of the federal system means that no one need worry about the power of the central government.

James Madison
The Federalist No. 14

In the first place it is to be remembered, that the general government is not to be charged with the whole power of making and administering laws. Its jurisdiction is limited to certain enumerated objects, which concern all the members of the republic, but which are not to be attained by the separate provisions of any. The subordinate governments [states] which can extend their care to all those other objects, which can be separately provided for, will retain their due authority and activity. Were it proposed by the plan of the Convention to abolish the governments of the particular States, its adversaries would have some ground for their objection, though it would not be difficult to shew that if they were abolished, the general government would be compelled by the principle of self-preservation, to reinstate them in their proper jurisdiction.

*   *   *

In No. 15 and No. 22 Hamilton argues that the Articles of Confederation are too weak.

Alexander Hamilton
The Federalist No. 15

The great and radical vice in the construction of the existing Confederation is in the principle of legislation for states or governments, in their corporate or collective capacities and as contradistinguished from the individuals of whom they consist. Though this principle does not run through all the powers delegated to the Union; yet it pervades and governs those, on which the efficacy of the rest depends. Except as to the rule of apportionment, the United States have an indefinite discretion to make requisitions for men and money; but they have no authority to raise either by regulations extending to the individual citizens of America. The consequence of this is, that though in theory their resolutions concerning those objects are laws, constitutionally binding on the members of the Union, yet in practice they are mere recommendations, which the States observe or disregard at their option. . . .

Government implies the power of making laws. It is essential to the idea of a law, that it be attended with a sanction; or, in other words, a penalty or punishment for disobedience. If there be no penalty annexed to disobedience, the resolutions or commands which pretend to be laws will in fact amount to nothing more than advice or recommendation. This penalty, whatever it may be, can only be inflicted in two ways; by the agency of the Courts and Ministers of Justice, or by military force; by the coertion of the magistracy, or by the coertion of arms. The first kind can evidently apply only to men—the last kind must of necessity be employed against bodies politic, or communities or States. It is evident, that there is no process of a court by which their observance of the laws can in the last resort be enforced. Sentences may be denounced against them for violations of their duty; but these sentences can only be carried into execution by the sword. In an association where the general authority is confined to the collective bodies of the communities that compose it, every breach of the laws must involve a state of war, and military execution must become the only instrument of civil obedience. Such a state of things can certainly not deserve the name of government, nor would any prudent man choose to commit his happiness to it.

There was a time when we were told that breaches, by the States, of the regulations of the federal authority were not to be expected—that a sense of common interest would preside over the conduct of the respective members, and would beget a full compliance with all the constitutional requisitions of the Union. This language at the present day would appear as wild as a great part of what we now hear from the same quarter will be thought, when we shall have received further lessons from that best oracle of wisdom, experience. It at all times betrayed an ignorance of the true springs by which human conduct is actuated, and belied the original inducements to the establishment of civil power. Why has government been instituted at all? Because the passions of men will not conform to the dictates of reason and justice, without constraint. Has it been found that bodies of men act with more rectitude or greater disinterestedness than individuals? The contrary of this has been inferred by all accurate observers of the conduct of mankind; and the inference is founded upon obvious reasons. Regard to reputation has a less active influence, when the infamy of a bad action is to be divided among a number, than when it is to fall singly upon one. A spirit of faction which is apt to mingle its poison in the deliberations of all bodies of men, will often hurry the persons of whom they are composed into improprieties and excesses, for which they would blush in a private capacity.

Alexander Hamilton
The Federalist No. 22

In addition to the defects already enumerated in the existing Federal system, there are others of not less importance, which concur in rendering it altogether unfit for the administration of the affairs of the Union. . . .

A circumstance, which crowns the defects of the confederation, remains yet to be mentioned—the want of a judiciary power. Laws are a dead letter without courts to expound and define their true meaning and operation. The treaties of the United States to have any force at all, must be considered as part of the law of the land. Their true import as far as respects individuals, must, like all other laws, be ascertained by judicial determinations. To produce uniformity in these determinations, they ought to be submitted in the last resort, to one SUPREME TRIBUNAL. And this tribunal ought to be instituted under the same authority which forms the treaties themselves. These ingredients are both indispensable. If there is in each State, a court of final jurisdiction, there may be as many different final determinations on the same point, as there are courts. There are endless diversities in the opinions of men. We often see not only different courts, but the Judges of the same court differing from each other. To avoid the confusion which would unavoidably result from the contradictory decisions of a number of independent judicatories, all nations have found it necessary to establish one court paramount to the rest—possessing a general superintendance, and authorised to settle and declare in the last resort, an uniform rule of civil justice.

This is the more necessary where the frame of the government is so compounded, that the laws of the whole are in danger of being contravened by the laws of the parts. In this case if the particular tribunals are invested with a right of ultimate jurisdiction, besides the contradictions to be expected from difference of opinion, there will be much to fear from the bias of local views and prejudices, and from the interference of local regulations. As often as such an interference was to happen, there would be reason to apprehend, that the provisions of the particular laws might be preferred to those of the general laws; for nothing is more natural to men in office, than to look with peculiar deference towards that authority to which they owe their official existence.

The treaties of the United States, under the present constitution, are liable to the infractions of thirteen different Legislatures, and as many different courts of final jurisdiction, acting under the authority of those Legislatures. The faith, the reputation, the peace of the whole union, are thus continually at the mercy of the prejudices, the passions, and the interests of every member of which it is composed. Is it possible that foreign nations can either respect or confide in such a government? Is it possible that the People of America will longer consent to trust their honor, their happiness, their safety, on so precarious a foundation?

* * *

In Federalist No. 23 Hamilton begins his argument for a strong central government, saying that certain powers should be without limit.

Alexander Hamilton
The Federalist No. 23

The authorities essential to the care of the common defence are these—to raise armies—to build up and equip fleets—to prescribe rules for the government of both—to direct their operations—to provide for their support. These powers ought to exist without limitation: *Because it is impossible to forsee or define the extent and variety of national exigencies, or the corresponding extent & variety of the means which may be necessary to satisfy them.* The circumstances that endanger the safety of nations are infinite; and for this reason no constitutional shackles can wisely be imposed on the power to which the care of it is committed. This power ought to be co-extensive with all the possible combinations of such circumstances; and ought to be under the direction of the same councils, which are appointed to preside over the common defence.

* * *

In Federalist No. 39 Madison argues that the new Constitution will be both republican (which he carefully defines) and federal. He specifically rejects the notion that it will be a national Constitution.

James Madison
The Federalist No. 39

Is . . . the general form and aspect of the government to be strictly republican? It is evident that no other form would be reconcileable with the genius of the people of America; with the fundamental principles of the revolution; or with that honorable determination, which animates every votary of freedom, to rest all our political experiments on the capacity of mankind for self-government. If the plan of the Convention therefore be found to depart from the republican character, its advocates must abandon it as no longer defensible.

What then are the distinctive characters of the republican form? . . .

If we resort for a criterion, to the different principles on which different forms of government are established, we may define a republic to be, or at least may bestow that name on, a government which derives all its powers directly or indirectly from the great body of the people; and is administered by persons holding their offices during pleasure, for a limited period, or during good behaviour. It is essential to such a government, that it be derived from the great body of the society, not from an inconsiderable proportion, or a favored class of it; otherwise a handful of tyrannical nobles, exercising their oppressions by a delegation of their powers, might aspire to the rank of republicans, and claim for their government the honorable title of republic. It is sufficient for such a government, that the persons administering it be appointed, either directly or indirectly, by the people; and that they hold their appointments by either of the tenures just specified; otherwise every government in the United States, as well as every other popular government that has been or can be well organized or well executed, would be degraded from the republican character. . . .

On comparing the Constitution planned by the Convention, with the standard here fixed, we perceive at once that it is in the most rigid sense conformable to it. The House of Representatives, like that of one branch at least of all the State Legislatures, is elected immediately by the great body of the people. The Senate, like the present Congress, and the Senate of Maryland, derives its appointment indirectly from the people. The President is indirectly derived from the choice of the people, according to the example in most of the States. Even the judges, with all other officers of the Union, will, as in the several States, be the choice, though a remote choice, of the people themselves. The duration of the appointments is equally conformable to the republican standard, and to the model of the State Constitutions. The House of Representatives is periodically elective as in all the States: and for the period of two years as in the State of South-Carolina. The Senate is elective for the period of six years; which is but one year more than the period of the Senate of Maryland; and but two more than that of the Senates of New-York and Virginia. The President is to continue in office for the period of four years; as in New-York and Delaware, the chief magistrate is elected for three years, and in South-Carolina for two years. In the other States the election is annual. In several of the States however, no constitutional provision is made for the impeachment of the Chief Magistrate. And in Delaware and Virginia, he is not impeachable till out of office. The President of the United States is impeachable at any time during his continuance in office. The tenure by which the Judges are to hold their places, is, as it unquestionably ought to be, that of good behaviour. The tenure of the ministerial offices generally will be a subject of legal regulation, conformably to the reason of the case, and the example of the State Constitutions.

Could any further proof be required of the republican complexion of this system, the most decisive one might be found in its absolute prohibition of titles of nobility, both under the Federal and the State Governments; and in its express guarantee of the republican form to each of the latter.

But it was not sufficient, say the adversaries of the proposed Constitution, for the Convention to adhere to the republican form. They ought, with equal care, to have preserved the *federal* form, which regards the union as a *confederacy* of sovereign States; instead of which, they have framed a *national government,* which regards the union as a *consolidation* of the States. And it is asked by what authority this bold and radical innovation was undertaken. The handle which has been made of this objection requires, that it should be examined with some precision.

Without enquiring into the accuracy of the distinction on which the objection is founded, it will be necessary to a just estimate of its force, first to ascertain the real character of the government in question; secondly, to enquire how far the Convention were authorised to propose such a government; and thirdly, how far the duty they owed to their country, could supply any defect of regular authority.

First. In order to ascertain the real character of the government it may be considered in relation to the foundation on which it is to be established; to the sources from which its ordinary powers are to be drawn; to the operation of those powers; to the extent of them; and to the authority by which future changes in the government are to be introduced.

On examining the first relation, it appears on one hand that the Constitution is to be founded on the assent and ratification of the people of America, given by deputies elected for the special purpose; but on the other, that this assent and ratification is to be given by the people, not as individuals composing one entire nation; but as composing the distinct and independent States to which they respectively belong. It is to be the assent and ratification of the several States, derived from the supreme authority in each State, the authority of the people themselves. The act therefore establishing the Constitution, will not be a *national* but a *federal* act.

That it will be a federal and not a national act, as these terms are understood by the objectors, the act of the people as forming so many independent States, not as forming one aggregate nation, is obvious from this single consideration that it is to result neither from the decision of a *majority* of the people of the Union, nor from that of a *majority* of the States. It must result from the *unanimous* assent of the several States that are parties to it, differing no other wise from their ordinary assent than in its being expressed, not by the legislative authority, but by that of the people themselves. Were the people regarded in this transaction as forming one nation, the will of the majority of the whole people of the United States, would bind the minority; in the same manner as the majority in each State must bind the minority; and the will of the majority must be determined either by a comparison of the individual votes; or by considering the will of a majority of the States, as evidence of the will of a majority of the people of the United States. Neither of these rules has been adopted. Each State in ratifying the Constitution, is considered as a sovereign body independent of all others, and only to be bound by its own voluntary act. In this relation then the new Constitution will, if established, be a *federal* and not a *national* Constitution.

The next relation is to the sources from which the ordinary powers of government are to be derived. The house of representatives will derive its powers from the people of America, and the people will be represented in the same proportion, and on the same principle, as they are in the Legislature of a particular State. So far the Government is *national* not *federal*. The Senate on the other hand will derive its powers from the States, as political and co-equal societies; and these will be represented on the principle of equality in the Senate, as they now are in the existing Congress. So far the government *federal*, not *national*. The executive power will be derived from a very compound source. The immediate election of the President is to be made by the States in their political characters. The votes allotted to them, are in a compound ratio, which considers them partly as distinct and co-equal societies; partly as unequal members of the same society. The eventual election, again is to be made by that branch of the Legislature which consists of the national representatives; but in this particular act, they are to be thrown into the form of individual delegations from so many distinct and co-equal bodies politic. From this aspect of the Government, it appears to be of a mixed character presenting at least as many *federal* as *national* features.

The difference between a federal and national Government as it relates to the *operation of the Government* is supposed to consist in this, that in the former, the powers operate on the political bodies composing the confederacy, in their political capacities: In the latter, on the individual citizens, composing the nation, in their individual capacities. On trying the Constitution by this criterion, it falls under the *national*, not the *federal* character; though perhaps not so compleatly, as has been understood. In several cases and particularly in the trial of controversies to which States may be parties, they must be viewed and proceeded against in their collective and political capacities only. So far the national countenance of the Government on this side seems to be disfigured by a few federal features. But this blemish is perhaps unavoidable in any plan; and the operation of the Government on the people in their individual capacities, in its ordinary and most essential proceedings, may on the whole designate it in this relation a *national* Government.

But if the government be national with regard to the *operation* of its powers, it changes its aspect again when we contemplate it in relation to the *extent* of its powers. The idea of a national Government involves in it, not only an authority over the individual citizens; but an indefinite supremacy over all persons and things, so far as they are objects of lawful Government. Among a people consolidated into one nation, this supremacy is compleatly vested in the national Legislature. Among communities united for particular purposes, it is vested partly in the general, and partly in the municipal Legislatures. In the former case, all local authorities are subordinate to the supreme; and may be controuled, directed or abolished by it at pleasure. In the latter the local or municipal authorities form distinct and independent portions of the supremacy, no more subject within their respective spheres to the general authority, than the general authority is subject to them, within its own sphere. In this relation then the proposed Government cannot be deemed a *national* one; since its jurisdiction extends to certain enumerated objects only, and leaves to the several States a residuary and inviolable sovereignty over all other objects. It is true that in controversies relating to the boundary between the two jurisdictions, the tribunal which is ultimately to decide, is to be established under the general Government. But this does not change the principle of the case. The decision is to be impartially made, according to the rules of the Constitution; and all the usual and most effectual precautions are taken to secure this impartiality. Some such tribunal is clearly essential to prevent an appeal to the sword, and a dissolution of the compact; and that it ought to be established under the general, rather than under the local Governments; or to speak more properly, that it could be safely established under the first alone, is a position not likely to be combated.

If we try the Constitution by its last relation, to the authority by which amendments are to be made, we find it neither wholly *national*, nor wholly *federal*. Were it wholly national, the supreme and ultimate authority would reside in the *majority* of the people of the Union; and this authority would be competent at all times, like that of a majority of every national society, to alter or abolish its established Government. Were it wholly federal on the other hand, the concurrence of each State in the Union would be essential to every alteration that would be binding on all. The mode provided by the plan of the Convention is not founded on either of these principles. In requiring more than a majority, and particularly, in computing the proportion by States, not by citizens, it departs from the *national*, and advances towards the *federal* character: In rendering the concurrence of less than the whole number of States sufficient, it loses again the *federal*, and partakes of the *national* character.

The proposed Constitution therefore is in strictness neither a national nor a federal constitution; but a composition of both. In its foundation, it is federal, not national; in the sources from which the ordinary powers of the Government are drawn, it is partly federal, and partly national: in the operation of these powers, it is national, not federal: In the extent of them again, it is federal, not national: And finally, in the authoritative mode of introducing amendments, it is neither wholly federal, nor wholly national.

* * *

In Federalist No. 45 and No. 46 Madison explores the relationship between the central government and the states under the Constitution.

James Madison
The Federalist No. 45

Having shewn that no one of the powers transferred to the federal Government is unnecessary or improper, the next question to be considered is whether the whole mass of them will be dangerous to the portion of authority left in the several States. . . .

Several important considerations have been touched in the course of these papers, which discountenance the supposition that the operation of the federal Government will by degrees prove fatal to the State Governments. The more I revolve the subject the more fully I am persuaded that the balance is much more likely to be disturbed by the preponderancy of the last than of the first scale. . . .

The State Governments will have the advantage of the federal Government, whether we compare them in respect to the immediate dependence of the one or the other; to the weight of personal influence which each side will possess; to the powers respectively vested in them; to the predilection and probable support of the people; to the disposition and faculty of resisting and frustrating the measures of each other.

The State Governments may be regarded as constituent and essential parts of the federal Government; whilst the latter is nowise essential to the operation or organisation of the former. Without the intervention of the State Legislatures, the President of the United States cannot be elected at all. They must in all cases have a great share in his appointment, and will perhaps in most cases of themselves determine it. The Senate will be elected absolutely and exclusively by the State Legislatures. Even the House of Representatives, though drawn immediately from the people, will be chosen very much under the influence of that class of men, whose influence over the people obtains for themselves an election into the State Legislatures. Thus each of the principal branches of the federal Government will owe its existence more or less to the favour of the State Governments, and must consequently feel a dependence, which is much more likely to beget a disposition too obsequious, than too overbearing towards them. On the other side, the component parts of the State Governments will in no instance be indebted for their appointment to the direct agency of the federal government, and very little if at all, to the local influence of its members.

The number of individuals employed under the Constitution of the United States, will be much smaller, than the number employed under the particular States. There will consequently be less of personal influence on the side of the former, than of the latter. . . .

The powers delegated by the proposed Constitution to the Federal Government, are few and defined. Those which are to remain in the State Governments are numerous and indefinite. The former will be exercised principally on external objects, as war, peace, negociation, and foreign commerce; with which last the power of taxation will for the most part be connected. The powers reserved to the several States will extend to all the objects, which, in the ordinary course of affairs, concern the lives, liberties and properties of the people; and the internal order, improvement, and prosperity of the State.

The operations of the Federal Government will be most extensive and important in times of war and danger; those of the State Governments, in times of peace and security. As the former periods will probably bear a small proportion to the latter, the State Governments will here enjoy another advantage over the Federal Government. The more adequate indeed the federal powers may be rendered to the national defence, the less frequent will be those scenes of danger which might favour their ascendency over the governments of the particular States.

If the new Constitution be examined with accuracy and candour, it will be found that the change which it proposes, consists much less in the addition of new powers to the Union, than in the invigoration of its original powers. The regulation of commerce, it is true, is a new power; but that seems to be an addition which few oppose, and from which no apprehensions are entertained. The powers relating to war and peace, armies and fleets, treaties and finance, with the other more considerable powers, are all vested in the existing Congress by the articles of Confederation. The proposed change does not enlarge these powers; it only substitutes a more effectual mode of administering them. The change relating to taxation, may be regarded as the most important: And yet the present Congress have as compleat authority to require of the States indefinite supplies of money for the common defence and general welfare, as the future Congress will have to require them of individual citizens; and the latter will be no more bound than the States themselves have been, to pay the quotas respectively taxed on them. Had the States complied punctually with the articles of confederation, or could their compliance have been enforced by as peaceable means as may be used with success towards single persons, our past experience is very far from countenancing an opinion that the State Governments would have lost their constitutional powers, and have gradually undergone an entire consolidation. To maintain that such an event would have ensued, would be to say at once, that the existence of the State Governments is incompatible with any system whatever that accomplishes the essential purposes of the Union.

James Madison
The Federalist No. 46

Resuming the subject of the last paper, I proceed to enquire whether the Federal Government or the State Governments will have the advantage with regard to the predilection and support of the people. Notwithstanding the different modes in which they are appointed, we must consider both of them, as substantially dependent on the great body of the citizens of the United States. I assume this position here as it respects the first, reserving the proofs for another place. The Federal and State Governments are in fact but different agents and trustees of the people, instituted with different powers, and designated for different purposes. The adversaries of the Constitution seem to have lost sight of the people altogether in their reasonings on this subject; and to have viewed these different establishments, not only as mutual rivals and enemies, but as uncontrouled by any common superior in their efforts to usurp the authorities of each other. These gentlemen must here be reminded of their error. They must be told that the ultimate authority, wherever the derivative may be found, resides in the people alone; and that it will not depend merely on the comparative ambition or address of the different governments, whether either, or which of them, will be able to enlarge its sphere of jurisdiction at the expence of the other. Truth no less than decency requires, that the event in every case, should be supposed to depend on the sentiments and sanction of their common constituents.

Many considerations, besides those suggested on a former occasion, seem to place it beyond doubt, that the first and most natural attachment of the people will be to the governments of their respective States. Into the administration of these, a greater number of individuals will expect to rise. From the gift of these a greater number of offices and emoluments will flow. By the superintending care of these, all the more domestic, and personal interests of the people will be regulated and provided for. With the affairs of these, the people will be more familiarly and minutely conversant. And with the members of these, will a greater proportion of the people have the ties of personal acquaintance and friendship, and of family and party attachments; on the side of these therefore the popular bias, may well be expected most strongly to incline. . . .

The remaining points on which I proposed to compare the federal and State governments, are the disposition, and the faculty they may respectively possess, to resist and frustrate the measures of each other.

It has been already proved, that the members of the federal will be more dependent on the members of the State governments, than the latter will be on the former. It has appeared also, that the prepossessions of the people on whom both will depend, will be more on the side of the State governments, than of the Federal Government. So far as the disposition of each, towards the other, may be influenced by these causes, the State governments must clearly have the advantage. But in a distinct and very important point of view, the advantage will lie on the same side. The prepossessions which the members themselves will carry into the Federal Government, will generally be favorable to the States; whilst it will rarely happen, that the members of the State governments will carry into the public councils, a bias in favor of the general government. . . .

Were it admitted however that the Federal Government may feel an equal disposition with the State governments to extend its power beyond the due limits, the latter would still have the advantage in the means of defeating such encroachments. If an act of a particular State, though unfriendly to the national government, be generally popular in that State, and should not too grossly violate the oaths of the State officers, it is executed immediately and of course, by means on the spot, and depending on the State alone. The opposition of the Federal Government, or the interposition of Federal officers, would but inflame the zeal of all parties on the side of the State, and the evil could not be prevented or repaired, if at all, without the employment of means which must always be resorted to with reluctance and difficulty. On the other hand, should an unwarrantable measure of the Federal Government be unpopular in particular States, which would seldom fail to be the case, or even a warrantable measure be so, which may sometimes be the case, the means of opposition to it are powerful and at hand. The disquietude of the people, their repugnance and perhaps refusal to co-operate with the officers of the Union, the frowns of the executive magistracy of the State, the embarrassments created by legislative devices, which would often be added on such occasions, would oppose in any State difficulties not to be despised; would form in a large State very serious impediments, and where the sentiments of several adjoining States happened to be in unison, would present obstructions which the Federal Government would hardly be willing to encounter.

But ambitious encroachments of the Federal Government, on the authority of the State governments, would not excite the opposition of a single State or of a few States only. They would be signals of general alarm. Every Government would espouse the common cause. A correspondence would be opened. Plans of resistance would be concerted. One spirit would animate and conduct the whole. The same combination in short would result from an apprehension of the federal, as was produced by the dread of a foreign yoke; and unless the projected innovations should be voluntarily renounced, the same appeal to a trial of force would be made in the one case, as was made in the other. But what degree of madness could ever drive the Federal Government to such an extremity? In the contest with Great Britain, one part of the empire was employed against the other. The more numerous part invaded the rights of the less numerous part. The attempt was unjust and unwise; but it was not in speculation absolutely chimerical. But what would be the contest in the case we are supposing? Who would be the parties? A few representatives of the people, would be opposed to the people themselves; or rather one set of representatives would be contending against thirteen sets of representatives, with the whole body of their common constituents on the side of the latter. . . .

The argument under the present head may be put into a very concise form, which appears altogether conclusive. Either the mode in which the Federal Government is to be constructed will render it sufficiently dependant on the people, or it will not. On the first supposition, it will be restrained by that dependence from forming schemes obnoxious to their constituents. On the other supposition it will not possess the confidence of the people, and its schemes of usurpation will be easily defeated by the State Governments; who will be supported by the people.

On summing up the considerations stated in this and the last paper, they seem to amount to the most convincing evidence, that the powers proposed to be lodged in the Federal Government, are as little formidable to those reserved to the individual States, as they are indispensibly necessary to accomplish the purposes of the Union; and that all those alarms which have been sounded, of a meditated or consequential annihilation of the State Governments, must, on the most favorable interpretation, be ascribed to the chimerical fears of the authors of them.

* * *

In Federalist No. 51 Madison examines checks and balances and separation of powers as means of limiting power.

James Madison
The Federalist No. 51

To what expedient then shall we finally resort for maintaining in practice the necessary partition of power among the several departments, as laid down in the constitution? The only answer that can be given is, that as all these exterior provisions are found to be inadequate, the defect must be supplied, by so contriving the interior structure of the government, as that its several constituent parts may, by their mutual relations, be the means of keeping each other in their proper places. Without presuming to undertake a full development of this important idea, I will hazard a few general observations, which may perhaps place it in a clearer light, and enable us to form a more correct judgment of the principles and structure of the government planned by the convention.

In order to lay a due foundation for that separate and distinct exercise of the different powers of government, which to a certain extent, is admitted on all hands to be essential to the preservation of liberty, it is evident that each department should have a will of its own; and consequently should be so constituted, that the members of each should have as little agency as possible in the appointment of the members of the others. Were this principle rigorously adhered to, it would require that all the appointments for the supreme executive, legislative, and judiciary magistracies, should be drawn from the same fountain of authority, the people, through channels, having no communication whatever with one another. Perhaps such a plan of constructing the several departments would be less difficult in practice than it may in contemplation appear. Some difficulties however, and some additional expence, would attend the execution of it. Some deviations therefore from the principle must be admitted. In the constitution of the judiciary department in particular, it might be inexpedient to insist rigorously on the principle; first, because peculiar qualifications being essential in the members, the primary consideration ought to be to select that mode of choice, which best secures these qualifications; secondly, because the permanent tenure by which the appointments are held in that department, must soon destroy all sense of dependence on the authority conferring them.

It is equally evident that the members of each department should be as little dependent as possible on those of the others, for the emoluments annexed to their offices. Were the executive magistrate, or the judges, not independent of the legislature in this particular, their independence in every other would be merely nominal.

But the great security against a gradual concentration of the several powers in the same department, consists in giving to those who administer each department, the necessary constitutional means, and personal motives, to resist encroachments of the others. The provision for defence must in this, as in all other cases, be made commensurate to the danger of attack. Ambition must be made to counteract ambition. The interest of the man must be connected with the constitutional rights of the place. It may be a reflection on human nature, that such devices should be necessary to controul the abuses of government. But what is government itself but the greatest of all reflections on human nature? If men were angels, no government would be necessary. If angels were to govern men, neither external nor internal controuls on government would be necessary. In framing a government which is to be administered by men over men, the great difficulty lies in this: You must first enable the government to controul the governed; and in the next place, oblige it to controul itself. A dependence on the people is no doubt the primary controul on the government; but experience has taught mankind the necessity of auxiliary precautions.

This policy of supplying by opposite and rival interests, the defect of better motives, might be traced through the whole system of human affairs, private as well as public. We see it particularly displayed in all the subordinate distributions of power; where the constant aim is to divide and arrange the several offices in such a manner as that each may be a check on the other; that the private interest of every individual, may be a centinel over the public rights. These inventions of prudence cannot be less requisite in the distribution of the supreme powers of the state.

But it is not possible to give to each department an equal power of self defence. In republican government the legislative authority, necessarily, predominates. The remedy for this inconveniency is, to divide the legislature into different branches; and to render them by different modes of election, and different principles of action, as little connected with each other, as the nature of their common functions, and their common dependence on the society, will admit. It may even be necessary to guard against dangerous encroachments by still further precautions. As the weight of the legislative authority requires that it should be thus divided, the weakness of the executive may require, on the other hand, that it should be fortified. An absolute negative, on the legislature, appears at first view to be the natural defence with which the executive magistrate should be armed. But perhaps it would be neither altogether safe, nor alone sufficient. On ordinary occasions, it might not be exerted with the requisite firmness; and on extraordinary occasions, it might be perfidiously abused. May not this defect of an absolute negative be supplied, by some qualified connection between this weaker department, and the weaker branch of the stronger department, by which the latter may be led to support the constitutional rights of the former, without being too much detached from the rights of its own department?

If the principles on which these observations are founded be just, as I persuade myself they are, and they be applied as a criterion, to the several state constitutions, and to the federal constitution, it will be found, that if the latter does not perfectly correspond with them, the former are infinitely less able to bear such a test.

There are moreover two considerations particularly applicable to the federal system of America, which place that system in a very interesting point of view.

First. In a single republic, all the power surrendered by the people, is submitted to the administration of a single government; and usurpations are guarded against by a division of the government into distinct and separate departments. In the compound republic of America, the power surrendered by the people, is first divided between two distinct governments, and then the portion allotted to each, subdivided among distinct and separate departments. Hence a double security arises to the rights of the people. The different governments will controul each other; at the same time that each will be controuled by itself.

Second. It is of great importance in a republic, not only to guard the society against the oppression of its rulers; but to guard one part of the society against the injustice of the other part. Different interests necessarily exist in different classes of citizens. If a majority be united by a common interest, the rights of the minority will be insecure. There are but two methods of providing against this evil: The one by creating a will in the community independent of the majority, that is, of the society itself; the other by comprehending in the society so many separate descriptions of citizens, as will render an unjust combination of a majority of the whole, very improbable, if not impracticable. The first method prevails in all governments possessing an hereditary or self appointed authority. This at best is but a precarious security; because a power independent of the society may as well espouse the unjust views of the major, as the rightful interests, of the minor party, and may possibly be turned against both parties. The second method will be exemplified in the federal republic of the United States. Whilst all authority in it will be derived from and dependent on the society, the society itself will be broken into so many parts, interests and classes of citizens, that the rights of individuals or of the minority, will be in little danger from interested combinations of the majority. In a free government, the security for civil rights must be the same as for religious rights. It consists in the one case in the multiplicity of interests, and in the other, in the multiplicity of sects. The degree of security in both cases will depend on the number of interests and sects; and this may be presumed to depend on the extent of country and number of people comprehended under the same government. This view of the subject must particularly recommend a proper federal system to all the sincere and considerate friends of republican government: Since it shews that in exact proportions as the territory of the union may be formed into more circumscribed confederacies or states, oppressive combinations of a majority will be facilitated, the best security under the republican form, for the rights of every class of citizens, will be diminished; and consequently, the stability and independence of some member of the government, the only other security, must be proportionally increased. Justice is the end of government. It is the end of civil society. It ever has been, and ever will be pursued, until it be obtained, or until liberty be lost in the pursuit. In a society under the forms of which the stronger faction can readily unite and oppress the weaker, anarchy may as truly be said to reign, as in a state of nature where the weaker individual is not secured against the violence of the stronger: And as in the latter state even the stronger individuals are prompted by the uncertainty of their condition, to submit to a government which may protect the weak as well as themselves. So in the former state, will the more powerful factions or parties be gradually induced by a like motive, to wish for a government which will protect all parties, the weaker as well as the more powerful. It can be little doubted, that if the state of Rhode Island was separated from the confederacy, and left to itself, the insecurity of rights under the popular form of government within such narrow limits, would be displayed by such reiterated oppressions of factious majorities, that some power altogether independent of the people would soon be called for by the voice of the very factions whose misrule had proved the necessity of it. In the extended republic of the United States, and among the great variety of interests, parties and sects which it embraces, a coalition of a majority of the whole society could seldom take place on any other principles than those of justice and the general good; and there being thus less danger to a minor from the will of the major party, there must be less pretext also, to provide for the security of the former, by introducing into the government a will not dependent on the latter; or in other words, a will independent of the society itself. It is no less certain than it is important, notwithstanding the contrary opinions which have been entertained, that the larger the society, provided it lie within a practicable sphere, the more duly capable it will be of self government. And happily for the *republican cause,* the practicable sphere may be carried to a very great extent, by a judicious modification and mixture of the *federal principle.*

* * *

In Federalist No. 62 Madison discusses the Senate.

James Madison
The Federalist No. 62

IV. The number of senators and the duration of their appointment come next to be considered. In order to form an accurate judgment on both these points, it will be proper to enquire into the purposes which are to be answered by a senate; and in order to ascertain these it will be necessary to review the inconveniencies which a republic must suffer from the want of such an institution.

First. It is a misfortune incident to republican government, though in a less degree than to other governments, that those who administer it, may forget their obligations to their constituents, and prove unfaithful to their important trust. In this point of view, a senate, as a second branch of the legislative assembly, distinct from, and dividing the power with, a first, must be in all cases a salutary check on the government. It doubles the security to the people, by requiring the concurrence of two distinct bodies in schemes of usurpation or perfidy, where the ambition or corruption of one, would otherwise be sufficient. This is a precaution founded on such clear principles, and now so well understood in the United States, that it would be more than superfluous to enlarge on it, I will barely remark that as the improbability of sinister combinations will be in proportion to the dissimilarity in the genius of the two bodies; it must be politic to distinguish them from each other by every circumstance which will consist with a due harmony in all proper measures, and with the genuine principles of republican government.

Secondly. The necessity of a senate is not less indicated by the propensity of all single and numerous assemblies, to yield to the impulse of sudden and violent passions, and to be seduced by factious leaders, into intemperate and pernicious resolutions. Examples on this subject might be cited without number; and from proceedings within the United States, as well as from the history of other nations. But a position that will not be contradicted need not be proved. All that need be remarked is that a body which is to correct this infirmity ought itself be free from it, and consequently ought to be less numerous. It ought moreover to possess great firmness, and consequently ought to hold its authority by a tenure of considerable duration.

Thirdly. Another defect to be supplied by a senate lies in a want of due acquaintance with the objects and principles of legislation. It is not possible that an assembly of men called for the most part from pursuits of a private nature, continued in appointment for a short time, and led by no permanent motive to devote the intervals of public occupation to a study of the laws, the affairs and the comprehensive interests of their country, should, if left wholly to themselves, escape a variety of important errors in the exercise of their legislative trust. It may be affirmed, on the best grounds, that no small share of the present embarrassments of America is to be charged on the blunders of our governments; and that these have proceeded from the heads rather than the hearts of most of the authors of them. What indeed are all the repealing, explaining and amending laws, which fill and disgrace our voluminous codes, but so many monuments of deficient wisdom; so many impeachments exhibited by each succeeding, against each preceding session; so many admonitions to the people of the value of those aids which may be expected from a well constituted senate?

A good government implies two things; first, fidelity to the object of government, which is the happiness of the people; secondly, a knowledge of the means by which that object can be best attained. Some governments are deficient in both these qualities: Most governments are deficient in the first. I scruple not to assert that in the American governments, too little attention has been paid to the last. The federal constitution avoids this error; and what merits particular notice, it provides for the last in a mode which increases the security for the first.

Fourthly. The mutability in the public councils, arising from a rapid succession of new members, however qualified they may be, points out in the strongest manner, the necessity of some stable institution in the government. Every new election in the states, is found to change one half of the representatives. From this change of men must proceed a change of opinions; and from a change of opinions, a change of measures. But a continual change even of good measures is inconsistent with every rule of prudence, and every prospect of success. The remark is verified in private life, and becomes more just as well as more important, in national transactions.

* * *

In Federalist No. 78 Hamilton discusses the judiciary, which was one of the major concerns of opponents of the Constitution.

Alexander Hamilton
The Federalist No. 78

We proceed now to an examination of the judiciary department of the proposed government. . . .

The manner of constituting it seems to embrace these several objects—1st. The mode of appointing the judges. 2d. The tenure by which they are to hold their places. 3d. The partition of the judiciary authority between different courts, and their relations to each other.

First. As to the mode of appointing the judges: This is the same with that of appointing the officers of the union in general. . . .

Second. As to the tenure by which the judges are to hold their places: This chiefly concerns their duration in office; the provisions for their support; and the precautions for their responsibility.

According to the plan of the convention, all the judges who may be appointed by the United States are to hold their offices *during good behaviour,* which is conformable to the most approved of the state constitutions; and among the rest, to that of this state [New York]. Its propriety having been drawn into question by the adversaries of that plan, is no light symptom of the rage for objection which disorders their imaginations and judgments. The standard of good behaviour for the continuance in office of the judicial magistracy is certainly one of the most valuable of the modern improvements in the practice of government. In a monarchy it is an excellent barrier to the despotism of the prince: In a republic it is a no less excellent barrier to the encroachments and oppressions of the representative body. And it is the best expedient which can be devised in any government, to secure a steady, upright and impartial administration of the laws.

Whoever attentively considers the different departments of power must perceive, that in a government in which they are separated from each other, the judiciary, from the nature of its functions, will always be the least dangerous to the political rights of the constitution; because it will be least in a capacity to annoy or injure them. The executive not only dispenses the honors, but holds the sword of the community. The legislature not only commands the purse, but prescribes the rules by which the duties and rights of every citizen are to be regulated. The judiciary on the contrary has no influence over either the sword or the purse, no direction either of the strength or of the wealth of the society, and can take no active resolution whatever. It may truly be said to have neither Force nor Will, but merely judgment; and must ultimately depend upon the aid of the executive arm even for the efficacy of its judgments.

This simple view of the matter suggests several important consequences. It proves incontestably that the judiciary is beyond comparison the weakest of the three departments of power; that it can never attack with success either of the other two; and that all possible care is requisite to enable it to defend itself against their attacks. It equally proves, that though individual oppression may now and then proceed from the courts of justice, the general liberty of the people can never be endangered from that quarter: I mean, so long as the judiciary remains truly distinct from both the legislative and executive. For I agree that "there is no liberty, if the power of judging be not separated from the legislative and executive powers." And it proves, in the last place, that as liberty can have nothing to fear from the judiciary alone, but would have every thing to fear from its union with either of the other departments, that as all the effects of such an union must ensue from a dependence of the former on the latter, notwithstanding a nominal and apparent separation; that as from the natural feebleness of the judiciary, it is in continual jeopardy of being overpowered, awed or influenced by its coordinate branches; and that as nothing can contribute so much to its firmness and independence, as permanency in office, this quality may therefore be justly regarded as an indispensable ingredient in its constitution; and in a great measure as the citadel of the public justice and the public security. . . .

Some perplexity respecting the right of the courts to pronounce legislative acts void, because contrary to the constitution, has arisen from an imagination that the doctrine would imply a superiority of the judiciary to the legislative power. It is urged that the authority which can declare the acts of another void, must necessarily be superior to the one whose acts may be declared void. As this doctrine is of great importance in all the American constitutions, a brief discussion of the grounds on which it rests cannot be unacceptable.

There is no position which depends on clearer principles, than that every act of a delegated authority, contrary to the tenor of the commission under which it is exercised, is void. No legislative act therefore contrary to the constitution can be valid. To deny this would be to affirm that the deputy is greater than his principal; that the servant is above his master; that the representatives of the people are superior to the people themselves; that men acting by virtue of powers may do not only what their powers do not authorise, but what they forbid.

If it be said that the legislative body are themselves the constitutional judges of their own powers, and that the construction they put upon them is conclusive upon the other departments, it may be answered, that this cannot be the natural presumption, where it is not to be collected from any particular provisions in the constitution. It is not otherwise to be supposed that the constitution could intend to enable the representatives of the people to substitute their *will* to that of their constituents. It is far more rational to suppose that the courts were designed to be an intermediate body between the people and the legislature, in order, among other things, to keep the latter within the limits assigned to their authority. The interpretation of the laws is the proper and peculiar province of the courts. A constitution is in fact, and must be, regarded by the judges as a fundamental law. It therefore belongs to them to ascertain its meaning as well as the meaning of any particular act proceeding from the legislative body. If there should happen to be an irreconcileable variance between the two, that which has the superior obligation and validity ought of course to be preferred; or in other words, the constitution ought to be preferred to the statue, the intention of the people to the intention of their agents.

Nor does this conclusion by any means suppose a superiority of the judicial to the legislative power. It only supposes that the power of the people is superior to both; and that where the will of the legislature declared in its statutes, stands in opposition to that of the people declared in the constitution, the judges ought to be governed by the latter, rather than the former. They ought to regulate their decisions by the fundamental laws, rather than by those which are not fundamental. . . .

That inflexible and uniform adherence to the rights of the constitution and of individuals, which we perceive to be indispensable in the courts of justice, can certainly not be expected from judges who hold their offices by a temporary commission. Periodical appointments, however regulated, or by whomsoever made, would in some way or other be fatal to their necessary independence. If the power of making them was committed either to the executive or legislature, there would be danger of an improper complaisance to the branch which possessed it; if to both, there would be an unwillingness to hazard the displeasure of either; if to the people, or to persons chosen by them for the special purpose, there would be too great a disposition to consult popularity, to justify a reliance that nothing would be consulted but the constitution and the laws.

There is yet a further and a weighty reason for the permanency of the judicial offices; which is deducible from the nature of the qualifications they require. It has been frequently remarked with great propriety, that a voluminous code of laws is one of the inconveniences necessarily connected with the advantages of a free government. To avoid an arbitrary discretion in the courts, it is indispensable that they should be bound down by strict rules and precedents, which serve to define and point out their duty in every particular case that comes before them; and it will readily be conceived from the variety of controversies which grow out of the folly and wickedness of mankind, that the records of those precedents must unavoidably swell to a very considerable bulk, and must demand long and laborious study to acquire a competent knowledge of them. Hence it is that there can be but few men in the society, who will have sufficient skill in the laws to qualify them for the stations of judges. And making the proper deductions for the ordinary depravity of human nature, the number must be still smaller of those who unite the requisite integrity with the requisite knowledge. These considerations apprise us, that the government can have no great option between fit characters; and that a temporary duration in office, which would naturally discourage such characters from quitting a lucrative line of practice to accept a seat on the bench, would have a tendency to throw the administration of justice into hands less able, and less well qualified to conduct it with utility and dignity. In the present circumstances of this country, and in those in which it is likely to be for a long time to come, the disadvantages on this score would be greater than they may at first sight appear; but it must be confessed that they are far inferior to those which present themselves under the other aspects of the subject.

Upon the whole there can be no room to doubt that the convention acted wisely in copying from the models of those constitutions which have established *good behaviour* as the tenure of their judicial offices in point of duration; and that so far from being blameable on this account, their plan would have been inexcuseably defective if it had wanted this important feature of good government. The experience of Great Britain affords an illustrious comment on the excellence of the institution.

* * *

In Federalist No. 84 Hamilton argues that a bill of rights is not merely not needed but dangerous.

Alexander Hamilton
The Federalist No. 84

In the course of the foregoing review of the constitution I have taken notice of, and endeavoured to answer, most of the objections which have appeared against it. There however remain a few which either did not fall naturally under any particular head, or were forgotten in their proper places. These shall now be discussed; but as the subject has been drawn into great length, I shall so far consult brevity as to comprise all my observations on these miscellaneous points in a single paper.

The most considerable of these remaining objections is, that the plan of the convention contains no bill of rights. . . .

A minute detail of particular rights is certainly far less applicable to a constitution like that under consideration, which is merely intended to regulate the general political interests of the nation, than to a constitution which has the regulation of every species of personal and private concerns. If therefore the loud clamours against the plan of the convention on this score, are well founded, no epithets of reprobation will be too strong for the constitution of this state [New York]. But the truth is, that both of them contain all, which in relation to their objects, is reasonably to be desired.

I go further, and affirm that bills of rights, in the sense and in the extent in which they are contended for, are not only unnecessary in the proposed constitution, but would even be dangerous. They would contain various exceptions to powers which are not granted; and on this very account, would afford a colourable pretext to claim more than were granted. For why declare that things shall not be done which there is no power to do? Why for instance, should it be said, that the liberty of the press shall not be restrained, when no power is given by which restrictions may be imposed? I will not contend that such a provision would confer a regulating power; but it is evident that it would furnish, to men disposed to usurp, a plausible pretence for claiming that power. They might urge with a semblance of reason, that the constitution ought not to be charged with the absurdity of providing against the abuse of an authority, which was not given, and that the provision against restraining the liberty of the press afforded a clear implication, that a power to prescribe proper regulations concerning it, was intended to be vested in the national government. This may serve as a specimen of the numerous handles which would be given to the doctrine of constructive powers, by the indulgence of an injudicious zeal for bills of rights.

On the subject of the liberty of the press, as much has been said, I cannot forbear adding a remark to two: In the first place, I observe that there is not a syllable concerning it in the constitution of this state, and in the next, I contend that whatever has been said about it in that of any other state, amounts to nothing. What signifies a declaration that "the liberty of the press shall be inviolably preserved?" What is the liberty of the press? Who can give it any definition which would not leave the utmost latitude for evasion? I hold it to be impracticable; and from this, I infer, that its security, whatever fine declarations may be inserted in any constitution respecting it, must altogether depend on public opinion, and on the general spirit of the people and of the government. And here, after all, as intimated upon another occasion, must we seek for the only solid basis of all our rights.

There remains but one other view of this matter to conclude the point. The truth is, after all the declamation we have heard, that the constitution is itself in every rational sense, and to every useful purpose, a bill of rights. The several bills of rights, in Great-Britain, form its constitution, and conversely the constitution of each state is its bill of rights. And the proposed constitution, if adopted, will be the bill of rights of the union. Is it one object of a bill of rights to declare and specify the political privileges of the citizens in the structure and administration of the government? This is done in the most ample and precise manner in the plan of the convention, comprehending various precautions for the public security, which are not to be found in any of the state constitutions. Is another object of a bill of rights to define certain immunities and modes of proceeding, which are relative to personal and private concerns? This we have seen has also been attended to, in a variety of cases, in the same plan. Adverting therefore to the substantial meaning of a bill of rights, it is absurd to allege that it is not to be found in the work of the convention. It may be said that it does not go far enough, though it will not be easy to make this appear; but it can with no propriety be contended that there is no such thing. It certainly must be immaterial what mode is observed as to the order of declaring the rights of the citizens, if they are to be found in any part of the instrument which establishes the government. And hence it must be apparent that much of what has been said on this subject rests merely on verbal and nominal distinctions, which are entirely foreign from the substance of the thing.

Source: The Federalist, on the new Constitution. By Publius (pseud.). New York: J. & A. McLean, 1788.

Alexander Hamilton (1757–1804) was a lawyer and was secretary of the treasury 1789–95. John Jay (1745–1829) was the chief justice of the Supreme Court 1789–95. James Madison (1751–1836) was the fourth president of the United States.

Other Supporters of Ratification

There were, of course, others who supported the ratification of the Constitution. James Wilson (1742–98), who was a delegate to the Constitutional Convention, was one of the most important. In this extract he presents the Constitution to the Pennsylvania ratification convention. His primary concern here is with the issue of national versus state power, which he presents in the general context of the need for government.

James Wilson
Presentation to the Pennsylvania Legislature

The system proposed, by the late Convention, for the government of the United States, is now before you. Of that Convention I had the honor to be a member. As I am the only member of that body who has the honor to be also a member of this, it may be expected that I should prepare the way for the deliberations of this assembly, by unfolding the difficulties which the late Convention were obliged to encounter; by pointing out the end which they proposed to accomplish; and by tracing the general principles which they have adopted for the accomplishment of that end.

To form a good system of government for a single city or state, however limited as to territory, or inconsiderable as to numbers, has been thought to require the strongest efforts of human genius. With what conscious diffidence, then, must the members of the Convention have revolved in their minds the immense undertaking which was before them. Their views could not be confined to a small or single community, but were expanded to a great number of states; several of which contain an extent of territory, and resources of population, equal to those of some of the most respectable kingdoms on the other side of the Atlantic. Nor were even these the only objects to be comprehended within their deliberations. Numerous states yet unformed, myriads of the human race, who will inhabit regions hitherto uncultivated, were to be affected by the result of their proceedings. It was necessary, therefore, to form their calculations on a scale commensurate to a large portion of the globe. . . .

To be left without guide or precedent was not the only difficulty in which the Convention were involved, by proposing to their constituents a plan of a confederate republic. They found themselves embarrassed with another, of peculiar delicacy and importance. I mean that of drawing a proper line between the national government and the governments of the several states. It was easy to discover a proper and satisfactory principle on the subject. Whatever object of government is confined, in its operation and effects, within the bounds of a particular state, should be considered as belonging to the government of that state; whatever object of government extends, in its operation or effects, beyond the bounds of a particular state, should be considered as belonging to the government of the United States. But though this principle be sound and satisfactory, its application to particular cases would be accompanied with much difficulty, because, in its application, room must be allowed for great discretionary latitude of construction of the principle. In order to lessen or remove the difficulty arising from discretionary construction on this subject, an enumeration of particular instances, in which the application of the principle ought to take place, has been attempted with much industry and care. It is only in mathematical science that a line can be described with mathematical precision. But I flatter myself that, upon the strictest investigation, the enumeration will be found to be safe and unexceptionable, and accurate, too, in as great a degree as accuracy can be expected in a subject of this nature. . . .

After all, it will be necessary that, on a subject so peculiarly delicate as this, much prudence, much candor, much moderation, and much liberality, should be exercised and displayed both by the federal government and by the governments of the several states. It is to be hoped that those virtues in government will be exercised and displayed, when we consider that the powers of the federal government and those of the state governments are drawn from sources equally pure. If a difference can be discovered between them, it is in favor of the federal government, because that government is founded on a representation of the whole Union; whereas the government of any particular state is founded only on the representation of a part, inconsiderable when compared with the whole. Is it not more reasonable to suppose that the counsels of the whole will embrace the interest of every part, than that the counsels of any part will embrace the interests of the whole? . . .

Having enumerated some of the difficulties which the Convention were obliged to encounter in the course of their proceedings, I shall next point out the end which they proposed to accomplish. Our wants, our talents, our affections, our passions, all tell us that we were made for a state of society. But a state of society could not be supported long or happily without some civil restraint. It is true that, in a state of nature, any one individual may act uncontrolled by others; but it is equally true that, in such a state, every other individual may act uncontrolled by him. Amidst this universal independence, the dissensions and animosities between interfering members of the society would be numerous and ungovernable. The consequence would be, that each member, in such a natural state, would enjoy less liberty, and suffer more interruption, than he would in a regulated society. Hence the universal introduction of governments of some kind or other into the social state. The liberty of every member is increased by this introduction; for each gains more by the limitation of the freedom of every other member, than he loses by the limitation of his own. The result is, that civil government is necessary to the perfection and happiness of man. In forming this government, and carrying it into execution, it is *essential* that the *interest* and *authority* of the whole community should be binding in every part of it.

The foregoing principles and conclusions are generally admitted to be just and sound with regard to the nature and formation of single governments, and the duty of submission to them. In some cases, they will apply, with much propriety and force, to states already formed. The advantages and necessity of civil government among individuals in society, are not greater or stronger than, in some situations and circumstances, are the advantages and necessity of a federal government among states. A natural and very important question now presents itself— Is such the situation, are such the circumstances, of the United States? A proper answer to this question will unfold some very interesting truths.

The United States may adopt any one of four different systems. They may become consolidated into one government, in which the separate existence of the states shall be entirely absolved. They may reject any plan of union or association, and act as separate and unconnected states. They may form two or more confederacies. They may unite in one federal republic. Which of these systems ought to have been formed by the Convention? To support, with vigor, a single government over the whole extend of the United States, would demand a system of the most unqualified and the most unremitted despotism. Such a number of separate states, contiguous in situation, unconnected and disunited in government, would be, at one time, the prey of foreign force, foreign influence, and foreign intrigue; at another, the victims of mutual rage, rancor, and revenge. Neither of these systems found advocates in the late Convention. I presume they will not find advocates in this. Would it be proper to divide the United States into two or more confederacies? It will not be unadvisable to take a more minute survey of this subject. Some aspects under which it may be viewed are far from being, at first sight, uninviting. Two or more confederacies would be each more compact and more manageable than a single one extending over the same territory. By dividing the United States into two or more confederacies, the great collision of interests apparently or really different and contrary in the *whole extent* of their dominion, would be broken, and, in a great measure, disappear, in the several parts. But these advantages, which are discovered from certain points of view, are greatly overbalanced by inconveniences that will appear on a more accurate examination. Animosities, and perhaps wars, would arise from assigning the extent, the limits, and the rights, of the different confederacies. The expenses of governing would be multiplied by the number of federal governments. The danger resulting from foreign influence and mutual dissensions, would not, perhaps, be less great and alarming in the instance of different confederacies, than in the instance of different though more numerous unassociated states.

These observations, and many others that might be made on the subject, will be sufficient to evince that a division of the United States into a number of separate confederacies would probably be an unsatisfactory and an unsuccessful experiment. The remaining system which the American states may adopt, is a union of them under one confederate republic. It will not be necessary to employ much time, or many arguments, to show that this is the most eligible system that can be proposed. By adopting this system, the vigor and decision of a wide-spreading monarchy may be joined to the freedom and beneficence of a contracted republic. The extent of territory, the diversity of climate and soil, the number, and greatness, and connection, of lakes and rivers with which the United States are intersected and almost surrounded,—all indicate an enlarged government to be fit and advantageous for them. The principles and dispositions of their citizens indicate that, in this government, liberty shall reign triumphant. Such, indeed, have been the general opinions and wishes entertained since the era of independence. If those opinions and wishes are as well founded as they have been general, the late Convention were justified in proposing to their constituents one confederate republic, as the best system of a national government for the United States.

In forming this system, it was proper to give minute attention to the interest of all the parts; but there was a duty of still higher import—to feel and to show a predominating regard to the superior interests of the whole. If this great principle had not prevailed, the plan before us would never have made its appearance. The same principle that was so necessary in forming it, is equally necessary in our deliberations, whether we should reject or ratify it.

Source: The Debates in the Several State Conventions on the Adoption of the Federal Constitution as Recommended by the General Convention at Philadelphia in 1787 Together With the Journal of the Federal Convention Luther Martin's Letter, Yates's Minutes, Congressional Opinions, Virginia and Kentucky Resolutions of '98–99, and Other Illustrations of the Constitution. 2nd edition. 5 volumes. Edited by Jonathan Elliot. Reprint, New York: Burt Franklin, [1974].

James Wilson (1742–98) was a lawyer and a politician.

Opponents of Ratification

The opponents of ratification have generally been ignored. Their arguments were mostly along the lines of those who supported the Articles of Confederation, but they were also deeply divided among themselves. Some argued for radically reduced government, while others felt that the national government under the proposed constitution was not strong enough. The former was the most common position. In the essay reprinted here, Melancton Smith (1744–98) summarizes the arguments against the Constitution.

Melancton Smith
An Address to the People of the State of New York

It would be easy to shew, that in the leading and most important objections that have been made to the plan, there has been and is an entire concurrence of opinion among writers, and in public bodies throughout the United States.

I have not time to fully illustrate this by a minute narration of particulars; but to prove that this is the case, I shall adduce a number of important instances.

It has been objected to that the new system, that it is calculated to, and will effect such a consolidation of the States, as to supplant and overturn the state governments. In this the minority of Pennsylvania, the opposition in Massachusetts, and all the writers of any ability or note in Philadelphia, New York, and Boston concur. It may be added, that this appears to have been the opinion of the Massachusetts convention, and gave rise to that article in the amendments proposed, which confines the general government to the exercise only of powers expressly given.

It has been said that the representation in the general legislature is too small to secure liberty, or to answer the intention of representation. In this there is an union of sentiments in the opposers.

The constitution has been opposed, because it gives to the legislature an unlimited power of taxation both with respect to direct and indirect taxes, a right to lay and collect taxes, duties, imposts and excises of every kind and description, and to any amount. In this there has been as general a concurrence of opinion as in the former.

The opposers to the constitution have said that it is dangerous, because the judicial power may extend to many cases which ought to be reserved to the decision of the State courts, and because the right of trial by jury is not secured in the judicial courts of the general government, in civil cases. All the opposers are agreed in this objection.

The power of the general legislature to alter and regulate the time, place and manner of holding elections, has been stated as an argument against the adoption of the system. It has been argued that this power will place in the hands of the general government, the authority, whenever they shall be disposed, and a favorable opportunity offers, to deprive the body of the people in effect, of all share in the government. The opposers to the constitution universally agree in this objection, and of such force is it, that most of its ardent advocates admit its validity, and those who have made attempts to vindicate it, have been reduced to the necessity of using the most trifling arguments to justify it.

The mixture of legislative, judicial, and executive powers in the senate; the little degree of responsibility under which the great officers of government will be held; and the liberty granted by the system to establish and maintain a standing army without any limitation or restriction, are also objected to the constitution; and in these there is a great degree of unanimity of sentiment in the opposers.

Source: An Address to the People of the State of New-York: Showing the necessity of making Amendments to the Constitution, proposed for the United States, previous to its Adoption. By a Plebeian [Melancton Smith]. New York, 1788.

Melancton Smith (1744–98) was an American businessman and a member of the Continental Congress 1785–88.

Minorities

AFRICAN AMERICANS

The debates regarding minorities continued. The Petition for Equal Education was an early argument for racial equality, as well as an argument that the petitioners were not getting services for the taxes they paid. This argument would have reminded its readers of the "no taxation without representation" position taken before the Revolution.

Petition for Equal Education, 1787

To the Honorable the Senate and House of Representatives of the Commonwealth of Massachusetts Bay, in General Court assembled.

The petition of a great number of blacks, freemen of this Commonwealth, humbly sheweth, that your petitioners are held in common with other freemen of this town and Commonwealth and have never been backward in paying our proportionate part of the burdens under which they have, or may labor under; and as we are willing to pay our equal part of these burdens, we are of the humble opinion that we have the right to enjoy the privileges of free men. But that we do not will appear in many instances, and we beg leave to mention one out of the many, and that is of the education of our children which now receive no benefit from the free schools in the town of Boston, which we think is a great grievance, as by woful experience we now feel the want of a common education. . . .

Source: *A Documentary History of the Negro People in the United States.* Edited by Herbert Aptheker. New York: Citadel Press, 1951.

INDIANS

The Treaty with the Six Nations of 1784 is an early example of a treaty that was made and almost immediately broken. It also establishes the principle of defining lands for the Indians, an approach that was to develop into the system of Indian reservations. The speech by Corn Tassel notes that the colonists want to force the natives to live a settled life under the rules and regulations that the colonists believe to be best. Corn Tassel argues for a form of multiculturalism.

Treaty with the Six Nations, 1784

Articles concluded at Fort Stanwix, on the twenty-second day of October, one thousand seven hundred and eighty-four, between Oliver Wolcott, Richard Butler, and Arthur Lee, Commissioners Plenipotentiary from the United States, in Congress assembled, on the one part, and the Sachems and Warriors of the Six Nations, on the other.

The United States of America give peace to the Senecas, Mohawks, Onondagas and Cayugas, and receive them into our protection upon the following conditions:

Article I.

Six hostages shall be immediately delivered to the commissioners by the said nations, to remain in possession of the United States, till all the prisoners, white and black, which were taken by the said Senecas, Mohawks, Onondagas and Cayugas, or by any of them, in the late war, from among the people of the United States, shall be delivered up.

Article II.

The Oneida and Tuscarora nations shall be secured in the possession of the lands on which they are settled.

Article III.

A line shall be drawn, beginning at the mouth of a creek about four miles east of Niagara, called Oyonwayea, or Johnston's Landing-Place, upon the lake named by the Indians Oswego, and by us Ontario; from thence southerly in a direction always four miles east of the carrying-path, between Lake Erie and Ontario, to the mouth of the Tehoseroron, or Buffaloe Creek on Lake Erie; thence south to the north boundary of the state of Pennsylvania; thence west to the end of the said north boundary; thence south along the west boundary of the said state, to the river Ohio; the said line from the mouth of the Oyonwayea to the Ohio, shall be the western boundary of the lands of the Six Nations, so that the Six Nations shall and do yield to the United States, all claims to the country west of the said boundary, and then shall be secured in the peaceful possession of the lands they inhabit east and north of the same, reserving only six miles square round the fort of Oswego, to the United States, for the support of the same.

Article IV.

The Commissioners of the United States, in consideration of the present circumstances of the Six Nations, and in execution of the humane and liberal views of the United States upon the signing of the above articles, will order goods to be delivered to the said Six Nations for their use and comfort.

Source: Indian Affairs: Laws and Treaties. Volume 2, *Treaties.* Washington, D.C.: Government Printing Office, 1904. Reprinted as *Indian Treaties 1778–1883.* Compiled and edited by Charles J. Kappler. New York: Interland Publishing Co., 1972.

Corn Tassel
Speech of 1785

It is a little surprising that when we entered into treaties with our brothers, the whites, their whole cry is *more land!* Indeed, formerly it seemed to be a matter of formality with them to demand what they knew we durst not refuse. But on the principles of fairness, of which we have received assurances during the conducting of the present treaty, and in the name of free will and equality, I must reject your demand.

Suppose, in considering the nature of your claim (and in justice to my nation I shall and will do it freely), I were to ask one of you, my brother warriors, under what kind of authority, by what law, or on what pretense he makes this exorbitant demand of nearly all the lands we hold between your settlements and our towns, as the cement and consideration of our peace.

Would he tell me that it is by right of conquest? No! If he did, I should retort on him that we had last marched over his territory; even up to this very place which he has *fortified* so far within his former limits; nay, that some of our young warriors (whom we have not yet had an opportunity to recall or give notice to, of the general treaty) are still in the woods, and continue to keep his people in fear, and that it was but till lately that these identical walls were your strongholds, out of which you durst scarcely advance.

If, therefore, a bare march, or reconnoitering a country is sufficient reason to ground a claim to it, we shall insist upon transposing the demand, and your relinquishing your settlements on the western waters and removing one hundred miles back towards the east, whither some of our warriors advanced against you in the course of last year's campaign.

Let us examine the facts of your present eruption into our country, and we shall discover your pretentions on that ground. What did you do? You marched into our territories with a superior force; our vigilance gave us no timely notice of your maneuvers; your numbers far exceeded us, and we fled to the stronghold of our extensive woods, there to secure our women and children.

Thus, you marched into our towns; they were left to your mercy; you killed a few scattered and defenseless individuals, spread fire and desolation wherever you pleased, and returned again to your own habitations. If you meant this, indeed, as a conquest you omitted the most essential point; you should have fortified the junction of the Holstein and Tennessee rivers, and have thereby conquered all the waters above you. But, as all are fair advantages during the existence of a state of war, it is now too late for us to suffer for your mishap of generalship!

Again, were we to inquire by what law or authority you set up a claim, I answer, *none!* Your laws extend not into our country, nor ever did. You talk of the law of nature and the law of nations, and they are both against you.

Indeed, much has been advanced on the want of what you term civilization among the Indians; and many proposals have been made to us to adopt your laws, your religion, your manners and your customs. But, we confess that we do not yet see the propriety, or practicability of such a reformation, and should be better pleased with beholding the good effect of these doctrines in your own practices than with hearing you talk about them, or reading your papers to us upon such subjects.

You say: Why do not the Indians till the ground and live as we do? May we not, with equal propriety, ask, Why the white people do not hunt and live as we do? You profess to think it no injustice to warn us not to kill our deer and other game from the mere love of waste; but it is very criminal in our young men if they chance to kill a cow or a hog for their sustenance when they happen to be in your lands. We wish, however, to be at peace with you, and to do as we would be done by. We do not quarrel with you for killing an occasional buffalo, bear or deer on our lands when you need one to eat; but you go much farther; your people hunt to gain a livelihood by it; they kill all our game; our young men resent the injury, and it is followed by bloodshed and war.

This is not a mere affected injury; it is a grievance which we equitably complain of and it demands a permanent redress.

The great God of Nature has placed us in different situations. It is true that he has endowed you with many superior advantages; but he has not created us to be your slaves. *We are a separate people!* He has given each their lands, under distinct considerations and circumstances; he has stocked yours with cows, ours with buffalo; yours with hog, ours with bear; yours with sheep, ours with deer. He has, indeed, given you an advantage in this, that your cattle are tame and domestic while ours are wild and demand not only a larger space for range, but art to hunt and kill them; they are, nevertheless, as much our property as other animals are yours, and ought not to be taken away without our consent, or for something equivalent.

Source: "Tatham's Characters among the North American Indians." *Annual of Biography and Obituary.* London, 1820.

CHAPTER 5

The New Nation,
1790–1840

✷ ✷ ✷

The ratification of the Constitution and the establishment of the new governmental system went relatively smoothly, but not without continuing conflict over the nature of the union and the rights of citizens under that union.

The Bill of Rights

The first manifestation of that continuing debate was the addition of the first ten amendments to the Constitution, the Bill of Rights. Americans tend to think of the Bill of Rights as an integral part of the Constitution, but it was added at the insistence of those opposed to the adoption of the Constitution and over the objections of those like James Madison (1751–1836) and Alexander Hamilton (1757–1804) who believed that a Bill of Rights was not needed. During the past forty years, the Bill of Rights has been at the center of political debate. Issues such as gun control, prayer in the schools, the treatment of suspects and prisoners, the natures of acceptable punishment, the powers of police to search cars stopped for traffic offenses, pornography, and the nature of acceptable political protest have all depended on interpretations of the Bill of Rights. Today, countries such as Canada, which did not have a written Bill of Rights, have adopted similar provisions, and other countries are considering adopting them.

The First Ten Amendments
The Bill of Rights

December 15, 1791

Amendment I

Congress shall make no law respecting an establishment of religion, or prohibiting the free exercise thereof; or abridging the freedom of speech, or of the press; or the right of the people peaceably to assemble, and to petition the Government for a redress of grievances.

Amendment II

A well regulated Militia, being necessary to the security of a free State, the right of the people to keep and bear Arms, shall not be infringed.

Amendment III

No Soldier shall, in time of peace be quartered in any house, without the consent of the Owner, nor in time of war, but in a manner to be prescribed by law.

Amendment IV

The right of the people to be secure in their persons, houses, papers, and effects, against unreasonable searches and seizures, shall not be violated, and no Warrants shall issue, but upon probable cause, supported by Oath or affirmation, and particularly describing the place to be searched, and the persons or things to be seized.

Amendment V

No person shall be held to answer for a capital, or otherwise infamous crime, unless on a presentment or indictment of a Grand Jury, except in cases arising in the land or naval forces, or in the Militia, when in actual service in time of War or public danger; nor shall any person be subject for the same offence to be twice put in jeopardy of life or limb; nor shall be compelled in any Criminal Case to be a witness against himself, nor be deprived of life, liberty, or property, without due process of law; nor shall private property be taken for public use, without just compensation.

Amendment VI

In all criminal prosecutions, the accused shall enjoy the right to a speedy and public trial, by an impartial jury of the State and district wherein the crime shall have been committed, which district shall have been previously ascertained by law, and to be informed of the nature and cause of the accusation; to be confronted with the witnesses against him; to have compulsory process for obtaining witnesses in his favor, and to have the Assistance of Counsel for his defence.

Amendment VII

In Suits at common law, where the value in controversy shall exceed twenty dollars, the right of trial by jury shall be preserved, and no fact tried by a jury, shall be otherwise reexamined in any Court of the United States, than according to the rules of the common law.

Amendment VIII

Excessive bail shall not be required, nor excessive fines imposed, nor cruel and unusual punishment inflicted.

Amendment IX

The enumeration in the Constitution, of certain rights, shall not be construed to deny or disparage others retained by the people.

Amendment X

The powers not delegated to the United States by the Constitution, nor prohibited by it to the States, are reserved to the States respectively, or to the people.

*   *   *

Two other early amendments were also found necessary. The Eleventh Amendment prohibits the Supreme Court from having original jurisdiction in a case brought against a state by a citizen of another state or another country. The amendment was passed after the Supreme Court claimed such jurisdiction.

The Eleventh Amendment

January 8, 1798

The Judicial power of the United States shall not be construed to extend to any suit in law or equity, commenced or prosecuted against one of the United States by Citizens of another State, or by Citizens or Subjects of any Foreign State.

* * *

The Twelfth Amendment changes the method of electing the vice president. Under the original Constitution, the vice president was the second highest vote-getter in the contest for president. Thus, in a race with two major candidates, the winner became president and the loser became vice president. This was quickly found to not work very well.

The Twelfth Amendment

September 25, 1804

The Electors shall meet in their respective states, and vote by ballot for President and Vice-President, one of whom, at least, shall not be an inhabitant of the same state with themselves; they shall name in their ballots the person voted for as President, and in distinct ballots the person voted for as Vice-President, and they shall make distinct lists of all persons voted for as President, and of all persons voted for as Vice President, and of the number of votes for each, which lists they shall sign and certify, and transmit sealed to the seat of the government of the United States, directed to the President of the Senate;—The President of the Senate shall, in the presence of the Senate and House of Representatives, open all the certificates and the votes shall then be counted;—The person having the greatest number of votes for President, shall be the President, if such number be a majority of the whole number of Electors appointed; and if no person have such majority, then from the persons having the highest numbers not exceeding three on the list of those voted for as President, the House of Representatives shall choose immediately, by ballot, the President. But in choosing the President, the votes shall be taken by states, the representation from each state having one vote; a quorum for this purpose shall consist of a member or members from two thirds of the states, and a majority of all the states shall be necessary to a choice. And if the House of Representatives shall not choose a President whenever the right of choice devolve upon them, before the fourth day of March next following, then the Vice-President shall act as President, as in the case of the death or other constitutional disability of the President. The person having the greatest number of votes as Vice-President, shall be the Vice-President, if such number be a majority of the whole number of Electors appointed, and if no person have a majority, then from the two highest numbers on the list, the Senate shall choose the Vice-President; a quorum for the purpose shall consist of two thirds of the whole number of Senators, and a majority of the whole number shall be necessary to a choice. But no person constitutionally ineligible to the office of President shall be eligible to that of Vice-President of the United States.

The Conflict over the Power of the Central Government

ALEXANDER HAMILTON

In the Federalist Papers, Alexander Hamilton had argued for a strong central government. As secretary of the treasury under George Washington, he argued that the Constitution had, in fact, established such a government. This position is best reflected in his argument on the constitutionality of a national bank, where he develops his theory that the central government has all the power it needs to fulfill its duties — the doctrine of implied powers.

Alexander Hamilton
Opinion as to the Constitutionality of the Bank of the United States

February 23, 1791

The Secretary of the Treasury having perused with attention the papers containing the opinions of the Secretary of State and the Attorney-General, concerning the constitutionality of the bill for establishing a national bank, proceeds, according to the order of the President, to submit the reasons which have induced him to entertain a different opinion.

It will naturally have been anticipated, that in performing this task he would feel uncommon solicitude. Personal considerations alone, arising from the reflection that the measure originated with him, would be sufficient to produce it. The sense which he has manifested of the great importance of such an institution to the successful administration of the department under his particular care, and an expectation of serious ill consequences to result from a failure of the measure, do not permit him to be without anxiety on public accounts. But the chief solicitude arises from a firm persuasion, that principles of construction like those espoused by the Secretary of State and the Attorney-General would be fatal to the just and indispensable authority of the United States.

In entering upon the argument, it ought to be premised that the objections of the Secretary of State and the Attorney-General are founded on a general denial of the authority of the United States to erect corporations. The latter, indeed, expressly admits, that if there be anything in the bill which is not warranted by the Constitution, it is the clause of incorporation.

Now it appears to the Secretary of the Treasury that this *general principle is inherent* in the very *definition* of government, and *essential* to every step of the progress to be made by that of the United States, namely: That every power vested in a government is in its nature *sovereign*, and includes, by *force* of the *term*, a right to employ all the *means* requisite and fairly applicable to the attainment of the *ends* of such power, and which are not precluded by restrictions and exceptions specified in the Constitution, or not immoral, or not contrary to the *essential ends* of political society.

This principle, in its application to government in general, would be admitted as an axiom, and it will be incumbent upon those who may incline to deny it, to prove a distinction, and to show that a rule which, in the general system of things, is essential to the preservation of the social order, is inapplicable to the United States.

The circumstance that the powers of sovereignty are in this country divided between the National and State governments, does not afford the distinction required. It does not follow from this, that each of the portion of *powers* delegated to the one or to the other, is not sovereign with *regard to its proper objects*. It will only *follow* from it, that each has sovereign power as to *certain things*, and not as to *other things*. To deny that the Government of the United States has sovereign power, as to its declared purposes and trusts, because its power does not extend to all cases, would be equally to deny that the State governments have sovereign power in any case, because their power does not extend to every case. The tenth section of the first article of the Constitution exhibits a long list of very important things which they may not do. And thus the United States would furnish the singular spectacle of a *political society* without *sovereignty*, or of a *people governed*, without *government*.

If it would be necessary to bring proof to a proposition so clear, as that which affirms that the powers of the Federal Government, as to *its objects*, were sovereign, there is a clause of its Constitution which would be decisive. It is that which declares that the Constitution, and the laws of the United States made in pursuance of it, and all treaties made, or which shall be made, under their authority, shall be the *supreme law of the land*. The power which can create the *supreme law of the land* in *any case*, is doubtless *sovereign* as to such case.

This general and indisputable principle puts at once an end to the *abstract* question, whether the United States have power to erect a corporation; that is to say, to give a *legal* or *artificial capacity* to one or more persons, distinct from the *natural.* For it is unquestionably incident to *sovereign power* to erect corporations, and consequently to *that* of the United States, in *relation* to the *objects* intrusted to the management of the government. The difference is this: where the authority of the government is general, it can create corporations in *all cases;* where it is confined to certain branches of legislation, it can create corporations *only* in those cases.

Here, then, as far as concerns the reasonings of the Secretary of State and the Attorney-General, the affirmative of the constitutionality of the bill might be permitted to rest. It will occur to the President, that the principle here advanced has been untouched by either of them.

For a more complete elucidation of the point, nevertheless, the arguments which they had used against the power of the government to erect corporations, however foreign they are to the great and fundamental rule which has been stated, shall be particularly examined. And after showing that they do not tend to impair its force, it shall also be shown that the power of incorporation, incident to the government in certain cases, does fairly extend to the particular case which is the object of the bill.

The first of these arguments is, that the foundation of the Constitution is laid on this ground: "That all powers not delegated to the United States by the Constitution, nor prohibited by it to the States, are reserved to the States, or to the people." Whence it is meant to be inferred, that Congress can in no case exercise any power not included in those enumerated in the Constitution. And it is affirmed, that the power of erecting a corporation is not included in any of the enumerated powers.

The main proposition here laid down, in its true signification, is not to be questioned. It is nothing more than a consequence of this republican maxim, that all government is a delegation of power. But how much is delegated in each case is a question of fact, to be made out by fair reasoning and construction, upon the particular provisions of the Constitution, taking as guides the general principles and general ends of governments.

It is not denied that there are *implied,* as well as *express powers,* and that the *former* are as effectually delegated as the *latter.* And for the sake of accuracy it shall be mentioned that there is another class of powers, which may be properly denominated *resulting powers.* It will not be doubted that if the United States should make a conquest of any of the territories of its neighbors, they would possess sovereign jurisdiction over the conquered territory. This would be rather a result from the whole mass of the powers of the government, and from the nature of political society, than a consequence of either of the powers specially enumerated.

But be this as it may, it furnishes a striking illustration of the general doctrine contended for; it shows an extensive case, in which a power of erecting corporations is either implied in, or would result from, some or all of the powers vested in the National Government. The jurisdiction acquired over such conquered country would certainly be competent to any species of legislation.

To return:—It is conceded that *implied powers* are to be considered as delegated equally with *express ones*. Then it follows, that as a power of erecting a corporation may as well be *implied* as any other thing, it may as well be employed as an *instrument* or *means* of carrying into execution any of the specified powers, as any other *instrument* or *means* whatever. The only question must be in this, as in every other case, whether the means to be employed, or, in this instance, the corporation to be erected, has a natural relation to any of the acknowledged objects or lawful ends of the government. Thus a corporation may not be erected by Congress for superintending the police of the city of Philadelphia, because they are not authorized to *regulate* the *police* of that city. But one may be erected in relation to the collection of taxes, or to the trade with foreign countries, or to the trade between the States, or with the Indian tribes; because it is the province of the Federal Government to *regulate* those objects, and because it is incident to a general *sovereign* or *legislative* power to *regulate* a thing, to employ all the means which relate to its regulation to the best and greatest advantage.

Source: *Papers on Public Credit, Commerce, and Finance.* By Alexander Hamilton. Edited by Samuel McKee, Jr. New York: Columbia University Press, 1934.

Alexander Hamilton (1757–1804) was a lawyer and was secretary of the treasury 1789–95.

THE ALIEN AND SEDITION ACTS

Under President John Adams (1735–1826), Congress passed acts that gave the president extraordinary powers over the citizenry. One act limited speech and publication deemed to defame any part of the U.S. government or to bring the U.S. government into disrepute. In an act concerning aliens, the president was given the authority to deport or imprison "all natives, citizens, denizens, or subjects" of any country at war with the United States. Another act extended the period before a person could become a citizen from five to fourteen years. The real purpose of the alien and sedition acts was to undercut the political power of Thomas Jefferson (1743–1826), whose followers tended to support the French Revolution, and who drew considerable support from newly naturalized citizens.

Chap. LXVI.—*An Act respecting Enemy Aliens.*

Section 1. *Be it enacted by the Senate and House of Representatives of the United States of America in Congress assembled,* That whenever there shall be a declared war between the United States and any foreign nation or government, or any invasion or predatory incursion shall be perpetrated, attempted, or threatened against the territory of the United States, by any foreign nation or government, and the President of the United States shall make public proclamation of the event, all natives, citizens, denizens, or subjects of the hostile nation or government, being males of the age of fourteen years and upwards, who shall be within the United States, and not actually naturalized, shall be liable to be apprehended, restrained, secured and removed, as alien enemies. And the President of the United States shall be, and he is hereby authorized, in any event, as aforesaid, by his proclamation thereof, or other public act, to direct the conduct to be observed, on the part of the United States, towards the aliens who shall become liable, as aforesaid; the manner and degree of the restraint to which they shall be subject, and in what cases, and upon what security their residence shall be permitted, and to provide for the removal of those, who, not being permitted to reside within the United States, shall refuse or neglect to depart therefrom; and to establish any other regulations which shall be found necessary in the premises and for the public safety: Provided, that aliens resident within the United States, who shall become liable as enemies, in the manner aforesaid, and who shall not be chargeable with actual hostility, or other crime against the public safety, shall be allowed, for the recovery, disposal, and removal of their goods and effects, and for their departure, the full time which is, or shall be stipulated by any treaty, where any shall have been between the United States, and the hostile nation or government, of which they shall be natives, citizens, denizens or subjects: and where no such treaty shall have existed, the President of the United States may ascertain and declare such reasonable time as may be consistent with the public safety, and according to the dictates of humanity and national hospitality.

Source: 1 Stat. 570 (1798)

An Act in addition to the act, entitled "An act for the punishment of certain crimes against the United States."

Section 1. *Be it enacted by the Senate and House of Representatives of the United States of America, in Congress assembled,* That if any persons shall unlawfully combine or conspire together, with intent to oppose any measure or measures of the government of the United States, which are or shall be directed by proper authority, or to impede the operation of any law of the United States, or to intimidate or prevent any person holding a place or office in or under the government of the United States, from undertaking, performing or executing his trust or duty; and if any person or persons, with intent as aforesaid, shall counsel, advise or attempt to procure any insurrection, riot, unlawful assembly, or combination, whether such conspiracy, threatening, counsel, advice, or attempt shall have the proposed effect or not, he or they shall be deemed guilty of a high misdemeanor, and on conviction, before any court of the United States having jurisdiction thereof, shall be punished by a fine not exceeding five thousand dollars, and by imprisonment during a term not less than six months nor exceeding five years; and further, at the discretion of the court may be holden to find sureties for his good behaviour in such sum, and for such time, as the said court may direct.

Sec 2. *And be it further enacted,* That if any person shall write, print, utter or publish, or shall cause or procure to be written, printed, uttered or published, or shall knowingly and willingly assist or aid in writing, printing, uttering or publishing any false, scandalous and malicious writing or writings against the government of the United States, or either house of the Congress of the United States, or the President of the United States, with intent to defame the said government, or either house of the said Congress, or the said President, or to bring them, or either of them, into contempt or disrepute; or to excite against them, or either or any of them, the hatred of the good people of the United States, or to stir up sedition within the United States, or to excite any unlawful combinations therein, for opposing or resisting any law of the United States, or any act of the President of the United States, done in pursuance of any such law, or of the powers in him vested by the constitution of the United States, or to resist, oppose, or defeat any such law or act, or to aid, encourage or abet any hostile designs of any foreign nation against the United States, their people or government, then such person, being thereof convicted before any court of the United States having jurisdiction thereof, shall be punished by a fine not exceeding two thousand dollars, and by imprisonment not exceeding two years.

Source: 1 Stat. 596 (1798).

THE KENTUCKY AND VIRGINIA RESOLUTIONS

Responding to the act establishing a national bank and to the alien and sedition acts, some states declared that such acts were null and void within their boundaries. These resolutions were one of the earliest assertions of states' rights after the adoption of the Constitution. Note that the first sentence of the Kentucky resolution asserts that the central or "General" government was the creation of

the states. (Kentucky was admitted to the Union in 1792.) Thomas Jefferson was the anonymous author of the Kentucky Resolution.

Kentucky Legislature
in the House of Representatives

November 10th, 1798.

RESOLVED, that the several States composing the United States of America, are not united on the principles of unlimited submission to their General Government; but that by compact under the style and title of a Constitution for the United States and of amendments thereto, they constituted a General Government for special purposes, delegated to that Government certain definite powers, reserving each State to itself, the residuary mass of right to their own self Government; and that whensoever the General Government assumes undelegated powers, its acts are unauthoritative, void, and of no force; That to this compact each State acceded as a State, and is an integral party, its co-States forming as to itself, the other party: That the Government created by this compact was not made the exclusive or final *judge* of the extent of the powers delegated to itself; since that would have made its discretion, and not the Constitution, the measure of its powers; but that as in all other cases of compact among parties having no common Judge, each party has an equal right to judge for itself, as well of infractions as of the mode and measure of redress.

II. Resolved, that the Constitution of the United States having delegated to Congress a power to punish treason, counterfeiting the securities and current coin of the United States, piracies and felonies committed on the High Seas, and offenses against the laws of nations, and no other crimes whatever, and it being true as a general principle, and one of the amendments to the Constitution having also declared, "that the powers not delegated to the United States by the Constitution, nor prohibited by it to the States, are reserved to the States respectively, or to the people," therefore also the same act of Congress passed on the 14th day of July, 1798, and entitled "An act in addition to the act entitled an act for the punishment of certain crimes against the United States," as also the act passed by them on the 27th day of June, 1798, entitled "An act to punish frauds committed on the Bank of the United States" (and all other their acts which assume to create, define, or punish crimes other than those enumerated in the Constitution) are altogether void and of no force, and that the power to create, define, and punish such other crimes is reserved, and of right appertains solely and exclusively to the respective States, each within its own Territory.

III. Resolved, that it is true as a general principle, and is also expressly declared by one of the amendments to the Constitution that "the powers not delegated to the United States by the Constitution, nor prohibited by it to the States, are reserved to the States respectively or to the people;" and that no power over the freedom of religion, freedom of speech, or freedom of the press being delegated to the United States by the Constitution, nor prohibited by it to the States, all lawful powers respecting the same did of right remain, and were reserved to the States, or to the people: That thus was manifested their determination to retain to themselves the right of judging how far the licentiousness of speech and of the press may be abridged without lessening their useful freedom, and how far those abuses which cannot be separated from their use, should be tolerated rather than the use be destroyed; and thus also they guarded against all abridgement by the United States of the freedom of religious opinions and exercises, and retained to themselves the right of protecting the same, as this state by a Law passed on the general demand of its Citizens, had already protected them from all human restraint or interference: And that in addition to this general principle and express declaration, another and more special provision has been made by one of the amendments to the Constitution which expressly declares, that "Congress shall make no law respecting an Establishment of religion, or prohibiting the free exercise thereof, or abridging the freedom of speech, or the press," thereby guarding in the same sentence, and under the same words, the freedom of religion, of speech, and of the press, insomuch, that whatever violates either, throws down the sanctuary which covers the others, and that libels, falsehoods, and defamation, equally with heresy and false religion, are withheld from the cognizance of federal tribunals. That therefore the act of the Congress of the United States passed on the 14th day of July 1798, entitled "An act in addition to the act for the punishment of certain crimes against the United States," which does abridge the freedom of the press, is not law, but is altogether void and of no effect.

IV. Resolved, that alien friends are under the jurisdiction and protection of the laws of the State wherein they are; that no power over them has been delegated to the United States, nor prohibited to the individual States distinct from their power over citizens; and it being true as a general principle, and one of the amendments to the Constitution having also declared, that "the powers not delegated to the United States by the Constitution nor prohibited by it to the States are reserved to the States respectively or to the people," the act of the Congress of the United States—passed on the 22d day of June, 1798, entitled "An act concerning aliens," which assumes power over alien friends not delegated by the Constitution, is not law, but is altogether void and of no force.

V. Resolved, that in addition to the general principle as well as the express declaration, that powers not delegated are reserved, another and more special provision inserted in the Constitution from abundant caution has declared, "that the *migration* or importation of such persons as any of the States now existing shall think proper to admit, shall not be prohibited by the Congress prior to the year 1808." That this Commonwealth does admit the migration of alien friends described as the subject of the said act concerning aliens; that a provision against prohibiting their migration, is a provision against all acts equivalent thereto, or it would be nugatory; that to remove them when migrated is equivalent to a prohibition of their migration, and is therefore contrary to the said provision of the Constitution and void.

VI. Resolved, that the imprisonment of a person under the protection of the Laws of this Commonwealth on his failure to obey the simple order of the President to depart out of the United States, as is undertaken by the said act entitled "An act concerning Aliens," is contrary to the Constitution, one amendment to which has provided, that "no person shall be deprived of liberty without due process of law," and that another having provided "that in all criminal prosecutions, the accused shall enjoy the right to a public trial by an impartial jury, to be informed of the nature and cause of the accusation, to be confronted with the witnesses against him, to have compulsory process for obtaining witness in his favour, and to have the assistance of counsel for his defence," the same act undertaking to authorize the President to remove a person out of the United States who is under the protection of the Law, on his own suspicion, without accusation, without jury, without public trial, without confrontation of the witnesses against him, without having witnesses in his favour, without defence, without counsel, is contrary to these provisions also of the Constitution, is therefore not law but utterly void and of no force.

That transferring the power of judging any person who is under the protection of the laws, from the Courts to the President of the United States, as is undertaken by the same act concerning Aliens, is against the article of the Constitution which provides, that "the judicial power of the United States shall be vested in Courts, the Judges of which shall hold their offices during good behaviour," and that the said act is void for that reason also; and it is further to be noted, that this transfer of Judiciary power is to that magistrate of the General Government who already possesses all the Executive, and a qualified negative in all the Legislative powers.

VII. Resolved, that the construction applied by the General Government (as is evinced by sundry of their proceedings) to those parts of the Constitution of the United States which delegate to Congress a power to lay and collect taxes, duties, imposts, and excises; to pay the debts, and provide for the common defence, and general welfare of the United States, and to make all laws which shall be necessary and proper for carrying into execution the powers vested by the Constitution in the Government of the United States, or any department thereof, goes to the destruction of all the limits prescribed to their power by the Constitution—That words meant by that instrument to be subsiduary only to the execution of the limited powers, ought not to be so construed as themselves to give unlimited powers, nor a part so to be taken, as to destroy the whole residue of the instrument: That the proceedings of the General Government under colour of these articles, will be a fit and necessary subject for revisal and correction at a time of greater tranquility, while those specified in the preceding resolutions call for immediate redress.

Source: The Debates in the Several State Conventions on the Adoption of the Federal Constitution as Recommended by the General Convention at Philadelphia in 1787 Together with the Journal of the Federal Convention, Luther Martin's Letter, Yates's Minutes, Congressional Opinions, Virginia and Kentucky Resolutions of '98–99, and Other Illustrations of the Constitution. 2nd edition. 5 volumes. Edited by Jonathan Elliot. Reprint, New York: Burt Franklin, [1974].

JEFFERSON'S FIRST INAUGURAL ADDRESS

In his first inaugural address, Jefferson responded to the problems that the United States had faced under President Adams.

Thomas Jefferson
First Inaugural Address

Friends and Fellow Citizens:

About to enter fellow citizens on the exercise of duties, which comprehend everything dear and valuable to you, it is proper you should understand what I deem the essential principle of this government and consequently those which ought to shape its administration.

I will compress them in the narrowest compass they will bear, stating the general principle, but not all its limitations.

Equal and exact justice to all men, of whatever state or persuasion, religion, or political:

Peace, commerce, and honest friendship with all nations, entangling alliances with none:

The support of the State governments in all their rights, as the most competent administrations for our domestic concerns, and the surest bulwarks against antirepublican tendencies:

The preservation of the General government, in its whole constitutional vigor, as the sheet anchor of our peace at home, and safety abroad.

A jealous care of the right of election by the people, a mild and safe corrective of abuses, which are lopped by the sword of revolution, where peaceable remedies are unprovided.

Absolute acquiescence in the decisions of the Majority—the vital principle of republics, from which is no appeal but to force, the vital principle and immediate parent of despotism.

A well disciplined militia, our best reliance in peace, and for the first moments of war, till regulars may relieve them: The Supremacy of the Civil over Military authority:

Economy in public expense, that labor may be lightly burthened:

The honest paiment of our debts and sacred preservation of the public faith:

Encouragement of Agriculture, and of Commerce as it's handmaid:

The diffusion of information, and arraignment of all abuses at the bar of the public reason:

Freedom of Religion, freedom of the press, and freedom of person under the protection of the Habeas corpus: And trial by juries, impartially selected.

These Principles form the bright constellation which has gone before us, and guided our steps, thro' an age of Revolution and Reformation: The wisdom of our Sages, and blood of our Heroes, have been devoted to their attainment: They should be the Creed of our political faith, the Text of civic instruction, the Touchstone by which to try the services of those we trust; and should we wander from them, in moments of error or alarm, let us hasten to retrace our steps and to regain the road which alone leads to Peace, Liberty and Safety.

Source: The Works of Thomas Jefferson. Edited by Paul L. Ford, 9:193–200. New York: G. P. Putnam's Sons, 1905.

Thomas Jefferson (1743–1826) was the third president of the United States.

Natural Aristocracy

Jefferson and Adams differed politically but remained friends and corresponded prodigiously until they both died on July 4, 1826. This 1813 letter from Jefferson to Adams expressed a common theme for both of them.

Thomas Jefferson
Letter to John Adams, October 28, 1813

I agree with you that there is a natural aristocracy among men. The grounds of this are virtue and talents. Formerly, bodily powers gave place among the *aristoi*. But since the invention of gunpowder has armed the weak as well as the strong with missile death, bodily strength like beauty, good humor, politeness, and other accomplishments has become but an auxiliary ground of distinction. There is also an artificial aristocracy, founded on wealth and birth, without either virtue or talents; for with these it would belong to the first class. The natural aristocracy I consider as the most precious gift of nature for the instruction, the trusts, and government of society. And, indeed, it would have been inconsistent in creation to have formed man for the social state and not to have provided virtue and wisdom enough to manage the concerns of the society. May we not even say that that form of government is best which provides the most effectually for a pure selection of these natural *aristoi* into offices of government? The artificial aristocracy is a mischievous ingredient in government, and provision should be made to prevent its ascendency. On the question of what is the best provision, you and I differ, but we differ as rational friends, using the free exercise of our own reason and mutually indulging its errors. You think it best to put the pseudo-*aristoi* into a separate chamber of legislation, where they may be hindered from doing mischief by their co-ordinate branches and where, also, they may be a protection to wealth against the agrarian and plundering enterprises of the majority of the people. I think that to give them power in order to prevent them doing mischief is arming them for it and increasing instead of remedying the evil.

Source: The Adams-Jefferson Letters: The Complete Correspondence between Thomas Jefferson and Abigail and John Adams. Edited by Lester J. Cappon, 2:91. Chapel Hill: Published for the Institute of Early American History and Culture at Williamsburg, Virginia, by the University of North Carolina Press, 1959).

Political Debate

Political debate on a variety of general issues was vigorous. The following selections from John Taylor (1753–1824) and Frances Wright (1795–1852), who occupied different positions on the political spectrum, illustrate two of the concerns of the time. Some may be surprised at the fact that Taylor felt the need to defend private property in 1820. And while one point in defending private property is to defend slavery, Taylor is more generally arguing against the centralization of power (such as the national bank) and the growing national involvement in the economy, which he saw as dangerous. Wright's argument for the education of women both physically and intellectually is a fairly early example of a continuing theme.

John Taylor
Construction Construed, and Constitutions Vindicated.
The Principles of Our Revolution.

These are the keys of construction, and the locks of liberty. The question to be considered is, whether our revolution was designed to establish the freedom both of religion and property, or only of the former.

It is strange that the human mind should have been expanded in relation to religion, and yet should retain narrow notions in relation to property. Objects unseen, and incapable of being explained by the information of the senses, afford less perfect materials for the exercise of reason, than those capable of being investigated by evidence, within the scope of the human understanding. As the difficulties opposed to the correction of religious fanaticism seemed less surmountable, whilst its effects were more pernicious, the zeal of philosophers was condensed in an effort to relieve mankind from an evil the most distressing; and their attention was diverted from another, at this period the most prominent. But having wrested religious liberty from the grasp of fanaticism, it now behooves them to turn their attention towards pecuniary fanaticism, and to wrest civil liberty from its tyranny also. Between an absolute power in governments over the religion and over the property of men, the analogy is exact, and their consequences must therefore be the same. Freedom of religion being the discovery by which religious liberty could only be established; freedom of property must be the only means also, for the establishment of civil liberty. Pecuniary fanaticism, undisciplined by constitutional principles, is such an instrument for oppression, as an undisciplined religious fanaticism. A power in governments to regulate individual wealth, will be directly guided by those very motives, which indirectly influenced all governments, possessed of a power to regulate religious opinions and rites. If we have only restrained one of these powers, we have most improvidently retained the other, under which mankind have groaned in all ages; and which at this time is sufficient to oppress or enslave the European nations, although they have drawn some of the teeth of religious fanaticism. An adoration of military fame, specious projects and eminent individuals, has in all ages brought on mankind a multitude of evils; and a sound freedom of property is the only mode that I know of, able to destroy the worship of these idols, by removing beyond their reach the sacrifices upon which themselves, and their proselytes, subsist.

Many princes have patronized literature, but none have patronized knowledge. Augustus was celebrated for the former species of munificence; yet the temporary splendors of imperial patronage were soon obscured by the bad principle of a tyranny over property; a principle, unpropitious to knowledge, because it was hostile to individual liberty. We must reason from a comparison between general or universal facts, and not from a contemplation of temporary exceptions, to come at truth; and when we discover that an absolute power over property, though occasionally exercised for the attainment of praise-worthy ends, is yet constantly attended by general evils, infinitely outweighing such particular benefits; we forbear to draw our conclusion from the partial cases, or decide erroneously. A truth, established by its universality, ought to be an overmatch for the sophistries of cupidity. The best general principle, under the destiny of mankind, is capable of producing partial evils. The freedom of the press, of religion, and of property, may occasionally produce inconveniences; but ought mankind therefore to transfer their approbation from these three foundations of civil liberty, to the instruments by which it is destroyed?

No form of government can foster a fanaticism for wealth, without being corrupted. The courtiers of republicks, able to exercise an absolute power over the national property, are more numerous and more vicious than the courtiers of kings, because access to patrons is easier; they have more occasion for partisans, and a multiplication of despots over property multiplies the channels of fraud. New ones also are frequently opened by a revolution of parties, and of patrons, who with their favorites and dependants, are in haste to bolster power or amass wealth, during the continuance of a fleeting authority. Against a propensity so mischievous, and so fatal to republicks, there seems to be no resource, but a constitutional prohibition of the power by which it is nurtured; and a rejection of precedents, by which infringements of so wholesome a prohibition are usually justified. Both reason and morality unite to impress upon nations, a necessity for imposing restraints upon a propensity, which may so easily be concealed under the most glittering robes of patriotism. What real patriot would feel himself molested, by restraints upon avarice and ambition? Are not both unfriendly to human happiness? Some patriots have sacrificed their lives for the happiness of their country. Is the sacrifice of an error, by which fraud and avarice are nurtured, too much to expect of ours?

A love of wealth, fostered by honest industry, is an ally both of moral rectitude, and national happiness, because it can only be gratified by increasing the fund for national subsistence, comfort, strength and prosperity; but a love of wealth, fostered by partial laws for enriching corporations and individuals, is allied to immorality and oppression, because it is gratified at the expense of industry, and diminishes its ability to work out national blessings.

Source: Construction Construed and Constitutions Vindicated. By John Taylor. Richmond, Va.: Shepherd and Pollard, 1820.

John Taylor (1753–1824), known as "John Taylor of Caroline," was a politician and agriculturalist. He was U.S. senator from Virginia 1792–94, 1803, and 1822–24.

Frances Wright
Education

In the education of women, New England seems hitherto to have been peculiarly liberal. The ladies of the eastern states are frequently possessed of the most solid acquirements, the modern and even the dead languages, and a wide scope of reading; the consequence is that their manners have the character of being more composed than those of my gay young friends in this quarter. I have already stated, in one of my earlier letters, that the public attention is now everywhere turned to the improvement of female education. In some states, colleges for girls are established under the eye of the legislature. . . .

In other countries it may seem of little consequence to inculcate upon the female mind "the principles of government, and the obligations of patriotism," but . . . in a country where a mother is charged with the formation of an infant mind that is to be called in future to judge of the laws and support the liberties of a republic, the mother herself should well understand those laws and estimate those liberties. Personal accomplishments and the more ornamental branches of knowledge should certainly in America be made subordinate to solid information. This is perfectly the case with respect to the men; as yet the women have been educated too much after the European manner. French, Italian, dancing, drawing engage the hours of the one sex (and this but too commonly in a lax and careless way), while the more appropriate studies of the other are philosophy, history, political economy, and the exact sciences. It follows, consequently, that after the spirits of youth have somewhat subsided, the two sexes have less in common in their pursuits and turn of thinking than is desirable. A woman of a powerful intellect will of course seize upon the new topics presented to her by the conversation of her husband. The less vigorous or the more thoughtless mind is not easily brought to forego trifling pursuits for those which occupy the stronger reason of its companion.

I must remark that in no particular is the liberal philosophy of the Americans more honorably evinced than in the place which is awarded to women. The prejudices still to be found in Europe, though now indeed somewhat antiquated, which would confine the female library to romances, poetry, and belleslettres, and female conversation to the last new publication, new bonnet, and *pas seul,* are entirely unknown here. The women are assuming their place as thinking beings, not in despite of the men, but chiefly in consequence of their enlarged views and exertions as fathers and legislators. . . .

The liberty here enjoyed by the young women often occasions some surprise to foreigners, who, contrasting it with the constraint imposed on the female youth of Paris or London, are at a loss to reconcile the freedom of the national manners with the purity of the national morals; but confidence and innocence are twin sisters, and should the American women ever resign the guardianship of their own virtue, the lawyers of these democracies will probably find as good occupation in prosecuting suits for divorce as those of any of the monarchies of Europe.

I often lament that in the rearing of women so little attention should be commonly paid to the exercise of the bodily organs; to invigorate the body is to invigorate the mind, and Heaven knows that the weaker sex have much cause to be rendered strong in both. In the happiest country their condition is sufficiently hard. Have they talents? It is difficult to turn them to account. Ambition? The road to honorable distinction is shut against them. A vigorous intellect? It is broken down by sufferings, bodily and mental. The lords of creation receive innumerable, incalculable advantages from the hand of nature, and it must be admitted that they everywhere take sufficient care to foster the advantages with which they are endowed. There is something so flattering to human vanity in the consciousness of superiority that it is little surprising if men husband with jealousy that which nature has enabled them to usurp over the daughters of Eve. Love of power more frequently originates in vanity than pride (two qualities, by the way, which are often confounded) and is, consequently, yet more peculiarly the sin of little than of great minds. Now an overwhelming proportion of human minds appertain to the former class and must be content to soothe their self-love by considering the weakness of others rather than their own strength. You will say this is severe; is it not true? In what consists the greatness of a despot? In his own intrinsic merits? No, in the degradation of the multitude who surround him. What feeds the vanity of a patrician? The consciousness of any virtue that he inherits with his blood? The list of his senseless progenitors would probably soon cease to command his respect if it did not enable him to command that of his fellow creatures. "But what," I hear you ask, "has this to do with the condition of women? Do you mean to compare men collectively to the despot and the patrician?" Why not? The vanity of the despot and the patrician is fed by the folly of their fellow men, and so is that of their sex collectively soothed by the dependence of women: it pleases them better to find in their companion a fragile vine, clinging to their firm trunk for support, than a vigorous tree with whose branches they may mingle theirs. I believe they sometimes repent of their choice when the vine has weighed the oak to the ground. It is difficult, in walking through the world, not to laugh at the consequences which, sooner or later, overtake men's follies, but when these are visited upon women I feel more disposed to sigh. Born to endure the worst afflictions of fortune, they are enervated in soul and body lest the storm should not visit them sufficiently rudely. Instead of essaying to counteract the unequal law of nature, it seems the object of man to visit it upon his weaker helpmate more harshly. It is well, however, that his folly recoils upon his own head, and that the fate of the sexes is so entwined that the dignity of the one must rise or fall with that of the other.

In America much certainly is done to ameliorate the condition of women, and as their education shall become, more and more, the concern of the state, their character may aspire in each succeeding generation to a higher standard. The republic, I am persuaded, will be amply repaid for any trouble or expense that may be thus bestowed. In her struggles for liberty much of her virtue emanated from the wives and daughters of her senators and soldiers, and to preserve to her sons the energy of freemen and patriots she must strengthen that energy in her daughters.

To invigorate the character, however, it is not sufficient to cultivate the mind. The body also must be trained to wholesome exercise, and the nerves braced to bear those extremes of climate which here threaten to enervate the more weakly frame. . . .

Now, though it is by no means requisite that the American women should emulate the men in the pursuit of the whale, the felling of the forest, or the shooting of wild turkeys, they might, with advantage, be taught in early youth to excel in the race, to hit a mark, to swim, and in short to use every exercise which could impart vigor to their frames and independence to their minds.

Source: Views of Society and Manners in America. By Frances Wright. 2nd edition. London: Longman, 1822.

Frances Wright (1795–1852) was a lecturer and writer concerned with women's rights, slavery, and the plight of workers, among other issues. She founded the Nashoba Community as a means of freeing slaves.

The Abolitionist Movement

The antislavery movement was beginning to pull together and become a real force in American politics. As the essay by Angelina Grimké (1805–79) illustrates, many women were active in the movement. As both Grimké's essay and the selection by William Lloyd Garrison (1805–79) illustrate, much of the antislavery movement self-consciously occupied a high moral ground, appealing to religious principles and eschewing violence, although this later changed for some abolitionists.

Grimké's appeal to women and her argument that women can help in the crusade against slavery fits nicely with Frances Wright's earlier argument that women had an active role in social reform. Wright was an abolitionist herself and founded a colony in Tennessee for the purpose of freeing slaves and educating them for freedom. The experiment was a failure, but Wright helped the slaves who resided there to move to Haiti and freedom.

Women did not have an easy time in the abolitionist movement. The antislavery movement split over the role of women in the movement; many—both men and women but predominantly the former—believed that women's role should be in the home and not on the platform. As a result, the Anti-Slavery Convention for American Women was formed. Its meeting, which began May 9, 1837, was both the first female convention and, with 10 percent of the delegates African Americans, the first broadly integrated meeting held in the United States.

At this meeting Grimké proposed the following motion:

> *Resolved,* That as certain rights and duties are common to all moral beings, the time has come for woman to move in that sphere which Providence has assigned her, and no longer remain satisfied in the circumscribed limits with which corrupt custom and a perverted application of Scripture have encircled her; therefore that it is the duty of woman, and the province of woman, to plead the cause of the oppressed in our land, and to do all that she can by her voice, and her pen, and her purse, and the influence of her example, to overthrow the horrible system of slavery.

On the whole, histories of the abolitionist movement have focused on the male leaders and ignored the female ones. But women like Abby Kelley (1811–87) shared the speakers' platform—along with the stones and bottles hurled at it—with white, male abolitionists such as Garrison and African-American abolitionists such as Frederick Douglass (1817?-95).

William Lloyd Garrison
Declaration of Sentiments

The Convention assembled in the city of Philadelphia, to organize a National Anti-Slavery Society, promptly seize the opportunity to promulgate the following Declaration of Sentiments, as cherished by them in relation to the enslavement of one-sixth portion of the American people. . . .

Those for whose emancipation we are striving—constituting at the present time at least one-sixth part of our countrymen—are recognized by law, and treated by their fellow-beings, as marketable commodities, as goods and chattels, as brute beasts; are plundered daily of the fruits of their toil without redress; really enjoy no constitutional nor legal protection from licentious and murderous outrages upon their persons; and are ruthlessly torn asunder—the tender babe from the arms of its frantic mother—the heart-broken wife from her weeping husband—at the caprice or pleasure of irresponsible tyrants. For the crime of having a dark complexion, they suffer the pangs of hunger, the infliction of stripes, the ignominy of brutal servitude. They are kept in heathenish darkness by laws expressly enacted to make their instruction a criminal offence.

These are the prominent circumstances in the condition of more than two millions of our people, the proof of which may be found in thousands of indisputable facts and in the laws of the slaveholding States.

Hence we maintain—that, in view of the civil and religious privileges of this nation, the guilt of its oppression is unequalled by any other on the face of the earth; and, therefore, that it is bound to repent instantly, to undo the heavy burdens, and to let the oppressed go free.

We further maintain—that no man has a right to enslave or imbrute his brother—to hold or acknowledge him, for one moment, as a piece of merchandise—to keep back his hire by fraud—or to brutalize his mind, by denying him the means of intellectual, social and moral improvement.

The right to enjoy liberty is inalienable. To invade it is to usurp the prerogative of Jehovah. Every man has a right to his own body—to the products of his own labor—to the protection of law—and to the common advantages of society. It is piracy to buy or steal a native African, and subject him to servitude. Surely, the sin is as great to enslave an American as an African.

Therefore we believe and affirm—that there is no difference, in principle, between the African slave trade and American slavery: That every American citizen who retains a human being in involuntary bondage as his property, is, according to Scripture (Ex. xxi. 16), a man-stealer:

That the slaves ought instantly to be set free, and brought under the protection of law:

That if they had lived from the time of Pharaoh down to the present period, and had been entailed through successive generations, their right to be free could never been alienated, but their claims would have constantly risen in solemnity:

That all those laws which are now in force, admitting the right of slavery, are therefore, before God, utterly null and void; being an audacious usurpation of the Divine prerogative, a daring infringement on the law of nature, a base overthrow of the very foundations of the social compact, a complete extinction of all the relations, endearments and obligations of mankind, and a presumptuous transgression of all the holy commandments; and that therefore they ought instantly to be abrogated.

We further believe and affirm—that all persons of color who possess the qualifications which are demanded of others, ought to be admitted forthwith to the enjoyment of the same privileges, and the exercise of the same prerogatives, as others; and that the paths of preferment, of wealth, and of intelligence, should be opened as widely to them as to persons of a white complexion.

We maintain that no compensation should be given to the planters emancipating their slaves:

Because it would be a surrender of the great fundamental principle, that man cannot hold property in man;

Because slavery is a crime, and therefore is not an article to be sold;

Because the holders of slaves are not the just proprietors of what they claim; freeing the slave is not depriving them of property, but restoring it to its rightful owner; it is not wronging the master, but righting the slave—restoring him to himself;

Because immediate and general emancipation would only destroy nominal, not real, property; it would not amputate a limb or break a bone of the slaves, but, by infusing motives into their breasts, would make them doubly valuable to the masters as free laborers; and

Because, if compensation is to be given at all, it should be given to the outraged and guiltless slaves, and not to those who have plundered and abused them.

We regard as delusive, cruel and dangerous any scheme of expatriation which pretends to aid, either directly or indirectly, in the emancipation of the slaves, or to be a substitute for the immediate and total abolition of slavery.

We fully and unanimously recognize the sovereignty of each State, to legislate exclusively on the subject of the slavery which is tolerated within its limits; we concede that Congress, under the present national compact, has no right to interfere with any of the slave States in relation to this momentous subject:

But we maintain that Congress has a right, and is solemnly bound, to suppress the domestic slave trade between the several States, and abolish slavery in those portions of our territory which the Constitution has placed under its exclusive jurisdiction.

We also maintain that there are, at the present time, the highest obligations resting upon the people of the free States to remove slavery by moral and political action, as prescribed in the Constitution of the United States. They are now living under a pledge of their tremendous physical force, to fasten the galling fetters of tyranny upon the limbs of millions in the Southern States; they are liable to be called at any moment to suppress a general insurrection of the slaves; they authorize the slaveowner to vote for three-fifths of his slaves as property, and thus enable him to perpetuate his oppression; they support a standing army at the South for its protection; and they seize the slave who has escaped into their territories, and sent him back to be tortured by an enraged master or a brutal driver. This relation to slavery is criminal, and full of danger: IT MUST BE BROKEN UP.

Done at Philadelphia, the 6th day of December, A. D. 1833.

Source: Selections from the Writings and Speeches of William Lloyd Garrison. New York: Negro Universities Press, 1968. Originally published in 1852 by R. F. Wallcut.

William Lloyd Garrison (1805–79) was a leading abolitionist.

Angelina Grimké
Appeal to the Christian Women of the South

Why appeal to *women* on this subject? *We* do not make the laws which perpetuate slavery. *No* legislative power is vested in *us; we* can do nothing to overthrow the system, even if we wished to do so. To this I reply, I know you do not make the laws, but I also know that *you are the wives and mothers, the sisters and daughters of those who do;* and if you really suppose *you* can do nothing to overthrow slavery, you are greatly mistaken. You can do much in every way: four things I will name. 1st. You can read on this subject. 2d. You can pray over this subject. 3d. You can speak on this subject. 4th. You can act on this subject. I have not placed reading before praying because I regard it more important, but because, in order to pray aright, we must understand what we are praying for; it is only then we can "pray with the understanding and the spirit also."

1. Read then on the subject of slavery. . . .

2. Pray over this subject. . . .

3. Speak on this subject. . . .

4. Act on this subject. Some of you *own* slaves yourselves. If you believe slavery is *sinful,* set them at liberty, "undo the heavy burdens and let the oppressed go free." If they wish to remain with you, pay them wages, if not let them leave you. Should they remain teach them, and have them taught the common branches of an English education; they have minds and those minds, *ought to be improved.* So precious a talent as intellect, never was given to be wrapt in a napkin and buried in the earth. It is the *duty* of all, as far as they can, to improve their own mental faculties, because we are commanded to love God with *all our minds,* as well as with all our hearts, and we commit a great sin, if we *forbid or prevent* that cultivation of the mind in others, which would enable them to perform this duty. Teach your servants then to read &c, and encourage them to believe it is their *duty* to learn, if it were only that they might read the Bible.

But some of you will say, we can neither free our slaves nor teach them to read, for the laws of our state forbid it. Be not surprised when I say such wicked laws *ought to be no barrier* in the way of your duty. . . .

But some of you may say, if we do free our slaves, they will be taken up and sold, therefore there will be no use in doing it. Peter and John might just as well have said, we will not preach the gospel, for if we do, we shall be taken up and put in prison, therefore there will be no use in our preaching. *Consequences,* my friends, belong no more to *you,* than they did to these apostles. Duty is ours and events are God's. If you think slavery is sinful, all *you* have to do is to set your slaves at liberty, do all you can to protect them, and in humble faith and fervent prayer, commend them to your common Father. He can take care of them; but if for wise purposes he sees fit to allow them to be sold, this will afford you an op-portunity of testifying openly, wherever you go, against the crime of *manstealing.* Such an act will be *clear robbery,* and if exposed, might, under the Divine direc-tion, do the cause of Emancipation more good, than anything that could hap-pen, for, "He makes even the wrath of man to praise him, and the remainder of wrath he will restrain." . . .

But you may say we are *women,* how can our hearts endure persecution? And why not? Have not women stood up in all the dignity and strength of moral courage to be the leaders of the people, and to bear a faithful testimony for the truth whenever the providence of God has called them to do so? . . .

And what, I would ask in conclusion, have *women* done for the great and glori-ous cause of Emancipation? Who wrote that pamphlet which moved the heart of Wilberforce to pray over the wrongs, and his tongue to plead the cause of the op-pressed African? It was a *woman,* Elizabeth Heyrick. Who labored assiduously to keep the sufferings of the slave continually before the British public? They were *women.* And how did they do it? By their needles, paint brushes and pens, by speaking the truth, and petitioning Parliament for the abolition of slavery. And what was the effect of their labors? Read it in the Emancipation bill of Great Brit-ain. Read it, in the present state of her West India Colonies. Read it, in the im-pulse which has been given to the cause of freedom, in the United States of America. Have English women then done so much for the negro, and shall American women do nothing? Oh no! Already are there sixty female Anti-Slavery Societies in operation. These are doing just what the English women did, telling the story of the colored man's wrongs, praying for his deliverance, and presenting his kneeling image constantly before the public eye on bags and needle-books, card-racks, pen-wipers, pin-cushion, &c. Even the children of the north are in-scribing on their handy work, "May the points of our needles prick the slavehold-er's conscience." Some of the reports of these Societies exhibit not only consider-able talent, but a deep sense of religious duty, and a determination to persevere through evil as well as good report, until every scourge, and every shackle, is bur-ied under the feet of the manumitted slave. . . .

The *women of the South can overthrow* this horrible system of oppression and cruelty, licentiousness and wrong. Such appeals to your legislatures would be ir-resistible, for there is something in the heart of man which *will bend under moral suasion.* There is a swift witness for truth in his bosom, which *will respond to truth* when it is uttered with calmness and dignity. If you could obtain but six signa-tures to such a petition in only one state, I would say, send up that petition, and be not in the least discouraged by the scoffs and jeers of the heartless, or the reso-lution of the house to lay it on the table. It will be a great thing if the subject can be introduced into your legislatures in any way, even by *women,* and *they will* be the most likely to introduce it there in the best possible manner, as a matter of *morals* and *religion,* not of expediency or politics. You may petition, too, the different ecclesiastical bodies of the slave states. Slavery must be attacked with the whole power of truth and the sword of the spirit. You must take it up on *Christian* ground, and fight against it with Christian weapons, whilst your feet are shod with the preparation of the gospel of peace. And *you are now* loudly called upon by the cries of the widow and the orphan, to arise and gird yourselves for this great moral conflict, with the whole armour of righteousness upon the right hand and on the left.

Source: The Anti-Slavery Examiner 1, no. 2 (September 1836): 16–26.

Angelina E. Grimké (1805–79) was an abolitionist and women's rights pioneer.

Minorities

As should already be clear, women in the early nineteenth century did not just stay at home and care for their families. They were actively involved in reform movements throughout the country, and not just in those directed at women. At the same time, women were also arguing for their rights and asserting their equality.

African Americans were also active in shaping American politics and culture. Benjamin Banneker (1731–1806), a respected astronomer and mathematician who helped the planner of the District of Columbia lay out the site, had a continuing correspondence with Thomas Jefferson. In the letter included here he argues that African Americans are intellectually equal to others.

WOMEN

Judith Sargent Murray
On the Equality of the Sexes

If upon mature consideration we adopt the idea, that nature is . . . partial in her distributions? Is it indeed a fact, that she hath yielded to one half of the human species so unquestionable a mental superiority? I know that to both sexes elevated understandings, and the reverse, are common. But, suffer me to ask, in what the minds of females are so notoriously deficient, or unequal. May not the intellectual powers be ranged under their four heads—imagination, reason, memory and judgement. The province of imagination has long since been surrendered up to us, and we have been crowned undoubted sovereigns of the regions of fancy. Invention is perhaps the most arduous effort of the mind; this branch of imagination hath been particularly ceded to us, and we have been time out of mind invested with the creative faculty. Observe the variety of fashions (here I bar the contemptuous smile) which distinguish and adorn the female world; how continually are they changing, insomuch that they almost render the whole man's assertion problematical, and we are ready to say, *there is something new under the sun.* Now, what a playfulness, what an exuberance of fancy, what strength of inventive imagination, doth this continual variation discover? Again, it hath been observed, that is the turpitude of the conduct of our sex, hath been ever so enormous, so extremely ready are we that the very first thought presents us with an apology so plausible, as to produce our actions even in an amiable light. Another instance of our creative powers, is our talent for slander; how ingenious are we at inventive scandal? what a formidable story can we in a moment fabricate merely from the force of a prolifick imagination? how many reputations, in the fertile brain of a female, have been utterly despoiled? how industrious are we at improving a hint? suspicion how easily do we convert into conviction, and conviction, embellished by the power of eloquence, stalks abroad to the surprise and confusion of unsuspecting innocence. Perhaps it will be asked if I furnish these facts as instances of excellency in our sex. Certainly not; but as proofs of a creative faculty, of a lively imagination. Assuredly great activity of mind is thereby discovered, and was this activity properly directed, what beneficial effects would follow. Is the needle and kitchen sufficient to employ the operations of a soul thus organized? I should conceive not. Nay, it is a truth that those very departments leave the intelligent principle vacant, and at liberty for speculation. Are we deficient in reason? We can only reason from what we know, and if opportunity of acquiring knowledge hath been denied us, the inferiority of our sex cannot fairly be deduced from thence. Memory, I believe, will be allowed us in common, since every one's experience must testify, that a loquacious old woman is as frequently met with, as a communicative old man; their subjects are alike drawn from the fund of other times, and the transactions of their youth, or of maturer life, entertain, or perhaps fatigue you, in the evening of their lives. "But our judgment is not so strong—we do not distinguish so well." Yet it may be questioned, from what doth this superiority, in this discrimination faculty of the soul, proceed. May we not trace its source in the difference of education, and continued advantages? Will it be said that the judgment of a male of two years old, is more sage than that of a female's of the same age? I believe the reverse is generally observed to be true. But from that period what partiality! how is the one exalted and the other depressed, by the contrary modes of education which are adopted! the one is taught to aspire, and the other is early confined and limited. As their years increase, the sister must be wholly domesticated, while the brother is led by the hand through all the flowery paths of science. Grant that their minds are by nature equal, yet who shall wonder at the *apparent* superiority, if indeed custom becomes *second nature;* nay if it taketh place of nature, and that it doth the experience of each day well evince. At length arrived at womanhood, the uncultivated fair one feels a void, which the employments allotted her are by no means capable of filling. What can she do? to books, she may not apply; or if she doth, *to those only of the novel kind,* lest she merit the appellation of a *learned lady;* and what ideas have been affixed to this term, the observation of many can testify. Fashion, scandal and sometimes what is still more reprehensible, are then called in to her relief; and who can say to what lengths the liberties she takes may proceed. Meantime she herself is most unhappy; she feels the want of a cultivated mind. Is she single, she in vain seeks to fill up time from sexual employments or amusements. Is she united to a person whose soul nature made equal to her own, education hath set him so far above her, that in those entertainments which are productive of such rational felicity, she is qualified to accompany him. She experiences a mortifying consciousness of inferiority, which embitters every enjoyment. Doth the person to whom her adverse fate hath consigned her, possess a mind incapable of improvement, she is equally wretched, in being so closely connected with an individual whom she cannot but despise. Now, was she permitted the same instructors as her brother, (with an eye however to their particular departments) for the employment of a rational mind an ample field would be opened. In astronomy she might catch a glimpse of the immensity of the Deity, and thence she would form amazing conceptions of the august and supreme Intelligence. In geography she would admire Jehovah in the midst of his benevolence; thus adapting this globe to the various wants and amusements of its inhabitants. In natural philosophy she would adore the infinite majesty of heaven, clothed in condescension; and as she traversed the reptile world, she would hail the goodness of a creating God. A mind, thus filled, would have little room for the trifles with which our sex are, with too much justice, accused of amusing themselves, and they would thus be rendered fit companions for those, who should one day wear them as their crown. Fashions, in their variety, would then give place to conjecturers, which might perhaps conduce to the improvement of the literary world; and there would be no leisure for slander or detraction. Reputation would not then be blasted, but serious speculations would occupy the lively imaginations of the sex. Unnecessary visits would be precluded, and that custom would only be indulged by way of relaxation, or to answer the demands of consanguinity and friendship. Females would become discreet, their judgments would be invigorated, and their partners for life being circumspectly chosen an unhappy Hymen would then be as rare, as is now the reverse.

Will it be urged that those acquirements would supersede our domestick duties, I answer that every requisite in female economy is easily attained; and, with truth I can add, that when once attained, they require no further *mental atten-*

tion. Nay, while we are pursuing the needle, or the superintendency of the family, I repeat, that our minds are at full liberty of reflection; that imagination may exert itself in full vigor; and that if a just foundation is early laid, our ideas will then be worthy of rational beings. If we were industrious we might easily find time to arrange them upon paper, or should avocations press too hard for such an indulgence, the hours allotted for conversation would at least become more refined and rational. Should it still be vociferated, "Your domestick employments are sufficient"—I would calmly ask, is it reasonable, that a candidate for immortality, for the joys of heaven, an intelligent being, who is to spend an eternity in contemplating the works of Deity, should at present be so degraded, as to be allowed no other ideas, than those which are suggested by the mechanism of a pudding, or the sewing of the seams of a garment? Pity that all such censurers of female improvement do not go one step further, and deny their future existence; to be consistent they surely ought.

Yes, ye lordly, ye haughty sex, our souls are by nature *equal* to yours; the same breath of God animates, enlivens, and invigorates us; and that we are not fallen lower than yourselves, let those witness who have greatly towered above the various discouragements by which they have been so heavily oppressed; and though I am unacquainted with the list of celebrated characters on either side, yet from the observations I have made in the contracted circle in which I have moved, I dare confidently believe, that from the commencement of time to the present day, there hath been as many females, as males, who, by the *mere force of natural powers,* have merited the crown of applause; who *thus unassisted,* have seized the wreath of fame. I know there are those who assert, that as the animal powers of the one sex are superior, of course their mental faculties also must be stronger; thus attributing strength of mind to the transient organization of this earth worn tenement. But if this reasoning is just, man must be content to yield the palm to many of the brute creation, since by not a few of his breathren of the field, he is far surpassed in bodily strength. Moreover, was this argument admitted, it would prove too much, for occular demonstration evinceth, that there are many robust masculine ladies, and effeminate gentlemen. Yet I fancy that Mr. Pope, though clogged with an enervated body, and distinguished by a diminutive stature, could nevertheless lay claim to greatness of soul; and perhaps there are many other instances which might be adduced to combat so unphilosophical an opinion. Do we not often see that when the clay built tabernacle is well nigh dissolved, when it is just ready to mingle with the parent-soil, the immortal inhabitant aspire to, and even attaineth heights the most sublime, and which were before wholly unexplored. Besides, were we to grant that animal strength proved anything, taking into consideration the accustomed impartiality of nature, we should be induced to imagine, that she had invested the female mind with superior strength as an equivalent for the bodily powers of man. But waving this however palpable advantage, for *equality* only, we wish to contend.

Source: *The Massachusetts Magazine,* March 1790.

Judith Sargent Murray (1751–1820) was the author of serious of essays in *The Massachusetts Magazine* (1792–94) and two plays produced in Boston.

AFRICAN AMERICANS

Benjamin Banneker
Letter to Thomas Jefferson, 1791

I am fully sensible of that freedom, which I take with you in the present occasion; a liberty which seemed to me scarcely allowable, when I reflected on that distinguished and dignified station in which you stand, and the almost general prejudice and prepossession, which is so prevalent in the world against those of my complexion.

I suppose it is a truth too well attested to you, to need a proof here, that we are a race of beings, who have long labored under the abuse and censure of the world; that we have long been looked upon with an eye of contempt; and that we have long been considered rather as brutish than human, and scarcely capable of mental endowments.

Sir, I hope I may safely admit, in consequence of that report which hath reached me, that you are a man less inflexible in sentiments of this nature, than many others; that you are measurably friendly, and well disposed towards us; and that you are willing and ready to lend your aid and assistance to our relief, from those many distresses, and numerous calamities, to which we are reduced.

Now Sir, if this is founded in truth, I apprehend you will embrace every opportunity, to eradicate that train of absurd and false ideas and opinions, which so generally prevails with respect to us; and that your sentiments are concurrent with mine, which are, that one universal Father hath given being to us all; and that he hath not only made us all of one flesh, but that he hath also, without partiality, afforded us all the same sensations and endowed us all with the same faculties; and that however variable we may be in society or religion, however diversified in situation or color, we are all in the same family and stand in the same relation to him. Sir, if these are sentiments of which you are fully persuaded, I hope you cannot but acknowledge, that it is the indispensable duty of those, who maintain for themselves the rights of human nature, and who possess the obligations of Christianity, to extend their power and influence to the relief of every part of the human race, from whatever burden or oppression they may unjustly labor under; and this, I apprehend, a full conviction of the truth and obligation of these principles should lead all to.

Sir, I have long been convinced, that if your love for yourselves, and for those inestimable laws, which preserved to you the rights of human nature, was founded on sincerity, you could not but be solicitous, that every individual, of whatever rank or distinction, might with you equally enjoy the blessings thereof; neither could you rest satisfied short of the most active effusion of your exertions, in order for the promotion from any state of degradation, to which the unjustifiable cruelty and barbarism of men may have reduced them.

Sir, I freely and cheerfully acknowledge, that I am of the African race, and in that color which is natural to them of the deepest dye; and it is under a sense of the most profound gratitude to the Supreme Ruler of the Universe, that I now confess to you, that I am not under that state of tyrannical thraldom, and inhuman captivity, to which too many of my brethren are doomed, but that I have abundantly tasted of the fruition of those blessings, which proceed from that free and unequalled liberty with which you are favored; and which, I hope, you will willingly allow you have mercifully received, from the immediate hand of that Being, from whom proceedeth every good and perfect Gift.

Sir, suffer me to recall to your mind that time, in which the arms and tyranny of the British crown were exerted, with every powerful effort, in order to reduce you to a state of servitude; look back, I entreat you, on the variety of dangers to which you were exposed; reflect on that time, in which every human aid appeared unavailable, and in which even hope and fortitude wore the aspect of inability to the conflict, and you cannot but be led to a serious and grateful sense of your miraculous and providential preservation; you cannot but acknowledge, that the present freedom and tranquility which you enjoy have mercifully received, and that it is the peculiar blessing of Heaven.

This, Sir, was a time when you clearly saw into the injustice of a state of slavery, and in which you had just apprehensions of the horror of its condition. It was now that your abhorrence thereof was so excited, that you publicly held forth this true and invaluable doctrine, which is worthy to be recorded and remembered in all succeeding ages: "We hold these truths to be self-evident, that all men are created equal; that they are endowed by their Creator with certain unalienable rights, and that among these are, life, liberty, and the pursuit of happiness."

Here was a time, in which your tender feelings for yourselves had engaged you thus to declare, you were then impressed with proper ideas of the great violation of liberty, and the free possession of those blessings, to which you were entitled by nature; but, Sir, how pitiable is it to reflect, that although you were so fully convinced of the benevolence of the Father of Mankind, and of his equal and impartial distribution of these rights and privileges, which he hath conferred upon them, that you should at the same time counteract his mercies, in detaining by fraud and violence so numerous a part of my brethren, under groaning captivity, and cruel oppression, that you should at the same time be found guilty of that most criminal act, which you professedly detested in others, with respect to yourselves,

I suppose that your knowledge of the situation of my brethren, is too extensive to need a recital here; neither shall I presume to prescribe methods by which they may be relieved, otherwise than by recommending to you and all others, to wean yourselves from those narrow prejudices which you have imbibed with respect to them, and as Job proposed to his friends, "put your soul in their souls' stead"; thus shall your hearts be enlarged with kindness and benevolence towards them; and thus shall you need neither the direction of myself or others, in what manner to proceed herein.

Source: A Documentary History of the Negro People in the United States. Edited by Herbert Aptheker. New York: Citadel, 1951.

Benjamin Banneker (1731–1806) was an African-American astronomer.

INDIANS

During this period, Indians were being expelled from U.S. territory, and President Andrew Jackson (1767–1845) justified this expulsion. Jackson, perhaps best known in this context for his statement that "the only good Indian is a dead Indian," argues for forcing Indians to leave their long-established homes.

Andrew Jackson
Argument for Indian Removal

I informed the Indians inhabiting parts of Georgia and Alabama that their attempt to establish an independent government would not be countenanced by the Executive of the United States, and advised them to emigrate beyond the Mississippi or submit to the laws of those States.

Our conduct toward these people is deeply interesting to our national character. Their present condition, contrasted with what they once were, makes a most powerful appeal to our sympathies. Our ancestors found them the uncontrolled possessors of these vast regions. By persuasion and force they have been made to retire from river to river and from mountain to mountain, until some of the tribes have become extinct and others have left but remnants to preserve for awhile their once terrible names. Surrounded by the whites with their arts of civilization, which by destroying the resources of the savage doom him to weakness and decay, the fate of the Mohegan, the Narragansett, and the Delaware is fast overtaking the Choctaw, the Cherokee, and the Creek. That this fate surely awaits them if they remain within the limits of the States does not admit of a doubt. Humanity and national honor demand that every effort should be made to avert so great a calamity. It is too late to inquire whether it was just in the United States to include them and their territory within the bounds of new States, whose limits they could control. That step can not be retraced. A State can not be dismembered by Congress or restricted in the exercise of her constitutional power. But the people of those States and of every State, actuated by feelings of justice and a regard for our national honor, submit to you the interesting question whether something can not be done, consistently with the rights of the States, to preserve this much-injured race.

As a means of effecting this end I suggest for your consideration the propriety of setting apart an ample district west of the Mississippi, and without the limits of any State of Territory now formed, to be guaranteed to the Indian tribes as long as they shall occupy it, each tribe having a distinct control over the portion designated for its use. There they may be secured in the enjoyment of governments of their own choice, subject to no other control from the United States than such as may be necessary to preserve peace on the frontier and between the several tribes. There the benevolent may endeavor to teach them, to raise up an interesting commonwealth, destined to perpetuate the race and to attest the humanity and justice of this Government.

This emigration should be voluntary, for it would be as cruel as unjust to compel the aborigines to abandon the graves of their fathers and seek a home in a distant land. But they should be distinctly informed that if they remain within the limits of the States they must be subject to their laws. In return for their obedience as individuals they will without doubt be protected in the enjoyment of those possessions which they have improved by their industry. But it seems to me visionary to suppose that in this state of things claims can be allowed on tracts of country on which they have neither dwelt nor made improvements, merely because they have seen them from the mountain or passed them in the chase. Submitting to the laws of the States, and receiving, like other citizens, protection in their persons and property, they will ere long become merged in the mass of our population.

Source: A Compilation of the Messages and Papers of the Presidents. Edited by James D. Richardson, 2:456–59. Washington: National Bureau of Literature and Art, 1908.

Andrew Jackson (1767–1845) was the seventh president of the United States.

CHAPTER 6

The Civil War Debates, 1841–1865

✳ ✳ ✳

Although there were issues other than slavery and the relative power of the states versus the national government during the period before the Civil War — or, as it is usually described in the South, the War Between the States — these issues dominated at the time and perhaps seem even more central in retrospect.

Slavery

Slavery was addressed directly both by those in favor of it, such as George Fitzhugh (1806–81), and by those opposed to it, such as Henry Garnet (1815–82) and Abraham Lincoln (1808–65). Fitzhugh was one of the few truly articulate advocates of slavery who was willing to write directly in its defense; most defenders of slavery did so indirectly by defending states' rights, as did John C. Calhoun (1782–1850).

Fitzhugh argued that the slave was better off than the northern factory worker and that slavery was a natural condition for inferior peoples. Calhoun rarely even mentioned slavery directly, but the purpose of his argument was to defend slavery through the defense of the South.

Garnet was an African American who was quite unusual in actually calling for a revolt of the slaves in the South and reminding them of previous such revolts. It is striking that there is not even the slightest suggestion in his essay that the slaves could expect active support in their revolution from free African Americans or whites from the North.

The most famous of the African-American abolitionists was Frederick Douglass (1817?-95), who escaped from slavery and became a well-known and respected lecturer and writer. In the essay reprinted here he argues that African Americans need to help themselves as well as being helped by whites.

George Fitzhugh
Cannibals All!
The Universal Trade

We are all, North and South, engaged in the White Slave Trade, and he who succeeds best is esteemed most respectable. It is far more cruel than the Black Slave Trade, because it exacts more of its slaves, and neither protects nor governs them. We boast that it exacts more when we say, "that the *profits* made from employing free labor are greater than those from slave labor," are the amount of the products of such labor, which the employer, by means of the command which capital or skill gives him, takes away, exacts, or "exploitates" from the free laborer. The profits of slave labor are that portion of the products of such labor which the power of the master enables him to appropriate. These profits are less, because the master allows the slave to retain a larger share of the results of his own labor than do the employers of free labor. But we not only boast that the White Slave Trade is more exacting and fraudulent (in fact, though not in intention) than Black Slavery; but we also boast that it is more cruel, in leaving the laborer to take care of himself and family out of the pittance which skill or capital have allowed him to retain. When the day's labor is ended, he is free, but is overburdened with the cares of family and household, which make his freedom an empty and delusive mockery. But his employer is really free, and may enjoy the profits made by others' labor, without a care, or a trouble, as to their well-being. The negro slave is free, too, when the labors of the day are over, and free in mind as well as body; for the master provides food, raiment, house, fuel, and everything else necessary to the physical well-being of himself and family. The master's labors commence just when the slave's end. No wonder men should prefer white slavery to capital, to negro slavery, since it is more profitable, and is free from all the cares and labors of black slave-holding. . . .

Probably, you are a lawyer, or a merchant, or a doctor, who has made by your business fifty thousand dollars, and retired to live on your capital. But, mark! not to spend your capital. That would be vulgar, disreputable, criminal. That would be, to live by your own labor; for your capital is your amassed labor. That would be to do as common working men do; for they take the pittance which their employers leave them to live on. They live by labor; for they exchange the results of their own labor for the products of other people's labor. It is, no doubt, an honest, vulgar way of living but not at all a respectable way. The respectable way is to make other people work for you, and to pay them nothing for so doing—and to have no concern about them after their work is done. Hence, white slave-holding is much more respectable than negro slavery—for the master works nearly as hard for the negro as he for the master. But you, my virtuous, respectable reader, exact three thousand dollars per annum from white labor (for your income is the product of white labor) and make not one cent of return in any form. You retain your capital, and never labor, and yet live in luxury on the labor of others. Capital commands labor, as the master does the slave. Neither pays for labor; but the master permits the slave to retain a larger allowance from the proceeds of his own labor, and hence "free labor is cheaper than slave labor." You, with the command over labor which your capital gives you, are a slave owner—a master, without the obligations of a master. They who work for you, who create your income, are slaves, without the rights of slaves. Slaves without a master! Whilst you were engaged in amassing your capital, in seeking to become independent, you were in the White Slave Trade. To become independent is to be able to make other people support you, without being obliged to labor for *them*. Now, what man in society is not seeking to attain this situation? He who attains it is a slave owner, in the worst sense. He who is in pursuit of it is engaged in the slave trade. You, reader, belong to the one or other class. The men without property, in free society, are theoretically in a worse condition than slaves. Practically, their condition corresponds with this theory, as history and statistics everywhere demonstrate. The capitalists, in free society, live in ten times the luxury and show that Southern masters do, because the slaves to capital work harder and cost less than negro slaves.

The negro slaves of the South are the happiest, and, in some sense, the freest people in the world. The children and the aged and infirm work not at all, and yet have all the comforts and necessaries of life provided for them. They enjoy liberty, because they are oppressed neither by care nor labor. The women do little hard work, and are protected from the despotism of their husbands by their masters. The negro men and stout boys work, on the average, in good weather, not more than nine hours a day. The balance of their time is spent in perfect abandon. Besides, they have their Sabbaths and holidays. White men, with so much of license and liberty, would die of ennui; but negroes luxuriate in corporeal and mental repose. With their faces upturned to the sun, they can sleep at any hour; and quiet sleep is the greatest of human enjoyments. "Blessed be the man who invented sleep." 'Tis happiness in itself—and results from contentment with the present, and confident assurance of the future. We do not know whether free laborers ever sleep. They are fools to do so; for, whilst they sleep, the wily and watchful capitalist is devising means to ensnare and exploitate them. The free laborer must work or starve. He is more of a slave than the negro, because he works longer and harder for less allowance than the slave, and has no holiday, because the cares of life with him begin when its labors end. He has no liberty, and not a single right. We know, 'tis often said, air and water are common property, which all have equal right to participate and enjoy; but this is utterly false. The appropriation of the lands carries with it the appropriation of all on or above the lands, *usque ad coelum, aut ad inferos* [even to heaven or to hell]. A man cannot breathe the air without a place to breathe it from, and all places are appropriated. All water is private property "to the middle of the stream," except the ocean, and that is not fit to drink.

Free laborers have not a thousandth part of the rights and liberties of negro slaves. Indeed, they have not a single liberty, unless it be the right or liberty to die. But the reader may think that he and other capitalists and employers are freer than negro slaves. Your capital would soon vanish, if you dared indulge in the liberty and abandon of negroes. You hold your wealth and position by the tenure of constant watchfulness, care, and circumspection. You never labor; but you are never free. . . .

Source: Cannibals All! or Slaves Without Masters. By George Fitzhugh. Richmond, Va., 1857.

George Fitzhugh (1806–81) was a proslavery writer.

Henry Garnet
A Memorial Discourse

Two hundred and twenty-seven years ago, the first of our injured race were brought to the shores of America. They came not with glad spirits to select their homes in the New World. They came not with their own consent, to find an unmolested enjoyment of the blessings of this fruitful soil. The first dealings they had with men calling themselves Christians, exhibited to them the worst features of corrupt and sordid hearts; and convinced them that no cruelty is too great, no villainy and no robbery too abhorrent for even enlightened men to perform, when influenced by avarice and lust. Neither did they come flying upon the wings of Liberty, to a land of freedom. But they came with broken hearts, from their beloved native land, and were doomed to unrequited toil and deep degradation. Nor did the evil of their bondage end at their emancipation by death. Succeeding generations inherited their chains, and millions have come from eternity into time, and have returned again to the world of spirits, cursed and ruined by American slavery.

The propagators of the system, or their immediate ancestors, very soon discovered its growing evil, and its tremendous wickedness, and secret promises were made to destroy it. The gross inconsistency of a people holding slaves, who had themselves "ferried o'er the wave" for freedom's sake, was too apparent to be entirely overlooked. The voice of Freedom cried, "Emancipate yourselves." Humanity supplicated with tears for the deliverance of the children of Africa. Wisdom urged her solemn plea. The bleeding captive plead his innocence, and pointed to Christianity who stood weeping at the cross. Jehovah frowned upon the nefarious institution, and thunderbolts, red with vengeance, struggled to leap forth to blast the guilty wretches who maintained it. But all was in vain. Slavery had stretched its dark wings of death over the land, the Church stood silently by—the priests prophesied falsely, and the people loved to have it so. Its throne is established, and now it reigns triumphant.

Nearly three millions of your fellow-citizens are prohibited by law and public opinion, (which in this country is stronger than law,) from reading the Book of Life. Your intellect has been destroyed as much as possible, and every ray of light they have attempted to shut out from your minds. The oppressors themselves have become involved in the ruin. They have become weak, sensual, and rapacious—they have cursed you—they have cursed themselves—they have cursed the earth which they have trod.

The colonists threw the blame upon England. They said that the mother country entailed the evil upon them, and that they would rid themselves of it if they could. The world thought they were sincere, and the philanthropic pitied them. But time soon tested their sincerity.

In a few years the colonists grew strong, and severed themselves from the British Government. Their independence was declared, and they took their station among the sovereign powers of the earth. The declaration was a glorious document. Sages admired it, and the patriotic of every nation reverenced the God-like sentiments which it contained. When the power of Government returned to their hands, did they emancipate the slaves? No; they rather added new links to our chains. Were they ignorant of the principles of Liberty? Certainly they were not. The sentiments of their revolutionary orators fell in burning eloquence upon their hearts, and with one voice they cried, Liberty or Death. Oh what a sentence was that! It ran from soul to soul like electric fire, and nerved the arm of thousands to fight in the holy cause of Freedom. Among the diversity of opinions that are entertained in regard to physical resistance, there are but a few found to gainsay that stern declaration. We are among those who do not. Slavery! How much misery is comprehended in that single word. What mind is there that does not shrink from its direful effects? Unless the image of God be obliterated from the soul, all men cherish the love of Liberty. The nice discerning political economist does not regard the sacred right more than the untutored African who roams in the wilds of Congo. Nor has the one more right to the full enjoyment of his freedom than the other. In every man's mind the good seeds of liberty are planted, and he who brings his fellow down so low, as to make him contented with a condition of slavery, commits the highest crime against God and man. Brethren, your oppressors aim to do this. They endeavor to make you as much like brutes as possible. When they have blinded the eyes of your mind—when they have embittered the sweet waters of life—then, and not till then, has American slavery done its perfect work. . . .

Brethren, it is as wrong for your lordly oppressors to keep you in slavery, as it was for the man thief to steal our ancestors from the coast of Africa. You should therefore now use the same manner of resistance, as would have been just in our ancestors when the bloody foot-prints of the first remorseless soul-thief was placed upon the shores of our fatherland. The humblest peasant is as free in the sight of God as the proudest monarch that ever swayed a sceptre. Liberty is a spirit sent out from God, and like its great Author, is no respecter of persons.

Brethren, the time has come when you must act for yourselves. It is an old and true saying that, "if hereditary bondmen would be free, they must themselves strike the blow". . . .

Tell them in language which they cannot misunderstand, of the exceeding sinfulness of slavery, and of a future judgment, and of the righteous retributions of an indignant God. Inform them that all you desire is FREEDOM, and that nothing else will suffice. Do this, and for ever after cease to toil for the heartless tyrants, who give you no other reward but stripes and abuse. If they then commence the work of death, they, and not you, will be responsible for the consequences. You had better all *die immediately,* than live slaves and entail your wretchedness upon your posterity. If you would be free in this generation, here is your only hope. However much you and all of us may desire it, there is not much hope of redemption without the shedding of blood. If you must bleed, let it all come at once—rather *die freemen, than live to be slaves.* . . .

Fellow men! Patient sufferers! behold your dearest rights crushed to the earth! See your sons murdered, and your wives, mothers and sisters doomed to prostitution. In the name of the merciful God, and by all that life is worth, let it no longer be a debatable question whether it is better to choose *Liberty or death.* . . .

Brethren, arise, arise! Strike for your lives and liberties. Now is the day and the hour. Let every slave throughout the land do this, and the days of slavery are numbered. You cannot be more oppressed than you have been—you cannot suffer greater cruelties than you have already. *Rather die free-men than live to be slaves.* Remember that you are FOUR MILLIONS!. . .

Let your motto be resistance! *resistance!* RESISTANCE! No oppressed people have ever secured their liberty without resistance. What kind of resistance you had better make, you must decide by the circumstances that surround you, and according to the suggestion of expediency. Brethren, adieu! Trust in the living God. Labor for the peace of the human race, and remember that you are FOUR MILLIONS.

Source: A Memorial Discourse. By Henry Garnet. Philadelphia, 1865.

Henry Garnet (1815–82) was an African-American minister who had been born a slave and was active in the abolitionist movement.

Frederick Douglass
What Are the Colored People Doing for Themselves?

The present is a time when every colored man in the land should bring this important question home to his own heart. It is not enough to know that white men and women are nobly devoting themselves to our cause; we should know what is being done among ourselves. That our white friends have done, and are still doing, a great and good work for us, is a fact which ought to excite in us sentiments of the profoundest gratitude; but it must never be forgotten that when they have exerted all their energies, devised every scheme, and done all they can do in asserting our rights, proclaiming our wrongs, and rebuking our foes, their labor is lost—yea, worse than lost, unless we are found in the faithful discharge of our anti-slavery duties. If there be one evil spirit among us, for the casting out of which we pray more earnestly than another, it is that lazy, mean and cowardly spirit, that robs us of all manly self-reliance, and teaches us to depend upon others for the accomplishment of that which we should achieve with our own hands. Our white friends can and are rapidly removing the barriers to our improvement, which themselves have set up; but the main work must be commenced, carried on, and concluded by ourselves. While in no circumstances should we undervalue or fail to appreciate the self-sacrificing efforts of our friends, it should never be lost sight of, that our destiny, for good or for evil, for time and for eternity, is, by an all-wise God, committed to us; and that all the helps or hindrances with which we may meet on earth, can never release us from this high and heaven-imposed responsibility. It is evident that we can be improved and elevated only just so fast and far as we shall improve and elevate ourselves. We must rise or fall, succeed or fail, by our own merits. If we are careless and unconcerned about our own rights and interests, it is not within the power of all the earth combined to raise us from our present degraded condition. . . .

We say the present is a time when every colored man should ask himself the question, What am I doing to elevate and improve my condition, and that of my brethren at large? . . .

It is a doctrine held by many good men, in Europe as well as in America, that every oppressed people will gain their rights just as soon as they prove themselves worthy of them; and although we may justly object to the extent to which this doctrine is carried, especially in reference to ourselves as a people, it must still be evident to all that there is a great truth in it.

One of the first things necessary to prove the colored man worthy of equal freedom, is an earnest and persevering effort on his part to gain it. We deserve no earthly or heavenly blessing, for which we are unwilling to labor. For our part, we despise a freedom and equality obtained for us by others, and for which we have been unwilling to labor. A man who will not labor to gain his rights, is a man who would not, if he had them, prize and defend them. What is the use of standing a man on his feet, if, when we let him go, his head is again brought to the pavement? Look out for ourselves as we will—beg and pray to our white friends for assistance as much as we will—and that assistance may come, and come at the needed time; but unless we, the colored people of America, shall set about the work of our own regeneration and improvement, we are doomed to drag on in our present miserable and degraded condition for ages. Would that we could speak to every colored man, woman and child in the land, and, with the help of Heaven, we would thunder into their ears their duties and responsibilities, until a spirit should be roused among them, never to be lulled till the last chain is broken. . . .

What we, the colored people, want, is *character,* and this nobody can give us. . . . We must get character for ourselves, as a people. A change in our political condition would do very little for us without this. Character is the important thing, and without it we must continue to be marked for degradation and stamped with the brand of inferiority. With character, we shall be powerful. Nothing can harm us when we get character. . . .

The fact that we are limited and circumscribed, ought rather to incite us to a more vigorous and persevering use of the elevating means within our reach, than to dishearten us. The means of education, though not so free and open to us as to white persons, are nevertheless at our command to such an extent as to make education possible; and these, thank God, are increasing. Let us educate our children, even though it should us subject to a coarser and scantier diet, and disrobe us of our few fine garments. "For the want of knowledge we are killed all the day." Get wisdom—get understanding, is a peculiarly valuable exhortation to us, and the compliance with it is our only hope in this land.—It is idle, a hollow mockery, for us to pray to God to break the oppressor's power, while we neglect the means of knowledge which will give us the ability to break this power.—God will help us when we help ourselves. Our oppressors have divested us of many valuable blessings and facilities for improvement and elevation; but, thank heaven, they have not yet been able to take from us the privilege of being honest, industrious, sober and intelligent. We may read and understand—we may speak and write—we may expose our wrongs—we may appeal to the sense of justice yet alive in the public mind, and by an honest, upright life, we may at last wring from a reluctant public the all-important confession, that we are men, worthy men, good citizens, good Christians, and ought to be treated as such.

Source: *The North Star,* July 14, 1848.

Frederick Douglass (1817?-95) was an orator and journalist. Born a slave, he taught himself to read and write and escaped when he was twenty-one.

State Power and National Power

The other central issue before the Civil War was a continuation of the long-standing debate over the relations between the states and the central government. The following selections include what is probably the single most eloquent statement of the sense of the nation, Abraham Lincoln's Gettysburg Address, and two statements of the Southern position.

The first of the defenses of the South is from John C. Calhoun's "A Disquisition on Government." Calhoun is best known for developing a theory of "concurrent majorities," which argues that each interest in society should have a veto over legislation. The obvious problem is the definition of *interest.* Many argue, however, that the pluralist system found in the United States today informally establishes the system that Calhoun proposed. That is an exaggeration, but there certainly is a system in which interests can retard legislation, even though there is no possibility of permanently vetoing legislation.

The second defense of the South is the Constitution of the Confederate States of America, which incorporates almost all the features of the U.S. Constitution, including all of the Bill of Rights. It differs in its clear establishment of slavery and in specific limitations on the national government.

John C. Calhoun
A Disquisition on Government

In order to have a clear and just conception of the nature and object of government, it is indispensable to understand correctly what that constitution or law of our nature is, in which government originates; or, to express it more fully and accurately, — that law, without which government would not, and with which, it must necessarily exist. Without this, it is as impossible to lay any solid foundation for the science of government, as it would be to lay one for that of astronomy, without a like understanding of that constitution or law of the material world, according to which the several bodies composing the solar system mutually act on each other, and by which they are kept in their respective spheres. The first question, accordingly, to be considered is, — What is that constitution or law of our nature, without which government would not exist, and with which its existence is necessary?

In considering this, I assume, as an incontestable fact, that man is so constituted as to be a social being. His inclinations and wants, physical and moral, irresistibly impel him to associate with his kind; and he has, accordingly, never been found, in any age or country, in any state other than the social. In no other, indeed, could he exist; and in no other, — were it possible for him to exist, — could he attain to a full development of his moral and intellectual faculties, or raise himself, in the scale of being, much above the level of the brute creation.

I next assume, also, as a fact not less incontestable, that, while man is so constituted as to make the social state necessary to his existence and the full development of his faculties, this state itself cannot exist without government. The assumption rests on universal experience. In no age or country has any society or community ever been found, whether enlightened or savage, without government of some description.

Having assumed these, as unquestionable phenomena of our nature, I shall, without further remark, proceed to the investigation of the primary and important question, — What is that constitution of our nature, which, while it impels man to associate with his kind, renders it impossible for society to exist without government?

The answer will be found in the fact, (not less incontestable than either of the others,) that, while man is created for the social state, and is accordingly so formed as to feel what affects others, as well as what affects himself, he is, at the same time, so constituted as to feel more intensely what affects him indirectly, than what affects him directly through others; or, to express it differently, he is so constituted, that his direct or individual affections are stronger than his sympathetic or social feelings. I intentionally avoid the expression, *selfish* feelings, as applicable to the former; because, as commonly used, it implies an unusual excess of the individual over the social feelings, in the person to whom it is applied; and, consequently, something depraved and vicious. My object is, to exclude such inference, and to restrict the inquiry exclusively to facts in their bearings on the subject under consideration, viewed as mere phenomena appertaining to our nature, — constituted as it is; and which are as unquestionable as is that of gravitation, or any other phenomenon of the material world.

In asserting that our individual are stronger than our social feelings, it is not intended to deny that there are instances, growing out of peculiar relations, — as that of a mother and her infant, — or resulting from the force of education and habit over peculiar constitutions, in which the latter have over-powered the former; but these instances are few, and always regarded as something extraordinary. The deep impression they make, whenever they occur, is the strongest proof that they are regarded as exceptions to some general and well understood law of our nature; just as some of the minor powers of the material world are apparently to gravitation.

I might go farther, and assert this to be a phenomenon, not of our nature only, but of all animated existence, throughout its entire range, as far as our knowledge extends. It would, indeed, seem to be essentially connected with the great law of self-preservation which pervades all that feels, from man down to the lowest and most insignificant reptile or insect. In none is it stronger than in man. His social feelings may, indeed, in a state of safety and abundance, combined with high intellectual and moral culture, acquire great expansion and force; but not so great as to overpower this all-pervading and essential law of animated existence.

But that constitution of our nature which makes us feel more intensely what affects us directly than what affects us indirectly through others, necessarily leads to conflict between individuals. Each, in consequence, has a greater regard for his own safety or happiness, than for the safety or happiness of others; and, where these come in opposition, is ready to sacrifice the interests of others to his own. And hence, the tendency to a universal state of conflict, between individual and individual; accompanied by the connected passions of suspicion, jealousy, anger and revenge, — followed by insolence, fraud and cruelty; — and, if not prevented by some controlling power, ending in a state of universal discord and confusion, destructive of the social state and the ends for which it is ordained. This controlling power, wherever vested, or by whomsoever exercised, is GOVERNMENT.

It follows, then, that man is so constituted, that government is necessary to the existence of society, and society to his existence, and the perfection of his faculties. It follows, also, that government has its origin in this twofold constitution of his nature; the sympathetic or social feelings constituting the remote, — and the individual or direct, the proximate cause. . . .

Government, although intended to protect and preserve society, has itself a strong tendency to disorder and abuse of its powers, as all experience and almost every page of history testify. The cause is to be found in the same constitution of our nature which makes government indispensable. The powers which it is necessary for government to possess, in order to repress violence and preserve order, cannot execute themselves. They must be administered by men in whom, like others, the individual are stronger than the social feelings. And hence, the powers vested in them to prevent injustice and oppression on the part of others, will, if left unguarded, be by them converted into instruments to oppress the rest of the community. That, by which this is prevented, by whatever name called, is what is meant by CONSTITUTION, in its most comprehensive sense, when applied to GOVERNMENT.

Having its origin in the same principle of our nature, *constitution* stands to *government,* as *government* stands to *society;* and, as the end for which society is ordained, would be defeated without government, so that for which government is ordained would, in a great measure, be defeated without constitution. But they differ in this striking particular. There is no difficulty in forming government. It is not even a matter of choice, whether there shall be one or not. Like breathing, it is not permitted to depend on our volition. Necessity will force it on all communities in some one form or another. Very different is the case as to constitution. Instead of a matter of necessity, it is one of the most difficult tasks imposed on man to form a constitution worthy of the name; while, to form a perfect one,—one that would completely counteract the tendency of government to oppression and abuse, and hold it strictly to the great ends for which it is ordained,—has thus far exceeded human wisdom, and possibly ever will. From this, another striking difference results. Constitution is the contrivance of man, while government is of Divine ordination. Man is left to perfect what the wisdom of the Infinite ordained, as necessary to preserve the race.

With these remarks, I proceed to the consideration of the important and difficult question: How is this tendency of government to be counteracted? Or, to express it more fully,—How can those who are invested with the powers of government be prevented from employing them, as the means of aggrandizing themselves, instead of using them to protect and preserve society? It cannot be done by instituting a higher power to control the government, and those who administer it. This would be but to change the seat of authority, and to make this higher power, in reality, the government; with the same tendency, on the part of those who might control its powers, to pervert them into instruments of aggrandizement. Nor can it be done by limiting the powers of government, so as to make it too feeble to be made an instrument of abuse; for, passing by the difficulty of so limiting its powers, without creating a power higher than the government itself to enforce the observance of the limitations, it is a sufficient objection that it would, if practicable, defeat the end for which government is ordained, by making it too feeble to protect and preserve society. The powers necessary for this purpose will ever prove sufficient to aggrandize those who control it, at the expense of the rest of the community. . . .

What I propose . . . is to explain on what principles government must be formed, in order to resist, by its own interior structure,—or, to use a single term, *organism,*—the tendency to abuse of power. This structure, or organism, is what is meant by constitution, in its strict and more usual sense; and it is this which distinguishes, what are called, constitutional governments from absolute. It is in this strict and more usual sense that I propose to use the term hereafter. How government, then, must be constructed, in order to counteract, through its organism, this tendency on the part of those who make and execute the laws to oppress those subject to their operation, is the next question which claims attention.

There is but one way in which this can possibly be done; and that is, by such an organism as will furnish the ruled with the means of resisting successfully this tendency on the part of the rulers to oppression and abuse. Power can only be resisted by power,—and tendency by tendency. Those who exercise power and those subject to its exercise, — the rulers and the ruled, — stand in antagonistic relations to each other. The same constitution of our nature which leads rulers to oppress the ruled, — regardless of the object for which government is ordained, — will, with equal strength, lead the ruled to resist, when possessed of the means of making peaceable and effective resistance. Such as organism, then, as will furnish the means by which resistance may be systematically and peaceably made on the part of the ruled, to oppression and abuse of power on the part of the rulers, is the first and indispensable step towards *forming* a constitutional government. And as this can only be effected by or through the right of suffrage, — (the right on the part of the ruled to choose their rulers at proper intervals, and to hold them thereby responsible for their conduct,) — the responsibility of the rulers to the ruled, through the right of suffrage, is the indispensable and primary principle in the *foundation* of a constitutional government. When this right is properly guarded, and the people sufficiently enlightened to understand their own rights and the interests of the community, and duly to appreciate the motives and conduct of those appointed to make and execute the laws, it is all-sufficient to give those who elect, effective control over those they have elected.

I call the right of suffrage the indispensable and primary principle; for it would be a great and dangerous mistake to suppose, as many do, that it is, of itself, sufficient to form constitutional governments. To this erroneous opinion may be traced one of the causes, why so few attempts to form constitutional governments have succeeded; and why, of the few which have, so small a number have had durable existence. It has led, not only to mistakes in the attempts to form such governments, but to their overthrow, when they have, by some good fortune, been correctly formed. So far from being, of itself, sufficient, — however well guarded it might be, and however enlightened the people, — it would, unaided by other provisions, leave the government as absolute, as it would be in the hands of irresponsible rulers; and with a tendency, at least as strong, towards oppression and abuse of its powers; as I shall next proceed to explain.

The right of suffrage, of itself, can do no more than give complete control to those who elect, over the conduct of those they have elected. In doing this, it accomplishes all it possibly can accomplish. This is its aim, — and when this is attained, its end is fulfilled. It can do no more, however enlightened the people, or however widely extended or well guarded the right may be. The sum total, then, of its effects, when most successful, is, to make those elected, the true and faithful representatives of those who elected them, — instead of irresponsible rulers, — as they would be without it; and thus, by converting it into an agency, and the rulers into agents, to divest government of all claims to sovereignty, and to retain it unimpaired to the community. But it is manifest that the right of suffrage, in making these changes, transfers, in reality, the actual control over the government, from those who make and execute the laws, to the body of the community;

and, thereby, places the powers of the government as fully in the mass of the community, as they would be if they, in fact, had assembled, made, and executed the laws themselves, without the intervention of representatives or agents. The more perfectly it does this, the more perfectly it accomplishes its ends; but in doing so, it only changes the seat of authority, without counteracting, in the least, the tendency of the government to oppression and abuse of its powers.

If the whole community had the same interests, so that the interests of each and every portion would be so affected by the action of the government, that the laws which oppressed or impoverished one portion, would necessarily oppress and impoverish all others,—or the reverse,—then the right of suffrage, of itself, would be all-sufficient to counteract the tendency of the government to oppression and abuse of its powers; and, of course, would form, of itself, a perfect constitutional government. The interest of all being the same, by supposition, as far as the action of the government was concerned, all would have like interests as to what laws should be made, and how they should be executed. All strife and struggle would cease as to who should be elected to make and execute them. The only question would be, who was most fit; who the wisest and most capable of understanding the common interest of the whole. This decided, the election would pass off quietly, and without party discord; as no one portion could advance its own peculiar interest without regard to the rest, by electing a favorite candidate.

But such is not the case. On the contrary, nothing is more difficult than to equalize the action of the government, in reference to the various and diversified interests of the community; and nothing more easy than to pervert its powers into instruments to aggrandize and enrich one or more interests by oppressing and impoverishing the others; and this too, under the operation of laws, couched in general terms;—and which, on their face, appear fair and equal. Nor is this the case in some particular communities only. It is so in all; the small and the great,—the poor and the rich,—irrespective of pursuits, productions, or degrees of civilization;—with, however, this difference, that the more extensive and populous the country, the more diversified the condition and pursuits of its population, and the richer, more luxurious, and dissimilar the people, the more difficult is it to equalize the action of the government,—and the more easy for one portion of the community to pervert its powers to oppress, and plunder the other. . . .

The right of suffrage, without some other provision, the next question for consideration is—What is that other provision? This demands the most serious consideration; for of all the questions embraced in the science of government, it involves a principle, the most important, and the least understood; and when understood, the most difficult of application in practice. It is, indeed, emphatically, that principle which *makes* the constitution, in its strict and limited sense.

From what has been said, it is manifest, that this provision must be of a character calculated to prevent any one interest, or combination of interests, from using the powers of government to aggrandize itself at the expense of the others. Here lies the evil: and just in proportion as it shall prevent, or fail to prevent it, in the same degree it will effect, or fail to effect the end intended to be accomplished. There is but one certain mode in which this result can be secured; and that is, by the adoption of some restriction or limitation, which shall so effectually prevent any one interest, or combination of interests, from obtaining the exclusive control of the government, as to render hopeless all attempts directed to that end. There is, again, but one mode in which this can be effected; and that is, by taking the sense of each interest or portion of the community, which may be unequally and injuriously affected by the action of the government, separately, through its own majority, or in some other way by which its voice may be fairly expressed; and to require the consent of each interest, either to put or to keep the government in action. This, too, can be accomplished only in one way,—and that is, by such an organism of the government,—and, if necessary for the purpose, of the community also,—as will, by dividing and distributing the powers of government, give to each division or interest, through its appropriate organ, either a concurrent voice in making and executing the laws, or a veto on their execution.

It is only by such as organism, that the assent of each can be made necessary to put the government in motion; or the power made effectual to arrest its action, when put in motion;—and it is only by the one or the other that the different interests, orders, classes, or portions, into which the community may be divided, can be protected, and all conflict and struggle between them prevented,—by rendering it impossible to put or to keep it in action, without the concurrent consent of all.

Such an organism as this, combined with the right of suffrage, constitutes, in fact, the elements of constitutional government. The one, by rendering those who make and execute the laws responsible to those on whom they operate, prevents the rulers from oppressing the ruled; and the other, by making it impossible for any one interest or combination of interests or class, or order, or portion of the community, to obtain exclusive control, prevents any one of them from oppressing the other. It is clear, that oppression and abuse of power must come, if at all, from the one or the other quarter. From no other can they come. It follows, that the two, suffrage and proper organism combined, are sufficient to counteract the tendency of government to oppression and abuse of power; and to restrict it to the fulfilment of the great ends for which it is ordained. . . .

There are two different modes in which the sense of the community may be taken; one, simply by the right of suffrage, unaided; the other, by the right through a proper organism. Each collects the sense of the majority. But one regards numbers only, and considers the whole community as a unit, having but one common interest throughout; and collects the sense of the greater number of the whole, as that of the community. The other, on the contrary, regards interests as well as numbers;—considering the community as made up of different and conflicting interests, as far as the action of the government is concerned; and takes the sense of each, through its majority or appropriate organ, and the united sense of all, as the sense of the entire community. The former of these I shall call the numerical, or absolute majority; and the latter, the concurrent, or constitutional majority. I call it the constitutional majority, because it is an essential element in every constitutional government,—be its form what it may. So great is the difference, politically speaking, between the two majorities, that they cannot be confounded, without leading to great and fatal errors; and yet the distinction between them has been so entirely overlooked, that when the term *majority* is used in political discussions, it is applied exclusively to designate the numerical,—as if there were no other. Until this distinction is recognized, and better understood, there will continue to be great liability to error in properly constructing constitutional governments, especially of the popular form, and of preserving them when properly constructed.

Source: A Disquisition on Government and a Discourse on the Constitution and Government of the United States. By John C. Calhoun. Edited by Richard K. Crallé. Volume 1 of *The Works of John C. Calhoun.* New York: Russell & Russell, 1968. Reprint of the 1851–56 edition.

John C. Calhoun (1782–1850) was an intellectual and political leader in the pre-Civil War South. He was vice president of the United States 1825–31.

Constitution of the Confederate States of America

March 11, 1861

We, the people of the Confederate States, each State acting in its sovereign and independent character, in order to form a permanent federal government, establish justice, insure domestic tranquillity, and secure the blessings of liberty to ourselves and our posterity—invoking the favor and guidance of Almighty God—do ordain and establish this Constitution for the Confederate States of America.

ART. I.

SEC. 1.—All legislative powers herein delegated shall be vested in a Congress of the Confederate States, which shall consist of a Senate and House of Representatives.

SEC. 2. (1) The House of Representatives shall be chosen every second year by the people of the several States; and the electors in each State shall be citizens of the Confederate States, and have the qualifications requisite for electors of the most numerous branch of the State Legislature; but no person of foreign birth, not a citizen of the Confederate States, shall be allowed to vote for any officer, civil or political, State or Federal.

(2) No person shall be Representative who shall not have attained the age of twenty-five years, and be citizen of the Confederate States, and who shall not, when elected, be an inhabitant of that State in which he shall be chosen.

(3) Representatives and direct taxes shall be apportioned among the several States which may be included within this Confederacy, according to their respective numbers, which shall be determined by adding to the whole number of free persons, including those bound to service for a term of years, and excluding Indians not taxed, three-fifths of all slaves. The actual enumeration shall be made within three years after the first meeting of the Congress of the confederate States, and within every subsequent term of ten years, in such manner as they shall by law direct. The number of Representatives shall not exceed one for every fifty thousand, but each State shall have at least one Representative; and until such enumeration shall be made, the State of South Carolina shall be entitled to choose six; the State of Georgia ten; the State of Alabama nine; the State of Florida two; the State of Mississippi seven; the State of Louisiana six; and the State of Texas six.

(4) When vacancies happen in the representation of any State, the Executive authority thereof shall issue writs of election to fill such vacancies.

(5) The House of Representatives shall choose their Speaker and other officers; and shall have the sole power of impeachment; except that any judicial or other federal officer resident and acting solely within the limits of any State, may be impeached by a vote of two-thirds of both branches of the Legislature thereof.

SEC. 3. (1) The Senate of the Confederate States shall be composed of two Senators from each State, chosen for six years by the Legislature thereof, at the regular session next immediately preceding the commencement of the term of service; and each Senator shall have one vote.

(2) Immediately after they shall be assembled, in consequence of the first election, they shall be divided as equally as may be into three classes. The seats of the Senators of the first class shall be vacated at the expiration of the second year; of the second class at the expiration of the fourth year; and of the third class at the expiration of the sixth year; so that one-third may be chosen every second year; and if vacancies happen by resignation or otherwise during the recess of the Legislature of any State, the Executive thereof may make temporary appointments until the next meeting of the Legislature, which shall then fill such vacancies.

(3) No person shall be a Senator, who shall not have attained the age of thirty years, and be inhabitant of the Confederate States; and who shall not, when elected, be an inhabitant of the State for which he shall be chosen.

(4) The Vice-President of the Confederate States shall be President of the Senate, but shall have no vote, unless they be equally divided.

(5) The Senate shall choose their other officers, and also a President *pro tempore*, in the absence of the Vice-President, or when he shall exercise the office of President of the Confederate States.

(6) The Senate shall have sole power to try all impeachments. When sitting for that purpose they shall be on oath or affirmation. When the President of the Confederate States is tried, the Chief-Justice shall preside; and no person shall be convicted without the concurrence of two-thirds of the members present.

(7) Judgment in cases of impeachment shall not extend further than removal from office, and disqualification to hold and enjoy any office of honor, trust, or profit, under the Confederate States; but the party convicted shall, nevertheless, be liable to and subject to indictment, trial, judgment, and punishment according to law.

SEC. 4 (1) The times, places, and manner of holding elections for Senators and Representatives, shall be prescribed in each State by the Legislature thereof, subject to the provisions of this Constitution; but the Congress may, at any time, by law, make or alter such regulations, except as to the times and places of choosing Senators.

(2) The Congress shall assemble at least once in every year; and such meeting shall be on the first Monday in December, unless they shall, by law, appoint a different day.

SEC. 5. (1) Each House shall be the judge of the elections, returns, and qualifications of its own members, and a majority of each shall constitute a quorum to do business; but a smaller number may adjourn from day to day, and may be authorized to compel the attendance of absent members, in such manner and under such penalties as each House may provide.

(2) Each House may determine the rules of its proceedings, punish its members for disorderly behavior, and, with the concurrence of two-thirds of the whole number, expel a member.

(3) Each House shall keep a journal of its proceedings, and from time to time publish the same, excepting such part as may in its judgment require secrecy, and the ayes and nays of the members of either House, on any question, shall, at the desire of one-fifth of those present, be entered on the journal.

(4) Neither House, during the session of Congress, shall, without the consent of the other, adjourn for more than three days, nor to any other place than that in which the two Houses shall be sitting.

SEC. 6. (1) The Senators and Representatives shall receive a compensation for their services, to be ascertained by law, and paid out of the Treasury of the Confederate States. They shall, in all cases except treason and breach of the peace, be privileged from arrest during their attendance at the session of their respective

Houses, and in going to and returning from the same; and for any speech or debate in either House, they shall not be questioned in any other place.

(2) No Senator or Representative shall, during the time for which he was elected, be appointed to any civil office under the authority of the Confederate States, which shall have been created, or the emoluments whereof shall have been increased during such time; and no person holding any office under the Confederate States shall be a member of either House during his continuance in office. But Congress may, by law, grant to the principal officer in each of the Executive Departments a seat upon the floor of either House, with the privilege of discussing any measure appertaining to his department.

SEC. 7. (1) All bills for raising revenue shall originate in the House of Representatives; but the Senate may propose or concur with amendments as on other bills.

(2) Every bill which shall have passed both Houses shall, before it becomes a law, be presented to the President of the Confederate States; if he approve he shall sign it; but if not, he shall return it with his objections to that House in which it shall have originated, who shall enter the objections at large on their journal, and proceed to reconsider it. If, after such reconsideration, two-thirds of that House shall agree to pass the bill, it shall be sent, together with the objections, to the other House, by which it shall likewise be reconsidered, and if approved by two-thirds of that House, it shall become a law. But in all cases, the votes of both Houses shall be determined by yeas and nays, and the names of the persons voting for and against the bill shall be entered on the journal of each House respectively. If any bill shall not be returned by the President within ten days (Sundays excepted) after it shall have been presented to him, the same shall be a law, in like manner as if he had signed it, unless the Congress, by their adjournment, prevent its return; in which case it shall not be a law. The President may approve any appropriation and disapprove any other appropriation in the same bill. In such case he shall, in signing the bill, designate the appropriations disapproved; and shall return a copy of such appropriations, with his objections, to the House in which the bill shall have originated; and the same proceedings shall then be had as in case of other bills disapproved by the President.

(3) Every order, resolution or vote, to which the concurrence of both Houses may be necessary (except on questions of adjournment) shall be presented to the President of the Confederate States; and before the same shall take effect shall be approved by him; or being disapproved by him, may be repassed by two-thirds of both Houses, according to the rules and limitations prescribed in case of a bill.

SEC. 8. — The Congress shall have power —

(1) To lay and collect taxes, duties, imposts, and excises, for revenue necessary to pay the debts, provide for the common defence, and carry on the Government of the Confederate States; but no bounties shall be granted from the treasury; nor shall any duties or taxes on importations from foreign nations be laid to promote

or foster any branch of industry; and all duties, imposts, and excises shall be uniform throughout the Confederate States.

(2) To borrow money on the credit of the Confederate States.

(3) To regulate commerce with foreign nations, and among the several States, and with the Indian tribes; but neither this, nor any other clause contained in the Constitution shall be construed to delegate the power to Congress to appropriate money for any internal improvement intended to facilitate commerce; except for the purpose of furnishing lights, beacons, and buoys, and other aids to navigation upon the coasts, and the improvement of harbors, and the removing of obstructions in river navigation, in all which cases, such duties shall be laid on the navigation facilitated thereby, as may be necessary to pay the costs and expenses thereof.

(4) To establish uniform laws of naturalization, and uniform laws on the subject of bankruptcies throughout the Confederate States, but no law of Congress shall discharge any debt contracted before the passage of the same.

(5) To coin money, regulate the value thereof, and of foreign coin, and fix the standard of weights and measures.

(6) To provide for the punishment of counterfeiting the securities and current coin of the Confederate States.

(7) To establish post-offices and post-routes; but the expenses of the Post-office Department, after the first day of March, in the year of our Lord eighteen hundred and sixty-three, shall be paid out of its own revenues.

(8) To promote the progress of science and useful arts, by securing for limited times to authors and inventors the exclusive right to their respective writings and discoveries.

(9) To constitute tribunals inferior to the Supreme Court.

(10) To define and punish piracies and felonies committed on the high seas, and offences against the law of nations.

(11) To declare war, grant letters of marque and reprisal, and make rules concerning captures on land and water.

(12) To raise and support armies; but no appropriation of money to that use shall be for a longer term than two years.

(13) To provide and maintain a navy.

(14) To make rules for government and regulation of the land and naval forces.

(15) To provide for calling forth the militia to execute the laws of the Confederate States; suppress insurrections, and repel invasions.

(16) To provide for organizing, arming, and disciplining the militia, and for governing such part of them as may be employed in the service of the Confederate States; reserving to the States, respectively, the appointment of the officers, and the authority of training the militia according to the discipline prescribed by Congress.

(17) To exercise exclusive legislation, in all cases whatsoever, over such district (not exceeding ten miles square) as may, by cession of one or more States, and the acceptance of Congress, become the seat of the Government of the Confederate States; and to exercise a like authority over all places purchased by the consent of the Legislature of the State in which the same shall be, for the erection of forts, magazines, arsenals, dock-yards, and other needful buildings, and

(18) To make all laws which shall be necessary and proper for carrying into execution the foregoing powers, and all other powers vested by this Constitution in the Government of the Confederate States, or in any department or officer thereof.

SEC. 9. (1) The importation of negroes of the African race, from any foreign country, other than the slaveholding States or Territories of the United States of America, is hereby forbidden; and Congress is required to pass such laws as shall effectually prevent the same.

(2) Congress shall also have power to prohibit the introduction of slaves from any State not a member of, or Territory not belonging to, this Confederacy.

(3) The privilege of the writ of *habeas corpus* shall not be suspended, unless when in cases of rebellion or invasion the public safety may require it.

(4) No bill of attainder, or *ex post facto* law, or law denying or impairing the right of property in negro slaves shall be passed.

(5) No capitation or other direct tax shall be laid unless in proportion to the census or enumeration hereinbefore directed to be taken.

(6) No tax or duty shall be laid on articles exported from any State, except by vote of two-thirds of both Houses.

(7) No preference shall be given by any regulation of commerce or revenue to the ports of one State over those of another.

(8) No money shall be drawn from the treasury but in consequence of appropriations made by law; and a regular statement and account of the receipts and expenditures of all public money shall be published from time to time.

(9) Congress shall appropriate no money from the treasury except by a vote of two-thirds of both Houses, taken by yeas and nays, unless it be asked and estimated for by some one of the heads of departments, and submitted to Congress by the President; or for the purpose of paying its own expenses and contingencies; or for the payment of claims against the Confederate States, the justice of which shall have been judicially declared by a tribunal for the investigation of claims against the Government, which it is hereby made the duty of Congress to establish.

(10) All bills appropriating money shall specify in federal currency the exact amount of each appropriation and the purposes for which it is made; and Congress shall grant no extra compensation to any public contractor, officer, agent, or servant, after such contract shall have been made or such service rendered.

(11) No title of nobility shall be granted by the Confederate States; and no person holding any office of profit or trust under them shall, without the consent of the Congress, accept of any present, emoluments, office, or title of any kind whatever, from any king, prince or foreign state.

(12) Congress shall make no law respecting an establishment of religion, or prohibiting the free exercise thereof; or abridging the freedom of speech or of the press; or the right of the people peaceably to assemble and petition the Government for a redress of grievances.

(13) A well-regulated militia being necessary to the security of a free State, the right of the people and keep and bear arms shall not be infringed.

(14) No soldier shall, in time of peace, be quartered in any house without the consent of the owner; nor in time of war, but in a manner prescribed by law.

(15) The right of the people to be secure in their persons, houses, papers, and against unreasonable searches and seizures, shall not be violated; and no warrant shall issue but upon probable cause, supported by oath or affirmation, and particularly describing the place to be searched, and the person or things to be seized.

(16) No person shall be held to answer for a capital or otherwise infamous crime, unless on a presentment or indictment of a grand jury, except in cases arising in the land or naval forces, or in the militia, when in actual service, in time of war, or public danger; nor shall any person be subject for the same offence to be twice put in jeopardy of life or limb; nor be compelled in any criminal case to be a witness against himself; nor be deprived of life, liberty, or property, without due process of law; nor shall any private property be taken for public use without just compensation.

(17) In all criminal prosecutions the accused shall enjoy the right to a speedy and public trial, by an impartial jury of the State and district wherein the crime shall have been committed, which district shall have been previously ascertained by law, and to be informed of the nature and cause of the accusation; to be confronted with the witnesses against him; to have compulsory process for obtaining witnesses in his favor; and to have the assistance of counsel for his defence.

(18) In suits at common law, where the value in controversy shall exceed twenty dollars, the right of trial by jury shall be preserved; and no fact so tried by a jury shall be otherwise reexamined in any court of the Confederacy, than according to the rules of the common law.

(19) Excessive bail shall not be required, nor excessive fines imposed, nor cruel or unusual punishment inflicted.

(20) Every law, or resolution having the force of law, shall relate to but one subject, and that shall be expressed in the title.

SEC. 10. (1) No State shall enter into any treaty, alliance, or confederation; grant letters of marque and reprisals; coin money; make any thing but gold and silver coin a tender in payment of debts; pass any bill of attainder, or *ex post facto* law, or law impairing the obligation of contracts; or grant any title of nobility.

(2) No State shall, without the consent of Congress, lay any imposts or duties on imports or exports, except what may be absolutely necessary for executing its inspection laws; and the net produce of all duties and imposts, laid by any State on imports or exports, shall be for the use of the Treasury of the Confederate States; and all such laws shall be subject to the revision and control of Congress.

(3) No state shall, without the consent of Congress, lay any duty of tonnage, except on sea-going vessels, for the improvement of its rivers and harbors navigated by the said vessels; but such duties shall not conflict with any treaties of the Confederate States with foreign nations; and any surplus of revenue, thus derived, shall, after making such improvement, be paid into the common treasury; nor shall any State keep troops or ships of war in time of peace, enter into any agreement or compact with another State, or with a foreign power, or engage in war, unless actually invaded, or in such imminent danger as will not admit of delay. But when any river divides or flows through two or more States, they may enter into compacts with each other to improve the navigation thereof.

ART. II.

SEC. I. (1) The Executive power shall be vested in a President of the Confederate States of America. He and the Vice-President shall hold their offices for the term of six years; but the President shall not be reeligible. The President and Vice-President shall be elected as follows:

(2) Each State shall appoint, in such manner as the Legislature thereof may direct, a number of electors equal to the whole number of Senators and Representatives to which the State may be entitled in Congress; but no Senator or Representative, or person holding an office of trust or profit under the Confederate States, shall be appointed an elector.

(3) The electors shall meet in their respective States and vote by ballot for President and Vice-President, one of whom, at least, shall not be an inhabitant of the same State with themselves; they shall name in their ballots the person voted for as President, and in distinct ballots the person voted for as Vice-President, and they shall make distinct lists of all persons voted for as President, and of all persons voted for as Vice-President, and of the number of votes for each; which list they shall sign, and certify, and transmit, sealed, to the Government of the Confederate States, directed to the President of the Senate. The President of the Senate shall, in the presence of the Senate and House of Representatives, open all the certificates, and the votes shall then be counted; the person having the greatest number of votes for President shall be the President, if such number be a majority of the whole number of electors appointed; and if no person shall have a major-

ity, then, from the persons having the highest numbers, not exceeding three, on the list of those voted for as President, the House of Representatives shall choose immediately, by ballot, the President. But, in choosing the President, the votes shall be taken by States, the Representative from each State having one vote; a quorum for this purpose shall consist of a member or members from two-thirds of the States, and a majority of all the States shall be necessary to a choice. And if the House of Representatives shall not choose a President, whenever the right of choice shall devolve upon them before the fourth day of March next following, then the Vice-President shall act as President, as in case of the death, or other constitutional disability of the President.

(4) The person having the greatest number of votes as Vice-President shall be the Vice-President, if such number be a majority of the whole number of electors appointed; and if no person have a majority, then from the two highest numbers on the list, the Senate shall choose the Vice-President; a quorum for the purpose shall consist of two-thirds of the whole number of Senators, and a majority of the whole number shall be necessary for a choice.

(5) But no person constitutionally ineligible to the office of President shall be eligible to that of Vice-President of the Confederate States.

(6) The Congress may determine the time of choosing the electors, and the day on which they shall give their votes; which day shall be the same throughout the Confederate Sates.

(7) No person except a natural born citizen of the Confederate States, or a citizen thereof, at the time of the adoption of this Constitution, or a citizen thereof born in the United States prior to the 20th December, 1860, shall be eligible to the office of President; neither shall any person be eligible to that office who shall not have attained the age of thirty-five years, and been fourteen years a resident within the limits of the Confederate States, as they may exist at the time of his election.

(8) In case of the removal of the President from office, or of his death, resignation, or inability to discharge the powers and duties of the said office, the same shall devolve on the Vice-President; and the Congress may, by law, provide for the case of the removal, death, resignation, or inability both of the President and the Vice-President, declaring what officer shall then act as president, and such officer shall then act accordingly until the disability be removed or a President shall be elected.

(9) The President shall, at stated times, receive for his services a compensation, which shall neither be increased nor diminished during the period for which he shall have been elected; and he shall not receive within that period any other emolument from the Confederate States, or any of them.

(10) Before he enters on the execution of the duties of his office, he shall take the following oath or affirmation:

"I do solemnly swear (or affirm) that I will faithfully execute the office of President of the Confederate States, and will, to the best of my ability, preserve, protect, and defend the Constitution thereof."

SEC. 2. (1) The President shall be commander-in-chief of the army and navy of the Confederate States, and of the militia of the several States, when called into the actual service of the Confederate States; he may require the opinion, in writing, of the principal officer in each of the Executive Departments, upon any subject relating to the duties of their respective offices; and he shall have power to grant reprieves and pardons for offences against the Confederate States, except in cases of impeachment.

(2) He shall have power, by and with the advice and consent of the Senate, to make treaties, provided two-thirds of the Senators present concur; and he shall nominate, and, by and with the advice and consent of the Senate, shall appoint ambassadors, other public ministers, and consuls, Judges of the Supreme Court, and all other officers of the Confederate States, whose appointments are not herein otherwise provided for, and which shall be established by law; but the Congress may by law vest the appointment of such inferior officers, as they think proper, in the President alone, in the courts of law, or in the heads of departments.

(3) The principal officer in each of the Executive Departments, and all persons connected with the diplomatic service, may be removed from office at the pleasure of the President. All other civil officers of the Executive Department may be removed at any time by the President, or other appointing power, when their services are unnecessary, or for dishonesty, incapacity, inefficiency, misconduct, or neglect of duty; and when so removed, the removal shall be reported to the Senate, together with the reasons therefor.

(4) The President shall have power to fill all vacancies that may happen during the recess of the Senate, by granting commissions which shall expire at the end of the next session; but no person rejected by the Senate shall be reappointed to the same office during their ensuing recess.

SEC. 3. (1) The President shall, from time to time, give to the Congress information of the state of the Confederacy, and recommend to their consideration such measures as he shall judge necessary and expedient; he may, on extraordinary occasions, convene both Houses, or either of them; and, in case of disagreement between them, with respect to the time of adjournment he may adjourn them to such time as he shall think proper; he shall receive ambassadors and other public ministers; he shall take care that the laws be faithfully executed, and shall commission all the officers of the Confederate States.

SEC. 4. (1) The President and Vice-President, and all civil officers of the Confederate States, shall be removed from office on impeachment for, or conviction of, treason, bribery, or other high crimes and misdemeanors.

ART. III.

SEC. I. (1) The judicial power of the Confederate States shall be vested in one Superior Court, and in such inferior courts as the Congress may from time to time ordain and establish. The judges, both of the Supreme and inferior courts, shall hold their offices during good behavior, and shall, at stated times, receive for their services a compensation, which shall not be diminished during their continuance in office.

SEC. 2. (1) The judicial power shall extend to all cases arising under the Constitution, the laws of the Confederate States, or treaties made or which shall be made under their authority; to all cases affecting ambassadors, other public ministers, and consuls; to all cases of admiralty or maritime jurisdiction; to controversies to which the Confederate States shall be a party; to controversies between two or more States; between a State and citizens of another State, where the State is plaintiff; between citizens claiming lands under grants of different States, and between a State or the citizen thereof, and foreign States, citizen, or subjects; but no State shall be sued by citizen or subject of any foreign State.

(2) In all cases affecting ambassadors, other public ministers, and consuls, and those in which a State shall be a party, the Supreme Court shall have original jurisdiction. In all the other cases before mentioned, the Supreme Court shall have appellate jurisdiction, both as to law and fact, with such exceptions, and under such regulations as the Congress shall make.

(3) The trial of all crimes, except in cases of impeachment, shall be by jury, and such trial shall be held in the State where the said crimes shall have been committed; but when not committed within any State, the trial shall be at such place or places as the Congress may by law have directed.

SEC. 3. (1) Treason against the Confederate States shall consist only in levying war against them, or in adhering to their enemies, giving them aid and comfort. No person shall be convicted of treason unless on the testimony of two witnesses to the same overt act, or on confession in open court.

(2) The Congress shall have power to declare the punishment of treason, but no attainder of treason shall work corruption of blood, or forfeiture, except during the life of the person attainted.

ART. IV.

SEC. I. (1) Full faith and credit shall be given in each State to the public acts, records, and judicial proceedings of every other State. And the Congress may, by general laws, prescribe the manner in which such acts, records, and proceedings shall be proved, and the effect thereof.

SEC. 2. (1) The citizens of each State shall be entitled to all the privileges and immunities of citizens of the several States, and shall have the right of transit and sojourn in any State of this Confederacy, with their slaves and other property; and the right of property in said slaves shall not be thereby impaired.

(2) A person charged in any State with treason, felony, or other crime against the laws of such State, who shall flee from justice, and be found in another State, shall, on demand of the executive authority of the State from which he fled, be delivered up to be removed to the State having jurisdiction of the crime.

(3) No slave or other person held to service or labor in any State or Territory of the Confederate States, under the laws thereof, escaping or unlawfully carried into another, shall, in consequence of any law or regulation therein, be discharged from such service or labor; but shall be delivered up on claim of the party to whom such slave belongs, or to whom such service or labor may be due.

SEC. 3. (1) Other States may be admitted into this Confederacy by a vote of two-thirds of the whole House of Representatives, and two-thirds of the Senate, the Senate voting by States; but no new State shall be formed or erected within the jurisdiction of any other States; nor any State be formed by the junction of two or more States, or parts of States, without the consent of the Legislatures of the States concerned as well as of the Congress.

(2) The Congress shall have power to dispose of and make all needful rules and regulations concerning the property of the Confederate States, including the lands thereof.

(3) The Confederate States may acquire new territory; and Congress shall have power to legislate and provide governments for the inhabitants of all territory belonging to the Confederate States, lying without the limits of the several States, and may permit them, at such times, and in such manner as it may by law provide, to form States to be admitted into the Confederacy. In all such territory, the institution of negro slavery, as it now exists in the Confederate States, shall be recognized and protected by Congress and by the territorial government; and the inhabitants of the several Confederate States and Territories shall have the right to take to such territory any slaves lawfully held by them in any of the States or Territories of the Confederate States.

(4) The Confederate States shall guarantee to every State that now is or hereafter may become a member of this Confederacy, a Republican form of Government, and shall protect each of them against invasion; and on application of the Legislature, (or of the Executive when the Legislature is not in session,) against domestic violence.

ART. V.

SEC. I. (1) Upon the demand of any three States, legally assembled in their several Conventions, the Congress shall summon a Convention of all the States, to take into consideration such amendments to the Constitution as the said States shall concur in suggesting at the time when the said demand is made; and should any of the proposed amendments to the Constitution be agreed on by the said Convention—voting by States—and the same be ratified by the Legislatures of two-thirds thereof—as the one or the other mode of ratification may be proposed by the general convention—they shall thenceforward form a part of this Constitution. But no State shall, without its consent, be deprived of its equal representation in the Senate.

ART. VI.

1.—The Government established by this Constitution is the successor of the Provisional Government of the Confederate States of America, and all the laws passed by the latter shall continue in force until the same shall be repealed or modified; and all the officers appointed by the same shall remain in office until their successors are appointed and qualified, or the offices abolished.

2. All debts contracted and engagements entered into before the adoption of this Constitution, shall be as valid against the Confederate States under this Constitution as under the Provisional Government.

3. This Constitution, and the laws of the Confederate States, made in pursuance thereof, and all treaties made, or which shall be made, under the authority of the Confederate States, shall be the supreme law of the land; and the judges in every State shall be bound thereby, any thing in the Constitution or laws of any State to the contrary notwithstanding.

4. The Senators and Representatives before mentioned, and the numbers of the several State Legislatures, and all executive and judicial offices, both of the Confederate States and of the several States, shall be bound, by oath or affirmation, to support this Constitution; but no religious test shall ever be required as a qualification to any office or public trust under the Confederate States.

5. The enumeration, in the Constitution, of certain rights, shall not be construed to deny or disparage others retained by the people of the several States.

6. The powers not delegated to the Confederate States by the Constitution, nor prohibited by it to the States, are reserved to the States, respectively, or to the people thereof.

ART. VII.

1.—The ratification of the conventions of five States shall be sufficient for the establishment of this Constitution between the States so ratifying the same.

2. When five States shall have ratified this Constitution in the manner before

specified, the Congress, under the provisional Constitution, shall prescribe the time for holding the election of President and Vice-President, and for the meeting of the electoral college, and for counting the votes and inaugurating the President. They shall also prescribe the time for holding the first election of members of Congress under this Constitution, and the time for assembling the same. Until the assembling of such Congress, the Congress under the provisional Constitution shall continue to exercise the legislative powers granted them; not extending beyond the time limited by the Constitution of the Provisional Government.

Adopted unanimously by the Congress of the Confederate States of South Carolina, Georgia, Florida, Alabama, Mississippi, Louisiana, and Texas, sitting in convention at the capitol, in the city of Montgomery, Ala., on the eleventh day of March, in the year eighteen hundred and sixty-one.

Source: A Compilation of the Messages and Papers of the Confederacy Including the Diplomatic Correspondences 1801–1865. Edited by James D. Richardson, 1:37–54. Nashville: United States Publishing Co., 1906.

Abraham Lincoln
Gettysburg Address
November 19, 1863

Fourscore and seven years ago our fathers brought forth on this continent a new nation, conceived in liberty, and dedicated to the proposition that all men are created equal.

Now we are engaged in a great civil war, testing whether that nation, or any nation so conceived and so dedicated, can long endure. We are met on a great battlefield of that war. We have come to dedicate a portion of that field as a final resting-place for those who here gave their lives that that nation might live. It is altogether fitting and proper that we should do this.

But, in a larger sense, we cannot dedicate—we cannot consecrate—we cannot hallow—this ground. The brave men, living and dead, who struggled here, have consecrated it far above our poor power to add or detract. The world will little note nor long remember what we say here, but it can never forget what they did here. It is for us, the living, rather, to be dedicated here to the unfinished work which they who fought here have thus far so nobly advanced. It is rather for us to be here dedicated to the great task remaining before us—that from these honored dead we take increased devotion to that cause for which they gave the last full measure of devotion; that we here highly resolve that these dead shall not have died in vain; that this nation, under God, shall have a new birth of freedom; and that government of the people, by the people, for the people, shall not perish from the earth.

Transcendentalism

The most important intellectual movement in the pre-Civil War nineteenth century was transcendentalism. Inspired by European, mostly German, romanticism, transcendentalism was a literary, philosophic, and religious movement centered around Concord, Massachusetts. Its leading figures were Ralph Waldo Emerson (1803–82) and Henry David Thoreau (1817–62), but the movement also included such figures as Bronson Alcott (1799–1888), now mostly remembered as the father of Louisa May Alcott (1832–88), but then recognized as a major educational theorist; George Ripley (1802–80), one of the founders of Brook Farm; William Ellery Channing (1780–1842), a leading Unitarian; Margaret Fuller (1810–50), a feminist and radical thinker; and Theodore Parker (1810–60), a Unitarian preacher and leading abolitionist.

Although transcendentalism is probably better characterized as a sensibility than a philosophy, transcendentalists found parallels to their thought in such disparate sources as German idealism and the Hindu scriptures. In the United States, transcendentalism was part of the rejection of Calvinism—a rejection that, at a deeper level, has never been entirely successful. But transcendentalism was not primarily a religious movement, at least not in any denominational sense. The focus for the transcendentalists was Nature, not God, perhaps best reflected in the sensuous love of nature found in Thoreau's *Walden, or Life in the Woods* (1854) and *A Week on the Concord and Merrimack Rivers* (1849).

Politically, the transcendentalists were individualists and social reformers. Emerson's "Politics," a selection from which appears below, shows the individual rather than government as the measure of right and wrong.

Ralph Waldo Emerson
Politics

The less government we have, the better—the fewer laws, and the less confided power. The antidote to this abuse of formal Government is the influence of private character, the growth of the Individual; the appearance of the principal to supersede the proxy; the appearance of the wise man, of whom the existing government is, it must be owned, a shabby imitation. That which all things tend to educe, which freedom, cultivation, intercourse, revolutions, go to form and deliver, is character; that is the end of nature, to reach unto this coronation of her king. To educate the wise man, the State exists; and with the appearance of the wise man, the State expires. The appearance of character makes the State unnecessary. The wise man is the State. He needs no army, fort, or navy,—he loves men too well; no bribe, or feast, or palace, to draw friends to him; no vantage ground, no favorable circumstance. He needs no library, for he has not done thinking; no church, for he is a prophet; no statute book, for he has the lawgiver; no money, for he is value; no road, for he is at home where he is; no experience, for the life of the creator shoots through him, and looks from his eyes. He has no personal friends, for he who has the spell to draw the prayer and piety of all men unto him needs not husband and educate a few, to share with him a select and poetic life. His relation to men is angelic; his memory is myrrh to them; his presence, frankincense and flowers. . . .

The tendencies of the times favor the idea of self-government, and leave the individual, for all code, to the rewards and penalties of his own constitution, which work with more energy than we believe, whilst we depend on artificial restraints. The movement in this direction has been very marked in modern history. Much has been blind and discreditable, but the nature of the revolution is not affected by the vices of the revolters; for this is a purely moral force. It was never adopted by any party in history, neither can be. It separates the individual from all party, and unites him, at the same time, to the race. It promises a recognition of higher rights than those of personal freedom, or the security of property. A man has a right to be employed, to be trusted, to be loved, to be revered. The power of love, as the basis of a State, has never been tried. We must not imagine that all things are lapsing into confusion, if every tender protestant be not compelled to bear his part in certain social conventions: nor doubt that roads can be built, letters carried, and the fruit of labor secured, when the government of force is at an end. Are our methods now so excellent that all competition is hopeless? Could not a nation of friends even devise better ways? On the other hand, let not the most conservative and timid fear anything from a premature surrender of the bayonet, and the system of force. For, according to the order of nature, which is quite superior to our will, it stands thus; there will always be a government of force, where men are selfish; and when they are pure enough to abjure the code of force, they will be wise enough to see how these public ends of the postoffice, of the highway, of commerce, and the exchange of property, of museums and libraries, of institutions to art and science, can be answered.

We live in a very low state of the world, and pay unwilling tribute to governments founded on force. There is not among the most religious and instructed men of the most religious and civil nations, a reliance on the moral sentiment, and a sufficient belief in the unity of things to persuade them that society can be maintained without artificial restraints, as well as the solar system, or that the private citizen might be reasonable, and a good neighbor, without the hint of a jail or a confiscation. What is strange, too, there never was in any man sufficient faith in the power of rectitude, to inspire him with the broad design of renovating the State on the principle of right and love. All those who have pretended this design have been partial reformers, and have admitted in some manner the supremacy of the bad State. I do not call to mind a single human being who has steadily denied the authority of the laws, on the simple ground of his own moral nature. Such designs, full of genius and full of fate as they are, are not entertained except avowedly as air pictures. If the individual who exhibits them dare to think them practicable, he disgusts scholars and churchmen; and men of talent, and women of superior sentiments, cannot hide their contempt. Not the less does nature continue to fill the heart of youth with suggestions in this enthusiasm, and there are now men — if indeed I can speak in the plural number, — more exactly, I will say, I have just been conversing with one man, to whom no weight of adverse experience will make it for a moment appear impossible, that thousands of human beings might exercise toward each other the grandest and simplest sentiments, as well as a knot of friends, or a pair of lovers.

Source: Essays. Second Series. By Ralph Waldo Emerson. Chicago: Geo. M. Hill, 1844.

Ralph Waldo Emerson (1803–82) was the most famous American essayist and lecturer of the nineteenth century.

*   *   *

One of the classic texts of American political thought and arguably the most famous U.S. political pamphlet was inspired by the debates over slavery and governmental power. Thoreau's essay defending civil disobedience was later to inspire Mahatma Gandhi (1869–1948) in India and, through Gandhi, Martin Luther King, Jr. (1929–65) in the United States. In it Thoreau makes the same argument as Emerson, but makes it much more strongly.

Henry David Thoreau
Civil Disobedience

I heartily accept the motto, — "That government is best which governs least;" and I should like to see it acted up to more rapidly and systematically. Carried out, it finally amounts to this, which also I believe, — "That government is best which governs not at all;" and when men are prepared for it, that will be the kind of government which they will have. Government is at best but an expedient; but most governments are usually, and all governments are sometimes, inexpedient.

The objections which have been brought against a standing army, and they are many and weighty, and deserve to prevail, may also at last be brought against a standing government. The standing army is only an arm of the standing government. The government itself, which is only the mode which the people have chosen to execute their will, is equally liable to be abused and perverted before the people can act through it. Witness the present Mexican war, the work of comparatively a few individuals using the standing government as their tool; for, in the outset, the people would not have consented to this measure.

This American government,—what is it but a tradition, though a recent one, endeavoring to transmit itself unimpaired to posterity, but each instant losing some of its integrity? It has not the vitality and force of a single living man; for a single man can bend it to his will. It is a sort of wooden gun to the people themselves. But it is not the less necessary for this; for the people must have some complicated machinery or other, and hear its din, to satisfy that idea of government which they have. Governments show thus how successfully men can be imposed on, even impose on themselves, for their own advantage. It is excellent, we must all allow. Yet this government never of itself furthered any enterprise, but by the alacrity with which it got out of its way. *It* does not keep the country free. *It* does not settle the West. It does not educate. The character inherent in the American people has done all that has been accomplished; and it would have done somewhat more, if the government had not sometimes got in its way. For government is an expedient by which men would fain succeed in letting one another alone; and, as has been said, when it is most expedient, the governed are most let alone by it. Trade and commerce, if they were not made of India-rubber, would never manage to bounce over the obstacles which legislators are continually putting in their way; and, if one were to judge these men wholly by the effects of their actions and not partly by their intentions, they would deserve to be classed and punished with those mischievous persons who put obstructions on the railroads.

But, to speak practically and as a citizen, unlike those who call themselves no-government men, I ask for, not *at once* no government, but at once a better government. Let every man make known what kind of government would command his respect, and that will be one step toward obtaining it.

After all, the practical reason why, when the power is once in the hands of the people, a majority are permitted, and for a long period continue, to rule is not because they are most likely to be in the right, nor because this seems fairest to the minority, but because they are physically the strongest. But a government in which the majority rule in all cases cannot be based on justice, even as far as men understand it. Can there not be a government in which majorities do not virtually decide right and wrong, but conscience?—in which majorities decide only those questions to which the rule of expediency is applicable? Must the citizen ever for a moment, or in the least degree, resign his conscience to the legislator?

Why has every man a conscience, then? I think that we should be men first, and subjects afterward. It is not desirable to cultivate a respect for the law, so much as for the right. The only obligation which I have a right to assume is to do at any time what I think right. It is truly enough said, that a corporation has no conscience; but a corporation of conscientious men is a corporation *with* a conscience. Law never made men a whit more just; and, by means of their respect for it, even the well-disposed are daily made the agents of injustice. A common and natural result of an undue respect for law is, that you may see a file of soldiers, colonel, captain, corporal, privates, powder-monkeys, and all, marching in admirable order over hill and dale to the wars, against their wills, ay, against their common sense and consciences, which makes it very steep marching indeed, and produces a palpitation of the heart. They have no doubt that it is a damnable business in which they are concerned; they are all peaceably inclined. Now, what are they? Men at all? or small movable forts and magazines, at the service of some unscrupulous man in power? Visit the Navy-Yard, and behold a marine, such a man as an American government can make, or such as it can make a man with its black arts, — a mere shadow and reminiscence of humanity, a man laid out alive and standing, and already, as one may say, buried under arms with funeral accompaniments, though it may be, —

"Not a drum was heard, not a funeral note,
    As his corse to the rampart we hurried;
Not a soldier discharged his farewell shot
    O'er the grave where our hero we buried."

The mass of men serve the state thus, not as men mainly, but as machines, with their bodies. They are the standing army, and the militia, jailors, constables, posse comitatus, etc. In most cases there is no free exercise whatever of the judgment or of the moral sense; but they put themselves on a level with wood and earth and stones; and wooden men can perhaps be manufactured that will serve the purpose as well. Such command no more respect than men of straw or a lump of dirt. They have the same sort of worth only as horses and dogs. Yet such as these even are commonly esteemed good citizens. Others — as most legislators, politicians, lawyers, ministers, and office-holders — serve the state chiefly with their heads; and, as they rarely make any moral distinctions, they are as likely to serve the Devil, without *intending* it, as God. A very few, as heroes, patriots, martyrs, reformers in the great sense, and *men,* serve the state with their consciences also, and so necessarily resist it for the most part; and they are commonly treated as enemies by it. A wise man will only be useful as a man, and will not submit to be "clay," and "stop a hole to keep the wind away," but leave that office to his dust at least: —

"I am too high-born to be propertied,
To be a secondary at control,
Or useful serving-man and instrument
To any sovereign state throughout the world."

He who gives himself entirely to his fellow-men appears to them useless and selfish; but he who gives himself partially to them is pronounced a benefactor and philanthropist.

How does it become a man to behave toward this American government to-day? I answer, that he cannot without disgrace be associated with it. I cannot for an instant recognize that political organization as *my* government which is the *slave's* government also.

All men recognize the right of revolution; that is, the right to refuse allegiance to, and to resist, the government, when its tyranny or its inefficiency are great and unendurable. But almost all say that such is not the case now. But such was the case, they think, in the Revolution of '75. If one were to tell me that this was a bad government because it taxed certain foreign commodities brought to its ports, it is most probable that I should not make an ado about it, for I can do without them. All machines have their friction; and possibly this does enough good to counterbalance the evil. At any rate, it is a great evil to make a stir about it. But when the friction comes to have its machine, and oppression and robbery are organized, I say, let us not have such a machine any longer. In other words, when a sixth of the population of a nation which has undertaken to be the refuge of liberty are slaves, and a whole country is unjustly overrun and conquered by a foreign army, and subjected to military law, I think that it is not too soon for honest men to rebel and revolutionize. What makes this duty the more urgent is the fact that the country so overrun is not our own, but ours is the invading army. . . .

Unjust laws exist: shall we be content to obey them, or shall we endeavor to amend them, and obey them until we have succeeded, or shall we transgress them at once? Men generally, under such a government as this, think that they ought to wait until they have persuaded the majority to alter them. They think that, if they should resist, the remedy would be worse than the evil. But it is the fault of the government itself that the remedy *is* worse than the evil. *It* makes it worse. Why is it not more apt to anticipate and provide for reform? Why does it not cherish its wise minority? Why does it cry and resist before it is hurt? Why does it not encourage its citizens to be on the alert to point out its faults and *do* better than it would have them? Why does it always crucify Christ, and excommunicate Copernicus and Luther, and pronounce Washington and Franklin rebels? . . .

If the injustice is part of the necessary friction of the machine of government, let it go, let it go: perchance it will wear smooth,—certainly the machine will wear out. If the injustice has a spring, or a pulley, or a rope, or a crank, exclusively for itself, then perhaps you may consider whether the remedy will not be worse than the evil; but if it is of such a nature that it requires you to be the agent of injustice to another, then, I say, break the law. Let your life be a counter friction to stop the machine. What I have to do is to see, at any rate, that I do not lend myself to the wrong which I condemn.

As for adopting the ways which the state has provided for remedying the evil, I know not of such ways. They take too much time, and a man's life will be gone. I have other affairs to attend to. I came into this world, not chiefly to make this a good place to live in, but to live in it, be it good or bad. A man has not everything to do, but something; and because he cannot do *everything*, it is not necessary that he should do *something* wrong. . . .

Under a government which imprisons any unjustly, the true place for a just man is also a prison. The proper place to-day, the only place which Massachusetts has provided for her freer and less desponding spirits, is in her prisons, to be put out and locked out of the State by her own act, as they have already put themselves out by their principles. It is there that the fugitive slave, and the Mexican prisoner on parole, and the Indian come to plead the wrongs of his race should find them; on that separate, but more free and honorable ground, where the State places those who are not *with* her, but against her,—the only house in a slave State in which a free man can abide with honor. If any think that their influence would be lost there, and their voices no longer afflict the ear of the State, that they would not be as an enemy within its walls, they do not know by how much truth is stronger than error, nor how much more eloquently and effectively he can combat injustice who has experienced a little in his own person. Cast your whole vote, not a strip of paper merely, but your whole influence. A minority is powerless while it conforms to the majority; it is not even a minority then; but it is irresistible when it clogs by its whole weight. If the alternative is to keep all just men in prison, or give up war and slavery, the State will not hesitate which to choose. If a thousand men were not to pay their tax-bills this year, that would not be a violent and bloody measure, as it would be to pay them, and enable the State to commit violence and shed innocent blood. This is, in fact, the definition of a peaceable revolution, if any such is possible. If the tax-gatherer, or any other public officer, asks me, as one has done, "But what shall I do?" my answer is, "If you really wish to do anything, resign your office." When the subject has refused allegiance, and the officer has resigned his office, then the revolution is accomplished. But even suppose blood should flow. Is there not a sort of blood shed when the conscience is wounded? Through this wound a man's real manhood and immortality flow out, and he bleeds to an everlasting death. I see this blood flowing now. . . .

I please myself with imagining a State at last which can afford to be just to all men, and to treat the individual with respect as a neighbor; which even would not think it inconsistent with its own repose if a few were to live aloof from it, not meddling with it, nor embraced by it, who fulfilled all the duties of neighbors and fellow-men. A State which bore this kind of fruit, and suffered it to drop off as fast as it ripened, would prepare the way for a still more perfect and glorious State, which also I have imagined, but not yet anywhere seen.

Source: "On the Duty of Civil Disobedience." By Henry David Thoreau. Originally published as "Resistance to Civil Government." *Aesthetic Papers,* No. 1. Edited by Elizabeth Peabody. Boston, 1849.

Henry David Thoreau (1817–62) was a naturalist and writer. He published his famous *Walden* in 1854. An advocate of civil disobedience, he influenced Mahatma Gandhi and Martin Luther King, Jr.

BROOK FARM

The transcendentalists were active in the feminist and abolitionist movements, and they participated in communal experiments designed to transform America. The most famous of these experiments at the time, and the one central to the transcendentalists, was Brook Farm, located in West Roxbury, Massachusetts. As Emerson wrote to the Scottish essayist Thomas Carlyle in 1840, "We are all a little wild here with numberless projects of social reform. Not a reading man but has a draft of a new Community in his waistcoat pocket. I am gently mad myself, and am resolved to live cleanly. George Ripley is talking up another colony of agriculturalists and scholars with whom he threatens to take the field and the book. [Ripley's project became Brook Farm.] One man renounces the use of animal food; & another of coin; & another of domestic hired service; & another of the state; & on the whole we have a commendable share of reason & hope." [1] Brook Farm is remembered in part because the novelist Nathaniel Hawthorne (1804–64) lived there briefly and unhappily and wrote one of his deservedly least-known novels, *The Blithedale Romance* (1852), about the experience.

Brook Farm was originally founded in 1841 as a reform community tied closely to the transcendentalists. In 1843 it converted to the ideas of the French utopian socialist Charles Fourier (1772–1837), but the changes required were not great. Reprinted here are the original agreement drawn up at the founding of the community, a statement that accompanied the new constitution adopted in 1844, and that new constitution. The community lasted until 1847.

Articles of Agreement and Association between the members of the Institute for Agriculture and Education.

In order more effectually to promote the great purposes of human culture; to establish the external relations of life on a basis of wisdom and purity; to apply the principles of justice and love to our social organization in accordance with the laws of Divine Providence; to substitute a system of brotherly cooperation for one of selfish competition; to secure to our children, and to those who may be entrusted to our care, the benefits of the highest physical, intellectual and moral education in the present state of human knowledge, the resources at our command will permit; to institute an attractive, efficient and productive system of industry; to prevent the exercise of worldly anxiety by the competent supply of our necessary wants; to diminish the desire of excessive accumulation by making the acquisition of individual property subservient to upright and disinterested uses; to guarantee to each other the means of physical support and of spiritual progress, and thus to impart a greater freedom, simplicity, truthfulness, refinement and moral dignity to our mode of life, —

We the undersigned, do unite in a Voluntary Association, to wit: —

ARTICLE 1. The name and style of the Association shall be "(The Brook Farm) Institute of Agriculture and Education." All persons who shall hold one or more shares in the stock of the Association, and shall sign the articles of agreement, or who shall hereafter be admitted by the pleasure of the Association, shall be members thereof.

ART. 2. No religious test shall ever be required of any member of the Association; no authority assumed over individual freedom of opinion by the Association, nor by any member over another; nor shall anyone be held accountable to the Association except for such acts as violate rights of the members, and the essential principles on which the Association is founded; and in such cases the relation of any member may be suspended, or discontinued, at the pleasure of the Association.

ART. 3. The members of this Association shall own and manage such real and personal estate, in joint stock proprietorship, as may, from time to time, be agreed on, and establish such branches of industry as may be deemed expedient and desirable.

ART. 4. The Association shall provide such employment for all of its members as shall be adapted to their capacities, habits and tastes, and each member shall select and perform such operation of labor, whether corporal or mental, as he shall deem best suited to his own endowments, and the benefit of the Association.

ART. 5. The members of this Association shall be paid for all labor performed under its direction and for its advantage, at a fixed and equal rate, both for men and women. This rate shall not exceed one dollar per day, nor shall more than ten hours in the day be paid for as a day's labor.

ART. 6. The Association shall furnish to all its members, their children and family dependents, house-rents, fuel, food and clothing, and all other comforts and advantages possible, at the actual cost, as nearly as the same can be ascertained; but no charge shall be made for education, medical or nursing attendance, or the use of the library, public rooms or baths to the members; nor shall any charge be paid for food, rent or fuel by those deprived of labor by sickness, nor for food of children under ten years of age, nor for anything on members over seventy years of age, unless at the special request of the individual by whom the charges are paid, or unless the credits in his favor exceed, or equal, the amount of such charges.

ART. 7. All labor performed for the Association shall be duly credited, and all articles furnished shall be charged, and a full settlement made with every member once every year.

ART. 8. Every child over ten years of age shall be charged for food, clothing, and articles furnished at cost, and shall be credited for his labor, not exceeding fifty cents per day, and on the completion of his education in the Association at the age of twenty, shall be entitled to a certificate of stock, to the amount of credits in his favor, and many be admitted a member of the Association.

ART. 9. Every share-holder in the joint-stock proprietorship of the Association, shall be paid on such stock, at the rate of five per cent, annually.

ART. 10. The net profits of the Association remaining in the treasury after the payments of all demands for interest on stock, labor performed, and necessary repairs, and improvements shall be divided into a number of shares corresponding with the number of days' labor, and every member shall be entitled to one share for every day's labor performed by him.

ART. 11. All payments may be made in certificates of stock at the option of the Association; but in any case of need, to be decided by himself, every member may be permitted to draw on the funds of the treasury an amount not exceeding the credits in his favor.

ART. 12. The Association shall hold an annual meeting for the choice of officers, and such other necessary business as shall come before them.

ART. 13. The officers of the Association shall be twelve directors, divided into four departments, as follows: first, General Direction; second, Direction of Agriculture; third, Direction of Education; fourth, Direction of Finance; consisting of three persons each, provided that the same persons may be a member of each Direction at the pleasure of the Association.

ART. 14. The Chairman of the General Direction shall be presiding officer in the Association, and together with the Direction of Finance, shall constitute a Board of Trustees, by whom the property of the Association shall be managed.

ART. 15. The General Direction shall oversee and manage the affairs of the Association so that every department shall be carried on in an orderly and efficient manner. Each department shall be under the general supervision of its own Direction, which shall select, and, in accordance with the General Direction, shall appoint, all such overseers, directors and agents, as shall be necessary to the complete and systematic organization of the department, and shall have full authority to appoint such persons to these stations as they shall judge best qualified for the same.

ART. 16. No Directors shall be deemed to possess any rank superior to the other members of the Association, nor shall be chosen in reference to any other consideration than their capacity to serve the Association; nor shall they be paid for their official service except at the rate of one dollar for ten hours in a day, actually employed in official duties.

ART. 17. The Association may, from time to time, adopt such rules and regulations, not inconsistent with the spirit and purpose of the Articles of Agreement, as shall be found expedient and necessary.

1844 Statement

All persons who are not familiar with the purposes of Association, will understand from this document that we propose a radical and universal reform rather than to redress any particular wrong, or to remove the sufferings of any single class of human beings. We do this in the light of universal principles in which all differences, whether of religion, or politics, or philosophy, are reconciled, and the dearest and most private hope of every man has the promise of fulfillment. Herein, let it be understood, we would remove nothing that is truly beautiful or venerable; we reverence the religious sentiment in all its forms, the family and whatever else has its foundation either in human nature or Divine Providence. The work we are engaged in is not destruction, but true conservation; it is not a mere resolution, but, as we are assured, a necessary step in the progress which no one can be blind enough to think has yet reached its limit.

We believe that humanity, trained by these long centuries of suffering and struggle, led on by so many saints and heroes and sages, is at length prepared to enter into that universal order toward which it has perpetually moved. Thus we recognize the worth of the whole past, and of every doctrine and institution it has bequeathed us; thus also we perceive that the present has its own high mission, and we shall only say what is beginning to be seen by all sincere thinkers, when we declare that the imperative duty of this time and this country, nay, more, that its only salvation and the salvation of civilized countries, lies in the reorganization of society according to the unchanging laws of human nature, and of universal harmony.

We look, then, to the generous and helpful of all classes for sympathy for encouragement and for actual aid; not to ourselves only, but to all who are engaged in this great work. And whatever may be the result of any special efforts, we can never doubt that the object we have in view will be finally attained; that human life shall yet be developed, not in discord and misery, but in harmony and joy, and that the perfected earth shall at last bear on her bosom a race of men worthy of the name.

1844 Constitution

The department of Industry shall be managed in groups and series as far as is practicable, and shall consist of three primary series, to wit: Agricultural, Mechanical and Domestic Industry. The chief of each group to be elected weekly, and the chief of each series once in two months by the members thereof, subject to the approval of the General Direction.

Persons wishing to become members must first reside on the place as applicants for one month.

Applicants who have passed acceptably through their term may become candidates, and remain in this new relation a month more, when they may be admitted as Associates.

Personal property may be received as stock by the Direction of Finance when it shall be deemed advantageous to the Association.

Persons shall, on becoming residents on the domain, deliver an exact inventory of all the furniture and implements which they may retain as private property, to be filed for reference in the office of the Direction.

New groups and series may be formed from time to time for the prosecution of different and new branches of industry.

Three hundred days shall be considered a year's labor. The hours of labor shall be from the first of October to the first of April at least eight hours daily, and from the first of April to the first of October at least ten hours daily, and no person shall be credited for labor beyond that time.

No debt shall be contracted in behalf of the Association by any person whatever.

Articles furnished to the Associates shall be charged at cost as nearly as the same can be ascertained.

The period of education shall extend from birth to the age of twenty years, and shall be divided into three stages: Infancy to six years, Pupilage from six to sixteen years, and Probation from sixteen to twenty. The education during probation shall be in the practical duties of Associates.

No public meeting for business or amusement shall be protracted beyond the hour of ten P.M.

Source: Brook Farm—Historic & Personal Memoirs. By John Thomas Codman. Boston: Arena, 1894.

Education

The nineteenth-century reform movement also focused on specific issues, one of which was education. The United States was the center of the development of mass public education, and one of its founders was Horace Mann.

Horace Mann
Tenth Annual Report (1846)

As an innovation upon all preëxisting policy and usages, the establishment of Free Schools was the boldest ever promulgated, since the commencement of the Christian era. As a theory, it could have been refuted and silenced by a more formidable array of argument and experience than was ever marshalled against any other opinion of human origin. But time has ratified its soundness. Two centuries now proclaim it to be as wise as it was courageous, as beneficent as it was disinterested. It was one of those grand mental and moral experiments whose effects cannot be determined in a single generation. But now, according to the manner in which human life is computed, we are the sixth generation from its founders, and have we not reason to be grateful both to God and man for its unnumbered blessings? The sincerity of our gratitude must be tested by our efforts to perpetuate and improve what they established. The gratitude of the lips only is an unholy offering. . . .

The alleged ground upon which the founders of our Free School system proceeded, when adopting it, did not embrace the whole argument by which it may be defended. Their insight was better than their reason. They assumed a ground, indeed, satisfactory and convincing to Protestants; but, at that time, only a small portion of Christendom was Protestant, and even now only a minority of it is so. The very ground on which our Free Schools were founded, therefore, if it were the only one, would be a reason with half of Christendom, at the present time, for their immediate abolition.

In later times, and since the achievement of American Independence, the universal and ever-repeated argument in favor of Free Schools has been, that the general intelligence which they are capable of diffusing, and which can be imparted by no other human instrumentality, is indispensable to the continuance of a republican government. This argument, it is obvious, assumes, as a postulatum, the superiority of a republican over all other forms of government, and, as a people, we religiously believe in the soundness, both of the assumption and of the argument founded upon it. But if this be all, then a sincere monarchist, a defender of arbitrary power, or a believer in the divine right of kings, would oppose Free Schools, for the identical reasons we offer in their behalf. A perfect demonstration of our doctrine, — that Free Schools are the only basis of republican institutions, — would be the perfection of reasoning to his mind, that they should be immediately exterminated.

Admitting, nay claiming for ourselves, the substantial justness and soundness of the general grounds on which our system was originally established and has since been maintained; yet it is most obvious that, unless some broader and more comprehensive principle can be found, the system of Free Schools will be repudiated by whole nations as impolitic and dangerous; and, even among ourselves, all who deny our premises will, of course, set at nought the conclusions to which they lead.

Again; the expediency of Free Schools is sometimes advocated on grounds of Political Economy. An educated people is a more industrious and productive people. Knowledge and abundance sustain to each other the relation of cause and effect. Intelligence is a primary ingredient in the Wealth of Nations. Where this does not stand at the head of the inventory, the items in a nation's valuation will be few, and the sum at the foot of the column insignificant.

The moralist, too, takes up the argument of the economist. He demonstrates that vice and crime are not only prodigals and spendthrifts of their own, but defrauders and plunderers of the means of others; that they would seize upon all the gains of honest industry, and exhaust the bounties of Heaven itself, without satiating their rapacity for new means of indulgence; and that often, in the history of the world, whole generations might have been trained to industry and virtue by the wealth which one enemy to his race has destroyed.

Source: Slavery: Letters and Speeches. By Horace Mann. New York: Burt Franklin, 1969. Originally published 1851.

Horace Mann (1796–1859) was an American educator.

Minorities

This period saw the beginnings of the reservation system. This is reflected in the Treaty with the Kickapoo of 1854. Also reprinted here is Chief Seattle's famous speech on the decline of the North American Indians. Whether it accurately portrays what Chief Seattle said or was made up by a later non-Indian, the speech reflects a common attitude of the Indians.[2] This can be seen in the similar statement by Cochise, whose request to be allowed to live out his life in the mountains was denied. When he died in 1874 he was secretly buried in the mountains.

Treaty with the Kickapoo, 1854

Articles of agreement and convention made and concluded at the city of Washington this eighteenth day of May, one thousand eight hundred and fifty-four, by George W. Manypenny, commissioner on the part of the United States, and the following named delegates of the Kickapoo tribe of Indians, viz: Pah-kah-kah or John Kennekuk, Kap-i-o-mah or the Fox Carrier, No-ka-wat or the Fox Hair; Pe-sha-gon or Tug made of Bear Skin, and Ke-wi-sah-tuk or Walking Bear or Squire, thereto duly authorized by said tribe.

ARTICLE 1. The Kickapoo tribe of Indians hereby cede, sell, and convey unto the United States all that country southwest of the Missouri River, which was provided as a permanent home, for them in the treaty of Castor Hill, of the twenty-fourth of October, one thousand eight hundred and thirty-two, and described in the supplemental article thereto, entered into at Fort Leavenworth, on the 26th of November, one thousand eight hundred and thirty-two, as follow: Beginning "on the Delaware line, where said line crosses the left branch of Salt Creek, thence down said creek to the Missouri River, thence up the Missouri River thirty miles when measured on a straight line, thence westwardly to a point twenty miles from the Delaware line, so as to include in the lands assigned to the Kickapoos, at least twelve hundred square miles;" saving and reserving, in the western part thereof, one hundred and fifty thousand acres for a future and permanent home, which shall be set off for, and assigned to, them by metes and bounds. *Provided,* That upon the return home of the delegates here contracting, and upon consultation with their people, and after an exploration if required by them, in company with their agent, a location to that extent can be found within said specified section of country suited to their wants and wishes. *And it is also further provided,* That should a suitable location, upon examination and consultation, to the full extent of one hundred and fifty thousand acres, not be found, within said western part of this cession, then the said delegates and agents shall be permitted to extend the location beyond the western line of the country herein ceded and north of the recent Delaware line over so much of the public domain, otherwise unappropriated, as shall make up the deficiency—or to make a selection entirely beyond the limits of the country at present occupied by the Kickapoos upon any lands of the United States, not otherwise appropriated, lying within the limits bounded by the said western line, by the recent Delaware northern line, and the waters of the Great Nemahaw River; and in either case they shall describe their selection, which must be made within six months from the date hereof, by metes and bounds, and transmit the description thereof, signed by said delegates and agent, to the Commissioner of Indian Affairs; and thereupon, the selection so made, shall be taken and deemed as the future permanent home of the Kickapoo Indians. It is expressly understood that the Kickapoos shall claim under this article no more than one hundred and fifty thousand acres of land; and if that quantity, or any portion thereof shall be selected, as provided above, outside of the reservation herein made, then said reservation, or a quantity equal to that which may be selected outside thereof, shall be, and the same is hereby, ceded and relinquished to the United States.

ARTICLE 2. In consideration whereof the United States agree to pay to the said Indians, under the direction of the President, and in such manner as he shall from time to time prescribe, the sum of three hundred thousand dollars, as follows: one hundred thousand dollars to be invested at an interest of five per centum per annum; the interest of which shall be annually expended for educational and other beneficial purposes. The remaining two hundred thousand dollars to be paid thus: Twenty-five thousand dollars in the month of October, one thousand eight hundred and fifty-four; twenty thousand dollars during the same month in each of the years one thousand eight hundred and fifty-five and one thousand eight hundred and fifty-six; fourteen thousand dollars during the same month in each of the years one thousand eight hundred and fifty-seven and one thousand eight hundred and fifty-eight; nine thousand dollars in the same month of each of the six years next succeeding that of one thousand eight hundred and fifty-eight; seven thousand dollars in the same month of each of the four years next succeeding the expiration of the last-named period of six years; and five thousand dollars in the same month of each of the five years next succeeding the last-named four years. And as the Kickapoos will remove to a new home, and will, therefore, require the principal portion of the annual payments for several years to aid in building houses, in breaking and fencing land, in buying stock, agricultural implements, and other articles needful for their comfort and civilization, it is understood that such portion of said annual payments as may be necessary, will be appropriated to and expended for such purposes.

ARTICLE 3. The President may cause to be surveyed, in the same manner in which the public lands are surveyed, the reservation herein provided for the Kickapoos; and may assign to each person, or family desiring it, such quantity of land as, in his opinion, will be sufficient for such person, or family, with the understanding that he, or they, will occupy, improve, and cultivate the same, and comply with such other conditions as the President may prescribe. The land thus assigned may hereafter be confirmed by patent to the parties, or their representatives, under such regulations and restrictions as Congress may impose.

ARTICLE 4. It is agreed that the United States shall pay to such of the Kickapoos, as have improvement upon the lands hereby ceded a fair compensation for the same—the value to be ascertained in such mode as shall be prescribed by the President.

ARTICLE 5. The debts of Indians contracted in their private dealings as individuals, whether to traders or others, shall not be paid out of the general fund.

ARTICLE 6. It is the desire of the Kickapoo Indians that their faithful friend and interpreter, Peter Cadue, should have a home provided for him and his family. It is therefore agreed that there shall be assigned to him a tract of land equal to one section, to be taken from the legal subdivisions of the surveyed land, and to include his present residence and improvement on Cadue's Creek, and the President is authorized to issue a patent to him for the same.

ARTICLE 7. It is agreed that all roads and highways laid out by authority of law shall have right of way through the reservation on the same terms as are provided by law when roads and highways are made through lands of citizens of the United States; and railroad companies, when the lines of their roads necessarily pass through the lands of the Kickapoos, shall have right of way on the payment of a fair compensation therefor in money.

ARTICLE 8. The Kickapoos release the United States from all claims or demands of any kind whatsoever, arising or which may hereafter arise under former treaties, and agree within twelve months after the ratification of this instrument, to remove and subsist themselves, without cost to the United States; in consideration of which release and agreement the United States agree to pay them the sum of twenty thousand dollars.

ARTICLE 9. The Kickapoos promise to use their best efforts to prevent the introduction and use of ardent spirits in their country, to encourage industry, thrift, and morality, and by every possible means to promote their advancement in civilization.

Source: *Indian Affairs: Laws and Treaties*. Volume 2, *Treaties*. Washington, D.C.: Government Printing Office, 1904. Reprinted as *Indian Treaties 1778–1883*. Compiled and edited by Charles J. Kappler. New York: Interland Publishing Co., 1972.

Chief Seattle
Our People Are Ebbing Away Like a Rapidly Receding Tide

Yonder sky that has wept tears of compassion upon my people for centuries untold, and which to us appears changeless and eternal, may change. Today is fair. Tomorrow it may be overcast with cloud. My words are like the stars that never change. Whatever Seattle says the great chief at Washington can rely upon with as much certainty as he can upon the return of the sun or the seasons. The White Chief says that Big Chief at Washington sends us greetings of friendship and good will. This is kind of him for we know he has little need of our friendship in return. His people are many. They are like the grass that covers vast prairies. My people are few. They resemble the scattering trees of a storm-swept plain. The Great—and I presume—good White Chief sends us word that he wishes to buy our lands but is willing to allow us enough to live comfortably. This indeed appears just, even generous, for the Red Man no longer has rights that he need respect, and the offer may be wise also, as we are no longer in need of an extensive country.

There was a time when our people covered the land as the waves of a wind-ruffled sea cover its shell-paved floor, but that time long since passed away with the greatness of tribes that are now but a mournful memory. I will not dwell on, nor mourn over, our untimely decay, nor reproach my pale face brothers with hastening it as we too may have been somewhat to blame.

Youth is impulsive. When our young men grow angry at some real or imaginary wrong, and disfigure their faces with black paint, it denotes that their hearts are black—and then they are often cruel and relentless, and our old men and old women are unable to restrain them. Thus it has ever been. Thus it was when the white man first began to push our forefathers westward. But let us hope that the hostilities between us may never return. We would have everything to lose and nothing to gain. Revenge by young braves is considered gain, even at the cost of their own lives, but old men who stay at home in times of war, and mothers who have sons to lose, know better.

Our good father at Washington—for I presume he is now our father as well as yours . . . sends us word that if we do as he desires he will protect us. His brave warriors will be to us a bristling wall of strength, and his wonderful ships of war will fill our harbors so that our ancient enemies far to the northward . . . will cease to frighten our women, children and old men. Then in reality will he be our father and we his children. But can that ever be? Your God is not our God! Your God loves your people and hates mine. He folds his strong protecting arms lovingly about the pale face and leads him by the hand as a father leads his infant son—but He has forsaken His red children—if they are really His. Our God, the Great Spirit, seems also to have forsaken us. Your God makes your people wax strong every day. Soon they will fill all the land. Our people are ebbing away like a rapidly receding tide that will never return. The white man's God can not love our people or He would protect them. They seem to be orphans who can look nowhere for help. How then can we be brothers? How can your God become our God and renew our prosperity and awaken in us dreams of returning greatness. If we have a common Heavenly Father He must be partial—for He came to His pale-face children. We never saw Him. He gave you laws but had no word for His red children whose teeming multitudes once filled this vast continent as stars fill the firmament. No. We are two distinct races with separate origins and separate destinies. There is little in common between us.

To us the ashes of our ancestors are sacred and their resting place is hallowed ground. You wander far from the graves of your ancestors and seemingly without regret. Your religion was written on tables of stone by the iron finger of your God so that you could not forget. The Red Man could never comprehend nor remember it. Our religion is the traditions of our ancestors—the dreams of our old men, given them in the solemn hours of night by the Great Spirit; and the visions of our sachems, and is written in the hearts of our people.

Your dead cease to love you and the land of their nativity as soon as they pass the portals of the tomb and wander away beyond the stars. They are soon forgotten and never return. Our dead never forget the beautiful world that gave them being. They will love its verdant valleys, its murmuring rivers, its magnificent mountains, sequestered vales and verdant-lined lakes and bays, and ever yearn in tender, fond affection over the lonely hearted living, and often return from the Happy Hunting Ground to visit, guide, console and comfort them.

Day and night can not dwell together. The Red Man has ever fled the approach of the White Man as the morning mist flees before the rising sun.

However, your proposition seems fair, and I think that my folks will accept it and will retire to the reservation you offer them. Then we will dwell apart in peace for the words of the Great White Chief seem to be the voice of Nature speaking to my people out of dense darkness.

It matters little where we pass the remnant of our days. They will not be many. The Indian's night promises to be dark. Not a single star of hope hovers above his horizon. Sad-voiced winds moan in the distance. Grim Nemesis seems to be on the Red Man's trail, and wherever he goes he will hear the approaching footsteps of his fell destroyer and prepare to stolidly meet his doom, as does the wounded doe that hears the approaching footsteps of the hunter.

A few more moons. A few more winters—and not one of the descendants of the mighty hosts that once moved over this broad land or lived in happy homes, protected by the Great Spirit, will remain to mourn over the graves of a people—

once more powerful and hopeful than yours. But why should I mourn at the untimely fate of my people? Tribe follows tribe, and nation follows nation, like the waves of the sea. It is the order of nature, and regret is useless. Your time of decay may be distant—but it will surely come, for even the White Man whose God walked and talked with him as friend with friend, can not be exempt from the common destiny. We may be brothers after all. We will see.

We will ponder your proposition and when we decide we will let you know. But should we accept it, I here and now make this condition—that we will not be denied the privilege without molestation, of visiting at any time the tombs of our ancestors, friends and children. Every part of this soil is sacred, in the estimation of my people. Every hillside, every valley, every plain and grove, has been hallowed by some sad or happy event in days long vanished. Even the rocks, which seem to be dumb and dead as they swelter in the sun along the silent shore thrill with memories of stirring events connected with the lives of my people, and the very dust upon which you now stand responds more lovingly to their footsteps than to yours, because it is rich with the dust of our ancestors and our bare feet are conscious of the sympathetic touch. Our departed braves, fond mothers, glad, happy-hearted maidens, and even the little children who lived here and rejoiced here for a brief season, still love these sombre solitudes and at eventide they grow shadowy of returning spirits. And when the last Red Man shall have perished, and the memory of my tribe shall have become a myth among the white man, these shores will swarm with the invisible dead of my tribe, and when your children's children think themselves alone in the field, the store, the shop, upon the highway, or in the silence of the pathless woods, they will not be alone. In all the earth there is no place dedicated to solitude. At night when the streets of your cities and villages are silent and you think them deserted, they will throng with the returning hosts that once filled them and still love this beautiful land. The White Man will never be alone.

Let him be just and deal kindly with my people, for the dead are not powerless. Dead—I say? There is no death. Only a change of worlds.

Source: "Chief Seattle and Angeline." By Clarence B. Bagley. *Washington Historical Quarterly* (October 1931). Speech of October 1855.

Chief Seattle (1788–1866) was a leader of the Duwamish-Suquamish tribe.

Cochise

Plea to Live in the Mountains

The sun has been very hot on my head and made me as in a fire; my blood was on fire, but now I have come into this valley and drunk of these waters and washed myself in them and they have cooled me. Now that I am cool I have come with my hands open to you to live in peace with you, I speak straight and do not wish to deceive or be deceived. I want a good, strong and lasting peace.

When God made the world he gave one part to the white man and another to the Apache. Why was it? Why did they come together? Now that I am to speak, the sun, the moon, the earth, the air, the waters, the birds and beasts, even the children unborn shall rejoice at my words. The white people have looked for me long. I am here! What do they want? They have looked for me long; why am I worth so much? If I am worth so much why not mark when I set my foot and look when I spit? The coyotes go about at night to rob and kill; I can not see them; I am not God. I am no longer chief of all the Apaches. I am no longer rich; I am but a poor man. The world was not always this way. I can not command the animals; if I would they would not obey me. God made us not as you; we were born like the animals, in the dry grass, not on beds like you. This is why we do as the animals, go about of a night and rob and steal. If I had such things as you have, I would not do as I do, for then I would not need to do so. There are Indians who go about killing and robbing. I do not command them. If I did, they would not do so. My warriors have been killed in Sonora. I came in here because God told me to do so. He said it was good to be at peace — so I came! I was going around the world with the clouds, and the air, when God spoke to my thought and told me to come in here and be at peace with all. He said the world was for us all; how was it?

When I was young I walked all over this country, east and west, and saw no other people than the Apaches. After many summers I walked again and found another race of people had come to take it. How is it? Why is it that the Apaches wait to die — that they carry their lives on their finger nails? They roam over the hills and plains and want the heavens to fall on them. The Apaches were once a great nation; they are now but few, and because of this they want to die and so carry their lives on their finger nails. Many have been killed in battle. You must speak straight so that your words may go as sunlight to our hearts. Tell me, if the Virgin Mary has walked throughout all the land, why has she never entered the wigwam of the Apache? Why have we never seen or heard her?

I have no father nor mother; I am alone in the world. No one cares for Cochise; that is why I do not care to live, and wish the rocks to fall on me and cover me up. If I had a father and a mother like you, I would be with them and they with me. When I was going around the world, all were asking for Cochise. Now he is here—you see him and hear him—are you glad? If so, say so. Speak, Americans and Mexicans, I do not wish to hide anything from you nor have you hide anything from me; I will not lie to you; do not lie to me. I want to live in these mountains; I do not want to go to Tularosa. That is a long ways off. The flies on those mountains eat out the eyes of the horses. The bad spirits live there. I have drunk of these waters and they cooled me; I do not want to leave here.

Source: "Reflections of an Interview with Cochise." By A. N. Ellis. *Kansas State Historical Society Reports* 13 (1913–14).

Cochise (1812?–74) was a chief of the Chirichua Apaches.

Women

This was also the period in which the women's movement began its first major advance. The two documents reprinted here are the "Declaration of Sentiments," the Declaration of Independence of the women's movement, and a famous speech by Sojourner Truth (1797–1883), an ex-slave, usually called "Ain't I a Woman." The "Declaration of Sentiments" was adopted by the first women's suffrage convention held in the United States, at Seneca Falls, New York, in 1848. The convention was called by Elizabeth Cady Stanton (1815–1902), Lucretia Mott (1793–1880), and others as a response to their not being allowed to participate in an international antislavery convention in London. When the purpose of their meeting was discovered, they were locked out of the hall in Seneca Falls, but they managed to break in and hold their meeting.

The speech by Sojourner Truth was given three years later at another women's rights convention. The version given here is the one reported by Frances D. Gage, which is the best known version. It is generally considered to reflect more conflict between Truth and her audience than was actually the case.

Declaration of Sentiments

When, in the course of human events, it becomes necessary for one portion of the family of man to assume among the people of the earth a position different from that which they have hitherto occupied, but one to which the laws of nature and of nature's God entitle them, a decent respect to the opinions of mankind requires that they should declare the causes that impel them to such a course.

We hold these truths to be self-evident: that all men and women are created equal; that they are endowed by their Creator with certain inalienable rights; that among these are life, liberty, and the pursuit of happiness; that to secure these rights governments are instituted, deriving their just powers from the consent of the governed. Whenever any form of government becomes destructive of these ends, it is the right of those who suffer from it to refuse allegiance to it, and to insist upon the institution of a new government, laying its foundation on such principles, and organizing its powers in such form, as to them shall seem most likely to effect their safety and happiness. Prudence indeed, will dictate that governments long established should not be changed for light and transient causes; and accordingly all experience hath shown that mankind are more disposed to suffer, while evils are sufferable, than to right themselves by abolishing the forms to which they were accustomed. But when a long train of abuses and usurpations, pursuing invariably the same object evinces a design to reduce them under absolute despotism, it is their duty to throw off such government, and to provide new guards for their future security. Such has been the patient sufferance of the women under this government, and such is now the necessity which constrains them to demand the equal station to which they are entitled.

The history of mankind is a history of repeated injuries and usurpations on the part of man toward woman, having in direct object the establishment of an absolute tyranny over her. To prove this, let facts be submitted to a candid world.

He has never permitted her to exercise her inalienable right to the elective franchise.

He has compelled her to submit to laws, in the formation of which she had no voice.

He has withheld from her rights which are given to the most ignorant and degraded men—both natives and foreigners.

Having deprived her of this first right of a citizen, the elective franchise, thereby leaving her without representation in the halls of legislation, he has oppressed her on all sides.

He has made her, if married, in the eye of the law, civilly dead.

He has taken from her all right in property, even to the wages she earns.

He has made her, morally, an irresponsible being, as she can commit many crimes with impunity, provided they be done in the presence of her husband. In the covenant of marriage, she is compelled to promise obedience to her husband, he becoming, to all intents and purposes, her master—the law giving him power to deprive her of her liberty, and to administer chastisement.

He has so framed the laws of divorce, as to what shall be the proper causes, and in case of separation, to whom the guardianship of the children shall be given, as to be wholly regardless of the happiness of women—the law, in all cases, going upon a false supposition of the supremacy of man, and giving all power into his hands.

After depriving her of all rights as a married woman, if single, and the owner of property, he has taxed her to support a government which recognizes her only when her property can be made profitable to it.

He has monopolized nearly all the profitable employments, and from those she is permitted to follow, she receives but a scanty remuneration. He closes against her all the avenues to wealth and distinction which he considers most honorable to himself. As a teacher of theology, medicine, or law, she is not known.

He has denied her the facilities for obtaining a thorough education, all colleges being closed against her.

He allows her in Church, as well as State, but a subordinate position, claiming Apostolic authority for her exclusion from the ministry, and, with some exceptions, from any public participation in the affairs of the Church.

He has created a false public sentiment by giving to the world a different code of morals for men and women, by which moral delinquencies which exclude women from society, are not only tolerated, but deemed of little account in man.

He has usurped the prerogative of Jehovah himself, claiming it as his right to assign for her a sphere of action, when that belongs to her conscience and to her God.

He has endeavored, in every way that he could, to destroy her confidence in her own powers, to lessen her self-respect, and to make her willing to lead a dependent and abject life.

Now, in view of this entire disfranchisement of one-half the people of this country, their social and religious degradation—in view of the unjust laws above mentioned, and because women do feel themselves aggrieved, oppressed, and fraudulently deprived of their most sacred rights, we insist that they have immediate admission to all the rights and privileges which belong to them as citizens of the United States.

In entering upon the great work before us, we anticipate no small amount of misconception, misrepresentation, and ridicule; but we shall use every instrumentality within our power to effect our object. We shall employ agents, circulate tracts, petition the State and National legislatures, and endeavor to enlist the pulpit and the press in our behalf. We hope this Convention will be followed by a series of Conventions embracing every part of the country.

Source: History of Woman Suffrage. Edited by Elizabeth Cady Stanton, Susan B. Anthony, and Matilda Joslyn Gage, 1:70–71. New York: Fowler & Wells, 1881.

Sojourner Truth: "Ain't I a Woman"
(Reminiscences of Frances D. Gage)

The leaders of the movement trembled on seeing a tall, gaunt black woman in a gray dress and white turban, surmounted with an uncouth sun-bonnet, march deliberately into the church, walk with the air of a queen up the aisle, and take her seat upon the pulpit steps. A buzz of disapprobation was heard all over the house, and there fell on the listening ear, "An abolition affair!" "Woman's rights and niggers!" "I told you so!" "Go it, darkey!"

I chanced on that occasion to wear my first laurels in public life as president of the meeting. At my request order was restored, and the business of the Convention went on. Morning, afternoon, and evening exercises came and went. Through all these sessions old Sojourner, quiet and reticent as the "Lybian Statue," sat crouched against the wall on the corner of the pulpit stairs, her sun-bonnet shading her eyes, her elbows on her knees, her chin resting upon her broad, hard palms. At intermission she was busy selling the "Life of Sojourner Truth," a narrative of her own strange and adventurous life. Again and again, timorous and trembling ones came to me and said, with earnestness, "Don't let her speak, Mrs Gage, it will ruin us. Every newspaper in the land will have our cause mixed up with abolition and niggers, and we shall be utterly denounced." My only answer was, "We shall see when the time comes."

The second day the work waxed warm. Methodist, Baptist, Episcopal, Presbyterian, and Universalist ministers came in to hear and discuss the resolutions presented. One claimed superior rights and privileges for man, on the ground of "superior intellect"; another, because of the "manhood of Christ; if God had desired the equality of woman, He would have given some token of His will through the birth, life, and death of the Saviour." Another gave us a theological view of the "sin of our first mother." There were very few women in those days who dared to "speak in meeting"; and the august teachers of the people were seemingly getting the better of us, while the boys in the galleries, and the sneerers among the pews, were hugely enjoying the discomfiture, as they supposed, of the "strong-minded." Some of the tender-skinned friends were on the point of losing dignity, and the atmosphere betokened a storm. When, slowly from her seat in the corner rose Sojourner Truth, who, till now, had scarcely lifted her head. "Don't let her speak!" gasped half a dozen in my ear. She moved slowly and solemnly to the front, laid her old bonnet at her feet, and turned her great speaking eyes to me. There was a hissing sound of disapprobation above and below. I rose and announced "Sojourner Truth," and begged the audience to keep silence for a few moments.

The tumult subsided at once, and every eye was fixed on this almost Amazon form, which stood nearly six feet high, head erect, and eyes piercing the upper air like one in a dream. At her first word there was a profound hush. She spoke in deep tones, which, though not loud, reached every ear in the house, and away through the throng at the doors and windows.

"Wall, chilern, whar dar is so much racket dar must be somethin' out o' kilter. I tink dat 'twixt de niggers of de Souf and de womin at de Norf, all talkin' 'bout rights, de white men will be in a fix pretty soon. But what's all dis here talkin' 'bout?

"Dat man ober dar say dat womin needs to be helped into carriages, and lifted ober ditches, and to hab de best place everywhar. Nobody eber helps me into carriages, or ober mud-puddles, or gibs me any best place!" And raising herself to her full height, and her voice to a pitch like rolling thunder, she asked, "And a'n't I a woman? Look at me! Look at my arm! (and she bared her right arm to the shoulder, showing her tremendous muscular power). I have ploughed, and planted, and gathered into barns, and no man could head me! And a'n't I a woman? I could work as much and eat as much as a man—when I could get it—and bear de lash as well! And a'n't I a woman? I have borne thirteen children, and see 'em mos' all sold off to slavery, and when I cried out with my mother's grief, none but Jesus heard me! And a'n't I a woman?

"Den dey talks 'bout dis ting in de head; what dis dey call it?" ("Intellect," whispered some one near.) "Dat's it, honey. What's dat got to do wid womin's rights or nigger's rights? If my cup won't hold but a pint, and yourn holds a quart, wouldn't ye be mean not to let me have my little half-measure full?" And she pointed her significant finger, and sent a keen glance at the minister who had made the argument. The cheering was long and loud.

"Den dat little man in black dar, he say women can't have as much rights as men, 'cause Christ wan't a woman! Whar did your Christ come from?" Rolling thunder couldn't have stilled that crowd, as did those deep, wonderful tones, as she stood there with outstretched arms and eyes of fire. Raising her voice still louder, she repeated, "Whar did your Christ come? From God and a woman! Man had nothin' to do wid Him." Oh, what a rebuke that was to that little man.

Turning again to another objector, she took up the defense of Mother Eve. I can not follow her through it all. It was pointed, and witty, and solemn; eliciting at almost every sentence deafening applause; and she ended by asserting: "If de fust woman God ever made was strong enough to turn de world upside down all alone, dese women togedder (and she glanced her eye over the platform) ought to be able to turn it back, and get it right side up again! And now dey is asking to do it, de men better let 'em." Long-continued cheering greeted this. "Bleeged to ye for hearin' on me, and now ole Sojourner han't got nothin' more to say."

Amid roars of applause, she returned to her corner, leaving more than one of us with streaming eyes, and hearts beating with gratitude. She had taken us up in her strong arms and carried us safely over the slough of difficulty turning the whole tide in our favor. I have never in my life seen anything like the magical influence that subdued the mobbish spirit of the day, and turned the sneers and jeers of an excited crowd into notes of respect and admiration. Hundreds rushed up to shake hands with her, and congratulate the glorious old mother, and bid her God-speed on her mission of "testifyin' agin concerning the wickedness of this 'ere people."

Source: History of Woman Suffrage. Edited by Elizabeth Cady Stanton, Susan B. Anthony, and Matilda Joslyn Gage, 1:115–17.New York: Fowler & Wells, 1881.

Sojourner Truth (1797–1883) was born a slave and became a noted lecturer and abolitionist.

Notes

1. *The Correspondence of Emerson and Carlyle,* edited by Joseph Slater (New York: Columbia University Press, 1946), 283–84. Letter of October 30, 1840.

2. For a discussion of the various speeches attributed to Chief Seattle and their origins, see Rudolf Kaiser, "Chief Seattle's Speech(es): American Origins and European Reception." In *Recovering the Word: Essays on Native American Literature,* edited by Brian Swann and Arnold Krupat (Berkeley: University of California Press, 1987), 497–536.

CHAPTER 7

Reconstruction, 1865–1877

✳ ✳ ✳

Celebrating America

Patriotism has been a strong force in American thought and culture. Walt Whitman (1819–92) is particularly noted for his poems celebrating American life. His "Starting from Paumanok" is a particularly strong statement of patriotism and reflects Whitman's belief that American democracy breaks down class and regional divisions. The first version of the poem was published in 1860.

Walt Whitman

Starting from Paumanok.

I

Starting from fish-shape Paumanok where I was born,
Well-begotten, and rais'd by a perfect mother,
After roaming many lands, lover of populous pavements,
Dweller in Mannahatta my city, or on southern savannas,
Or a soldier camp'd or carrying my knapsack and gun, or a miner
  in California,
Or rude in my home in Dakota's woods, my diet meat, my drink
  from the spring,
Or withdrawn to muse and meditate in some deep recess,
Far from the clank of crowds intervals passing rapt and happy,
Aware of the fresh free giver the flowing Missouri, aware of mighty
  Niagara,
Aware of the buffalo herds grazing the plains, the hirsute and
  strong-breasted bull,
Of earth, rocks, Fifth-month flowers experienced, stars, rain, snow,
  my amaze,

Having studied the mocking-bird's tones and the flight of the
    mountain-hawk,
And heard at dawn the unrivall'd one, the hermit thrush from the
    swamp-cedars,
Solitary, singing in the West, I strike up for a New World.

2

Victory, union, faith, identity, time,
The indissoluble compacts, riches, mystery,
Eternal progress, the kosmos, and the modern reports,

This then is life,
Here is what has come to the surface after so many throes and
    convulsions.

How curious! how real!
Underfoot the divine soil, overhead the sun.

See revolving the globe,
The ancestor-continents away group'd together,
The present and future continents north and south, with the
    isthmus between.

See, vast trackless spaces,
As in a dream they change, they swiftly fill,
Countless masses debouch upon them,
They are now cover'd with the foremost people, arts, institutions,
    known.

See, projected through time,
For me an audience interminable.

With firm and regular step they wend, they never stop,
Successions of men, Americanos, a hundred millions,
One generation playing its part and passing on,
Another generation playing its part and passing on in its turn,
With faces turn'd sideways or backward towards me to listen,
With eyes retrospective towards me.

3

Americanos! conquerors! marches humanitarian!
Foremost! century marches! Libertad! masses!
For you a programme of chants.

Chants of the prairies,
Chants of the long-running Mississippi, and down to the Mexican
    sea,
Chants of Ohio, Indiana, Illinois, Iowa, Wisconsin and Minnesota,
Chants going forth from the centre from Kansas, and thence equi-
    distant,
Shooting in pulses of fire ceaseless to vivify all. . . .

6

I will make a song for these States that no one State may under
    any circumstances be subjected to another State,
And I will make a song that there shall be comity by day and by
    night between all the States, and between any two of them,
And I will make a song for the ears of the President, full of weap-
    ons with menacing points. . . .

12

Democracy! near at hand to you a throat is now inflating itself
    and joyfully singing.

Ma femme! for the brood beyond us and of us,
For those who belong here and those to come,
I exultant to be ready for them will now shake out carols stronger
    and haughtier than have ever yet been heard upon earth.

I will make the songs of passion to give them their way,
And your songs outlaw'd offenders, for I scan you with kindred
    eyes, and carry you with me the same as any.

I will make the true poem of riches,
To earn for the body and the mind whatever adheres and goes
    forward and is not dropt by death;
I will effuse egotism and show it underlying all, and I will be the
    bard of personality,
And I will show of male and female that either is but the equal
    of the other,
And sexual organs and acts! do you concentrate in me, for I am
    determin'd to tell you with courageous clear voice to prove
    you illustrious,
And I will show that there is no imperfection in the present, and
    can be none in the future,

And I will show that whatever happens to anybody it may be
　　turn'd to beautiful results,
And I will show that nothing can happen more beautiful than
　　death,
And I will thread a thread through my poems that time and events
　　are compact,
And that all the things of the universe are perfect miracles, each
　　as profound as any.

I will not make poems with reference to parts,
But I will make poems, songs, thoughts, with reference to ensemble,
And I will not sing with reference to a day, but with reference to
　　all days,
And I will not make a poem nor the least part of a poem but has
　　reference to the soul,
Because having look'd at the objects of the universe, I find there
　　is no one nor any particle of one but has reference to the soul.

14

Whoever you are, to you endless announcements!

Daughter of the lands did you wait for your poet?
Did you wait for one with a flowing mouth and indicative hand?
Toward the male of the States, and toward the female of the States,
Exulting words, words to Democracy's lands.

Interlink'd, food-yielding lands!
Land of coal and iron! land of gold! land of cotton, sugar, rice!
Land of wheat, beef, pork! land of wool and hemp! land of the
　　apple and the grape!
Land of the pastoral plains, the grass-fields of the world! land of
　　those sweet-air'd interminable plateaus!
Land of the herd, the garden, the healthy house of adobie!
Lands where the north-west Columbia winds, and where the south-
　　west Colorado winds!
Land of the eastern Chesapeake! land of the Delaware!
Land of Ontario, Erie, Huron, Michigan!
Land of the Old Thirteen! Massachusetts land! land of Vermont
　　and Connecticut!
Land of the ocean shores! land of sierras and peaks!
Land of boatmen and sailors! fishermen's land!

Inextricable lands! the clutch'd together! the passionate ones!

The side by side! the elder and younger brothers! the bony-limb'd!

The great women's land! the feminine! the experienced sisters
    and the inexperienced sisters!

Far breath'd land! Arctic braced! Mexican breez'd! the diverse!
    the compact!

The Pennsylvanian! the Virginian! the double Carolinian!

O all and each well-loved by me! my intrepid nations! O I at
    any rate include you all with perfect love!

I cannot be discharged from you! not from one any sooner than
    another!

O death! O for all that, I am yet of you unseen this hour with
    irrepressible love,

Walking New England, a friend, a traveller,

Splashing my bare feet in the edge of the summer ripples on Pau-
    manok's sands,

Crossing the prairies, dwelling again in Chicago, dwelling in every
    town,

Observing shows, births, improvements, structures, arts,

Listening to orators and oratresses in public halls,

Of and through the States as during life, each man and woman
    my neighbor,

The Louisianian, the Georgian, as near to me, and I as near to
    him and her,

The Mississippian and Arkansian yet with me, and I yet with any
    of them,

Yet upon the plains west of the spinal river, yet in my house of
    adobie,

Yet returning eastward, yet in the Seaside State or in Maryland,

Yet Kanadian cheerily braving the winter, the snow and ice wel-
    come to me,

Yet a true son either of Maine or of the Granite State, or the Nar-
    ragansett Bay State, or the Empire State,

Yet sailing to other shores to annex the same, yet welcoming every
    new brother,

Hereby applying these leaves to the new ones from the hour they
    unite with the old ones,

Coming among the new ones myself to be their companion and
    equal, coming personally to you now,

Enjoining you to acts, characters, spectacles, with me.

On my way a moment I pause,

Here for you! and here for America!

Still the present I raise aloft, still the future of the States I
harbinge glad and sublime,

And for the past I pronounce what the air holds of the red
aborigines.

The red aborigines,

Leaving natural breaths, sounds of rain and winds, calls as of birds
and animals in the woods, syllabled to us for names,

Okonee, Koosa, Ottawa, Monongahela, Sauk, Natchez, Chatta-
hoochee, Kaqueta, Oronoco,

Wabash, Miami, Saginaw, Chippewa, Oshkosh, Walla-Walla,

Leaving such to the States they melt, they depart, charging the
water and the land with names. . . .

See, steamers steaming through my poems,

See, in my poems immigrants continually coming and landing,

See, in arriere, the wigwam, the trail, the hunter's hut, the flat-boat,
the maize-leaf, the claim, the rude fence, and the backwoods
village,

See, on the one side the Western Sea and on the other the Eastern
Sea, how they advance and retreat upon my poems as
upon their own shores,

See, pastures and forests in my poems—see, animals wild and
tame—see, beyond the Kaw, countless herds of buffalo
feeding on short curly grass,

See, in my poems, cities, solid, vast, inland, with paved streets,
with iron and stone edifices, ceaseless vehicles, and commerce,

See, the many-cylinder'd steam printing-press—see, the electric
telegraph stretching across the continent,

See, through Atlantica's depths pulses American Europe reaching,
pulses of Europe duly return'd,

See, the strong and quick locomotive as it departs, panting, blowing
the steam-whistle,

See, ploughmen ploughing farms—see, miners digging mines—
see, the numberless factories,

See, mechanics busy at their benches with tools—see from among
them superior judges, philosophs, Presidents, emerge, drest
in working dresses,

See, lounging through the shops and fields of the States, me well-
    belov'd, close-held by day and night,
Here the loud echoes of my songs there—read the hints come at last.

Source: *Leaves of Grass*. By Walt Whitman. New York: Carlton House, n.d. [1891–92].

Walt Whitman (1819–92) was one of the most important poets in the United States. He thought of himself as a poet of democracy, and many of his poems have patriotic themes.

*   *   *

Although there were other developments, the period after the Civil War was dominated by issues related to rebuilding the Union and to the status of the freed slaves. Reconstruction had to deal with the fact that the war had left four million landless ex-slaves, as well as half a million landless whites, in a setting where the economic and social structure had been destroyed.

Our understanding of the period called Reconstruction has undergone major shifts over time. Until the 1890s, Reconstruction was generally seen as a positive force. From the 1890s to the 1960s, racism dominated the interpretations. The South had lost the war, but it won the peace through the development of myths about the Southern past, films such as *Birth of a Nation* and *Gone with the Wind*, and the general acceptance of Social Darwinism and the racism that went with it. Southern labels for the participants in Reconstruction stuck: "Carpetbaggers" were the well-educated, generally conscientious and honest administrators from the North, and the "Scalawags" were the Southerners (usually opponents of the war) who worked with them. African-American legislators and elected officials were depicted as stupid and corrupt, although they were in fact generally well educated and no more corrupt than the people they replaced.

The Emancipation Proclamation

The Emancipation Proclamation of 1863 was the first official government act freeing slaves. Although rightly seen as the first step to ending slavery, it was limited to those states and parts of states in actual rebellion at the time, as listed in the fifth paragraph. Thus, it did not affect slavery in areas loyal to the Union, and it had no legal effect in places where it did apply because these were part of the Confederate States of America and operated under its laws.

Abraham Lincoln
Emancipation Proclamation

Whereas, on the twenty-second day of September, in the year of our Lord one thousand eight hundred and sixty-two, a proclamation was issued by the President of the United States, containing, among other things, the following, to wit:

"That on the first day of January, in the year of our Lord one thousand eight hundred and sixty-three, all persons held as slaves within any state or designated part of a state, the people whereof shall then be in rebellion against the United States, shall be then, thenceforward, and forever, free; and the Executive Government of the United States, including the military and naval authority thereof, will recognize and maintain the freedom of such persons, and will do no act or acts to repress such persons, or any of them, in any efforts they may make for their actual freedom.

"That the Executive will, on the first day of January aforesaid, by proclamation, designate the states and parts of states, if any, in which the people thereof, respectively, shall then be in rebellion against the United States; and the fact that any state, or the people thereof, shall on that day be in good faith represented in the Congress of the United States, by members chosen thereto at elections wherein a majority of the qualified voters of such states shall have participated, shall, in the absence of strong countervailing testimony, be deemed conclusive evidence that such state, and the people thereof, are not then in rebellion against the United States."

Now, therefore, I, Abraham Lincoln, President of the United States, by virtue of the power in me vested as commander-in-chief of the army and navy of the United States, in time of actual armed rebellion against the authority and government of the United States, and as a fit and necessary war measure for suppressing said rebellion, do, on this first day of January, in the year of our Lord one thousand eight hundred and sixty-three, and in accordance with my purpose so to do, publicly proclaimed for the full period of one hundred days from the day first above mentioned, order and designate as the states and parts of states wherein the people thereof, respectively, are this day in rebellion against the United States, the following, to wit:

Arkansas, Texas, Louisiana (except the parishes of St. Bernard, Plaquemines, Jefferson, St. Johns, St. Charles, St. James, Ascension, Assumption, Terre Bonne, Lafourche, St. Mary, St. Martin, and Orleans, including the city of New Orleans), Mississippi, Alabama, Florida, Georgia, South Carolina, North Carolina, and Virginia (except the forty-eight counties designated as West Virginia, and also the counties of Berkeley, Accomac, Northampton, Elizabeth City, York, Princess Ann, and Norfolk, including the cities of Norfolk and Porstmouth) and which excepted parts are for the present left precisely as if this proclamation were not issued.

And by virtue of the power and for the purpose aforesaid, I do order and declare that all persons held as slaves within said designated states and parts of states are, and henceforward shall be, free, and that the Executive Government of the United States, including the military and naval authorities thereof, will recognize and maintain the freedom of said persons.

And I hereby enjoin upon the people so declared to be free to abstain from all violence, unless in necessary self-defense; and I recommend to them that, all cases when allowed, they labor faithfully for reasonable wages.

And I further declare and make known that such persons, of suitable condition, will be received into the armed service of the United States to garrison forts, positions, stations, and other places, and to man vessels of all sorts in said service.

And upon this act, sincerely believed to be an act of justice, warranted by the Constitution upon military necessity, I invoke the considerate judgment of mankind and the gracious favor of Almighty God.

In witness whereof, I have hereunto set my hand and caused the seal of the United States to be affixed. Done at the city of the Washington this first day of January, in the year of our Lord one thousand eight hundred and sixty-three, and of the Independence of the United States of America the eighty-seventh.

Source: 12 Stat. (1865) 1268.

Abraham Lincoln (1808–65) was the sixteenth president of the United States.

The Problems of Freedom

During the war Congress passed various laws intended to deal with the postwar era. "An Act to guarantee . . . a Republican Government" set up procedures for the re-establishment of state governments in those states that had joined the Confederate States of America. Note the voting restrictions in Section 4.

An Act to guarantee to certain States whose governments have been usurped or overthrown a republican form of government.

Be it enacted by the Senate and House of Representatives of the United States of America in Congress assembled, That in the States declared in rebellion against the United States the President shall, by and with the advice and consent of the Senate, appoint for each a provisional governor, whose pay and emoluments shall not exceed that of a brigadier-general of volunteers, who shall be charged with the civil administration of such State until a State government therein shall be recognized as hereinafter provided.

Sec. 2. And be it further enacted, That so soon as the military resistance to the United States shall have been suppressed in any such State and the people thereof shall have sufficiently returned to their obedience to the Constitution and the laws of the United States the provisional governor shall direct the marshal of the United States, as speedily as may be, to name a sufficient number of deputies, and to enroll all white male citizens of the United States resident in the State in their respective counties, and to request each one to take the oath to support the Constitution of the United States, and in his enrollment to designate those who take and those who refuse to take that oath, which rolls shall be forthwith returned to the provisional governor; and if the persons taking that oath shall amount to a majority of the persons enrolled in the State, he shall, by proclamation, invite the loyal people of the State to elect delegates to a convention charged to declare the will of the people of the State relative to the reestablishment of a State government, subject to and in conformity with the Constitution of the United States.

Sec. 3. And be it further enacted, That the convention shall consist of as many members as both houses of the last constitutional State legislature, apportioned by the provisional governor among the counties, parishes, or districts of the State, in proportion to the white population returned as electors by the marshal in compliance with the provisions of this act. The provisional governor shall, by proclamation, declare the number of delegates to be elected by each county, parish, or election district; name a day of election not less than thirty days thereafter; designate the places of voting in each county, parish, or district, conforming as nearly as may be convenient to the places used in the State elections next preceding the rebellion; appoint one or more commissioners to hold the election at each place of voting, and provide an adequate force to keep the peace during the election.

Sec. 4. And be it further enacted, That the delegates shall be elected by the loyal white male citizens of the United States of the age of 21 years, and resident at the time in the county, parish, or district in which they shall offer to vote, and enrolled as aforesaid, or absent in the military service of the United States, and who shall take and subscribe the oath of allegiance to the United States in the form contained in the act of Congress of July 2, 1862; and all such citizens of the United States who are in the military service of the United States shall vote at the headquarters of their respective commands, under such regulations as may be prescribed by the provisional governor for the taking and return of their votes; but no person who has held or exercised any office, civil or military, State or Confederate, under the rebel usurpation, or who has voluntarily borne arms against the United States, shall vote or be eligible to be elected as delegate at such election.

Sec. 5. *And be it further enacted,* That the said commissioners, or either of them, shall hold the election in conformity with this act, and, so far as may be consistent therewith, shall proceed in the manner used in the State prior to the rebellion. The oath of allegiance shall be taken and subscribed on the poll book by every voter in the form above prescribed, but every person known by or proved to the commissioners to have held or exercised any office, civil or military, State or Confederate, under the rebel usurpation, or to have voluntarily borne arms against the United States, shall be excluded though he offer to take the oath; and in case any person who shall have borne arms against the United States shall offer to vote, he shall be deemed to have borne arms voluntarily unless he shall prove the contrary by the testimony of a qualified voter. The poll book, showing the name and oath of each voter, shall be returned to the provisional governor by the commissioners of election, or the one acting, and the provisional governor shall canvass such returns and declare the person having the highest number of votes elected.

Sec. 6. *And be it further enacted,* That the provisional governor shall, by proclamation, convene the delegates elected as aforesaid at the capital of the State on a day not more than three months after the election, giving at least thirty days' notice of such day. In case the said capital shall in his judgment be unfit, he shall in his proclamation appoint another place. He shall preside over the deliberations of the convention and administer to each delegate, before taking his seat in the convention, the oath of allegiance to the United States in the form above prescribed.

Sec. 7. *And be it further enacted,* That the convention shall declare on behalf of the people of the State their submission to the Constitution and laws of the United States, and shall adopt the following provisions, hereby prescribed by the United States in the execution of the constitutional duty to guarantee a republican form of government to every State, and incorporate them in the constitution of the State; that is to say:

First. No person who has held or exercised any office, civil or military (except offices merely ministerial and military offices below the grade of colonel), State or Confederate, under the usurping power, shall vote for or be a member of the legislature or governor.

Second. Involuntary servitude is forever prohibited, and the freedom of all persons is guaranteed in said State.

Third. No debt, State or Confederate, created by or under the sanction of the usurping power shall be recognized or paid by the state.

Sec. 8. *And be it further enacted,* That when the convention shall have adopted those provisions it shall proceed to reestablish a republican form of government and ordain a constitution containing those provisions, which, when adopted, the convention shall by ordinance provide for submitting to the people of the State entitled to vote under this law, at an election to be held in the manner prescribed by the act for the election of delegates, but at a time and place named by the convention, at which election the said electors, and none others, shall vote directly for or against such constitution and form of State government. And the returns of said election shall be made to the provisional governor, who shall canvass the same in the presence of the electors, and if a majority of the votes cast shall be for the constitution and form of government, he shall certify the same, with a copy thereof, to the President of the United States, who, after obtaining the assent of Congress, shall, by proclamation, recognize the government so established, and none other, as the constitutional government of the State; and from the date of such recognition, and not before, Senators and Representatives and electors for President and Vice-President may be elected in such State, according to the laws of the State and of the United States.

Source: H.R. 244, 38th Congress, first session (1863).

* * *

One of the most important programs established during the war was the Freedmen's Bureau, which was to set up procedures for the transition from slavery to freedom. The American Freedmen's Inquiry Commission reported on the situation during the war and made proposals for the post-war period. Selections from its report follow.

The Commission's perception of slavery led it to stress the problems arising from the dependence on and obedience to the master and the lack of family ties. At the same time the report argues that the ex-slaves are capable of rapidly adjusting to freedom as long as they are helped through a transition period, found work, and educated. Very little of this was actually done. Programs were established to educate both the poor whites and the ex-slaves but few were actually implemented. The intended land reform either was not carried out or was quickly reversed.

American Freedmen's Inquiry Commission

New York, June 30, 1863.

Section I.—*Negroes as refugees.*
(District of Columbia, Eastern Virginia, and North Carolina.)

All the investigations and inquiries the Commission have made throughout the above sections of country, all the evidence they have there collected in connection with the character and condition of the negro population, who from all quarters find refuge within our lines, tend to this—that these refugees need not be, except for a very brief period, any burden whatever on the Government, but that, on the contrary, they may speedily become, under a system of supervision not difficult either to arrange or to conduct, provided the proper persons be employed, auxiliaries to the Government in its prosecution of the war, to the full as efficient as if the same number of loyal whites had emigrated into the Northern States.

The evidence before the Commission establishes beyond cavil the fact that these refugees are, with rare exceptions, loyal men, putting faith in the Government, looking to it for guidance and protection, willing to work for moderate wages if promptly paid, docile and easily managed, not given to quarreling among themselves, of temperate habits, cheerful and uncomplaining under hard labor whenever they are treated with justice and common humanity, and (in the Southern climate) able and willing, on the average, to work as long and as hard as white laborers, whether foreign or native born.

The circumstances which have thrown them, for a time, on the care of the government for support are such as operate equally upon indigent whites arrested in their ordinary course of labor by the operations of the war, and it is a mistake to suppose that assistance has been needed or obtained exclusively by persons of color in consequence of such disturbance. In some places the number of poor whites succored has been greater than that of poor blacks. In November last Major-General Butler was feeding in New Orleans 32,000 whites, 17,000 of whom were British-born subjects, and only 10,000 negroes, these last chiefly women and children, the able-bodied negro men being usually employed on the abandoned plantations.

Nor, where relief has been required by both whites and blacks, have the latter usually applied for or received, in proportion to numbers, nearly as much as the former. Mr. Vincent Colyer, appointed by General Burnside at New Berne, N. C., superintendent of the poor, white and black, reports that while 7,500 colored persons and 1,800 white persons received relief through his instrumentality, the average proportion dealt out in each of the staple articles of food—as flour, beef, bacon, bread, &c.—was about as one for each colored person relieved to sixteen for each white person to whom such relief was granted. At the time this occurred work was offered to both blacks and whites; to the whites at the rate of $12 a month, and to the blacks at the rate of $8 a month.

Under any circumstances, and in all large societies, even during a normal and peaceful condition of things, there will be found a certain amount of vagrancy and a certain number of indigent poor, disabled, or improvident, to whom it is a custom and a duty to extend relief. Beyond this, except as an expedient for the time being, the Commission believe that the refugee freedmen need no charitable assistance. In the city of Washington, containing 16,000 free colored persons, these support their own poor without almshouse aid, and scarcely a beggar is found among them.

The vices chiefly apparent in these refugees are such as appertain to their former social condition. Men who are allowed no property do not learn to respect the rights of property. Men who are subjected to despotic rule acquire the habit of shielding themselves from arbitrary punishment by subterfuges, or by a direct departure from the truth. In the case of women living under a system in which the conjugal relation is virtually set at naught, the natural result is that the instinct of chastity remains undeveloped or becomes obscured.

Thus, stealing is a common vice among these people when temptation occurs. Thus, they have the habit of lying when they deem a lie necessary to please a white superior or a defense against blame or punishment; under other circumstances they are as truthful as the average of uneducated white people. Thus, too, many colored women think it more disgraceful to be black than to be illegitimate, for it is especially in regard to white men that their ideas and habits as to this matter are perverted. A case came to the knowledge of the Commission, in which a mulatto girl deemed it beneath her to associate with her half-sister, a black and the daughter of her mother's husband, her own father being a white man. Such ideas and the habits thereby engendered render it highly important that freedmen's villages, particularly when they are chiefly inhabited by women and children, should be at a distance from any military encampment and should be strictly guarded. And as there are no sentinels so strict as the negroes themselves, the Commission believe, for this and other reasons, that colored guards will be found the most suitable and efficient for such service; and they recommend that in every case they be substituted for whites.

The testimony of the more intelligent among the superintendents is to the effect that the vices above referred to are not obstinately rooted, and that each one of them may be gradually eradicated by a proper appeal to the self-respect of the newly-made freedman, and by a strict recognition of his rights. He is found quite ready to copy whatever he believes are the rights and obligations of what he looks up to as the superior race, even if these prove a restraint upon the habits of license belonging to his former condition.

An officer on General Dix's staff, acting as provost-judge at Fortress Monroe, related to the Commission in graphic terms with what earnestness and conscious pride of his new position a negro sworn as witness for the first time in his life stood up to take the oath and deliver his testimony.

As to the false ideas touching chastity above referred to, the Commission believe that these can be in a great measure corrected by bringing practically to the notice of the refugees as soon as they come under the care of the superintendent the obligations of the married state in civilized life. Debarred as slaves from any legal union, often from any permanent connection, unable to contract a marriage that is not liable to be broken up at the will of the master, they usually regard it as a privilege appertaining to emancipation to be married "as white folks are." The Commission think that while compulsion in regard to this matter should be avoided, a judicious superintendent will, as a general rule, find no difficulty in inducing refugees when bringing with them those whom they acknowledge to be their wives and children, to consent to a ceremony which, while it legitimizes these relations, imposes upon the husband and father the legal obligation to support his family. This obligation and the duties connected with the family relation of civilized life should be carefully explained to these people, and while they remain under our care should be strictly maintained among them. The evidence before the Commission proves that with few exceptions they show themselves prompt to acknowledge and ready to fulfill such obligations.

If, however, cases should occur in which a refugee proves refractory and refuses to acknowledge as his wife, or to marry, the woman with whom he has been living and who is the mother of his children, he should no longer be allowed to cohabit with her or to live with the children; but if the proof of his previous relationship to them be sufficient, he should be compelled to contribute to their support from his wages in the same manner as if they were his family by legal marriage. All this is especially necessary in connection with a proper system of allotment from wages. . . .

Sufficient evidence is before the Commission that colored refugees in general place a high value both on education for their children and religious instruction for themselves. In Alexandria and in various other places it came to the knowledge of the Commission that one of the first acts of the negroes when they found themselves free was to establish schools at their own expense; and in every instance where schools and churches have been provided for them they have shown lively gratitude and the greatest eagerness to avail themselves of such opportunities of improvement.

As a general rule, they are more zealously devotional than the white race; they have more resignation and more reliance on Divine Providence. They have also more superstitions. These, however, the Commission think, should not be hardly dealt with. It is of more importance sympathizingly to meet and encourage in these untaught people the religious sentiment which sways them than to endeavor in a spirit of proselytism to replace their simple faith in the Divine goodness and protection by dogmas of a more elaborate and polemical character. Practically, as regards the Christian graces of kindness and humility, we have as much to learn from them as they from us.

It is desirable that as soon as possible their schools and their churches be supported in whole or in part by themselves.

Medical aid they need in the outset and it should be provided for them; but here, too, the principle of self-support should be introduced as soon as circumstances permit. Vaccination ought to be strictly attended to.

Section II.—*Negroes as refugees.*
(South Carolina and Florida.)

What has been stated in the foregoing pages as to the refugees that have crossed our lines from Eastern Virginia and North Carolina, though true in the main also of South Carolina and Florida negroes, is to be received with some modification as regards the former slave population of these two last-named States, especially South Carolina.

This is one of the States in which the system of negro slavery seems to have reached its farthest development with the least modification from contact with external civilization. There it appears to have run out nearer to its logical consequences than in any other we have visited. There it has been darkening in its shades of inhumanity and moral degradation from year to year, exhibiting, more and more, increased cruelty, a more marked crushing out, in the case of the negro race, of the humanizing relations of civilized life, and a closer approach, in practice, to a monstrous maxim; the same which a Chief Justice of the Supreme Court, perverting history, alleges to have been the sentiment of the civilized world when the U.S. Constitution was adopted, and in the spirit of which he assumes (in virtue of such perversion) that Constitution to have been framed, namely, that "the negro has no rights which the white man is bound to respect" [*Dred Scott* v. *John F.A. Sandford* (23 Howard 407)]. The evidence before the Commission shows that half a century ago its phase was much milder than on the day when South Carolina seceded. It is the uniform testimony of all emancipated South Carolinian slaves above the age of sixty that their youth was spent under a state of things which, compared to that of the last thirty years, was merciful and considerate. As a general rule, these old men are more bright and intelligent than the younger field hands, in many of whom a stolid, sullen despondency attests the stupefying influence of slave-driving under its more recent phase.

The disintegration of the family relation is one of the most striking and most melancholy indications of this progress of barbarism. The slave was not permitted to own a family name; instances occurred in which he was flogged for presuming to use one. He did not eat with his children or with their mother; "there was no time for that." In portions of this State, at least, a family breakfast or dinner table was a thing so little known among these people that ever since their enfranchisement it has been very difficult to break them of the life-long habit that each should clutch the dish containing his portion and skulk off into a corner, there to devour it in solitude. The entire day, until after sunset, was spent in the field; the night in huts of a single room, where all ages and both sexes herded promiscuously. Young girls of fifteen, some of an earlier age, became mothers, not only without marriage, but often without any pretense of fidelity to which even a slave could give that name. The church, it is true, interposed her protest; but the master, save in exceptional cases, did not sustain it, tacitly sanctioning a state of morality under which ties of habitual affection could not assume a form dangerous or inconvenient to despotic rule.

The men, indeed, frequently asked from their masters the privilege of appropriating to themselves those of the other sex. Sometimes it was granted, sometimes — when the arrangement was deemed unprofitable — it was refused. Some cases there were in which a slaveholder, prompted by his own sense of morality or religion or urged thereto by a pious wife, suffered these connections of his slaves to have the sanction of religious ceremony. But it is evident that to connect even with such a quasi-marriage the idea of sacredness or religious duty was inconsistent with that legal policy of the slave States which forbade to render indissoluble among slaves a relation which tomorrow it might be for the interest of their owners to break up.

The maternal relation was often as little respected as the marital. On many plantations, where the system was most thoroughly carried out, pregnancy neither exempted from corporal punishment nor procured a diminution of the daily task; and it was a matter of occasional occurrence that the woman was overtaken by the pains of labor in the field, and the child born between the cotton rows. Humane masters, however, were wont to diminish the task as pregnancy advanced, and commonly gave three, occasionally four, weeks' exemption from labor after child birth. The mother was usually permitted to suckle her child during three months only; and the cases were rare in which relaxation from labor was allowed during that brief period. On the other hand, instances have occurred in which the more severe drove the negress into the field within forty-eight hours after she became a mother, there to toil until the day of the next birth.

A noble exception, among others, to such a system of inhumanity, gratefully testified to by the negroes who enjoyed it, was to be found on the plantation of ex-Governor Aiken, one of the largest and most influential planters in the State. His habitual clemency, it is said, gave umbrage to many of his neighbor planters as endangering their authority under a severer rule.

Under such a slave system as this, where humanity is the exception, the iron enters deep into the soul. Popular songs are the expression of the inner life; and the negro songs of South Carolina are, with scarcely an exception, plaintive, despondent, and religious. When there mingles a tone of mournful exultation, it has reference to the future glories of Zion, not to worldly hopes. . . .

The chief object of ambition among the refugees is to own property, especially to possess land, if it be only a few acres, in their own State. Colonel Higginson testified to his conviction that the effect of bounty land would be much greater on the colored than on the white soldier. They delight in the idea.

Working for wages, they soon get an idea of accumulation. Savings banks will be popular with them whenever their confidence is won.

The negro of Florida occupies an intermediate place between the slaves of North Carolina and those of South Carolina. He is more enterprising and more self-reliant than the latter. As a general rule, he enlists more willingly and makes an excellent soldier. Many of them were employed as lumbermen and in other vocations better calculated to call out their intelligence than the monotonous labor of the cotton-field. . . .

Section V. — *Character of organization proposed.*

On one point the Commission are already agreed, namely, that a scheme of guardianship or protection for one race of men against another race inhabiting the same country cannot become a permanent institution. If the necessity for the constant operation of such a scheme could be proved, the proof would amount to this, that the two races cannot in perpetuity inhabit the same country at all, and that the one must ultimately give way to the other.

The Commission, therefore, adopt the opinion that all special governmental measures, particularly those involving continuous expenditure, whether for the relief of poor southern whites or of poor refugee blacks, or for the guardianship of such refugees, should be more or less temporary in their character, and should be prepared and administered in that idea and intent.

In this view of the case, the Commission state with satisfaction that in the course of their inquiries they have found unmistakable indications that the negro slave of the South, though in some respects resembling a child from the dependence in which he has been trained and the unreasoning obedience which has been exacted from him, and therefore, in many cases, seeking and needing for a season encouragement and direction, is by no means devoid of practical sagacity in the common affairs of life, and usually learns readily and quickly to shift for himself. This, the Commission think, it is just and desirable that he should be led to do at as early a period as is practicable, without further reliance for aid or guidance on the Government. . . .

It is proper for the Commission here to say that scarcely anything is more essential to the good government and improvement of these refugees than that the wages they earn should be promptly and regularly paid. Nothing so encourages their influx from rebeldom as this, and it is most desirable that a freedman should learn as speedily as possible that emancipation means neither idleness nor gratuitous work, but fair labor for fair wages.

If additional argument in favor of such regularity of payment were needed, it is to be found in the fact well known to those who have had experience with these people as laborers, that where they are regularly paid a single threat suffices, in place of all other punishment, to check laziness and other delinquency—the threat, namely, of dismissal. But if the payment of wages be uncertain or delayed for months, such a threat has no force; and the foreman has no hold over those whose work he directs. In every case in which complaints were made to the Commission of the inefficiency of freedmen's labor they found, on inquiry, that wages had been withheld form these men for months. White laborers would not work at all under such circumstances.

In connection with this regular payment of wages, and also with the suggestion heretofore made, that the refugees acknowledging wives and children should be legally married, the Commission recommend a system of allotment, under which each married laborer or soldier shall be required at the time his pay is received to cede a part of it, proportioned to the size of this family, for their support in all cases where that family is left dependent on the Government. In cases where the freedman shall have provided a home and support for his own family, the amount to be allotted can properly be a matter of recommendation only; yet such recommendation will probably in almost all cases be as effectual as a positive requisition. . . .

The importance of enlightened instruction, educational and religious, to these uneducated people, cannot be overestimated. It is pleasant to the Commission to be able to state their convictions, that the freedmen, in every district of country they have visited, eager to obtain for themselves, but especially for their children, those privileges of education which have hitherto been jealously withheld from them, may already be depended upon to support, in part, both teachers and pastors. The benevolent and religious societies of the North are aiding liberally in this good work, and the opinion of some of those who have taken a leading part in these philanthropic efforts (as expressed to the Commission) is that, with the aid of the freedmen themselves, they will be able for the present and until the number of refugee freedmen shall materially increase, to supply in most cases the necessary literary and religious instruction. If in the organization of the various superintendencies this opinion should prove to be correct, it is well. But organized efforts of private benevolence are usually uncertain in their duration, and a greatly increased immigration of refugees may so augment the number of freedmen needing instruction that the demand for school teaching and pastoral care will exceed the supply. In that case it may be necessary in certain locations that Government for the time being detail a chaplain to take the religious charge of a residency, and that it pay the salaries of the necessary teachers until the freedmen's schools become self-supporting. . . .

The organization proposed will be incomplete in these parts of the superintendencies here spoken of, in which the ordinary courts of justice are suspended, unless temporary provision be made for a magistracy, through whose action these people may learn the important lesson that the obedience which, as slaves, they paid to the will of a master, must now be rendered by them as freedmen to established law, care being taken not to encourage them to become litigious. . . .

They further recommend that the proper department superintendent be vested with authority to bring to conciliation and settlement all difficulties arising between freedmen, except where resort to a provost-judge or other legal tribunal becomes necessary. Where a case of difficulty occurring between a freedman and a white man goes before a provost-marshal or provost-judge, or before any regularly established legal tribunal, it should be made the duty of the department superintendent so far to act as friend and adviser for the freedman as to see to it that his case is fairly presented and tried, and to this end, in important cases, where necessary, to employ legal counsel. In all these cases the department superintendent should give such counsel and advice as shall tend to justice between the parties, acting in person when practicable, but, if necessary, he may be allowed to appoint the appropriate resident superintendent to act for him as deputy during his absence in the settlement of minor cases.

It should be specially recommended to the department superintendent, in the settlement of all personal difficulties between these people, to act as arbitrator rather than as formal judge, adopting the general principles governing courts of conciliation. And it is confidently believed by the Commission that if he shall succeed in gaining the confidence of the freedmen under his charge he will, with rare exceptions, be able amicably and satisfactorily to adjust such difficulties without further resort to law.

Source: The War of Rebellion: A Compilation of the Official Records of the Union and Confederate Armies. Washington, D.C.: Government Printing Office, 1899.

THE POSTWAR AMENDMENTS AND CIVIL RIGHTS ACT OF 1866

Immediately after the Civil War various amendments to the Constitution and bills were passed that were intended to correct the evils of slavery. This is the period frequently called Radical Reconstruction. The first, and most basic, act was the passage of the Thirteenth Amendment outlawing slavery.

Amendment XIII

December 18, 1865

Section 1. Neither slavery nor involuntary servitude, except as a punishment for crime whereof the party shall have been duly convicted, shall exist within the United States, or any place subject to their jurisdiction.
Section 2. Congress shall have power to enforce this article by appropriate legislation.

* * *

The concern with the rights of ex-slaves continued with the Civil Rights Act of 1866, which gave ex-slaves all the rights of citizens of the United States and gave the federal courts the power to deal with cases brought under the act. It was vetoed by President Andrew Johnson but passed over his veto.

Civil Rights Act of 1866

THIRTY-NINTH CONGRESS. SESS. I. CH. 31. 1866

CHAP. XXXI.—An Act to protect all Persons in the United States in their Civil Rights, and furnish the Means of their Vindication.

Be it enacted by the Senate and House of Representatives of the United States of America in Congress assembled, That all persons born in the United States and not subject to any foreign power, excluding Indians not taxed, are hereby declared to be citizens of the United States; and such citizens, of every race and color, without regard to any previous condition of slavery or involuntary servitude, except as a punishment for crime whereof the party shall have been duly convicted, shall have the same right, in every State and Territory in the United States, to make and enforce contracts, to sue, be parties, and give evidence, to inherit, purchase, lease, sell, hold, and convey real and personal property, and to full and equal benefit of all laws and proceedings for the security of person and property, as is enjoyed by white citizens, and shall be subject to like punishment, pains, and penalties, and to none other, any law, statute, ordinance, regulation, or custom, to the contrary notwithstanding.

Sec. 2. And be it further enacted, That any person who, under color of any law, statute, ordinance, regulation, or custom, shall subject, or cause to be subjected, any inhabitant of any State or Territory to the deprivation of any right secured or protected by this act, or to different punishment, pains, or penalties on account of such person having at any time been held in a condition of slavery or involuntary servitude, except as a punishment for crime whereof the party shall have been duly convicted, or by reason of his color or race, than is prescribed for the punishment of white persons, shall be deemed guilty of a misdemeanor, and, on conviction, shall be punished by fine not exceeding one thousand dollars, or imprisonment not exceeding one year, or both, in the discretion of the court.

Source: 19 Stat. 27 (1866).

* * *

At least in part because the leaders of the so-called Radical Reconstruction recognized the opposition to change represented by Johnson's veto of the Civil Rights Act, the Fourteenth Amendment to the Constitution was passed. The Fourteenth Amendment has been one of the most controversial and, at times, far reaching of all amendments to the Constitution.

Section 1 was designed to ensure that the provisions of the Bill of Rights applied to the states. Specifically it was designed to eliminate the so-called *Dred Scott* decision (*Dred Scott* v. *Sandford,* 19 How. 393 [U.S. 1857]), which barred African Americans from citizenship, and to keep the states from denying equal rights to the new citizens.

Section 2 removes the Constitutional formula that counted slaves as three-fifths of a person in apportioning the number of representatives in each state and establishes a penalty for any state that limits the right to vote. Sections 3 and 4 clarify certain postwar issues. Section 5 is the standard clause giving Congress the power to enforce the amendment.

In practice, however, for most of its history the Supreme Court interpreted the Fourteenth Amendment as applying only to property questions, and it became a kind of Bill of Rights for business. This approach lasted until 1954.

The Fifteenth Amendment, adopted two years later, grants the vote to ex-slaves. Since women are not mentioned, only men were enfranchised by this amendment. Some advocates of women's rights had hoped to combine the two issues, but supporters of the amendment that passed believed that adding the vote for women would make it too "extreme" and bring about its defeat. This caused a split between the advocates of rights for women and those for ex-slaves, groups that generally had been united throughout the abolition campaign. In some senses, this split has never been healed.

Amendment XIV

July 21, 1868

Section 1. All persons born or naturalized in the United States, and subject to the jurisdiction thereof, are citizens of the United States and of the State wherein they reside. No State shall make or enforce any law which shall abridge the privileges or immunities of citizens of the United States; nor shall any State deprive any person of life, liberty, or property, without due process of law; nor deny to any person within its jurisdiction the equal protection of the laws.

Section 2. Representatives shall be apportioned among the several States according to their respective numbers, counting the whole number of persons in each State, excluding Indians not taxed. But when the right to vote at any election for the choice of electors for President and Vice President of the United States, Representatives in Congress, the Executive and Judicial officers of a State, or the members of the Legislature thereof, is denied to any of the male inhabitants of such State, being twenty-one years of age, and citizens of the United States, or in any way abridged, except for participation in rebellion, or other crime, the basis of representation therein shall be reduced in the proportion which the number of such male citizens shall bear to the whole number of male citizens twenty-one years of age in such State.

Section 3. No person shall be a Senator or Representative in Congress, or elector of President and Vice President, or hold any office, civil or military, under the United States, or under any State, who, having previously taken an oath, as member of Congress, or as an officer of the United States, or as a member of any State, to support the Constitution of the United States, shall have engaged in insurrection or rebellion against the same, or given aid or comfort to the enemies thereof. But Congress may by a vote of two thirds of each House, remove such disability.

Section 4. The validity of the public debt of the United States, authorized by law, including debts incurred for payment of pensions and bounties for services in suppressing insurrection or rebellion, shall not be questioned. But neither the United States nor any State shall assume or pay any debt or obligation incurred in aid of insurrection or rebellion against the United States, or any claim for the loss or emancipation of any slave; but all such debts, obligations and claims shall be held illegal and void.

Section 5. The Congress shall have power to enforce, by appropriate legislation, the provisions of this article.

Amendment XV

March 30, 1870

Section 1. The right of citizens of the United States to vote shall not be denied or abridged by the United States or by any State on account of race, color, or previous condition of servitude.

Section 2. The Congress shall have power to enforce this article of appropriate legislation.

*   *   *

The ineffectiveness of the Fourteenth Amendment can be seen in the following 1873 petition to Congress from the National Convention of Colored Persons to protect their civil rights.

Petition to Congress for Civil Rights
Memorial of the National Convention of Colored Persons, Praying
To be protected in their civil rights.
December 19, 1873. — Ordered to lie on the table and be printed.
National Civil-Rights Convention,
Washington, D.C., December, 1873.

We regret the necessity which compels us to again come before you and say "we are aggrieved." We are authorized to say to those in authority, to Congress, to the people whom it represents, that there are nearly five millions of American citizens who are shamefully outraged; who are thus treated without cause. The recognitions made within a few years respecting in part our rights, make us more sensitive as to the denial of the rest.

Late declarations recognizing our entitlement to all of our rights, with essential ones withheld, render the grievances even more intolerable. Our grievances are many; our inconveniences through the denial of rights are great; but we shall refer only to those that may be affected through the action of Congress, by statutes forbidding them under penalties. We shall take it for granted that action will be had by Congress, protecting us from invidious distinctions in the enjoyment of common carriers, hotels and other public places of convenience and refreshment, in public places of amusement, and in enjoying other civil rights, but there are indications that there may be some objection made to Federal action against discrimination as to race and color in the management of public instruction, and in impaneling juries, the objectors alleging that it is unconstitutional for Congress to legislate to affect these cases. We propose to notice these objections briefly. They come from lawyers, who, like men in other callings, have their thoughts circumscribed by their training and habits of reflection. We do not feel bound, in a matter involving rights, to be circumscribed thereby. Language should be used, whenever it may without outraging it, to best subserve equity and justice. A decision of the supreme judiciary is binding and irrevocable, as affecting the particular case adjudicated, but is to be regarded only as a light which may be used, say, should be, in any other case before that judiciary, to assist in finding a proper solution of the case. It has no imperative binding force upon any subsequent case.

The force of recorded decisions as to the powers of Congress is somewhat impaired, because they were rendered under a bias or influence differing from the present.

The interest of slavery, a state institution, was so great and overshadowing as to subjugate church as well as state, morality as well as the laws of the land; decisions were rendered in its interests; it was ever keen, active, resolute, extremely suspicious. The State-rights theory, one essential to slavery, was persistently urged. How it was adhered to may be seen in its producing the late rebellion, its graveyard. Therefore the leanings of legal minds, through decisions and opinions made popular by this State-rights theory, must not be permitted to have the controlling sway some lawyers are disposed to give them; hence we are emboldened to take exceptions to the theory that Congress may not interpose except in the United States courts to secure unto a citizen an impartial jury. We affirm there is no prohibitory clause of the Constitution denying this right. On the other hand, we affirm that it ranges itself among the powers delegated to Congress, at least by implication; that it is a power inherent in the Government from its character, one supported by the principles of common law. It is in maintenance of a national right. We are at a loss to find the part of the constitution which admits Congress to go as far as it has gone in protecting the civil rights of citizens in the several States, assented to by objecting Senators, but which forbids its going far enough to effectually protect the civil rights of a citizen wherever the stars and stripes have sway.

If Congress may throw the protecting arm of the law around any citizen of the United States, in every State, so as to forbid any denial or discrimination in hotels and in public conveyances on account of race and color, it certainly may do so in protecting him from invidious rules impairing the right of property; it may say the common school, paid for and owned by all citizens in common, shall not be made to serve to the degradation and humiliation of any class thereof; that a branch of the Government, maintained to train the child as to his proper relation to his Government and his fellow-citizens, must not therein be trained in opposition to the Government's fundamental principles. . . .

This same argument applies to the constituting of juries, and we shall apply it in considering whether Congress has the right to secure to any citizen the benefit of an impartial jury of his peers.

Article 1st, section 8th, of the Constitution, says: "Congress shall have power to make all laws which shall be necessary and proper for carrying into execution the powers vested by the Constitution in the Government of the United States." The Constitution further says: "The Constitution, and the laws of the United States which shall be made in pursuance thereof, are the supreme law of the land, and the judges in every State shall be bound thereby." The Constitution, by implication as well as by direct words, affirms an impartial jury to be a constitutional right, of course to be maintained as such, to be a supreme law of the land, anything in the constitution and laws of any State to the contrary notwithstanding; which amounts to a prohibition on a State from refusing an impartial jury. From all of which it is evident, as well as from the binding force of the common law in securing an impartial jury, that Congress has power to protect, by law, the citizen in this great national and common right under civilized government.

The fact that federal legislation has been had and acquiesced in, and judicial decisions have enforced the same, establishing the theory that the National Government may interpose and regulate the judiciary of the States, restraining them from proscribing citizens because of their race or color, as, for instance, actions had under the present existing civil-rights laws, which regulate the receiving of testimony in the several States, shows that the power exists to protect us from the injustice of which we complain. . . .

It is not complete liberty and exact equality to be compelled to go to a proscribed school; to be tried by a jury from which every individual of the class to which the party tried belongs is excluded because he is of that class. The republican party, now in power, said there should be efficient and appropriate State and Federal legislation against the same. It is quite significant that the opponents of the republicans in the presidential canvass went into it with a platform which, as to civil rights, was not opposed to this position of the republicans.

Source: U.S. Senate, 43rd Congress, 1st session, *Miscellaneous Document Number 21* (1873–74).

BLACK CODES

Radical Reconstruction did not last long. Its major accomplishments—the Freedmen's Bureau and the Thirteenth, Fourteenth, and Fifteenth Amendments—were rapidly undercut by the overriding desire to reestablish the union and by the racism that permeated both the North and the South. The white South was allowed to control its own future with virtually no punishment

even of the Confederate leaders. Slavery was abolished, but various forms of involuntary servitude replaced slavery. This can be seen in the following examples, two of the many Black Codes that were passed during this period. Note that under the Mississippi code former slave owners were given preference in forced apprenticeships.

South Carolina Black Code

VIII. One who is a pauper, or a charge to the public, shall not be competent to contract marriage. Marriage between a white person and a person of color, shall be illegal and void.

IX. The marriage of an apprentice shall not, without the consent of the master, be lawful.

XLVIII. Visitors or other persons shall not be invited, or allowed by the servant, to come or remain upon the premises of the master, without his express permission.

XLIX. Servants shall not be absent from the premises without the permission of the master.

Mechanics, Artisans and Shop-keepers

LXXI. No person of color shall pursue or practice the art, trade or business of an artisan, mechanic or shop-keeper, or any other trade, employment or business (besides that of husbandry, or that of a servant under a contract for services or labor) on his own account and for his own benefit, or in partnership with a white person, or as agent or servant of any person, until he shall have obtained a license therefor from the Judge of the District Court, which license shall be good for one year only. This license the Judge may grant upon petition of the applicant, and upon being satisfied of his skill and fitness, and of his good moral character, and upon payment, by the applicant, to the Clerk of the District Court of one-hundred dollars, if a shop-keeper or pedlar, to be paid annually, and ten dollars if a mechanic artisan, or to engage in any other trade, also to be paid annually: *Provided, however,* That upon complaint being made and proved to the District Judge of an abuse of such license, he shall revoke the same, and: *Provided, also,* That no person of color shall practice any mechanical art or trade, unless he shows that he has served an apprenticeship in such trade or art, or is now practicing such trade or art.

Source: 1865 South Carolina Acts 291–304.

It shall be the duty of all sheriffs, justices of the peace, and other civil officers . . . to report to the probate courts of their respective counties semi-annually, at the January and July terms of said courts, all freedmen, free negroes, and mulattoes, under the age of eighteen, in their respective counties, beats or districts, who are orphans, or whose parent or parents have not the means or who refuse to provide for and support said minors; and thereupon it shall be the duty of said probate court to order the clerk of said court to apprentice said minors to some competent and suitable person, having a particular care to the interest of said minor: *Provided,* that the former owner of said minors shall have the preference when, in the opinion of the court, he or she shall be a suitable person for that purpose. . . .

That no freedman, free negro or mulatto, not in the military service of the United States government, and not licensed so to do by the board of police of his or her county, shall keep or carry fire-arms of any kind, or any ammunition, dirk or bowie knife. . . .

Source: 1865 Mississippi Laws 82.

Anarcho-Capitalism

Although the central focus of political activity in this period was Reconstruction and opposition to it, other currents of thought were also emerging. One of the contributions of the United States to the history of political thought is anarcho-capitalism. Although it is now recognized as an important theory, few people are aware that its history reaches back to the 1860s.

Lysander Spooner
No Treason. No. I

The question of treason is distinct from that of slavery; and is the same that it would have been, if free States, instead of slave States, had seceded.

On the part of the North, the war was carried on, not to liberate the slaves, but by a government that had always perverted and violated the Constitution, to keep the slaves in bondage; and was still willing to do so, if the slaveholders could be thereby induced to stay in the Union.

The principle, on which the war was waged by the North, was simply this: That men may rightfully be compelled to submit, to, and support, a government that they do not want; and that resistance, on their part, makes them traitors and criminals.

No principle, that is possible to be named, can be more self-evidently false than this; or more self-evidently fatal to all political freedom. Yet it triumphed in the field, and is now assumed to be established. If it be really established, the number of slaves, instead of having been diminished by the war, has been greatly increased; for a man, thus subjected to a government that he does not want, is a slave. And there is no difference, in principle—but only in degree—between political and chattel slavery. The former, no less than the latter, denies a man's ownership of himself and the products of his labor; and asserts that other men may own him, and dispose of him and his property, for their uses, and at their pleasure.

Previous to the war, there were some grounds for saying that—in theory, at least, if not in practice—our government was a free one; that it rested on consent. But nothing of that kind can be said now, if the principle on which the war was carried on by the North, is irrevocably established.

If that principle be *not* the principle of the Constitution, the fact should be known. If it *be* the principle of the Constitution, the Constitution itself should be at once overthrown.

Notwithstanding all the proclamations we have made to mankind, within the last ninety years, that our government rested on consent, and that was the only rightful basis on which any government could rest, the late war has practically demonstrated that our government rests upon force—as much as so any government that ever existed.

The North has thus virtually said to the world: It was all very well to prate of consent, so long as the objects to be accomplished were to liberate ourselves from our connexion with England, and also to coax a scattered and jealous people into a great national union; but now that those purposes have been accomplished, and the power of the North has become consolidated, it is sufficient for us—as for all governments—simply to say: *Our power is our right.*

In proportion to her wealth and population, the North has probably expended more money and blood to maintain her power over an unwilling people, than any other government ever did. And in her estimation, it is apparently the chief glory of her success, and an adequate compensation for all her own losses, and an ample justification for all her devastation and carnage of the South, that all pretence of any necessity for consent to the perpetuity or power of the government, is (as she thinks) forever expunged from the minds of the people. In short, the North exults beyond measure in the proof she has given, that a government, professedly resting on consent, will expend more life and treasure in crushing dissent, than any government, openly founded on force, has everdone.

And she claims that she has done all this in behalf of liberty! In behalf of free government! In behalf of the principle that government should rest on consent! . . .

Manifestly this one thing (to say nothing of others) is necessarily implied in the idea of a government's resting on consent, viz: *the separate, individual consent of every man who is required to contribute, either by taxation or personal service, to the support of the government.* All this, or nothing, is necessarily implied, because one man's consent is just as necessary as any other man's. If, for example, A claims that his consent is necessary to the establishment or maintenance of government, he thereby necessarily admits that B's and every other man's rights are just as good as his own. On the other hand, if he denies that B's or any other particular man's consent is necessary, he thereby necessarily admits that neither his own, nor any other man's is necessary; and that government need not be founded on consent at all.

There is, therefore, no alternative but to say, either that the separate, individual consent of every man, *who is required to aid, in any way, in supporting the government, is necessary, or that the consent of no one is necessary.*

Clearly this individual consent is indispensable to the idea of treason; for if a man has never consented or agreed to support a government, he breaks no faith in refusing to support it. And if he makes war upon it, he does so as an open enemy and not as a traitor—that is, as a betrayer, or treacherous friend.

All this, or nothing, was necessarily implied in the Declaration made in 1776. If the necessity for consent, then announced, was a sound principle in favor of three millions of men, it was an equally sound one in favor of three men, or of one man. If the principle was a sound one in behalf of men living on a separate continent, it was an equally sound one in behalf of a man living on a separate farm, or in a separate house.

Source: No Treason. No. 1. By Lysander Spooner. Boston, 1867.

Lysander Spooner (1808–87) was a lawyer, an abolitionist, and an anarchist.

Minorities

INDIANS

The restrictions on the Indians continued to worsen. The treaty with the Nez Percé forced the tribe onto a reservation and restricts the amount of land that they could hold off the reservation. The selections from Buffalo Bird Woman and Crazy Horse reflect back on the former way of life of the Indians.

Treaty with the Nez Percés

Whereas certain amendments are desired by the Nez Percé tribe of Indians to their treaty concluded at the council ground in the valley of the Lapwai, in the Territory of Washington, on the ninth day of June, in the year of our Lord one thousand eight hundred and sixty-three; and whereas the United States are willing to assent to said amendments; it is therefore agreed by and between Nathaniel G. Taylor, commissioner, on the part of the United States, thereunto duly authorized, and Lawyer, Timothy, and Jason, chiefs of said tribe, also being thereunto duly authorized, in manner and form following, that is to say: ARTICLE I. That all lands embraced within the limits of the tract set apart for the exclusive use and benefit of said Indians by the 2d article of said treaty of June 9th, 1863, which are susceptible of cultivation and suitable for Indian farms, which are not now occupied by the United States for military purposes, or which are not required for agency or other buildings and purposes provided for by existing treaty stipulations, shall be surveyed as provided in the 3d article of said treaty of June 9th, 1863, and as soon as the allotments shall be plowed and fenced, and as soon as schools shall be established as provided by existing treaty stipulations, such Indians now residing outside the reservation as may be decided upon by the agent of the tribe and the Indians themselves, shall be removed to and located upon allotments within the reservation: *Provided, however,* That in case there should not be a sufficient quantity of suitable land within the boundaries of the reservation to provide allotments for those now there and those residing outside the boundaries of the same, then those residing outside, or as many thereof as allotments cannot be provided for, may remain upon the lands now occupied and improved by them, provided, that the land so occupied does not exceed twenty acres for each and every male person who shall have attained the age of twenty-one years or is the head of a family, and the tenure of those remaining upon lands outside the reservation shall be the same as is provided in said 3d article of said treaty of June 9th, 1863, for those receiving allotments within the reservation; and it is further agreed that those now residing outside of the boundaries of the reservation and who may continue to so reside shall be protected by the military authorities in their rights upon the allotments occupied by them, and also in the privilege of grazing their animals upon surrounding unoccupied lands. ARTICLE 2. It is further agreed between the parties hereto that the stipulations contained in the 8th article of the treaty of June 9th, 1863, relative to timber, are hereby annulled as far as the same provides that the United States shall be permitted to use thereof in the maintaining of forts or garrisons, and that the said Indians shall have the aid of the military authorities to protect the timber upon their reservation, and that none of the same shall be cut or removed without the consent of the head-chief of the tribe, together with the consent of the agent and superintendent of Indian affairs, first being given in writing, which written consent shall state the part of the reservation upon which the timber is to be cut, and also the quantity, and the price to be paid therefor. ARTICLE 3. It is further hereby stipulated and agreed that the amount due said tribe for school purposes and for the support of teachers that has not been expended for that purpose since the year 1864, but has been used for other purposes, shall be ascertained and the same shall be re-imbursed to said tribe by appropriation by Congress, and shall be set apart and invested in United States bonds and shall be held in trust by the United States, the interest on the same to be paid to said tribe annually for the support of teachers.

In testimony whereof the said Commissioner on the part of the United States and the said chiefs representing said Nez Percé tribe of Indians have hereunto set their hands and seals this 13th day of August, in the year of our Lord one thousand eight hundred and sixty-eight, at the city of Washington, D.C.

Source: Indian Affairs: Laws and Treaties. Volume 2, *Treaties.* Washington, D.C.: Government Printing Office, 1904. Reprinted as *Indian Treaties 1778–1883.* Compiled and edited by Charles J. Kappler. New York: Interland Publishing Co., 1972.

Buffalo Bird Woman

Gone Forever

I am an old woman now. The buffaloes and black-tail deer are gone, and our Indian ways are almost gone. Sometimes I find it hard to believe that I ever lived them.

My little son grew up in the white man's school. He can read books, and he owns cattle and has a farm. He is a leader among our Hidatsa people, helping teach them to follow the white man's road.

He is kind to me. We no longer live in an earth lodge, but in a house with chimneys; and my son's wife cooks by a stove.

But for me, I cannot forget our old ways.

Often in summer I rise at daybreak and steal out to the cornfields; and as I hoe the corn I sing to it, as we did when I was young. No one cares for our corn songs now.

Sometimes at evening I sit, looking out on the big Missouri. The sun sets, and dusk steals over the water. In the shadows I seem again to see our Indian village, with smoke curling upward from the earth lodges; and in the river's roar I hear the yells of the warriors, the laughter of little children as of old. It is but an old woman's dream. Again I see but shadows and hear only the roar of the river; and tears come into my eyes. Our Indian life, I know, is gone forever.

Source: "Waheenee: An Indian Girl's Story Told by Herself to Gilbert L. Wilson." *North Dakota History* 38 (Winter/Spring 1971).

Buffalo Bird Woman was a member of the Hidatsa tribe.

Crazy Horse
I Have Spoken

My friend, I do not blame you for this. Had I listened to you this trouble would not have happened to me. I was not hostile to the white man. Sometimes my young men would attack the Indians who were their enemies and took their ponies. They did it in return.

We had buffalo for food, and their hides for clothing and our tipis. We preferred hunting to a life of idleness on the reservations, where we were driven against our will. At times we did not get enough to eat, and we were not allowed to leave the reservation to hunt.

We preferred our own way of living. We were no expense to the government then. All we wanted was peace and to be left alone. Soldiers were sent out in the Winter, who destroyed our villages. Then "Long Hair" [General Custer] came in the same way. They say we massacred him, but he would have done the same to us had we not defended ourselves and fought to the last. Our first impulse was to escape with our squaws and papooses, but we were so hemmed in that we had to fight.

After that I went up on Tongue River with a few of my people and lived in peace. But the government would not let me alone. Finally, . . . I came here . . . to talk with Big White Chief, but was not given a chance. They tried to confine me, I tried to escape, and a soldier ran his bayonet into me.

I have spoken.

Source: Twenty Years among Our Savage Indians. By J. Leo Humfreville. Hartford, Conn.: Hartford Publishing Co., 1897.

Crazy Horse was a leader of the Ogalala Sioux and hero of the Battle of Little Big Horn. He died in 1877. These are supposed to be his last words.

WOMEN

The women's movement, frequently thought to have disappeared between the Civil War and the suffrage movement, continued throughout the entire period. In the piece included here, Victoria Woodhull argues for the establishment of a women's political party.

Bradwell v. *Illinois* (16 Wall [1872]) was a failed suit by a woman requesting that she be allowed to practice law in Illinois. The Supreme Court argued that the ability to be admitted to the bar was not a right of a citizen of the United States, and that therefore the states must be left to decide such cases. Hence, even if the Fourteenth Amendment applied to the states, she would have lost her case. In the excerpt reprinted here, Justice Joseph Bradley, in a concurring opinion, went further.

Susan B. Anthony's "Statement to the Court" is her response to being found guilty of voting.

Victoria C. Woodhull
A New Political Party and A New Party Platform

At the Suffrage Convention held in Apollo Hall, May 11th and 12th, 1871, by request of Mrs. Lucretia Mott, the following Platform of Principles of a Just Government was read by Victoria C. Woodhull, and is embodied in this history that it may have a wide circulation in all its bearings on the future of this country.

Suffrage is a common right of citizenship. Women have the right of suffrage. Logically it cannot be escaped. Syllogistically it is self-evident, thus:

First—All persons—men and women—are citizens.
Second—Citizens have the right to vote.
Third—Women have the right to vote.

Though the right to vote be now denied, it must eventually be accorded. Women can be neither Democrats nor Republicans. They must be something more than Democratic or Republican. They must be humanitarian. They must become a positive element in governmental affairs. They have thought little; they must be brought to think more. To suggest food for thought, a new party and a new platform is proposed for the consideration of women and men: the party, the Cosmopolitical—the platform a series of reforms, to wit:

A reform in representation, by which all Legislative Bodies and the Presidential Electoral College shall be so elected that minorities as well as majorities shall have direct representation. . . .

A reform in the tenure of office, by which the Presidency shall be limited to one term, with a retiring life pension, and a permanent seat in the Federal Senate, where his Presidential experience may become serviceable to the nation, and on the dignity and life emolument of Presidential Senator he shall be placed above all other political position, and be excluded from all professional pursuits.

A radical reform in our Civil Service, by which the Government, in its executive capacity, shall at all times secure faithful and efficient officers, and the people trustworthy servants, whose appointment shall be entirely removed from, and be made independent of, the influence and control of the legislative branch of the Government, and who shall be removed for "cause" only, and who shall be held strictly to frequent public accounting to superiors for all their official transactions, which shall for ever dispose of the corrupt practices induced by the allurements of the motto of present political parties, that "to the victor belong the spoils," which is a remnant of arbitrarily assumed authority, unworthy of a government emanating from the whole people. . . .

A complete reform in commercial and navigation laws, by which American built or purchased ships and American seamen shall be practically protected by the admission of all that is required for construction of the first, or the use and maintenance of either, free in bond or on board.

A reform in the relations of the employer and employed, by which shall be secured the practice of the great natural law, of one-third of time to labour, one-third to recreation, and one-third to rest, that by this, intellectual improvement and physical development may go on to that perfection which the Almighty Creator designed.

A reform in the principles of protection and revenue, by which the largest home and foreign demand shall be created and sustained for products of American industry of every kind; by which this industry shall be freed from the ruinous effects consequent upon frequent changes in these systems; by which shall be secured that constant employment to working-men and working-women throughout the country which will maintain them upon an equality in all kinds and classes of industry; by which a continuous prosperity—which, if not so marked by rapid accumulation, shall possess the merit of permanency—will be secured to all, which in due time will reduce the cost of all products to a minimum value; by which the labouring poor shall be relieved of the onerous tax, now indirectly imposed upon them by Government; by which the burden of governmental support shall be placed where it properly belongs, and by which an unlimited national wealth will gradually accumulate, the ratio of taxation upon which will become so insignificant in amount as to be no burden to the people.

A reform by which the power of legislative bodies to levy taxes shall be limited to the actual necessities of the legitimate functions of Government in its protection of the rights of persons, property and nationality; and by which they shall be deprived of the power to exempt any property from taxation; or to make any distinctions directly or indirectly among citizens in taxation for the support of Government; or to give or loan the public property or credit to individuals or corporations to promote any enterprise whatever.

A reform in the system of criminal jurisprudence, by which the death penalty shall no longer be inflicted; and by which, during that term, a portion of the prison employment shall be for, and the product thereof be faithfully paid over to, the support of the criminal's family; and by which our so-called prisons shall be virtually transformed into vast reformatory workshops, from which the unfortunate may emerge to be useful members of society, instead of the alienated citizens they now are.

The institution of such supervisatory control and surveillance over the now low orders of society as shall compel them to industry, and provide for the helpless, and thus banish those institutions of pauperism and beggary which are fastening upon the vitals of society, and are so prolific of crime and suffering in certain communities.

The organization of a general system of national education which shall positively secure to every child of the country such an education in the arts, sciences and general knowledge as will render them profitable and useful members of society, and the entire proceeds of the public domain should be religiously devoted to this end. . . .

Thus in the best sense do I claim to be the friend and exponent of the most complete equality to which humanity can attain; of the broadest individual freedom compatible with the public good, and that supreme justice which shall know no distinction among citizens upon any ground whatever, in the administration and the execution of the laws; and also, to be a faithful worker in the cause of human advancement; and especially to be the co-labourer with those who strive to better the condition of the poor and friendless; to secure to the great mass of working people the just reward of their toil. I claim from these, and from all others in the social scale, that support in the bold political course I have taken which shall give me the strength and the position to carry out these needed reforms, which shall secure to them, in return, the blessings which the Creator designed the human race should enjoy.

If I obtain this support, woman's strength and woman's will, with God's support, if He vouchsafe it, shall open to them, and to this country, a new career of greatness in the race of nations, which can only be secured by that fearless course of truth from which the nations of the earth, under despotic male governments, have so far departed.

Source: The Arguments for Women's Electoral Rights under Amendments XIV and XV of the Constitution of the United States. By Victoria Woodhull. London: Norman, 1887. Reprinted in *The Victoria Woodhull Reader.* Edited by Madeline B. Stern. Weston, Mass.: MS Press, 1974.

Victoria Claflin Woodhull (1838–1927) was editor of *Woodhull and Claflin's Weekly* with her sister Tennessee Claflin (1846–1923). They advocated rights for women, a single standard of morality, free love, and spiritualism.

". . . [T]he civil law, as well as nature herself, has always recognized a wide difference in the respective spheres and destinies of man and woman. Man is, or should be, woman's protector and defender. The natural and proper timidity and delicacy which belongs to the female sex evidently unfits it for many of the occupations of civil life. The constitution of the family organization, which is founded in the divine ordinance, as well as in the nature of things, indicates the domestic sphere as that which properly belongs to the domain and functions of womanhood. The harmony, not to say identity, of interests and views which belong or should belong to the family institution, is repugnant to the idea of a woman adopting a distinct and independent career from that of her husband. So firmly fixed was this sentiment in the founders of the common law that it became a maxim of that system of jurisprudence that a woman had no legal existence separate from her husband, who was regarded as her head and representative in the social state; and, notwithstanding some recent modifications of this civil status, many of the special rules of law flowing from and dependent upon this cardinal principle still exist in full force in most states. One of these is, that a married woman is incapable, without her husband's consent, of making contracts which shall be binding on her or him. This very incapacity was one circumstance which the supreme court of Illinois deemed important in rendering a married woman incompetent fully to perform the duties and trusts that belong to the office of an attorney and counselor.

It is true that many women are unmarried and not affected by any of the duties, complications, and incapacities arising out of the married state, but these are exceptions to the general rule. The paramount destiny and mission of woman are to fulfill the noble and benign offices of wife and mother. This is the law of the Creator. And the rules of civil society must be adapted to the general constitution of things, and cannot be based upon exceptional cases.

Source: 16 Wall (1872) 130–42.

Susan B. Anthony
Statement to the Court

The Court: The prisoner will stand up. Has the prisoner anything to say why sentence shall not be pronounced?

Miss Anthony: Yes, your honor, I have many things to say; for in your ordered verdict of guilty, you have trampled under-foot, every vital principle of our government. My natural rights, my civil rights, my political rights, are all alike ignored. Robbed of the fundamental privilege of citizenship, I am degraded from the status of a citizen to that of a subject; and not only myself individually, but all of my sex, are, by your honor's verdict, doomed to political subjection under this so-called republican government.

Judge Hunt: The Court can not listen to a rehearsal of arguments the prisoner's counsel has already consumed three hours in presenting.

Miss Anthony: May it please your honor, I am not arguing the question, but simply stating the reasons why sentence can not, in justice, be pronounced against me. Your denial of my citizen's right to vote is the denial of my right of consent as one of the governed, the denial of my right of representation as one of the taxed, the denial of my right to a trial by a jury of my peers as an offender against law, therefore, the denial of my sacred rights to life, liberty, property, and—

Judge Hunt: The Court can not allow the prisoner to go on.

Miss Anthony: But your honor will not deny me this one and only poor privilege of protest against this high-handed outrage upon my citizen's rights. May it please the Court to remember that since the day of my arrest last November, this is the first time that either myself or any person of my disfranchised class has been allowed a word of defense before judge or jury—

Judge Hunt: The prisoner must sit down; the Court can not allow it.

Miss Anthony: Of all my prosecutors, from the 8th Ward corner grocery politician, who entered the complaint, to the United States Marshal, Commissioner, District Attorney, District Judge, your honor on the bench, not one is my peer, but each and all are my political sovereigns; and had your honor submitted my case to the jury, as was clearly your duty, even then I should have had just cause of protest, for not one of those men was my peer; but, native or foreign, white or black, rich or poor, educated or ignorant, awake or asleep, sober or drunk, each and every man of them was my political superior; hence, in no sense, my peer. Even, under such circumstances, a commoner of England tried before a jury of lords, would have far less cause to complain than [have] I, a woman, tried before a jury of men. Even my counsel, the Hon. Henry R. Selden, who has argued my cause so ably, so earnestly, so unanswerably before your honor, is my political sovereign. Precisely as no disfranchised person is entitled to sit upon a jury, and no woman is entitled to the franchise, so, none but a regularly admitted lawyer is allowed to practice in the courts, and no woman can gain admission to the bar— hence, jury, judge, counsel, must all be of the superior class.

Judge Hunt: The Court must insist—the prisoner has been tried according to the established forms of law.

Miss Anthony: Yes, your honor, but by forms of law all made by men, interpreted by men, administered by men, in favor of men, and against women; and hence, your honor's ordered verdict of guilty, against a United States citizen for the exercise of "that citizen's right to vote," simply because that citizen was a woman and not a man. But, yesterday, the same man-made forms of law declared it a crime punishable with $1,000 fine and six months' imprisonment, for you, or me, or any of us, to give a cup of cold water, a crust of bread, or a night's shelter to a panting fugitive as he was tracking his way to Canada. And every man or woman in whose veins coursed a drop of human sympathy violated that wicked law, reckless of consequences, and was justified in so doing. As then the slaves who got their freedom [had to] take it over, or under, or through the unjust forms of law, precisely so now must women, to get their right to a voice in this Government, take it; and I have taken mine, and mean to take it at every possible opportunity.

Judge Hunt: The Court orders the prisoner to sit down. It will not allow another word.

Miss Anthony: When I was brought before your honor for trial, I hoped for a broad and liberal interpretation of the Constitution and its recent amendments, that should declare all United States citizens under its protecting aegis—that should declare equality of rights the national guarantee to all persons born or naturalized in the United States. But failing to get this justice—failing, even, to get a trial by a jury not of my peers—I ask not leniency at your hands—but rather the full rigors of the law.

Judge Hunt: The Court must insist—(Here the prisoner sat down.)

Judge Hunt: The prisoner will stand up. (Here Miss Anthony arose again.) The sentence of the Court is that you pay a fine of one hundred dollars and the costs of the prosecution.

Miss Anthony: May it please your honor, I shall never pay a dollar of your unjust penalty. All the stock in trade I possess is a $10,000 debt, incurred by publishing my paper— *The Revolution*—four years ago, the sole object of which was to educate all women to do precisely as I have done, rebel against your man-made, unjust, unconstitutional forms of law, that tax, fine, imprison, and hang women, while they deny them the right of representation in the Government; and I shall work on with might and main to pay every dollar of that honest debt, but not a penny shall go to this unjust claim. And I shall earnestly and persistently continue to urge all women to the practical recognition of the old revolutionary maxim, that "Resistance to tyranny is obedience to God."

Source: History of Woman Suffrage. Edited by Elizabeth Cady Stanton, Susan B. Anthony, and Matilda Joslyn Gage, 2: 687–89. New York: Fowler & Wells, 1881.

Susan B. Anthony (1820–1906) was one of the leading advocates of women's suffrage.

CHAPTER 8

The Rise of Industrialism, 1878–1900

✳ ✳ ✳

Reconstruction was followed by a period of social strife. The war had accelerated the growth of industrialism in the North; the cities were expanding, and immigration was rapidly increasing. These forces produced a situation in which a few people were conspicuously wealthy while many were extremely poor. Such a situation is likely to explode periodically in violence, as it did in the last part of the nineteenth century.

Labor and agricultural groups worked — sometimes together and sometimes in opposition to each other — to publicize their plight and propose alternatives. African Americans and immigrants were the most common scapegoats.

American Anarchism

As noted in the previous chapter, anarchism plays an important role in American political thought that it rarely has had in other countries. In the late nineteenth century, anarchism was an active and important part of the U.S. labor movement.

The most important anarchist thinker of the period was Benjamin R. Tucker (1854–1939), editor of *Liberty*, a long-lived newspaper. Tucker, as his first editorial shows, opposed both church and state and both capitalism and socialism.

Benjamin R. Tucker
Liberty's Declaration of Purpose

LIBERTY enters the field of journalism to speak for herself because she finds no one willing to speak for her. She hears no voice that always champions her; she knows no pen that always writes in her defence; she sees no hand that is always lifted to avenge her wrongs or vindicate her rights. Many claim to speak in her name, but few really understand her. Still fewer have the courage and the opportunity to consistently fight for her. Her battle, then, is her own, to wage and win. She accepts it fearlessly and with a determined spirit.

Her foe, Authority, takes many shapes, but, broadly speaking, her enemies divide themselves into three classes: first, those who abhor her both as a means and as an end of progress, opposing her openly, avowedly, sincerely, consistently, universally; second, those who profess to believe in her as a means of progress, but who accept her only so far as they think she will subserve their own selfish interests, denying her and her blessings to the rest of the world; third, those who distrust her as a means of progress, believing in her only as an end to be obtained by first trampling upon, violating, and outraging her. These three phases of opposition to Liberty are met in almost every sphere of thought and human activity. Good representatives of the first are seen in the Catholic Church, and the Russian autocracy; of the second, in the Protestant Church and the Manchester school of politics and political economy; of the third, in the atheism of Gambetta and the socialism of Karl Marx.

Through these forms of authority another line of demarcation runs transversely, separating the divine from the human; or better still, the religious from the secular. Liberty's victory over the former is well-nigh achieved. Last century Voltaire brought the authority of the supernatural into disrepute. The Church has been declining ever since. Her teeth are drawn, and though she still seems to show here and there vigorous signs of life, she does so in the violence of the death-agony upon her, and soon her power will be felt no more. It is human authority that hereafter is to be dreaded, and the State, its organ, that in the future is to be feared. Those who have lost their faith in gods only to put it in governments; those who have ceased to be Church-worshippers only to become State-worshippers; those who have abandoned pope for king or czar, and priest for president or parliament,—have indeed changed their battle-ground, but none the less are foes of Liberty still. The Church has become an object of derision; the State must be made equally so. The State is said by some to be a "necessary evil"; it must be made unnecessary. This century's battle, then, is with the State: the State, that debases man; the State, that prostitutes woman; the State, that corrupts children; the State, that trammels love; the State, that stifles thought; the

State, that monopolizes land; the State, that limits credit; the State, that restricts exchange; the State, that gives idle capital the power of increase, and, through interest, rent, profit, and taxes, robs industrious labor of its products. . . .

Monopoly and privilege must be destroyed, opportunity afforded, and competition encouraged. This is Liberty's work, and "Down with Authority" her war-cry.

Source: Liberty 1, no. 1 (August 6, 1881): 1.

Benjamin R. Tucker (1854–1939) was an individualist anarchist best known for editing the journal *Liberty.*

THE HAYMARKET AFFAIR

In the conflicts between labor and capital, the most important incident from the point of view of radical labor was the Haymarket bombing in Chicago in 1884. The labor movement generally believed that the bomb was set off by the police. No one ever seems to have believed that the people arrested were guilty of anything other than their political beliefs. Some of those people were executed. While recent scholarship has shown that the police probably did not plant the bomb, it is equally clear that the executed people were innocent of any crime.[1]

Reprinted here are speeches given at the trial by two of the accused. August Spies (1855–87) was executed. Michael Schwab (1853–98) was pardoned in 1893 by Governor John Peter Altgeld (1847–1902). Although Altgeld lost reelection due to this pardon, he considered it his most noteworthy achievement, and it is the only act for which he is still remembered.

Address of Michael Schwab

What is Anarchy?

Is it not strange that when Anarchy was tried nobody ever told what Anarchy was? Even when I was on the witness stand, and asked the State's attorney for a definition of Anarchy, he declined to give it. But in their speeches he and his associates spoke very frequently about Anarchy, and it appeared that they understood it to be something horrible—arson, rapine, murder. In so speaking, Mr. Grinnell and his associates did not speak the truth. They searched the *Alarm* and the *Arbeiter-Zeitung*, and hunted articles written years before the month of May, 1886. In the columns of these papers, it is very often stated what we, the Anarchists, understood by the term Anarchy. And we are the only competent judges in this matter. As soon as the word is applied to us and our doctrine, it carries with it the meaning which we, the Anarchists, saw fit to give it. "Anarchy" is

Greek, and means, verbatim: without rulership; not being ruled. According to our vocabulary, Anarchy is a state of society in which all human beings do right for the simple reason that it is right, and hate wrong because it is wrong. In such a society, no laws, no compulsion will be necessary. The attorney for the State was wrong when he said: "Anarchy is dead." Anarchy, up to the present day, has existed only as a doctrine, and Mr. Grinnell has not the power to kill any doctrine whatever. You may call Anarchy, as defined by us, an idle dream, but that dream was dreamed by Gottfried Ephraim Lessing, one of the three great German poets and the most celebrated German critic of the last century. If Anarchy were the thing the State's attorney makes it out to be, how could it be that such eminent scholars as Prince Kropotkin and the greatest living geographer, Elisee Reclus, were avowed Anarchists, even editors of Anarchistic newspapers? Anarchy is a dream, but only in the present. It will be realized. Reason will grow in spite of all obstacles. Who is the man that has the cheek to tell us that human development has already reached its culminating point? I know that our ideal will not be accomplished this or next year, but I know that it will be accomplished as near as possible, some day, in the future. It is entirely wrong to use the word Anarchy as synonymous with violence. Violence is one thing and Anarchy another. In the present state of society violence is used on all sides, and, therefore, we advocated the use of violence against violence only, as a necessary means of defense. . . . I have not the slightest idea who threw the bomb on the Haymarket, and had no knowledge of any conspiracy to use violence on that or any other night.

Source: The Famous Speeches of the Eight Chicago Anarchists in Court When asked if they had anything to say why sentence of death should not be passed upon them October 7, 8 and 9, 1886. Chicago: Lucy E. Parsons, [1886].

Michael Schwab (1853–98) was one of the three men found guilty in the Haymarket bombing who were pardoned by Illinois Governor John Peter Altgeld after six years in jail.

Address of August Spies

Anarchism does not mean bloodshed; does not mean robbery, arson, etc. These monstrosities are, on the contrary, the characteristic features of capitalism. Anarchism means peace and tranquillity to all. Anarchism, or Socialism, means the re-organization of society upon scientific principles and the abolition of causes which produce vice and crime. Capitalism first produces these social diseases and then seeks to cure them by punishment.

Source: The Famous Speeches of the Eight Chicago Anarchists in Court When asked if they had anything to say why sentence of death should not be passed upon them October 7, 8 and 9, 1886. Chicago: Lucy E. Parsons, [1886].

August Spies (1855–87) was a German immigrant to the United States who became a labor activist. He was executed as a result of the Haymarket riots.

American Socialism

Industrial relations produced escalating conflict. One of the responses to this conflict was a form of American socialism that was briefly immensely influential both in the United States and throughout the world. Nationalism, as it was called because even in the late nineteenth century socialism was an unacceptable word in the United States, was the inspiration of a Massachusetts novelist.

In 1888 Edward Bellamy (1850–98), an author from Springfield, Massachusetts, published a utopian novel called *Looking Backward 2000–1887* in which he described a future society. The novel was an immense success and was the best-selling American novel for many years.

The greatest changes in Bellamy's future Boston were in economics and politics. The most fundamental economic changes were in the ownership of the means of production and the organization of labor. Through the development of monopoly capitalism, enterprises became larger and larger and were simply taken over by the state. Labor was nationalized. As a result, no one had to worry about a job or food, clothes or housing; everyone had the time, the energy, the freedom, and the inclination to pursue a great diversity of intellectual interests. The future Boston is a completely transformed city.

Edward Bellamy
Looking Backward

At my feet lay a great city. Miles of broad streets, shaded by trees and lined with fine buildings, for the most part not in continuous blocks but set in larger or smaller enclosures, stretched in every direction. Every quarter contained large open squares filled with trees, among which statues glistened and fountains flashed in the late afternoon sun. Public buildings of a colossal size and an architectural grandeur unparalleled in my day raised their stately piles on every side. . . .

The movement toward the conduct of business by larger and larger aggregations of capital, the tendency toward monopolies, which had been so desperately and vainly resisted, was recognized at last, in its true significance, as a process which only needed to complete its logical evolution to open a golden future to humanity.

Early in the last century the evolution was completed by the final consolidation of the entire capital of the nation. The industry and commerce of the country, ceasing to be conducted by a set of irresponsible corporations and syndicates of private persons at their caprice and for their profit, were intrusted to a single syndicate representing the people, to be conducted in the common interest for the common profit. The nation, that is to say, organized as the one great business corporation in which all other corporations were absorbed; it became the one capitalist in the place of all other capitalists, the sole employer, the final monopoly in which all previous and lesser monopolies were swallowed up, a monopoly in the profits and economies of which all citizens shared. The epoch of trusts had ended in The Great Trust. In a word, the people of the United States concluded to assume the conduct of their own business, just as one hundred odd years before they had assumed the conduct of their own government, organizing now for industrial purposes on precisely the same grounds that they had then organized for political purposes. At last, strangely late in the world's history, the obvious fact was perceived that no business is so essentially the public business as the industry and commerce on which the people's livelihood depends, and that to entrust it to private persons to be managed for private profit is a folly similar in kind, though vastly greater in magnitude, to that of surrendering the functions of political government to kings and nobles to be conducted for their personal gratification. . . .

While the internal organizations of different industries, mechanical and agricultural, differ according to their peculiar conditions, they agree in a general division of their workers into first, second, and third grades, according to ability, and these grades are in many cases subdivided into first and second classes. According to his standing as an apprentice a young man is assigned his place as a first, second, or third grade worker. Of course only men of unusual ability pass directly from apprenticeship into the first grade of the workers. The most fall into the lower grades, working up as they grow more experienced, at the periodical regradings. These regradings take place in each industry at intervals corresponding with the length of the apprenticeship to that industry, so that merit never need wait long to rise, nor can any rest on past achievements unless they would drop into a lower rank. One of the notable advantages of a high grading is the privilege it gives the worker in electing which of the various branches or processes of his industry he will follow as his specialty. Of course it is not intended that any of these processes shall be disproportionately arduous, but there is often much difference between them, and the privilege of election is accordingly highly prized. So far as possible, indeed, the preferences even of the poorest workmen are considered in assigning them their line of work, because not only their happiness but their usefulness is thus enhanced. While, however, the wish of the lower grade man is consulted so far as the exigencies of the service permit, he is considered only after the upper grade men have been provided for, and often he has to put up with second or third choice, or even with an arbitrary assignment when help is needed. This privilege of election attends every regrading, and when a man loses his grade he also risks having to exchange the sort of work he likes for some other less to his taste. The results of each regrading, giving the standing of every man in his industry, are gazetted in the public prints, and those who have won promotion since the last regrading receive the nation's thanks and are publicly invested with the badge of their new rank. . . .

It is obviously important that not only the good but also the indifferent and poor workmen should be able to cherish the ambition of rising. Indeed, the number of the latter being so much greater, it is even more essential that the ranking system should not operate to discourage them than that it should stimulate the others. It is to this end that the grades are divided into classes. The grades as well as the classes being made numerically equal at each regrading, there is not at any time, counting out the officers and the unclassified and apprentice grades, over one-ninth of the industrial army in the lowest class, and most of this number are recent apprentices, all of whom expect to rise. Those who remain during the entire term of service in the lowest class are but a trifling fraction of the industrial army, and likely to be as deficient in sensibility to their position as in ability to better it. . . .

A credit corresponding to his share of the annual product of the nation is given to every citizen on the public books at the beginning of each year, and a credit card is issued him with which he procures at the public storehouses, found in every community, whatever he desires whenever he desires it. This arrangement . . . totally obviates the necessity for business transactions of any sort between individuals and consumers. . . .

When the nation became the sole employer, all the citizens, by virtue of their citizenship, became employees, to be distributed according to the needs of industry. . . . Our entire social order is so wholly based upon and deduced from it that if it were conceivable that a man could escape from it, he would be left with no possible way to provide for his existence. . . .

Now the entire field of productive and constructive industry is divided into ten great departments, each representing a group of allied industries, each particular industry being in turn represented by a subordinate bureau, which has a complete record of the plant and force under its control, of the present product, and means of increasing it. The estimates of the distributive department, after adoption by the administration, are sent as mandates to the ten great departments, which allot them to the subordinate bureaus representing the particular industries, and these set the men at work. Each bureau is responsible for the task given it, and this responsibility is enforced by departmental oversight and that of the administration; nor does the distributive department accept the product without its own inspection; while even if in the hands of the consumer an article turns out unfit, the system enables the fault to be traced back to the original workman. The production of the commodities for actual public consumption does not, of course, require by any means all the national force of workers. After the necessary contingents have been detailed for the various industries, the amount of labor left for other employment is expended in creating fixed capital, such as buildings, machinery, engineering works, and so forth. . . .

[The labor system is called the industrial army and is organized like an army— the term of service is twenty-four years, from twenty-one to forty-five. This is, of course, much less than the current working life let alone that in 1887. In addition, the work day is much shorter; therefore, each individual has a great deal of free time.]

Every family in the ward has a room set apart in this great building for its permanent and exclusive use for a small annual rental. For transient guests and individuals there is accommodation on another floor. If we expect to dine here, we put in our orders the night before, selecting anything in market, according to the daily reports in the papers. The meal is as expensive or as simple as we please, though of course everything is vastly cheaper as well as better if it would be prepared at home. There is actually nothing which our people take more interest in than the perfection of the catering and cooking done for them. . . .

[T]he line of promotion for the meritorious lies through three grades to the officer's grade, and thence up through the lieutenancies to the captaincy or foremanship, and superintendency or colonel's rank. Next, with an intervening grade in some of the larger trades, come the general of the guild, under whose immediate control all the operations of the trade are conducted. This officer is at the head of the national bureau representing his trade, and is responsible for its work to the administration. The general of his guild holds a splendid position, and one which amply satisfies the ambition of most men, but above his rank, which may be compared . . . to that of a general of division or major-general, is that of the chiefs of the ten great departments, or groups of allied trades. The chiefs of these ten grand divisions of the industrial army may be compared to your commanders of army corps, or lieutenant-generals, each having from a dozen to a score of generals of separate guilds reporting to him. Above these ten great officers, who form his council, is the general-in-chief, who is the President of the United States. . . .

Supposing some of my neighbors or myself think we ought to have a newspaper reflecting our opinions, and devoted especially to our locality, trade, or profession. We go about among the people till we get the names of such a number that their annual subscriptions will meet the cost of the paper, which is little or big according to the largeness of its constituency. The amount of the subscriptions marked off the credits of the citizens guarantees the nation against loss in publishing the paper, its business being that of publisher purely, with no option to refuse the duty required. The subscribers to the paper now elect somebody as editor, who, if he accepts the office, is discharged from other service during his incumbency. Instead of paying a salary to him the subscribers pay the nation an indemnity equal to the cost of his support for taking him away from the general service. . . .

[The entire structure is unchanging, and politically, little happens. There are no longer state governments, and little legislation is passed.] It is rarely that Congress, even when it meets, considers new laws of consequence, and then it only has power to commend them to the following Congress, lest anything be done hastily. . . .

[Women] have a woman general-in-chief and are under exclusively feminine régime. This general, as also the higher officers, is chosen by the body of women who have passed the time of service, in correspondence with the manner in which the chiefs of the masculine army and the President of the nation are elected. The general of the women's army sits in the cabinet of the President and has a veto on measures respecting women's work, pending appeals to Congress. . . . [W]e have women on the bench, appointed by the general of the women, as well as men. Causes in which both parties are women are determined by women judges, and where a man and a woman are parties to a case, a judge of either sex must consent to the verdict. . . .

Source: Looking Backward 2000–1887. By Edward Bellamy. Boston: Ticknor and Co., 1888.

Edward Bellamy (1850–98) was a journalist and novelist who is best known for his utopian novel *Looking Backward.*

* * *

Although much has been left out, these brief excerpts point to the central institutions and mention two areas for which Bellamy was widely criticized and which he changed in *Equality* (1897), a sequel to *Looking Backward*. First, he democratized the political system. Second, he totally changed the treatment of women.

Social Darwinism

Intellectual justification for the divisions in society was provided by Social Darwinism. Social Darwinists argued, generally counter to Charles Darwin's own position, that life is a struggle for survival within the human species and that those who prosper deserve to do so. Therefore, as a corollary, those who fail deserve to fail. In the United States this theory was used to justify manifest destiny, racism, sexism, and the anti-immigrant and antilabor positions. It also gave theoretical support to the development of capitalism. One of capitalism's most important advocates was William Graham Sumner (1849–1910), whose essay

"The Absurd Effort to Make the World Over" is reprinted here. The title alone expresses Sumner's attitude toward reformers and radicals such as Bellamy, who is directly attacked in the essay. Sumner believed that competition is a law of nature.

Social Darwinists preached middle-class values that, they contended, would lead to an improvement in society. Sumner contended that poverty would be eliminated through the sober and industrious worker who also taught his (women were not to be workers) children to be that way.

William Graham Sumner
The Absurd Effort to Make the World Over

It will not probably be denied that the burden of proof is on those who affirm that our social condition is utterly diseased and in need of radical regeneration. My task at present, therefore, is entirely negative and critical: to examine the allegations of fact and the doctrines which are put forward to prove the correctness of the diagnosis and to warrant the use of the remedies proposed.

The propositions put forward by social reformers nowadays are chiefly of two kinds. There are assertions in historical form, chiefly in regard to the comparison of existing with earlier social states, which are plainly based on defective historical knowledge, or at most on current stock historical dicta which are uncritical and incorrect. Writers very often assert that something never existed before because they do not know that it ever existed before, or that something is worse than ever before because they are not possessed of detailed information about what has existed before. The other class of propositions consists of dogmatic statements which, whether true or not, are unverifiable. This class of propositions is the pest and bane of current economic and social discussion. Upon a more or less superficial view of some phenomenon a suggestion arises which is embodied in a philosophical proposition and promulgated as a truth. From the form and nature of such propositions they can always be brought under the head of "ethics." This word at least gives them an air of elevated sentiment and purpose, which is the only warrant they possess. It is impossible to test or verify them by any investigation or logical process whatsoever. It is therefore every difficult for anyone who feels a high responsibility for historical statements, and who absolutely rejects any statement which is unverifiable, to find a common platform for discussion or to join issue satisfactorily in taking the negative. . . .

If it is said that the employed class are under much more stringent discipline than they were thirty years ago or earlier, it is true. It is not true that there has been any qualitative change in this respect within thirty years, but it is true that a movement which began at the first settlement of the country has been advancing with constant acceleration and has become a noticeable feature within our time. This movement is the advance in the industrial organization. The first settlement was made by agriculturists, and for a long time there was scarcely any organization. There were scattered farmers, each working for himself, and some small towns with only rudimentary commerce and handicrafts. As the country has filled up, the arts and professions have been differentiated and the industrial organization has been advancing. This fact and its significance has hardly been noticed at all; but the stage of the industrial organization existing at any time, and the rate of advance in its development, are the absolutely controlling social facts. Nine-tenths of the socialistic and semi-socialistic, and sentimental or ethical, suggestions by which we are overwhelmed come from failure to understand the phenomena of the industrial organization and its expansion. It controls us all because we are all in it. It creates the conditions of our existence, sets the limits of our social activity, regulates the bonds of our social relations, determines our conceptions of good and evil, suggests our life-philosophy, molds our inherited political institutions, and reforms the oldest and toughest customs, like marriage and property. I repeat that the turmoil of heterogeneous and antagonistic social whims and speculations in which we live is due to the failure to understand what the industrial organization is and its all-pervading control over human life, while the traditions of our school of philosophy lead us always to approach the industrial organization, not from the side of objective study, but from that of philosophical doctrine. Hence it is that we find that the method of measuring what we see happening by what are called ethical standards, and of proposing to attack the phenomena by methods thence deduced is so popular. . . .

If it is said that there are some persons in our time who have become rapidly and in a great degree rich, it is true; if it is said that large aggregations of wealth in the control of individuals is a social danger, it is not true.

The movement of the industrial organization which has just been described has brought out a great demand for men capable of managing great enterprises. Such have been called "captains of industry." The analogy with military leaders suggested by this name is not misleading. The great leaders in the development of the industrial organization need those talents of executive and administrative skill, power to command, courage, and fortitude, which were formerly called for in military affairs and scarcely anywhere else. The industrial army is also as dependent on its captains as a military body is on its generals. One of the worst features of the existing system is that the employees have a constant risk in their employer. If he is not competent to manage the business with success, they suffer with him. Capital also is dependent on the skill of the captain of industry for the certainty and magnitude of its profits. Under these circumstances there has been a great demand for men having the requisite ability for this function. As the organization has advanced, with more impersonal bonds of coherence and wider scope of operations, the value of this functionary has rapidly increased. The possession of the requisite ability is a natural monopoly. Consequently, all the conditions have concurred to give to those who possessed this monopoly excessive and constantly advancing rates of remuneration.

Another social function of the first importance in an intense organization is the solution of those crises in the operation of it which are called the conjuncture of the market. It is through the market that the lines of relation run which preserve the system in harmonious and rhythmical operation. The conjuncture is the momentary sharper misadjustment of supply and demand which indicates that a redistribution of productive effort is called for. The industrial organization needs to be insured against these conjunctures, which, if neglected, produce a crisis and catastrophe; and it needs that they shall be anticipated and guarded against as far as skill and foresight can do it. The rewards of this function for the bankers and capitalists who perform it are very great. The captains of industry and the capitalists who operate on the conjuncture, therefore, if they are successful, win, in these days, great fortunes in a short time. There are no earnings which are more legitimate or for which greater services are rendered to the whole industrial body. The popular notions about this matter really assume that all the wealth accumulated by these classes of persons would be here just the same if they had not existed. They are supposed to have appropriated it out of the common stock. This is so far from being true that, on the contrary, their own wealth would not be but for themselves; and besides that, millions more of wealth, many-fold greater than their own, scattered in the hands of thousands, would not exist but for them. . . .

But it is repeated until it has become a commonplace which people are afraid to question, that there is some social danger in the possession of large amounts of wealth by individuals. I ask, Why? . . . It would be easy . . . to show what good is done by accumulations of capital in a few hands—that is, under close and direct management, permitting prompt and accurate application; also to tell what harm is done by loose and unfounded denunciations of any social component or any social group. . . .

Great figures are set out as to the magnitude of certain fortunes and the proportionate amount of the national wealth held by a fraction of the population, and eloquent exclamation-points are set against them. If the figures were beyond criticism, what would they prove? Where is the rich man who is oppressing anybody? If there was one, the newspapers would ring with it. The facts about the accumulation of wealth do not constitute a plutocracy. . . . Wealth, in itself considered, is only power, like steam, or electricity, or knowledge. The question of its good or ill turns on the question how it will be used. To prove any harm in aggregations of wealth it must be shown that great wealth is, as a rule, in the ordinary course of social affairs, put to a mischievous use. This cannot be shown beyond the very slightest degree, if at all. . . .

Assuming, however, that the charges against the existing "capitalistic"—that is, industrial—order of things are established, it is proposed to remedy the ill by reconstructing the industrial system on the principles of democracy. Once more we must untangle the snarl of half ideas and muddled facts.

Democracy is, of course, a word to conjure with. We have a democratic-republican political system, and we like it so well that we are prone to take any new step which can be recommended as "democratic" or which will round out some "principle" of democracy to a fuller fulfillment. Everything connected with this domain of political thought is crusted over with false historical traditions, cheap philosophy, and undefined terms, but it is useless to try to criticize it. The whole drift of the world for five hundred years has been toward democracy. That drift, produced by great discoveries and inventions, and by the discovery of a new continent, has raised the middle class out of the servile class. In alliance with the crown they crushed the feudal classes. They made the crown absolute in order to do it. Then they turned against the crown and, with the aid of the handicraftsmen and peasants, conquered it. Now the next conflict which must inevitably come is that between the middle capitalist class and the proletariat, as the word has come to be used. If a certain construction is put on this conflict, it may be called that between democracy and plutocracy, for it seems that industrialism must be developed into plutocracy by the conflict itself. That is the conflict which stands before civilized society today. All the signs of the times indicate its commencement, and it is big with fate to mankind and to civilization.

Although we cannot criticise democracy profitably, it may be said of it, with reference to our present subject, that up to this time democracy never has done anything, either in politics, social affairs, or industry, to prove its power to bless mankind. If we confine our attention to the United States, there are three difficulties with regard to its alleged achievements, and they all have the most serious bearing on the proposed democratization of industry.

1. The time during which democracy has been tried in the United States is too short to warrant any inferences. A century or two is a very short time in the life of political institutions, and if the circumstances change rapidly during the period the experiment is vitiated.

2. The greatest question of all about American democracy is whether it is a cause or a consequence. It is popularly assumed to be a cause, and we ascribe to its beneficent action all the political vitality, all the easiness of social relations, all the industrial activity and enterprise which we experience and which we value and enjoy. I submit, however, that, on a more thorough examination of the matter, we shall find that democracy is a consequence. There are economic and sociological causes for our political vitality and vigor, for the ease and elasticity of our

social relations, and for our industrial power and success. Those causes have also produced democracy, given it success, and have made its faults and errors innocuous. Indeed, in any true philosophy, it must be held that in the economic forces which control the material prosperity of a population lie the real causes of its political institutions, its social class-adjustments, its industrial prosperity, its moral code, and its world-philosophy. If democracy and the industrial system are both products of the economic conditions which exist, it is plainly absurd to set democracy to defeat those conditions in the control of industry. If, however, it is not true that democracy is a consequence, and I am well aware that very few people believe it, then we must go back to the view that democracy is a cause. That being so, it is difficult to see how democracy, which has had a clear field here in America, is not responsible for the ills which Mr. Bellamy and his comrades in opinion see in our present social state, and it is difficult to see the grounds of asking us to intrust it also with industry. The first and chief proof of success of political measures and systems is that, under them, society advances in health and vigor and that industry develops without causing social disease. If this has not been the case in America, American democracy has not succeeded. Neither is it easy to see how the masses, if they have undertaken to rule, can escape the responsibilities of ruling, especially so far so the consequences affect themselves. If, then, they have brought all this distress upon themselves under the present system, what becomes of the argument for extending the system to a direct and complete control of industry?

3. It is by no means certain that democracy in the United States has not, up to this time, been living on a capital inherited from aristocracy and industrialism. We have no pure democracy. Our democracy is limited at every turn by institutions which were developed in England in connection with industrialism and aristocracy, and these institutions are of the essence of our system. While our people are passionately democratic in temper and will not tolerate a doctrine that one man is not as good as another, they have common sense enough to know that he is not; and it seems that they love and cling to the conservative institutions quite as strongly as they do to the democratic philosophy. They are, therefore, ruled by men who talk philosophy and govern by the institutions. Now it is open to Mr. Bellamy to say that the reason why democracy in America seems to be open to the charge made in the last paragraph, of responsibility for all the ill which he now finds in our society, is because it has been infected with industrialism (capitalism); but in that case he must widen the scope of his proposition and undertake to purify democracy before turning industry over to it. The socialists generally seem to think that they make their undertakings easier when they widen their scope, and make them easiest when they propose to remake everything; but in truth social tasks increase in difficulty in an enormous ratio as they are widened in scope.

The question, therefore, arises, if it is proposed to reorganize the social system on the principles of American democracy, whether the institutions of industrialism are to be retained. If so, all the virus of capitalism will be retained. It is forgotten, in many schemes of social reformation in which it is proposed to mix what we like with what we do not like, in order to extirpate the latter, that each must undergo a reaction from the other, and that what we like may be extirpated by what we do not like. We may find that instead of democratizing capitalism we have capitalized democracy—that is, have brought in plutocracy. Plutocracy is a political system in which the ruling force is wealth. The denunciation of capital which we hear from all the reformers is the most eloquent proof that the greatest power in the world today is capital. They know that it is, and confess it most when they deny it most strenuously. At present the power of capital is social and industrial, and only in a small degree political. So far as capital is political, it is on account of political abuses, such as tariffs and special legislation on the one hand and legislative strikes on the other. These conditions exist in the democracy to which it is proposed to transfer the industries. What does that mean except bringing all the power of capital once for all into the political arena and precipitating the conflict of democracy and plutocracy at once? Can anyone imagine that the masterfulness, the overbearing disposition, the greed of gain, and the ruthlessness in methods, which are the faults of the master of industry at his worst, would cease when he was a functionary of the State, which had relieved him of risk and endowed him with authority? Can anyone imagine that politicians would no longer be corruptly fond of money, intriguing, and crafty when they were charged, not only with patronage and government contracts, but also with factories, stores, ships, and railroads? Could we expect anything except that, when the politician and the master of industry were joined in one, we should have the vices of both unchecked by the restraints of either? In any socialistic state there will be one set of positions which will offer chances of wealth beyond the wildest dreams of avarice; *viz.*, on the governing committees. Then there will be rich men whose wealth will indeed be a menace to social interests, and instead of industrial peace there will be such war as no one has dreamed of yet: the war between the political ins and outs—that is, between those who are on the committee and those who want to get on it.

We must not drop the subject of democracy without one word more. The Greeks already had occasion to notice a most serious distinction between two principles of democracy which lie at its root. . . . There is one democratic principle which means that each man should be esteemed for his merit and worth, for just what he is, without regard to birth, wealth, rank, or other adventitious circumstances. The other principle is that each one of us ought to be equal to all the others in what he gets and enjoys. The first principle is only partially realizable, but, so far as it goes, it is elevating and socially progressive and profitable. The second is not capable of an intelligible statement. The first is a principle of industrialism. It proceeds from and is intelligible only in a society built on the industrial virtues, free endeavor, security of property, and repression of the baser vices; that is, in a society whose industrial system is built on labor and exchange. The other is only a rule of division for robbers who have to divide plunder or monks who have to divide gifts. If, therefore, we want to democratize industry in the sense of the first principle, we need only perfect what we have now, especially on its political side. If we try to democratize it in the sense of the other principle, we corrupt politics at one stroke; we enter upon an industrial enterprise which will waste capital and bring us all to poverty, and we set loose greed and envy as ruling social passions.

If this poor old world is as bad as they say, one more reflection may check the zeal of the headlong reformer. It is at any rate a rough old world. It has taken its trend and curvature and all its twists and tangles from a long course of formation. All its wry and crooked gnarls and knobs are therefore stiff and stubborn. If we puny men by our arts can do anything at all to straighten them, it will only be by modifying the tendencies of some of the forces at work, so that, after a sufficient time, their action may be changed a little and slowly the lines of movement may be modified. This effort, however, can at most be only slight, and it will take a long time. In the meantime spontaneous forces will be at work, compared with which our efforts are like those of a man trying to deflect a river, and these forces will have changed the whole problem before our interferences have time to make themselves felt. The great stream of time and earthly things will sweep on just the same in spite of us. It bears with it now all the errors and follies of the past, the wreckage of all the philosophies, the fragments of all the civilizations, the wisdom of all the abandoned ethical systems, the debris of all the institutions, and the penalties of all the mistakes. It is only in imagination that we stand by and look at and criticize it and plan to change it. Everyone of us is a child of his age and cannot get out of it. He is in the stream and is swept along with it. Therefore the tide will not be changed by us. It will swallow up both us and our experiments. It will absorb the efforts at change and take them into itself as new but trivial components, and the great movement of tradition and work will go on unchanged by our fads and schemes. The things which will change it are the great discoveries and inventions, the new reactions inside the social organism, and the changes in the earth itself on account of changes in the cosmical forces. These causes will make of it just what, in fidelity to them, it ought to be. The men will be carried along with it and be made by it. The utmost they can do by their cleverness will be to note and record their course as they are carried along, which is what we do now, and is that which leads us to the vain fancy that we can make or guide the movement. That is why it is the greatest folly of which a man can be capable, to sit down with a slate and pencil to plan out a new social world.

Source: Forum 17 (March 1894): 92–102.

William Graham Sumner (1849–1910) was a social scientist who was one of the foremost advocates of Social Darwinism.

The Anti-Trust Movement

While Bellamy thought that the development of monopolies could be turned into an advantage, others felt that monopolies struck at the heart of competitive capitalism and should be broken up. The first result was the Sherman Anti-Trust Act. The bill was used both to break up monopolies and to declare labor unions illegal. The status of unions was an issue for many years and has recently returned as one.

Sherman Anti-Trust Act

CHAP. 647—An act to protect trade and commerce against unlawful restraints and monopolies.

Be it enacted by the Senate and House of Representatives of the United States of America in Congress assembled,

Sec. 1. Every contract, combination in the form of trust or otherwise, or conspiracy, in restraint of trade or commerce among the several States, or with foreign nations is hereby declared to be illegal. Every person who shall make any such contract or engage in any such combination or conspiracy, shall be deemed guilty of a misdemeanor, and, on conviction thereof, shall be punished by fine, not exceeding five thousand dollars, or by imprisonment not exceeding one year, or by both said punishments, in the discretion of the court.

Sec. 2. Every person who shall monopolize, or attempt to monopolize. or combine or conspire with any other person or persons, to monopolize any part of the trade or commerce among the several States, or with foreign nations, shall be deemed guilty of a misdemeanor, and, on conviction thereof, shall be punished by fine, not exceeding five thousand dollars, or by imprisonment not exceeding one year, or by both said punishments, in the discretion of the court.

Source: 26 Stat. 209 (1890).

Manifest Destiny

Social Darwinism supported the belief held by many Americans in their role as a chosen people to rule the continent. In the latter part of the nineteenth century this attitude was expressed through the belief in manifest destiny.

Albert J. Beveridge
Manifest Destiny

God has not been preparing the English-speaking and Teutonic peoples for a thousand years for nothing but vain and idle self-contemplation and self-admiration. No. He made us master organizers of the world to establish system where chaos reigned. He has given us the spirit of progress to overwhelm the forces of reaction throughout the earth. He has made us adept in government that we may administer government among savage and senile peoples. Were it not for such a force as this the world would relapse into barbarism and night. And of all our race He has marked the American people as His chosen nation to finally lead in the redemption of the world.

Source: Congressional Record, 56th Congress, 1st session, January 9, 1900.

Albert J. Beveridge (1862–1927) was a member of the U.S. Senate 1899–1911.

Other Reform Movements

Rising and consolidating industrialism produced as many reform movements as had the so-called age of reform earlier in the nineteenth century. The main difference is that the late-nineteenth-century reform movements were more focused on economic relations, whereas the earlier period included more of what might be called life-style reforms.

Populism and unionism were the most influential of the reform movements at the end of the century. The union movement has clearly shaped American thought and practice ever since, even though its influence is currently at an ebb. Populism struck a chord that still resonates in American thought. American politicians are still frequently labeled populists if they make appeals to a broad sweep of the population. Populism is based on the assumption that "the people" know what is best for them. The term used to refer specifically to those politicians who appealed to the lower classes, but it now can include the appeals to the middle class. Populism was often racist.

This section includes selections from the Knights of Labor, one of the earliest

labor unions in the United States; Coxey's Army, a demonstration of the unemployed in 1894; and various facets of populism. Also included is one of the most famous speeches of the time, "The Cross of Gold" by William Jennings Bryan (1860–1925). In this speech Bryan argued that the monetary system was a terrible burden on the American economy.

Knights of Labor

Constitution

Preamble

The recent alarming development and aggression of aggregated wealth, which, unless checked, will inevitably lead to the pauperization and hopeless degradation of the toiling masses, render it imperative, if we desire to enjoy the blessings of life, that a check should be placed upon its power and upon unjust accumulation, and a system adopted which will secure to the laborer the fruits of his toil; and as this much-desired object can only be accomplished by the thorough unification of labor, and the united efforts of those who obey the divine injunction that "In the sweat of thy brow shall thou eat bread," we have formed the [Knights of Labor] with a view of securing the organization and direction, by co-operative effort, of the power of the industrial classes; and we submit to the world the objects sought to be accomplished by our great organization, calling upon all who believe in securing "the greatest good to the greatest number" to aid and assist us:

I. To bring within the folds of organization every department of productive industry, making knowledge a standpoint for action, and industrial and moral worth, not wealth, the true standard of individual and national greatness.

II. To secure to the toilers a proper share of the wealth that they create; more of the leisure that rightfully belongs to them; more societary advantages; more of the benefits, privileges and emoluments of the world; in a word, all those rights and privileges necessary to make them capable of enjoying, appreciating, defending and perpetuating the blessings of good government.

III. To arrive at the true condition of the producing masses in their educational, moral and financial condition, by demanding from the various governments the establishment of Bureaus of Labor Statistics.

IV. The establishment of co-operative institutions, productive and distributive.

V. The reserving of the public lands—the heritage of the people—for the actual settler; not another acre for railroads or speculators.

VI. The abrogation of all laws that do not bear equally upon capital and labor, the removal of unjust technicalities, delays and discriminations in the administration of justice, and the adopting of measures providing for the health and safety of those engaged in mining, manufacturing or building pursuits.

VII. The enactment of laws to compel chartered corporations to pay their employes weekly, in full, for labor performed during the preceding week, in the lawful money of the country.

VIII. The enactment of laws giving mechanics and laborers a first lien on their work for their full wages.

IX. The abolishment of the contract system on national, State and municipal work.

X. The substitution of arbitration for strikes, whenever and wherever employers and employes are willing to meet on equitable grounds.

XI. The prohibition of the employment of children in workshops, mines and factories before attaining their fourteenth year.

XII. To abolish the system of letting out by contract the labor of convicts in our prisons and reformatory institutions.

XIII. To secure for both sexes equal pay for equal work.

XIV. The reduction of the hours of labor to eight per day, so that the laborers may have more time for social enjoyment and intellectual improvement, and be enabled to reap the advantages conferred by the labor-saving machinery which their brains have created.

Source: Thirty Years of Labor 1859–1889. By Terence V. Powderly. New York: Augustus M. Kelley, 1967. Originally published 1890.

Southern Alliance and Knights of Labor

St. Louis, Mo., *December 6, 1889*

Agreement made this day by and between the undersigned committee representing the National Farmers Alliance and Industrial Union on the one part, and the undersigned committee representing the Knights of Labor on the other part . . . for the purpose of giving practical effect to the demands herein set forth, the legislative committees of both organizations will act in concert before Congress for the purpose of securing the enactment of laws in harmony with the demands mutually agreed.

And it is further agreed, in order to carry out these objects, we will support for office only such men as can be depended upon to enact these principles in statute law uninfluenced by party caucus.

The demands hereinbefore referred to are as follows:

1. That we demand abolition of national banks and the substitution of legal tender treasury notes in lieu of national bank notes, issued in sufficient volume to do the business of the country on a cash system; regulating the amount needed on a per capita basis as the business interests of the country expands; and that all money issued by the Government shall be legal tender in payment of debts, both public and private.

2. That we demand that Congress shall pass such laws as shall effectually prevent the dealing in futures of all agricultural and mechanical productions; preserving a stringent system of procedure in trials as shall secure the prompt conviction, and imposing such penalties as shall secure the most perfect compliance with the law.

3. That we demand the free and unlimited coinage of silver.

4. That we demand the passage of laws prohibiting the alien ownership of land, and that Congress take early steps to devise some plan to obtain all lands now owned by aliens and foreign syndicates; and that all lands now held by railroad and other corporations in excess of such as is actually used and needed by them, be reclaimed by the Government and held for actual settlers only.

5. Believing in the doctrine of "equal rights to all and special privileges to none," we demand that taxation, National or State, shall not be used to build up one interest or class at the expense of another.

We believe that the money of the country should be kept as much as possible in the hands of the people, and hence we demand that all revenues, National, State or county, shall be limited to the necessary expenses of the Government economically and honestly administered.

6. That Congress issue a sufficient amount of fractional paper currency to facilitate exchange through the medium of the United States mail.

7. We demand that the means of communication and transportation shall be owned and operated in the interest of the people as is the United States postal system.

Source: The National Economist 3 (December 21, 1889): 214–15.

Jacob S. Coxey
Address of Protest

The Constitution of the United States guarantees to all citizens the right to peaceably assemble and petition for redress of grievances, and furthermore declares that the right of free speech shall not be abridged.

We stand here to-day to test these guarantees of our Constitution. . . . We stand here to-day on behalf of millions of toilers whose petitions have been buried in committee rooms, whose prayers have been unresponded to, and whose opportunities for honest, remunerative, productive labor have been taken from them by unjust legislation, which protects idlers, speculators, and gamblers: we come to remind the Congress here assembled of the declaration of a United States Senator, "that for a quarter of a century the rich have been growing richer, the poor poorer, and that by the close of the present century the middle class will have disappeared as the struggle for existence becomes fierce and relentless."

We stand here to remind Congress of its promise of returning prosperity should the Sherman act be repealed. We stand here to declare by our march of over 400 miles through difficulties and distress, a march unstained by even the slightest act which would bring the blush of shame to any, that we are law-abiding citizens, and as men our actions speak louder than words. We are here to petition for legislation which will furnish employment for every man able and willing to work; for legislation which will bring universal prosperity and emancipate our beloved country from financial bondage to the descendents of King George. We have come to the only source which is competent to aid the people in their day of dire distress. We are here to tell our Representatives, who hold their seats by grace of our ballots, that the struggle for existence has become too fierce and relentless. We come and throw up our defenseless hands, and say, help, or we and our loved ones must perish. We are engaged in a bitter and cruel war with the enemies of mankind—a war with hunger, wretchedness, and despair, and we ask Congress to heed our petitions and issue for the nation's good a sufficient volume of the same kind of money which carried the country through one awful war and saved the life of the nation.

In the name of justice, through whose impartial administration only the present civilization can be maintained and perpetuated, by the powers of the Constitution of our country upon which the liberties of the people must depend, and in the name of the commonweal of Christ, whose representatives we are, we enter a most solemn and earnest protest against this unnecessary and cruel usurpation and tyranny, and this enforced subjugation of the rights and privileges of American citizenship. We have assembled here in violation of no just laws to enjoy the privileges of every American citizen. . . .

We have come here through toil and weary marches, through storms and tempests, over mountains, and amid the trials of poverty and distress, to lay our grievances at the doors of our National Legislature and ask them in the name of Him whose banners we bear, in the name of Him who plead for the poor and oppressed, that they should consider the conditions of the starving unemployed of our land, and enact such laws as will give them employment, bring happier conditions to the people, and the smile of contentment to our citizens.

Source: *Congressional Record*, 53rd Congress, 2nd session (May 9, 1894): 4512.

Jacob S. Coxey (1854–1951) was known as General Coxey for his leadership of a march by the unemployed—known as Coxey's Army—on Washington, D.C., to call for government relief during the depression of 1893.

William Jennings Bryan
Cross of Gold Speech

And now, my friends, let me come to the paramount issue. If they ask us why it is that we say more on the money question than we say upon the tariff question, I reply that, if protection has slain its thousands, the gold standard has slain its tens of thousands. If they ask us why we do not embody in our platform all the things that we believe in, we reply that when we have restored the money of the Constitution all other necessary reforms will be possible; but that until this is done there is no other reform that can be accomplished.

Why is it that within three months such a change has come over the country? Three months ago, when it was confidently asserted that those who believe in the gold standard would frame our platform and nominate our candidates, even the advocates of the gold standard did not think that we could elect a president. And they had good reason for their doubt, because there is scarcely a State here today asking for the gold standard which is not in the absolute control of the Republican party. But note the change. Mr McKinley was the most popular man among the Republicans, and three months ago everybody in the Republican party prophesied his election. How is today? Why, the man who was once pleased to think that he looked like Napoleon—that man shudders today when he remembers that he was nominated on the anniversary of the battle of Waterloo. Not only that, but as he listens he can hear with ever-increasing distinctness the sound of the waves as they beat upon the lonely shores of St. Helena.

Why this change? Ah, my friends, is not the reason for the change evident to any one who will look at the matter? No private character, however pure, no personal popularity, however great, can protect from the avenging wrath of an indignant people a man who will declare that he is in favor of fastening the gold standard upon this country, or who is willing to surrender the right of self-government and place the legislative control of our affairs in the hands of foreign potentates and powers.

We go forth confident that we shall win. Why? Because upon the paramount issue of this campaign there is not a spot of ground upon which the enemy will dare to challenge battle. If they tell us that the gold standard is a good thing, we shall point to their platform and tell them that their platform pledges the party to get rid of the gold standard and substitute bimetallism. If the gold standard is a good thing, why try to get rid of it? I call your attention to the fact that some of the very people who are in this convention today and who tell us that we ought to declare in favor of international bimetallism — thereby declaring that the gold standard is wrong and that the principle of bimetallism is better — these very people four months ago were open and avowed advocates of the gold standard, and were then telling us that we could not legislate two metals together, even with the aid of all the world. If the gold standard is a good thing, we ought to declare in favor of its retention and not in favor of abandoning it; and if the gold standard is a bad thing why should we wait until other nations are willing to help us to let go? Here is the line of battle, and we care not upon which issue they force the fight; we are prepared to meet them on either issue or on both. If they tell us that the gold standard is the standard of civilization, we reply to them that this, the most enlightened of all the nations of the earth, has never declared for a gold standard and that both the great parties this year are declaring against it. If the gold standard is the standard of civilization, why, my friends, should we not have it? If they come to meet us on that issue we can present the history of our nation. More than that; we can tell them that they will search the pages of history in vain to find a single instance where the common people of any land have ever declared themselves in favor of the gold standard. They can find where the holders of fixed investments have declared for a gold standard, but not where the masses have. . . .

You come to us and tell us that the great cities are in favor of the gold standard; we reply that the great cities rest upon our broad and fertile prairies. Burn down your cities and leave our farms, and your cities will spring up again as if by magic; but destroy our farms and the grass will grow in the streets of every city in the country.

Source: The First Battle: A Story of the Campaign of 1896. By William Jennings Bryan, 199–206. Chicago: W. B. Conkey Co., 1896.

William Jennings Bryan (1860–1925) was the losing Democratic presidential candidate in 1896, 1900, and 1908. He was a member of the House of Representative 1891–95 and secretary of state 1913–15. He was a gifted orator.

Minorities

AFRICAN AMERICANS

The last part of the nineteenth century saw both the rise of movements to better the position of African Americans and the *Plessy* v. *Ferguson* Supreme Court decision that made segregation legal. Booker T. Washington (1856–1915) recognized the weakness of African Americans in American politics at the time and suggested ways to develop better lives without rocking the boat too much.

Booker T. Washington
Atlanta Exposition Address

Mr. President and Gentlemen of the Board of Directors and Citizens.

One-third of the population of the South is of the Negro race. No enterprise seeking the material, civil, or moral welfare of this section can disregard this element of our population and reach the highest success. I but convey to you, Mr. President and Directors, the sentiment of the masses of my race when I say that in no way have the value and manhood of the American Negro been more fittingly and generously recognized than by the managers of this magnificent Exposition at every stage of its progress. It is a recognition that will do more to cement the friendship of the two races than any occurrence since the dawn of our freedom.

Not only this, but the opportunity here afforded will awaken among us a new era of industrial progress. Ignorant and inexperienced, it is not strange that in the first years of our new life we began at the top instead of at the bottom; that a seat in Congress or the state legislature was more sought than real estate or industrial skill; that the political convention of stump speaking had more attractions than starting a dairy farm or truck garden.

A ship lost at sea for many days suddenly sighted a friendly vessel. From the mast of the unfortunate vessel was seen a signal, "Water, water; we die of thirst!" The answer from the friendly vessel at once came back, "Cast down your bucket where you are." A second time the signal, "Water, water; send us water!" ran up from the distressed vessel, and was answered, "Cast down your bucket where you are." And a third and fourth signal for water was answered, "Cast down your bucket where you are." The captain of the distressed vessel, at last heeding the injunction, cast down his bucket, and it came up full of fresh, sparkling water from the mouth of the Amazon River. To those of my race who depend on bettering their condition in a foreign land or who underestimate the importance of cultivating friendly relations with the Southern white man, who is their next-door neighbour, I would say: "Cast down your bucket where you are"—cast it down in making friends in every manly way of the people of all races by whom we are surrounded.

Cast it down in agriculture, mechanics, in commerce, in domestic service, and in the professions. And in this connection it is well to bear in mind that whatever other sins the South may be called to bear, when it comes to business, pure and simple, it is in the South that the Negro is given a man's chance in the commercial world, and in nothing is this Exposition more eloquent than in emphasizing this chance. Our greatest danger is that in the great leap from slavery to freedom we may overlook the fact that the masses of us are to live by the productions of our hands, and fail to keep in mind that we shall prosper in proportion as we learn to dignify and glorify common labour and put brains and skill into the common occupations of life; shall prosper in proportion as we learn to draw the line between the superficial and the substantial, the ornamental gewgaws of life and the useful. No race can prosper till it learns that there is as much dignity in tilling a field as in writing a poem. It is at the bottom of life we must begin, and not at the top. Nor should we permit our grievances to overshadow our opportunities.

To those of the white race who look to the incoming of those of foreign birth and strange tongue and habits for the prosperity of the South, were I permitted I would repeat what I say to my own race, "Cast down your bucket where you are." Cast it down among the eight millions of Negroes whose habits you know, whose fidelity and love you have tested in days when to have proved treacherous meant the ruin of your firesides, Cast down your bucket among these people who have, without strikes and labour wars, tilled your fields, cleared your forests, builded your railroads and cities, and brought forth treasures from the bowels of the earth, and helped make possible this magnificent representation of the progress of the South. Casting down your bucket among my people, helping and encouraging them as you are doing on these grounds, and to education of head, hand, and heart, you will find that they will buy your surplus land, make blossom the waste places in your fields, and run your factories. While doing this, you can be sure in the future, as in the past, that you and your families will be surrounded by the most patient, faithful, law-abiding, and unresentful people that the world has seen. As we have proved our loyalty to you in the past, in nursing your children, watching by the sick-bed of your mothers and fathers, and often following them with tear-dimmed eyes to their graves, so in the future, in our humble way, we shall stand by you with a devotion that no foreigner can approach, ready to lay down our lives, if need be, in defence of yours, interlacing our industrial, commercial, civil, and religious life with yours in a way that shall make the interests of both races one. In all things that are purely social we can be as separate as the fingers, yet one as the hand in all things essential to mutual progress.

There is no defence or security for any of us except in the highest intelligence and development of all. If anywhere there are efforts tending to curtail the fullest growth of the Negro, let these efforts be turned into stimulating, encouraging, and making him the most useful and intelligent citizen. Effort or means so in-

vested will pay a thousand per cent. interest. These efforts will be twice blessed—
"blessing him that gives and him that takes." . . .

Nearly sixteen millions of hands will aid you in pulling the load upward, or
they will pull against you the load downward. We shall constitute one-third and
more of the ignorance and crime of the South, or one-third its intelligence and
progress; we shall contribute one-third to the business and industrial prosperity
of the South, or we shall prove a veritable body of death, stagnating, depressing,
retarding every effort to advance the body politic.

Gentlemen of the Exposition, as we present to you our humble effort at an exhibition of our progress, you must not expect overmuch. Starting thirty years ago
with ownership here and there in a few quilts and pumpkins and chickens (gathered from miscellaneous sources), remember the path that has led from these to
the inventions and production of agricultural implements, buggies, steam-en-
gines, newspapers, books, statuary, carving, paintings, the management of drug-
stores and banks, has not been trodden without contact with thorns and thistles.
While we take pride in what we exhibit as a result of our independent efforts, we
do not for a moment forget that our part in this exhibition would fall far short
of your expectations but for the constant help that has come to our educational
life, not only from the Southern states, but especially from Northern philanthro-
pists, who have made their gifts a constant stream of blessing and encouragement.

The wisest among my race understand that the agitation of questions of social
equality is the extremest folly, and that progress in the enjoyment of all the privileges that will come to us must be the result of severe and constant struggle rather
than of artificial forcing. No race that has anything to contribute to the markets
of the world is long in any degree ostracized. It is important and right that all
privileges of the law be ours, but it is vastly more important that we be prepared
for the exercises of these privileges. The opportunity to earn a dollar in a factory
just now is worth infinitely more than the opportunity to spend a dollar in an op-
era-house.

In conclusion, may I repeat that nothing in thirty years has given us more hope
and encouragement, and drawn us so near to you of the white race, as this opportunity offered by the Exposition; and here bending, as it were, over the altar that
represents the results of the struggles of your race and mine, both starting practically empty-handed three decades ago, I pledge that in your effort to work out
the great and intricate problem which God has laid at the doors of the South, you
shall have at all times the patient, sympathetic help of my race; only let this be
constantly in mind, that, while from representations in these buildings of the
product of field, of forest, of mine, of factory, letters, and art, much good will
come, yet far above and beyond material benefits will be that higher good, that,

let us pray God, will come, in a blotting out of sectional differences and racial animosities and suspicions, in a determination to administer absolute justice, in a
willing obedience among all classes to the mandates of law. This, this, coupled
with our material prosperity, will bring into our beloved South a new heaven and
a new earth.

Source: In *Up from Slavery: An Autobiography.* By Booker T. Washington, 218–37. New
York: A. L. Burt, 1901.

Booker T. Washington (1856–1915) was the founder of the Tuskegee Institute and one of the
most prominent advocates of education for African Americans.

Plessy v. Ferguson

This case turns upon the constitutionality of an act of the general assembly of
the state of Louisiana, passed in 1890, providing for separate railway carriages for
the white and colored races. Acts 1890, No. 111, p. 152.

The first section of the statute enacts "that all railway companies carrying passengers in their coaches in this state, shall provide equal but separate accommodations for the white, and colored races, by providing two or more passenger
coaches for each passenger train, or by dividing the passenger coaches by a partition so as to secure separate accommodations: provided, that this section shall
not be construed to apply to street railroads. No person or persons shall be permitted to occupy seats in coaches, other than the ones assigned to them, on account of the race they belong to."

By the second section it was enacted "that, the officers of such passenger trains
shall have power and are hereby required to assign each passenger to the coach or
compartment used for the race to which such passenger belongs; any passenger
insisting on going into a coach or compartment to which by race he does not belong, shall be liable to a fine of twenty-five dollars, or in lieu thereof to imprisonment for a period of not more than twenty days in the parish prison, and any officer of any railroad insisting on assigning a passenger to a coach or compartment
other than the one set aside for the race to which said passenger belongs, shall be
liable to a fine of twenty-five dollars, or in lieu thereof to imprisonment for a period of not more than twenty days in the parish prison; and should any passenger
refuse to occupy the coach or compartment to which he or she is assigned by the
officer of such railway, said officer shall have power to refuse to carry such passenger on his train, and for such refusal neither he nor the railway company which
he represents shall be liable for damages in any of the courts of this state."

The third section provides penalties for the refusal or neglect of the officers, directors, conductors, and employes of railway companies to comply with the act,

with a proviso that "nothing in the act shall be construed as applying to nurses attending children of the other race." The fourth section is immaterial.

The information filed in the criminal district court charged, in substance, that Plessy, being a passenger between two stations within the state of Louisiana, was assigned by officers of the company to the coach used for the race to which he belonged, but he insisted upon going into a coach used by the race to which he did not belong. Neither in the information nor plea was his particular race or color averred.

The petition for the writ of prohibition averred that petitioner was seven-eighths Caucasian and one-eighth African blood; that the mixture of colored blood was not discernible in him; and that he was entitled to every right, privilege, and immunity secured to citizens of the United States of the white race; and that, upon such theory, he took possession of a vacant seat in a coach where passengers of the white race were accommodated, and was ordered by the conductor to vacate said coach, and take a seat in another, assigned to persons of the colored race, and, having refused to comply with such demand, he was forcibly ejected, with the aid of a police officer, and imprisoned in the parish jail to answer a charge of having violated the above act.

The constitutionality of this act is attacked upon the ground that it conflicts both with the thirteenth amendment of the constitution, abolishing slavery, and the fourteenth amendment, which prohibits certain restrictive legislation on the part of the states.

1. That it does not conflict with the thirteenth amendment, which abolished slavery and involuntary servitude, except as a punishment for crime, is too clear for argument. . . .

2. By the fourteenth amendment, all persons born or naturalized in the United States, and subject to the jurisdiction thereof, are made citizens of the United States and of the state wherein they reside; and the states are forbidden from making or enforcing any law which shall abridge the privileges or immunities of citizens of the United States, or shall deprive any person of life, liberty, or property without due process of law, or deny to any person within their jurisdiction the equal protection of the laws.

The proper construction of this amendment was first called to the attention of this court in the Slaughter-House Cases, 16 Wall 36, which involved, however, not a question of race, but one of exclusive privileges. The case did not call for any expression of opinion as to the exact rights it was intended to secure to the colored race, but it was said generally that its main purpose was to establish the citizenship of the negro, to give definitions of citizenship of the United States and of the states, and to protect from the hostile legislation of the states the privileges and immunities of citizens of the United States, as distinguished from those of citizens of the states.

The object of the amendment was undoubtedly to enforce the absolute equality of the two races before the law, but, in the nature of things, it could not have been intended to abolish distinctions based upon color, or to enforce social, as distinguished from political, equality, or a commingling of the two races upon terms unsatisfactory to either. Laws permitting, and even requiring, their separation, in places where they are liable to be brought into contact, do not necessarily imply the inferiority of either race to the other, and have been generally, if not universally, recognized as within the competency of the state legislatures in the exercise of their police power. The most common instance of this is connected with the establishment of separate schools for white and colored children, which have been held to be a valid exercise of the legislative power even by courts of states where the political rights of the colored race have been longest and most earnestly enforced. . . .

So far, then, as a conflict with the fourteenth amendment is concerned, the case reduces itself to the question whether the statute of Louisiana is a reasonable regulation, and with respect to this there must necessarily be a large discretion on the part of the legislature. In determining the question of reasonableness, it is at liberty to act with reference to the established usages, customs, and traditions of the people, and with a view to the promotion of their comfort, and the preservation of the public peace and good order. Gauged by this standard, we cannot say that a law which authorizes or even requires the separation of the two races in public conveyances is unreasonable, or more obnoxious to the fourteenth amendment than the acts of congress requiring separate schools for colored children in the District of Columbia, the constitutionality of which does not seem to have been questioned, or the corresponding acts of state legislatures.

Mr. Justice Harlan dissenting.

In respect of civil rights, common to all citizens, the constitution of the United States does not, I think, permit any public authority to know the race of those entitled to be protected in the enjoyment of such rights. Every true man has pride of race, and under appropriate circumstances, when the rights of others, his equals before the law, are not to be affected, it is his privilege to express such pride and to take such action based upon it as to him seems proper. But I deny that any legislative body or judicial tribunal may have regard to the race of citizens when the civil rights of those citizens are involved. Indeed, such legislation as that here in question in inconsistent not only with that equality of rights which pertains to citizenship, national and state, but with the personal liberty enjoyed by every one within the United States.

The thirteenth amendment does not permit the withholding or the deprivation of any right necessarily inhering in freedom. It not only struck down the institution of slavery as previously existing in the United States, but it prevents the imposition of any burdens or disabilities that constitute badges of slavery or servitude. It decreed universal civil freedom in this country. This court has so adjudged. But, that amendment having been found inadequate to the protection of the rights of those who had been in slavery, it was followed by the fourteenth amendment, which added greatly to the dignity and glory of American citizenship, and to the security of personal liberty, by declaring that "all persons born or naturalized in the United States, and subject to the jurisdiction thereof, are citizens of the United States and of the state wherein they reside," and that "no state shall make or enforce any law which shall abridge the privileges or immunities of citizens of the United States; nor shall any state deprive any person of life, liberty or property without due process of law, nor deny to any person within its jurisdiction the equal protection of the laws." These two amendments, if enforced according to their true intent and meaning, will protect all the civil rights that pertain to freedom and citizenship. Finally, and to the end that no citizen should be denied, on account of his race, the privilege of participating in the political control of his country, it was declared by the fifteenth amendment that "the right of citizens of the United States to vote shall not be denied or abridged by the United States or by any state on account of race, color or previous condition of servitude."

These notable additions to the fundamental law were welcomed by the friends of liberty throughout the world. They removed the race line from our governmental systems. They had, as this court has said, a common purpose, namely to secure "to a race recently emancipated, a race that through many generations have been held in slavery, all the civil rights that the superior race enjoy." They declared, in legal effect, this court has further said, "that the law in the states shall be the same for the black as for the white; that all persons, whether colored or white, shall stand equal before the laws of the states; and in regard to the colored race, for whose protection the amendment was primarily designed, that no discrimination shall be made against them by law because of their color." We also said: "The words of the amendment, it is true, are prohibitory, but they contain a necessary implication of a positive immunity or right, most valuable to the colored race, — the right to exemption from unfriendly legislation against them distinctively as colored; exemption from legal discriminations, implying inferiority in civil society, lessening the security of their enjoyment of the rights which others enjoy; and discriminations which are steps towards reducing them to the condition of a subject race." It was, consequently, adjudged that a state law that excluded citizens of the colored race from juries, because of their race, however, well qualified in other respects to discharge the duties of jurymen, was repugnant to the fourteenth amendment. . . .

At the present term, referring to the previous adjudications, this court declared that "underlying all of those decisions is the principle that the constitution of the United States, in its present form, forbids, so far as civil and political rights are concerned, discrimination by the general government or the states against any citizen because of his race. All citizens are equal before the law." Gibson v. State, 162 U.S. 565, 16 Sup. Ct. 904.

The decisions referred to show the scope of the recent amendments of the constitution. They also show that it is not within the power of a state to prohibit colored citizens, because of their race, from participating as jurors in the administration of justice. . . .

I am of opinion that the statute of Louisiana is inconsistent with the personal liberty of citizens, white and black, in that state, and hostile to both the spirit and letter of the constitution of the United States. If laws of like character should be enacted in the several states of the Union, the effect would be in the highest degree mischievous. Slavery, as an institution tolerated by law, would, it is true, have disappeared from our country; but there would remain a power in the states, by sinister legislation, to interfere with the full enjoyment of the blessings of freedom, to regulate civil rights, common to all citizens, upon the basis of race, and to place in a condition of legal inferiority a large body of American citizens, now constituting a part of the political community, called the "People of the United States," for whom, and by whom through representatives, our government is administered. Such a system is inconsistent with the guaranty given by the constitution to each state of a republican form of government, and may be stricken down by congressional action, or by the courts in the discharge of their solemn duty to maintain the supreme law of the land, anything in the constitution or laws of any state to the contrary notwithstanding.

For the reason stated, I am constrained to withhold my assent from the opinion and judgment of the majority.

Source: 163 U.S. (1896).

INDIANS

Sitting Bull comments on the treaties. Black Elk (1863–1950) remembers the past Indian way of life and the effect of the meeting between the Indians and their conquerors.

Sitting Bull

Opinion of Treaties

Friends and Relatives: Our minds are again disturbed by the Great Father's representatives, the Indian Agent, the squaw-men, the mixed-bloods, the interpreters and favorite ration-chiefs. What is it they want of us at this time? They want us to give up another chunk of our tribal land. This is not the first time or the last time. They will try to gain possession of the last piece of ground we possess. They are again telling us what they intend to do if we agree to their wishes. Have we ever set a price on our land and received such a value? No, we never did. What we got under the former treaties were promises of all sorts. They promised how we are going to live peaceably on the land we still own and how they are going to show us the new ways of living—even told us how we can go to heaven when we die, but all that we realized out of the agreements with the Great Father was, we are dying off in expectation of getting things promised us.

One thing I wish to state at this time is, something tells me that the Great Father's representatives have again brought with them a well-worded paper, containing just what they want but ignoring our wishes in the matter. It is this that they are attempting to drive us to. Our people are blindly deceived. Some are in favour of the proposition, but we who realize that our children and grandchildren may live a little longer, must necessarily look ahead and flatly reject the proposition. I, for one, am bitterly opposed to it. The Great Father has proven himself an *unktomi* [trickster] in our past dealings.

When the White People invaded our Black Hills country our treaty agreements were still in force but the Great Father has ignored it—pretending to keep out the intruders through military force, and at last failing to keep them out they had to let them come and take possession of our best part of our tribal possession. Yet the Great Father maintains a very large standing army that can stop anything.

Therefore I do not wish to consider any proposition to cede any portion of our tribal holdings to the Great Father. If I agree to dispose of any part of our land to the white people I would feel guilty of taking food away from our children's mouths, and I do not wish to be that mean. There are things they tell us sound good to hear, but when they have accomplished their purpose they will go home and will not try to fulfill our agreements with them.

My friends and relatives, let us stand as one family, as we did before the white people led us astray.

Source: New Sources of Indian History 1850–91. Edited by Stanley Vestal, 303–4. Norman: University of Oklahoma Press, 1934.

Sitting Bull (1834?-90) was a Sioux medicine man.

Black Elk
Early Boyhood

When I was older, I learned what the fighting was about that winter and next summer. Up on the Madison Fork the Wasichus [whites] had found much of the yellow metal that they worship and that makes them crazy, and they wanted to have a road up through our country to the place where the yellow metal was; but my people did not want the road. It would scare the bison and make them go away, and also it would let the other Wasichus come in like a river. They told us that they wanted only to use a little land, as much as a wagon would take between the wheels; but our people knew better. And when you look about you now, you can see what it was they wanted.

Once we were happy in our own country and we were seldom hungry, for then the two-leggeds and the four-leggeds lived together like relatives, and there was plenty for them and for us. But the Wasichus came, and they have made little islands for us and other little islands for the four-leggeds, and always these islands are becoming smaller, for around them surges the gnawing flood of the Wasichu; and it is dirty with lies and greed.

Source: Black Elk Speaks: Being the Life Story of a Holy Man of the Ogalala Sioux as told through John G. Neihardt (Flaming Rainbow). Lincoln: University of Nebraska Press, 1979.

Black Elk (1863–1950) was a Native American autobiographer and cultural historian. *Black Elk Speaks* is one of the most important documents for understanding the life of the Plains Indians during the nineteenth century.

WOMEN

Elizabeth Cady Stanton (1815–1902) cites Genesis 1:26–28 as providing a basis for gender equality.

Elizabeth Cady Stanton
The Book of Genesis

Genesis i: 26, 27, 28

26 And God said, Let us make man in our image, after our likeness: and let them have dominion over the fish of the sea, and over the fowl of the air, and over the cattle, and over all the earth, and over every creeping thing that creepeth upon the earth.

27 So God created man in his own image, in the image of God created he him; male and female created he them.

28 And God blessed them, and God said unto them, Be fruitful, and multiply, and replenish the earth, and subdue it; and have dominion over the fish of the sea, and over the fowl of the air, and over every living thing that moveth upon the earth.

Here is the sacred historian's first account of the advent of woman; a simultaneous creation of both sexes, in the image of God. It is evident from the language that there was consultation in the Godhead, and that the masculine and feminine elements were equally represented. . . .

The first step in the elevation of woman to her true position, as an equal factor in human progress, is the cultivation of the religious sentiment in regard to her dignity and equality, the recognition by the rising generation of an ideal Heavenly Mother, to whom their prayers should be addressed, as well as to a Father.

If language has any meaning, we have in these texts a plain declaration of the existence of the feminine element in the Godhead, equal in power and glory with the masculine. The Heavenly Mother and Father! "God created man in his *own image, male and female.*" Thus scripture, as well as science and philosophy, declares the eternity and equality of sex—the philosophical fact, without which there could have been no perpetuation of creation, no growth or development in the animal, vegetable, or mineral kingdoms, no awakening nor progressing, in the world of thought. The masculine and feminine elements, exactly equal and balancing each other, are as essential to the maintenance of the equilibrium of the universe as positive and negative electricity, the centripetal and centrifugal forces, the laws of attraction which bind together all we know of this planet whereon we dwell and of the system in which we revolve.

In the great work of creation the crowning glory was realized, when man and woman were evolved on the sixth day, the masculine and feminine forces in the image of God, that must have existed eternally, in all forms of matter and mind. . . .

The above texts plainly show the simultaneous creation of man and woman, and their equal importance in the development of the race. All those theories based on the assumption that man was prior in the creation, have no foundation in Scripture.

As to woman's subjection, on which both the canon and the civil law delight to dwell, it is important to note that equal dominion is given to woman over every living thing, but not one word is said giving man dominion over woman.

Here is the first title deed to this green earth giving alike to the sons and daughters of God. No lesson of woman's subjection can be fairly drawn from the first chapter of the Old Testament.

Source: The Woman's Bible. Part I. Comments on Genesis, Exodus, Leviticus, Numbers and Deuteronomy. By Elizabeth Cady Stanton. New York: European Publishing Co., 1895.

Elizabeth Cady Stanton (1815–1902) was one of the founders of the first women's rights conventions in Seneca Falls, New York, in 1848.

Notes

1. See Paul Avrich, *The Haymarket Affair* (Princeton, N.J.: Princeton University Press, 1984).

CHAPTER 9

The Progressive Era,
1900–1928

✳ ✳ ✳

The period from the beginning of the century to the collapse of the stock market in 1929 is a complex and varied one. The first part of this period, usually known as the Progressive Era, saw the completion of many of the reform movements that developed at the end of the previous century. A national income tax was established; the U.S. Senate was for the first time directly elected by the people; prohibition was passed in 1919 (and repealed in 1933); and women got the vote in 1920. Each of these amendments to the Constitution reflects a strand in the tapestry of Progressive Era reform.

Although the Sixteenth Amendment, which allowed Congress to collect taxes on income, is probably now the least popular amendment, it reflects one of the themes of this book in that the ability to collect income taxes significantly changes the power relations between the national government and the states. That ability gave the national government the means to institute other reforms, although it did little until the Depression except to spend money on some infrastructure projects.

Obviously the change in the method of electing the Senate was also part of a shift of power away from the states. In this case the power shift was to the voters in each state and was one of the two major Progressive Era attempts to empower the people; the other was the enfranchisement of women, which came seven years later.

Prohibition is now considered the great failure among amendments to the Constitution, but at the time many people thought of prohibition as the most important reform possible. The proponents of the prohibition of "the manufacture, sale, or transportation of intoxicating liquors" believed that this measure would eliminate poverty, abuse within the family, prostitution, and numerous other social ills. They believed that alcohol was the single cause of these problems, and that it would be relatively easy to eliminate. We now know that one-dimensional explanations of social problems are inadequate and that some laws simply can not be enforced. At the time, however, prohibition played much the same role now played by the phrase "family values."

Amendment XVI

February 25, 1913

The Congress shall have the power to lay and collect taxes on incomes, from whatever source derived, without apportionment among the several States, and without regard to any census or enumeration.

Amendment XVII

May 31, 1913

Section 1. The Senate of the United States shall be composed of two Senators from each State, elected by the people thereof, for six years; and each Senator shall have one vote. The electors in each State shall have the qualifications requisite for electors of the most numerous branch of the State Legislatures.

Section 2. When vacancies happen in the representation of any State in the Senate, the executive authority of such State shall issue writs of election to fill such vacancies; Provided, That the Legislature of any State may empower the executive thereof to make temporary appointment until the people fill the vacancies by election as the Legislature may direct.

Section 3. This amendment shall not be so construed as to affect the election or term of any Senator chosen before it becomes valid as part of the Constitution.

Amendment XVIII

January 29, 1919

Section 1. After one year from the ratification of this article, the manufacture, sale, or transportation of intoxicating liquors within, the importation thereof into, or the exportation thereof from the United States and all territory subject to the jurisdiction thereof, for beverage purposes, is hereby prohibited.

Section 2. The Congress and the several States shall have concurrent power to enforce this article by appropriate legislation.

Section 3. This article shall be inoperative unless it shall have been ratified as an amendment to the Constitution by the legislatures of the several States, as provided in the Constitution, within seven years from the date of the submission hereof to the States by the Congress.

Women's Rights

Today the Progressive Era amendment thought of as a real milestone in American history is the Nineteenth Amendment, in which women won the vote. Like Prohibition, however, the amendment was a sore disappointment for many supporters of the women's rights movement. They had hoped for a more radical change in the position of women in American society. What these women wanted can be seen in the work of Charlotte Perkins Gilman (1860–1935), now recognized as one of the most important feminist writers of the turn of the century. Her *Women and Economics* (1898) was the first work to look seriously at the role of women in the economy. In the essay reprinted here she reflects on the variety of roles women play in American society. The selection by Suzanne La Follette (1894?–1983) reflects an early response to the realization that obtaining the vote would not solve all of women's problems.

Amendment XIX

August 26, 1920

Section 1. The rights of the citizens of the United States to vote, shall not be denied or abridged by the United States or by any State on account of sex.

Section 2. Congress shall have power to enforce this article by appropriate legislation.

Charlotte Perkins Gilman

The Home
Lines of Advance

It will be helpful and encouraging for us to examine the development of the home to this date, and its further tendencies; that we may cease to regret here, and learn to admire there; that we may use our personal powers definitely to resist the undertow of habit and prejudice, and definitely to promote all legitimate progress.

There is a hopelessness in the first realisation of this old-world obstacle still stationary in our swift to-day; but there need not be. While apparently as strong as ever, it has in reality been undermined on every side by the currents of evolution; its whilom prisoners have been stimulated and strengthened by the unavoidable force of those same great currents, and little remains to do beyond the final opening of one's own eyes to the facts—not one's grandmother's eyes, but one's *own*—and the beautiful work of reconstruction.

Examine the main root of the whole thing—the exclusive confinement of women to the home, to their feminine functions and a few crude industries; and see how rapidly that condition is changing. The advance of women, during the last hundred years or so, is a phenomenon unparalleled in history. Never before has so large a class made as much progress in so small a time. From the harem to the forum is a long step, but she has taken it. From the ignorant housewife to the president of a college is a long step, but she has taken it. From the penniless dependent to the wholly self-supporting and often other-supporting business woman, is a long step, but she has taken it. She who knew so little is now the teacher; she who could do so little is now the efficient and varied producer; she who cared only for her own flesh and blood is now active in all wide good works around the world. She who was confined to the house now travels freely, the foolish has become wise, and the timid brave. Even full political equality is won in more than one country and state; it is a revolution of incredible extent and importance, and its results are already splendidly apparent.

This vast number of human beings formerly as separate as sand grains and as antagonistic as the nature of their position compelled, are now organising, from house to club, from local to general, in federations of city, state, nation, and world. The amount of social energy accumulated by half of us is no longer possible of confinement to that half; the woman has inherited her share, and has grown so large and strong that her previous surroundings can no longer contain or content her. . . .

The girls of to-day, in any grade of society, are pushing out to do things instead of being content to merely eat things, wear things, and dust things. The honourable instinct of self-support is taking the place of the puerile acceptance of gifts, and beyond self-support comes the still nobler impulse to give to others; not corrupting charity, but the one all-good service of a life's best work. Measuring the position of woman as it has been for all the years behind us up to a century or so ago with what it is today, the distance covered and the ratio of progress is incredible. It rolls up continually, accumulatively; and another fifty years will show more advance than the past five hundred.

This alone is enough to guarantee the development of the home. No unchanging shell can contain a growing body, something must break; and the positive force of growth is stronger than the negative force of mere adhesion of particles. A stronger, wiser, nobler woman must make a better home. . . .

Our houses are threaded like beads on a string, tied, knotted, woven together, and in the cities even built together; one solid house from block-end to block-end; their boasted individuality maintained by a thin partition wall. The tenement, flat, and apartment house still further group and connect us; and our claim of domestic isolation becomes merely another domestic myth. Water is a household necessity and was once supplied by household labour, the women going to the wells to fetch it. Water is now supplied by the municipality, and flows among our many homes as one. Light is equally in common; we do not have to make it for ourselves.

Where water and light are thus fully socialised, why are we so shy of any similar progress in the supply of food? Food is no more a necessity than water. If we are willing to receive our water from an extra-domestic pipe—why not our food? The one being a simple element and the other a very complex combination makes a difference, of course; but even so we may mark great progress. Some foods, more or less specific, and of universal use, were early segregated, and the making of them became a trade, as in breadstuffs, cheese, and confectionery. Where this has been done we find great progress, and an even standard of excellence. In America, where the average standard of bread-making is very low, we regard "baker's bread" as a synonym for inferiority; but even here . . . the baker bears comparison with the domestic cook. It is the maintenance of the latter that keeps the former down; where the baker is the general dependence he makes better bread.

Our American baker's bread has risen greatly in excellence as we make less and less at home. All the initial processes of the food supply have been professionalized. . . .

The sacred domestic rite of eating may be still performed in the sanctuary, but the once equally sacred, subsidiary art of cooking is swiftly going out of it. As to eating at home, so dear a habit, so old a habit, old enough to share with every beast that drags her prey into her lair, that she and her little ones may gnaw in safety; this remains strongly in evidence, and will for some time yet. But while it reigns unshaken in our minds let us follow, open-eyed, the great human distinction of eating together. To share one's food, to call guest and friend to the banquet, is not a custom of any animal save those close allies in social organisation, the ants and their compeers. Not only do we permit this, but it is our chiefest joy and pride. From the child playing tea-party to the Lord Mayor's Banquet, the human race shows a marked tendency to eat together. It is our one great common medium—more's the pity that we have none better as yet! To share food is the first impulse of true hospitality, the largest field of artificial extravagance. Moreover, in actual fact, in the working world, food is eaten together by almost all men at noon; and by women and men in what they call "social life" almost daily. In recent years, in our cities, this habit increases widely, swiftly; men, women, and families eat together more and more; and the eating-house increases in excellence commensurately. . . .

Turning to the other great domestic industry, the care of children, we may see hopeful signs of growth. The nursemaid is improving. Those who can afford it are beginning to see that the association of a child's first years with low-class ignorance cannot be beneficial. There is a demand for "trained nurses" for children; even in rare cases the employment of some Kindergarten ability. Among the very poor the day-nursery and Kindergarten are doing slow, but beautiful work. The President of Harvard demands that more care and money be spent on the primary grades in education; and all through our school systems there is a healthy movement. Child-study is being undertaken at last. Pedagogy is being taught as a science. In our public parks there is regular provision made for children; and in the worst parts of the cities an incipient provision of playgrounds.

There is no more brilliant hope on earth today than this new thought about the child. In what does it consist? In recognising "the child," children as a class, children as citizens with rights to be guaranteed only by the state; instead of our previous attitude toward them of absolute personal ownership — the unchecked tyranny, or as unchecked indulgence, of the private home. Children are at last emerging from the very lowest grade of private ownership into the safe, broad level of common citizenship. That which no million separate families could give their millions of separate children, the state can give, and does. Our progress, so long merely mechanical, is at last becoming personal, touching the people and lifting them as one.

Now what is all this leading to? What have we to hope — or to dread — in the undeniable lines of development here shown? What most of us dread is this: that we shall lose our domestic privacy; that we shall lose our family dinner table; that woman will lose "her charm;" that we shall lose our children; and the child lose its mother. We are mortally afraid of separation. . . .

The home, if it grows on in normal lines, will not be of the same size and relative density as it was in ancient times; but it will be as truly home to the people of today. In trying to maintain by force the exact limits and characteristics of the primitive home, we succeed only in making a place modern man is not at home in. . . .

Try to consider it first with the woman out for working hours. This is an impassable gulf to the average mind. "Home, with the woman out — there is no such thing!" cries it. The instant assumption is that she will never be in, in which case I am willing to admit that there would be no home. Suppose we retrace our steps a little and approach the average mind more gradually. Can it imagine a home, a real happy home, with the woman out of it for one hour a day? Can it, encouraged by this step, picture the home as still enduring while the woman is out of it two hours a day? Is there any exact time of attendance required to make a home? First mother and child, then father; this is the family, and the place where they live is the home.

Now the father goes out every day; does the home cease to exist because of his hours away from it? It is still his home, he still loves it, he maintains it, he lives in it, only he has a "place of business" elsewhere. At a certain stage of growth the children are out of it, between say 8.30 and 3.30. Does it cease to be home because of their hours away from it? Do they not love it and live in it—*while they are there?* Now if, while the father was out, and the children were out, the mother should also be out, would the home disappear into thin air?

It is home *while the family are in it.* When the family are out of it it is only a house; and a house will stand up quite solidly for some eight hours of the family's absence. Incessant occupation is not essential to a home. If the father has wife and children with him in the home when he returns to it, need it matter to him that the children are wisely cared for in schools during his absence; or that his wife is duly occupied elsewhere while they are so cared for?

Two "practical obstacles" intervene; first, the "housework"; second, the care of children below school age. The housework is fast disappearing into professional hands. When that is utterly gone, the idle woman has but one excuse—the babies. This is a very vital excuse. The baby is the founder of the home. If the good of the baby required the persistent, unremitting care of the mother in the home, then indeed she must remain there. No other call, no other claim, no other duty, can be weighed for a moment against this all-important service—the care of the little child.

But we have already seen that if there is one thing more than another the home fails in, it is just this. If there is one duty more than another the woman fails in, it is just this. Our homes are not planned nor managed in the interest of little children; and the isolated homebound mother is in no way adequate to their proper rearing. This is not disputable on any side. The death rate of little children during the years they are wholly in the home and mother's care proves it beyond question. The wailing of little children who live—or before they die—wailing from bodily discomfort, nervous irritation, mental distress, punishment—a miserable sound, so common, so expected, that it affects the price of real estate, tenants not wishing to live near little children on account of their cries—this sound of world-wide anguish does not seem to prove much for the happiness of these helpless inmates of the home.

Such few data as we have of babies and young children in properly managed day nurseries, give a far higher record of health and happiness. Not the sick baby in the pauper hospital, not the lonely baby in the orphan asylum; but the baby who has not lost his mother, but who adds to mother's love, calm, wise, experienced professional care.

A newborn baby leads a far happier, healthier, more peaceful existence in the hands of the good trained nurse, than it does when those skilled hands are gone, and it is left on the trembling knees of the young, untrained mother.

"But the nurse does not love it!" we wildly protest. What if she does not? Cannot the mother love it *while the nurse takes care of it?* This is the whole position in a nutshell. Nothing is going to prevent the mother from loving her children in one deep, ceaseless river of calm affection, with such maternal transports as may arise from time to time in addition; but nothing ought to prevent the child's being properly taken care of while the love is going on.

Source: The Home—Its Work and Influence. By Charlotte Perkins Gilman. New York: Charlton, 1910.

Charlotte Perkins Gilman (1860–1935) was a feminist economist, novelist, social critic, and activist.

Suzanne La Follette
Concerning Women

Women are at present under certain disabilities which legal equality with men can hardly be expected to remove. Those disabilities are:

1. Economic: Women are the victims of unjust discriminations in industry and the professions in regard to training, opportunities, tenure of employment, and wages. They are also victimized by ill-considered "welfare" legislation sponsored by benevolent persons, and by male workers whose purpose is to rid themselves of unwelcome competition.

If legal equality of the sexes were established, women might be able, under the law, to force public industrial schools to give them equal opportunities for training; they might also be able to enforce a demand for equal pay with men for equal work. It is even conceivable that they might force employers to lay off workers, during periods of depression, on a proportional basis—men and women together, in proportion to the number of each sex employed. All this, however, would entail unremitting vigilance, and great effort in getting legal enactments; it would also entail a great deal of governmental machinery, with all the waste and ineffectiveness implied by the terms; and it would leave the general labour-problem precisely where it is at present. As for the matter of opportunity, so long as industry is in the hands of private concerns, I see no way by which employers can be forced under an equal-rights law to employ women where they prefer to employ men. Nor is there any certainty that legal equality will save working women from having the race "safeguarded" at their expense. But if land were put freely in competition with industry for the employment of labour, all these disabilities would disappear. Women would enjoy the same freedom as men to get their living by their labour, and since there would be no such thing as a labour-surplus, their wage, like that of men, would be the full product of their labour, and not that share which employers or governmental boards thought fit to grant them. There would be no need for reformers or other benevolent persons to secure them fair hours and conditions of labour, or to get them excluded from hazardous employments; for there is no way to make a worker accept onerous conditions of labour from an employer if he have an ever-present alternative of going out and creating more agreeable conditions by working for himself. The worker whose independent position makes it possible to refuse to work an excessive number of hours or under unhealthful or dangerous or disagreeable conditions, will simply refuse, and there will be an end of it. Thus employers, instead of being prevented from exploiting women beyond a certain point, would be rendered incapable of exploiting anyone in any degree. Nor would male workers longer have any incentive to avail themselves of "protective" legislation in order to reduce the competition of women with men in the labour-market; for it is only where opportunity is artificially restricted that there are "not enough jobs to go around."

Certain direct consequences of the economic inferiority of women might be expected to disappear when that inferiority no longer existed. Foremost among these is the demoralizing temptation to get their living by their sex. Prostitution would disappear from a society which offered women ample opportunity to earn their living without doing violence to their selective sexual disposition. Marriage would no longer be degraded to the level of a means of livelihood, as it is today for a great many women; for economic security would no longer in any wise depend upon it. This being the case, the expectation now put upon women to undertake marriage as a profession would disappear, and marriage would come to be regarded in the light of a condition, freely and voluntarily assumed by both sexes, who would jointly and equally undertake its responsibilities. Under such circumstances, one might confidently expect a further modification of institutionalized marriage which would remove all those privileges and disabilities now legally enforced on either party by virtue of the contract. The idea that woman's place is the home—which implies that marriage, for her, necessarily involves acquiescence in a traditional sexual division of labour and a traditional mode of life—with all its disabling economic and psychological consequences, would disappear from a society in which she was able freely to choose her occupation according to her abilities. Thus, from the status of a class regarded as being divinely ordained to be the world's housekeepers, women would emerge into the status of human beings, free to consult their interests and inclinations in the ordering of their lives, without regard to traditional expectations which, being no longer enforced by economic or legal sanctions, would have no longer any power over them.

2. Psychological: Those prejudices and superstitions which now hamper women in their development and in the ordering of their lives, might be expected to disappear from a free society. In so far as they are the consequences of woman's subjection, they would yield before her emergence into the status of a human being, sharing equally with man in the freedom of opportunity that would result from the establishment of economic justice, and the increased cultural advantages that freedom of opportunity would bring. In so far as they are the outgrowth of primitive ignorance and superstition they would yield before the increased intelligence and enlightenment which might be expected to result from the abundance and leisure afforded to every human being by economic freedom. Thus those artificial differentiations between the sexes which have been built up by fear, by superstitions, and by masculine dominance, would tend to disappear. Women would no longer be regarded as extra-human beings endowed with superhuman powers for good or ill; they would no longer be regarded exclusively or chiefly as a function, being no longer forced to occupy that status; theories of their mental and spiritual inferiority based on the results of centuries of subjection would yield before a more humane and scientific attitude; and as freedom promoted individuation among women, it would become evident that the traditional notions concerning the feminine nature were drawn from qualities which, having been bred by their subjection, should have been regarded as characteristics not of a sex but of a class.

3. Social: The superstitious notion that woman's honour is a matter of sex would disappear with the masculine dominance from which it resulted. When women need no longer depend on marriage for their living or their social position, they will no longer be under any great compulsion to make their sexual relations conform to standards which have been adapted to suit the interests, desires and tastes of men. Being economically independent of men, they will be at liberty to consult their own interests, desires and tastes, in this as in other matters. They may desire to preserve those habits of virginity before marriage and chastity after it, which have been imposed upon them under masculine dominance; but they will be under no external compulsion to do so. When they have no longer a professional interest in conforming to the conventional moral code, their sexual relations will cease to be regarded as falling within the purview of morality at all; rather they will be, as those of men have been, a question of manners. For when a moral precept no longer has social or economic sanctions to enforce it, its observance ceases to be a matter of worldly interest or expediency, and becomes a

matter of personal taste. Then, if it be not sound, it will be repudiated; if it be sound, the individual who allows himself to be guided by it will profit spiritually by doing so, because his obedience will respond to his own instinct for what is good, rather than to an external pressure.

Source: Concerning Women. By Suzanne La Follette. New York: Albert and Charles Boni, 1926.

Suzanne La Follette (1894?–1983) was an early feminist who became active in anti-Communist causes.

Pragmatism

One of the most important philosophical movements in American history flowered during this period. Pragmatism originally developed in the writings of Charles Sanders Peirce (1839–1914) with a concern with the effects that might have "practical bearings" on the way we conceptualize the world. Peirce did not draw any political conclusions from his approach. William James (1842–1910) used the term, which Peirce abandoned, to refer to a method of philosophy in which we look at the practical effects of holding one notion as opposed to another. John Dewey (1859–1952) developed the theory and applied it both to politics and to educational theory. His work on the latter was more influential.

Education was one of the central concerns of the Progressive Era, and Dewey became its most influential thinker. In the following essay Dewey raises issues that are still with us and are still being hotly debated, such as who should control the public schools. Many teachers take Dewey's position—educators do not control the schools, but they should. But the position receiving the most attention currently is the argument, most frequently stated by conservatives, that the problem with the schools is that they are run by professional educators who set themselves up against the wishes of the community.

Such questions go to the heart of democratic theory. Who should have the greatest influence in shaping the minds of the next generation? Should parents—well or poorly educated—be able to determine what their children are taught? Should professional educators be able to run schools as they see fit? What is the role of the community in controlling the content of education?

Dewey believed that the school should provide an ideal environment in which students could both be educated and learn the skills needed to function in the adult world. He deeply influenced more than a generation of educational theory and practice. Many blame him, and particularly his emphasis on the empowerment of students, for the problems they see in our schools.

John Dewey
Democracy in Education

Modern life means democracy, democracy means freeing intelligence for independent effectiveness—the emancipation of mind as an individual organ to do
its own work. We naturally associate democracy, to be sure, with freedom of action, but freedom of action without freed capacity of thought behind it is only
chaos. If external authority in action is given up, it must be because internal authority of truth, discovered and known to reason, is substituted.

How does the school stand with reference to this matter? Does the school as an
accredited representative exhibit this trait of democracy as a spiritual force? Does
it lead and direct the movement? Does it lag behind and work at cross-purpose? I
find the fundamental need of the school today dependent upon its limited recognition of the principle of freedom of intelligence. This limitation appears to me
to affect both of the elements of school life: teacher and pupil. As to both, the
school has lagged behind the general contemporary social movement; and much
that is unsatisfactory, much of conflict and of defect, comes from the discrepancy
between the relatively undemocratic organization of the school, as it affects the
mind of both teacher and pupil, and the growth and extension of the democratic
principle in life beyond school doors. . . .

I. *As to the teacher.*—If there is a single public-school system in the United
States where there is official and constitutional provision made for submitting
questions of methods of discipline and teaching, and the questions of the curriculum, text-books, etc., to the discussion and decision of those actually engaged
in the work of teaching, that fact has escaped my notice. Indeed, the opposite situation is so common that it seems, as a rule, to be absolutely taken for granted as
the normal and final condition of affairs. The number of persons to whom any
other course has occurred as desirable, or even possible—to say nothing of necessary—is apparently very limited. But until the public school system is organized in such a way that every teacher has some regular and representative way in
which he or she can register judgment upon matters of educational importance,
with the assurance that this judgment will somehow affect the school system, the
assertion that the present system is not, from the internal standpoint, democratic
seems to be justified. Either we come here upon some fixed and inherent limitation of the democratic principle, or else we find in this fact an obvious discrepancy between the conduct of the school and the conduct of social life—a discrepancy so great as to demand immediate and persistent effort at reform. . . .

All other reforms are conditioned upon reform in the quality and character of
those who engage in the teaching profession. The doctrine of the man behind the

gun has become familiar enough, in recent discussion, in every sphere of life. Just because education is the most personal, the most intimate, of all human affairs, there, more than anywhere else, the sole ultimate reliance and final source of power are in the training, character, and intelligence of the individual. If any scheme could be devised which would draw to the calling of teaching persons of force of character, of sympathy with children, and consequent interest in the problems of teaching and of scholarship; no one need be troubled for a moment about other educational reforms, or the solution of other educational problems. But as long as a school organization which is undemocratic in principle tends to repel from all but the higher portions of the school system those of independent force, of intellectual initiative, and of inventive ability, or tends to hamper them in their work after they find their way into the schoolroom, so long all other reforms are compromised at their source and postponed indefinitely for fruition.

2. *As to the learner.*—The undemocratic suppression of the individuality of the teacher goes naturally with the improper restriction of the intelligence of the mind of the child. The mind, to be sure, is that of a child, and yet, after all, it is mind. To subject mind to an outside and ready-made material is a denial of the ideal of democracy, which roots itself ultimately in the principle of moral, self-directing individuality. Misunderstanding regarding the nature of the freedom that is demanded for the child is so common that it may be necessary to emphasize the fact that it is primarily intellectual freedom, free play of mental attitude, and operation which are sought. If individuality were simply a matter of feelings, impulses, and outward acts independent of intelligence, it would be more than a dubious matter to urge a greater degree of freedom for the child in the school. . . . Reform of education in the direction of greater play for the individuality of the child means the securing of conditions which will give outlet, and hence direction, to a growing intelligence. It is true that this freed power of mind with reference to its own further growth cannot be obtained without a certain leeway, a certain flexibility, in the expression of even immature feelings and fancies. But it is equally true that it is not a riotous loosening of these traits which is needed, but just that kind and degree of freedom from repression which are found to be necessary to secure the full operation of intelligence. . . .

What is primarily required for that direct inquiry which constitutes the essence of science is first-hand experience; an active and vital participation through the medium of all the bodily organs with the means and materials of building up first-hand experience. Contrast this first and most fundamental of all the demands for an effective use of mind with what we find in so many of our elementary and high schools. There first-hand experience is at a discount; in its stead are summaries and formulas of the results of other people. Only very recently has any positive provision been made within the schoolroom for any of the modes of activity and for any of the equipment and arrangement which permit and require the extension of original experiences on the part of the child. The school has literally been dressed out with hand-me-down garments—with intellectual suits which other people have worn.

Secondly, in that freed activity of mind which we term "science" there is always a certain problem which focusses effort, which controls the collecting of facts that bear upon the question, the use of observation to get further data, the employing of memory to supply relevant facts, the calling into play of imagination, to yield fertile suggestion and construct possible solutions of the difficulty. . . .

The remedy here, as in other phases of our social democracy, is not to turn back, but to go farther—to carry the evolution of the school to a point where it becomes a place for getting and testing experience, as real and adequate to the child upon his existing level as all the resources of laboratory and library afford to the scientific man upon his level. What is needed is not any radical revolution, but rather an organization of agencies already found in the schools. It is hardly too much to say that not a single subject or instrumentality is required which is not already found in many schools of the country. All that is required is to gather these materials and forces together and unify their operation. Too often they are used for a multitude of diverse and often conflicting aims. If a single purpose is provided, that of freeing the processes of mental growth, these agencies will at once fall into their proper classes and reinforce each other. . . .

Politically we have found that this country could not endure half free and half slave. We shall find equally great difficulty in encouraging freedom, independence, and initiative in every sphere of social life, while perpetuating in the school dependence upon external authority. The forces of social life are already encroaching upon the school institutions which we have inherited from the past, so that many of its main stays are crumbling. Unless the outcome is to be chaotic, we must take hold of the organic, positive principle involved in democracy, and put that in entire possession of the spirit and work of the school.

In education meet the three most powerful motives of human activity. Here are found sympathy and affection, the going out of the emotions to the most appealing and the most rewarding object of love—a little child. Here is found also the flowering of the social and institutional motive, interest in the welfare of society and in its progress and reform by the surest and shortest means. Here, too, is found the intellectual and scientific motive, the interest in knowledge, in scholarship, in truth for its own sake, unhampered and unmixed with any alien ideal. Copartnership of these three motives—of affection, of social growth, and of scientific inquiry—must prove as nearly irresistible as anything human when they are once united. And, above all else, recognition of the spiritual basis of democracy, the efficacy and responsibility of freed intelligence, is necessary to secure this union.

Source : *The Elementary School Teacher* 4, no. 4 (December 1903): 193–204.

John Dewey (1859–1952) was an educational theorist and philosopher.

Industrial Strife

Another issue central to the period was the continuing conflict between capital and labor. Political thought ranged across the political spectrum, and a variety of the positions are represented here. The Industrial Workers of the World (I.W.W.) is an organization dedicated to bringing all workers within one union; it was most successful before the Depression. The "Socialist Party Platform of 1912" shows the position of an American socialist political party early in the century. A number of such parties competed with each other and with the two main parties. The coming of World War I temporarily limited their development, but some of these parties had a resurgence after the war.

The testimony by Louis Brandeis (1865–1941) before the Congressional Commission on Industrial Relations in 1916 illustrates the reformist perspective. Emma Goldman's "Anarchism" (1917) is one of the most famous essays by one of the most important radical figures of all time. Goldman (1869–1940) was an outspoken and hardworking advocate for free speech, birth control, women's rights, and the rights of workers and immigrants; she was a deeply feared opponent of the U.S. government. She was constantly harassed and finally illegally deported.

Thorstein Veblen (1857–1929) was another important social critic. His complex language made him a less popular writer than some others, but his analyses of the American social and economic system were always effective.

Manifesto on Organizing the Industrial Workers of the World

Social relations and groupings only reflect mechanical and industrial conditions. The great facts of present industry are the displacement of human skill by machines and the increase of capitalist power through concentration in the possession of the tools with which wealth is produced and distributed.

Because of these facts trade division among laborers and competition among capitalists are alike disappearing. Class divisions grow ever more fixed and class antagonisms more sharp. Trade lines have been swallowed up in a common servitude of all workers to the machines which they tend. New machines, ever replacing less productive ones, wipe out whole trades and plunge new bodies of workers into the evergrowing army of tradeless, hopeless unemployed. As human beings and human skill are displaced by mechanical progress, the capitalists need use the workers only during that brief period when muscles and nerves respond most intensely. The moment the laborer no longer yields the maximum of profits, he is thrown upon the scrap pile, to starve alongside the discarded machine. A dead line has been drawn, and an age limit established, to cross which, in this world of monopolized opportunities, means condemnation to industrial death.

The worker, wholly separated from the land and the tools, with his skill of craftsmanship rendered useless, is sunk in the uniform mass of wage slaves. He sees his power of resistance broken by craft divisions, perpetuated from outgrown industrial stages. His wages constantly grow less as his hours grow longer and monopolized prices grow higher. Shifted hither and thither by the demands of profit-takers, the laborer's home no longer exists. In this hopeless condition he is forced to accept whatever humiliating conditions his master may impose. He is subjected to a physical and intellectual examination more searching than was the chattel slave when sold from the auction block. Laborers are no longer classified by differences in trade skill, but the employer assigns them according to the machines to which they are attached. These divisions, far from representing differences in skill or interests among the laborers, are imposed by the employers that workers may be pitted against one another and spurred to greater exertion in the shop, and that all resistance to capitalist tyranny may be weakened by artificial distinctions.

While encouraging these outgrown divisions among the workers the capitalists carefully adjust themselves to the new conditions. They wipe out all differences among themselves and present a united front in their war upon labor. Through employers' associations, they seek to crush, with brutal force, by the injunctions of the judiciary, and the use of military power, all efforts at resistance. Or when the other policy seems more profitable, they conceal their daggers beneath the Civic Federation and hoodwink and betray those whom they would rule and exploit. Both methods depend for success upon the blindness and internal dissensions of the working class. The employers' line of battle and methods of warfare correspond to the solidarity of the mechanical and industrial concentration, while laborers still form their fighting organizations on lines of long-gone trade divisions. . . .

This worn out and corrupt system offers no promise of improvement and adaptation. There is no silver lining to the clouds of darkness and despair settling down upon the world of labor.

This system offers only a perpetual struggle for slight relief within wage slavery. It is blind to the possibility of establishing an industrial democracy, wherein there shall be no wage slavery, but where the workers will own the tools which they operate, and the product of which they alone will enjoy.

It shatters the ranks of the workers into fragments, rendering them helpless and impotent on the industrial battlefield.

Separation of craft from craft renders industrial and financial solidarity impossible.

Union men scab upon union men; hatred of worker for worker is engendered, and the workers are delivered helpless and disintegrated into the hands of the capitalists.

Craft jealousy leads to the attempt to create trade monopolies.

Prohibitive initiation fees are established that force men to become scabs against their will. Men whom manliness or circumstances have driven from one trade are thereby fined when they seek to transfer membership to the union of a new craft.

Craft divisions foster political ignorance among the workers, thus dividing their class at the ballot box, as well as in the shop, mine and factory.

Craft unions may be and have been used to assist employers in the establishment of monopolies and the raising of prices. One set of workers are thus used to make harder the conditions of life of another body of laborers.

Craft divisions hinder the growth of class consciousness of the workers, foster the idea of harmony of interests between employing exploiter and employed slave. They permit the association of the misleaders of the workers with the capitalists in the Civic Federations, where plans are made for the perpetuation of capitalism, and the permanent enslavement of the workers through the wage system.

Previous efforts for the betterment of the working class have proven abortive because limited in scope and disconnected in action.

Universal economic evils afflicting the working class can be eradicated only by a universal working-class movement. Such a movement of the working class is impossible while separate craft and wage agreements are made favoring the employer against other crafts in the same industry, and while energies are wasted in fruitless jurisdiction struggles which serve only to further the personal aggrandizement of union officials.

A movement to fulfill these conditions must consist of one great industrial union embracing all industries — providing for craft autonomy locally, industrial autonomy internationally, and working-class unity generally.

It must be founded on the class struggle, and its general administration must be conducted in harmony with the recognition of the irrepressible conflict between the capitalist class and the working class.

It should be established as the economic organization of the working class, without affiliation with any political party.

All power should rest in a collective membership.

Local, national and general administration, including union labels, buttons, badges, transfer cards, initiation fees, and per capita tax should be uniform throughout.

All members must hold membership in the local, national or international union covering the industry in which they are employed, but transfers of membership between unions, local, national, or international, should be universal.

Workingmen bringing union cards from industrial unions in foreign countries should be freely admitted into the organization.

Source: Report of the New York State Joint Legislative Committee Investigating Sedition (Lusk Committee), 1:903–6.

Socialist Party Platform of 1912

The representatives of the Socialist party, in National Convention at Indianapolis, declare that the capitalist system has outgrown its historical function, and has become utterly incapable of meeting the problems now confronting society. We denounce this outgrown system as incompetent and corrupt and the source of unspeakable misery and suffering to the whole working class.

Under this system the industrial equipment of the nation has passed into the absolute control of plutocracy, which exacts an annual tribute of hundreds of millions of dollars from the producers. Unafraid of any organized resistance, it stretches out its greedy hands over the still undeveloped resources of the nation — the land, the mines, the forests and the waterpowers of every state in the Union.

In spite of the multiplication of labor-saving machines and improved methods in industry, which cheapen the cost of production, the share of the producers grows ever less, and the prices of all the necessities of life steadily increase. The boasted prosperity of this nation is for the owning class alone. To the rest it means only greater hardship and misery. The high cost of living is felt in every home. Millions of wage-workers have seen the purchasing power of their wages decrease until life has become a desperate battle for mere existence.

Multitudes of unemployed walk the streets of our cities or trudge from state to state awaiting the will of the masters to move the wheels of industry.

The farmers in every state are plundered by the increasing prices exacted for tools and machinery and by extortionate rents, freight rates and storage charges.

Capitalist concentration is mercilessly crushing the class of small business men and driving its members into the ranks of propertyless wage-workers. The overwhelming majority of the people of America are being forced under a yoke of bondage by this soulless industrial despotism.

It is this capitalist system that is responsible for the increasing burden of armaments, the poverty, slums, child labor, most of the insanity, crime and prostitution, and much of the disease that afflicts mankind.

Under this system the working class is exposed to poisonous conditions, to frightful and needless perils to life and limb, is walled around with court decisions, injunctions and unjust laws, and is preyed upon incessantly for the benefit of the controlling oligarchy of wealth. Under it also, the children of the working class are doomed to ignorance, drudging toil and darkened lives. . . .

The Socialist party is the political expression of the economic interests of the workers. Its defeats have been their defeats and its victories their victories. It is a party founded on the science and laws of social development. It proposes that, since all social necessities today are socially produced, the means of their production and distribution shall be socially owned and democratically controlled. . . .

WORKING PROGRAM.

As measures calculated to strengthen the working class in its fight for the realization of its ultimate aim, the co-operative commonwealth, and to increase its power of resistance against capitalist oppression, we advocate and pledge ourselves and our elected officers to the following program:

COLLECTIVE OWNERSHIP.

1. The collective ownership and democratic management of railroads, wire and wireless telegraphs and telephones, express services, steamboat lines and all other social means of transportation and communication and of all large-scale industries.

2. The immediate acquirement by the municipalities, the states or the federal government of all grain elevators, stock yards, storage warehouses, and other distributing agencies, in order to reduce the present extortionate cost of living.

3. The extension of the public domain to include mines, quarries, oil wells, forests and water power.

4. The further conservation and development of natural resources for the use and benefit of all the people:

(a) By scientific forestation and timber protection.

(b) By the reclamation of arid and swamp tracts.

(c) By the storage of flood waters and the utilization of water power.

(d) By the stoppage of the present extravagant waste of the soil and of the products of mines and oil wells.

(e) By the development of highway and waterway systems.

5. The collective ownership of land wherever practicable, and in cases where such ownership is impracticable, the appropriation by taxation of the annual rental value of all land held for speculation or exploitation.

6. The collective ownership and democratic management of the banking and currency system.

UNEMPLOYMENT.

The immediate government relief of the unemployed by the extension of all useful public works. All persons employed on such works to be engaged directly by the government under a workday of not more than eight hours and at not less than the prevailing union wages. The government also to establish employment bureaus; to lend money to states and municipalities without interest for the purpose of carrying on public works, and to take such other measures within its power as will lessen the widespread misery of the workers caused by the misrule of the capitalist class.

INDUSTRIAL DEMANDS.

The conservation of human resources, particularly of the lives and well-being of the workers and their families:

1. By shortening the workday in keeping with the increased productiveness of machinery.

2. By securing to every worker a rest period of not less than a day and a half in each week.

3. By securing a more effective inspection of workshops, factories and mines.

4. By forbidding the employment of children under sixteen years of age.

5. By the co-operative organization of the industries in the federal penitentiaries for the benefit of the convicts and their dependents.

6. By forbidding the interstate transportation of the products of child labor, of convict labor and of all uninspected factories and mines.

7. By abolishing the profit system in government work, and substituting either the direct hire of labor or the awarding of contracts to co-operative groups of workers.

8. By establishing minimum wage scales.

9. By abolishing official charity and substituting a non-contributory system of old-age pensions, a general system of insurance by the state of all its members against unemployment and invalidism and a system of compulsory insurance by employers of their workers, without cost to the latter, against industrial diseases, accidents and death.

POLITICAL DEMANDS.

1. The absolute freedom of press, speech and assemblage.

2. The adoption of a graduated income tax, the increase of the rates of the present corporation tax and the extension of inheritance taxes, graduate in proportion to the value of the estate and to nearness of kin—the proceeds of these taxes to be employed in the socialization of industry.

3. The abolition of the monopoly ownership of patents and the substitution of collective ownership, with direct rewards to inventors by premiums or royalties.

4. Unrestricted and equal suffrage for men and women.

5. The adoption of the initiative, referendum and recall and of proportional representation, nationally as well as locally.

6. The abolition of the Senate and of the veto power of the President.

7. The election of the President and the Vice-President by direct vote of the people.

8. The abolition of the power usurped by the Supreme Court of the United States to pass upon the constitutionality of the legislation enacted by Congress or by a referendum vote of the whole people.

9. The abolition of the present restrictions upon the amendment of the constitution, so that that instrument may be made amendable by a majority of the voters in the country.

10. The granting of the right of suffrage in the District of Columbia with representation in Congress and a democratic form of municipal government for purely local affairs.

11. The extension of democratic government to all United States territory.

12. The enactment of further measures for general education and particularly for vocational education in useful pursuits. The Bureau of Education to be made a department.

13. The enactment of further measures for the conservation of health. The creation of an independent bureau of health, with such restrictions as will secure full liberty to all schools of practice.

14. The separation of the present Bureau of Labor from the Department of Commerce and Labor and its elevation to the rank of a department.

15. Abolition of all federal district courts and the United States Circuit Courts of Appeals. State courts to have jurisdiction in all cases arising between citizens of the several states and foreign corporations. The election of all judges for short terms.

16. The immediate curbing of the power of the courts to issue injunctions.

17. The free administration of the law.

18. The calling of a convention for the revision of the constitution of the United States.

Such measures of relief as we may be able to force from capitalism are but a preparation of the workers to seize the whole powers of government, in order that they may thereby lay hold of the whole system of socialized industry and thus come to their rightful inheritance.

Source: National Party Platforms 1840–1968. Compiled by Kirk H. Porter and Donald Bruce Johnson. Urbana: University of Illinois Press, 1970.

Louis Brandeis

Testimony

CHAIRMAN WALSH. Does the fact that many large corporations with thousands of stockholders, among whom are large numbers of employees, in any way whatever affect the policy of large corporations? . . .

MR. BRANDEIS. My observation leads me to believe that while there are many contributing causes to unrest, that there is one case which is fundamental. That is the necessary conflict—the contrast between our political liberty and our industrial absolutism. We are as free politically, perhaps, as free as it is possible for us to be. Every male has his voice and vote; and the law has endeavored to enable, and has succeeded practically, in enabling him to exercise his political franchise without fear. He therefore has his part; and certainly can secure an adequate part in the government of the country in all of its political relations; that is, in all relations which are determined directly by legislation or governmental administration.

On the other hand, in dealing with industrial problems the position of the ordinary worker is exactly the reverse. The individual employee has no effective voice or vote. And the main objection, as I see it, to the very large corporation is, that it makes possible—and in many cases makes inevitable—the exercise of industrial absolutism. It is not merely the case of the individual worker against the employer which, even if he is a reasonably sized employer, presents a serious situation calling for the interposition of a union to protect the individual. But we have the situation of an employer so potent, so well organized, with such concentrated forces and with such extraordinary powers of reserve and the ability to endure against strikes and other efforts of a union, that the relatively loosely organized masses of even strong unions are unable to cope with the situation. We are dealing here with a question, not of motive, but of condition. Now, the large corporation and the managers of the powerful corporation are probably in large part actuated by motives just the same as the employer of a tenth of their size. Neither of them, as a rule, wishes to have his liberty abridged; but the smaller concern usually comes to the conclusion that it is necessary that it should be, where an important union must be dealt with. But when a great financial power has developed—when there exists these powerful organizations, which can successfully summon forces from all parts of the country, which can afford to use tremendous amounts of money in any conflict to carry out what they deem to be their business principle, and can also afford to suffer large losses—you have necessarily a condition of inequality between the two contending forces. Such contests, though undertaken with the best motives and with strong conviction on the part of the corporate managers that they are seeking what is for the best interests not only of the company but of the community, lead to absolutism. The result, in the cases of these large corporation, may be to develop a benevolent absolutism, but it is an absolutism all the same; and it is that which makes the great corporation so dangerous. There develops within the State a state so powerful that the ordinary social and industrial forces existing are insufficient to cope with it.

I noted . . . that the question . . . put to me concerning the employees of these large corporations related to their physical condition. Their mental condition is certainly equally important. Unrest, to my mind, never can be removed—and fortunately never can be removed—by mere improvement of the physical and material condition of the workingman. If it were possible we should run great risk of improving their material condition and reducing their manhood. We must bear in mind all the time, that however much we may desire material improvement and must desire it for the comfort of the individual, that the United States is a democracy, and that we must have above all things, men. It is the development of manhood to which any industrial and social system should be directed. We Americans are committed not only to social justice in the sense of avoiding things which bring suffering and harm, like unjust distribution of wealth; but we are committed primarily to democracy. The social justice for which we are striving is an incident of our democracy, not the main end. It is rather the result of democracy—perhaps its finest expression—but it rests upon democracy, which implies the rule by the people. And therefore the end for which we must strive is the attainment of rule by the people, and that involves industrial democracy as well as political democracy. That means that the problem of a trade should be no longer the problems of the employer alone. The problems of his business, and it is not the employer's business alone, are the problem of all in it. The union cannot shift upon the employer the responsibility for conditions, nor can the employer insist upon determining, according to his will, the conditions which shall exist. The problems which exist are the problems of the trade; they are the problems of employer and employee. Profit sharing, however liberal, cannot meet the situation. That would mean merely dividing the profits of business. Such a division may do harm or it might do good, dependent on how it is applied.

There must be a division not only of profits, but a division also of responsibilities. The employees must have the opportunity of participating in the decisions as to what shall be their condition and how the business shall be run. They must learn also in sharing that responsibility that they, too, must bear the suffering arising from grave mistakes, just as the employer must. But the right to assist in making the decisions, the right of making their own mistakes, if mistakes there must be, is a privilege which should not be denied to labor. We must insist upon labor sharing the responsibilities for the result of the business.

Now, to a certain extent we are gradually getting it—in smaller business. The grave objection to the large business is that, almost inevitably, the form of organisation, the absentee stockholdings and its remote directorship prevent participation, ordinarily, of the employees in such management. The executive officials become stewards in charge of the details of the operation of the business, they alone coming into direct relation with labor. Thus we lose that necessary co-operation which naturally flows from contact between employers and employees— and which the American aspirations for democracy demand. It is in the resultant absolutism that you will find the fundamental cause of prevailing unrest; no matter what is done with the superstructure, no matter how it may be improved in one way or the other, unless we eradicate that fundamental difficulty, unrest will not only continue, but, in my opinion, will grow worse. . . .

In dealing with the problem of industrial democracy there underlies all of the difficulties the question of the concentration of power. This factor so important in connection with the subject of credit and in connection with the subject of trusts and monopolies is no less important in treating the labor problem. As long as there is such concentration of power no effort of the workingmen to secure democratization will be effective. The statement that size is not a crime is entirely correct when you speak of it from the point of motive. But size may become such a danger in its results to the community that the community may have to set limits. A large part of our protective legislation consists of prohibiting things which we find are dangerous, according to common experience. Concentration of power has been shown to be dangerous in a democracy, even though that power may be used beneficently. For instance, on our public highways we put a limit on the size of an autotruck, no matter how well it is run. It may have the most skillful and considerate driver, but its mere size may make it something which the community cannot tolerate, in view of the other uses of the highway and the danger inherent in its occupation to so large an extent by a single vehicle.

Source: United States Commission on Industrial Relations: Final Report and Testimony, United States Senate, 64th Congress, 1st Session (1916), 87658-63.

Louis D. Brandeis (1856–1941) was an important lawyer, social critic, and Justice of the Supreme Court (1916–39). He was particularly concerned with the effects of capitalism, especially trusts, on the American economy. As a lawyer, he is remembered for the "Brandeis brief," which was mostly economic and social data showing the effects of the operation of laws.

Emma Goldman

Anarchism
What It Really Stands For

The history of human growth and development is at the same time the history of the terrible struggle of every new idea heralding the approach of a brighter dawn. In its tenacious hold on tradition, the Old has never hesitated to make use of the foulest and cruelest means to stay the advent of the New, in whatever form or period the latter may have asserted itself. Nor need we retrace our steps into the distant past to realize the enormity of opposition, difficulties, and hardships placed in the path of every progressive idea. The rack, the thumbscrew, and the knout are still with us; so are the convict's garb and the social wrath, all conspiring against the spirit that is serenely marching on.

Anarchism could not hope to escape the fate of all other ideas of innovation. Indeed, as the most revolutionary and uncompromising innovator, Anarchism must needs meet with the combined ignorance and venom of the world it aims to reconstruct.

To deal even remotely with all that is being said and done against Anarchism would necessitate the writing of a whole volume. I shall therefore meet only two of the principal objections. In so doing, I shall attempt to elucidate what Anarchism really stands for.

The strange phenomenon of the opposition to Anarchism is that it brings to light the relation between so-called intelligence and ignorance. And yet this is not so very strange when we consider the relativity of all things. The ignorant mass has in its favor that it makes no pretense of knowledge or tolerance. Acting, as it always does, by mere impulse, its reasons are like those of a child. "Why?" "Because." Yet the opposition of the uneducated to Anarchism deserves the same consideration as that of the intelligent man.

What, then, are the objections? First, Anarchism is impractical, though a beautiful idea. Second, Anarchism stands for violence and destruction, hence it must be repudiated as vile and dangerous. Both the intelligent man and the ignorant mass judge not from a thorough knowledge of the subject, but either from hearsay or false interpretation.

A practical scheme, says Oscar Wilde, is either one already in existence, or a scheme that could be carried out under the existing conditions; but it is exactly the existing conditions that one objects to, and any scheme that could accept these conditions is wrong and foolish. The true criterion of the practical, therefore, is not whether the latter can keep intact the wrong or foolish; rather is it whether the scheme has vitality enough to leave the stagnant waters of the old, and build, as well as sustain, new life. In the light of this conception, Anarchism is indeed practical. More than any other idea, it is helping to do away with the wrong and foolish; more than any other idea, it is building and sustaining new life.

The emotions of the ignorant man are continuously kept at a pitch by the most blood-curdling stories about Anarchism. Not a thing too outrageous to be employed against this philosophy and its exponents. Therefore Anarchism represents to the unthinking what the proverbial bad man does to the child, — a black monster bent on swallowing everything; in short, destruction and violence.

Destruction and violence! How is the ordinary man to know that the most violent element in society is ignorance; that its power of destruction is the very thing Anarchism is combating? Nor is he aware that Anarchism, whose roots, as it were, are part of nature's forces, destroys, not healthful tissue, but parasitic growths that feed on the life's essence of society. It is merely clearing the soil from weeds and sagebrush, that it may eventually bear healthy fruit.

Someone has said that it requires less mental effort to condemn than to think. The widespread mental indolence, so prevalent in society, proves this to be only too true. Rather than to go to the bottom of any given idea, to examine into its origin and meaning, most people will either condemn it altogether, or rely on some superficial or prejudicial definition of non-essentials.

Anarchism urges man to think, to investigate, to analyze every proposition; but that the brain capacity of the average reader be not taxed too much, I also shall begin with a definition, and then elaborate on the latter.

> ANARCHISM:—The philosophy of a new social order based on liberty
> unrestricted by man-made law; the theory that all forms of government rest
> on violence, and are therefore wrong and harmful, as well as unnecessary.

The new social order rests, of course, on the materialistic basis of life; but while all Anarchists agree that the main evil today is an economic one, they maintain that the solution of that evil can be brought about only through the consideration of *every phase* of life, — individual, as well as the collective; the internal, as well as the external phases. . . .

Anarchism is the great liberator of man from the phantoms that have held him captive; it is the arbiter and pacifier of the two forces for individual and social harmony. To accomplish that unity, Anarchism has declared war on the pernicious influences which have so far prevented the harmonious blending of individual and social instincts, the individual and society.

Religion, the dominion of the human mind; Property, the dominion of human needs; and Government, the dominion of human conduct, represent the stronghold of man's enslavement and all the horrors it entails. Religion! How it dominates man's mind, how it humiliates and degrades his soul. God is everything, man is nothing, says religion. But out of that nothing God has created a kingdom so despotic, so tyrannical, so cruel, so terribly exacting that naught but gloom and tears and blood have ruled the world since gods began. Anarchism rouses man to rebellion against this black monster. Break your mental fetters, says Anarchism to man, for not until you think and judge for yourself will you get rid of the dominion of darkness, the greatest obstacle to all progress.

Property, the dominion of man's needs, the denial of the right to satisfy his needs. Time was when property claimed a divine right, when it came to man with the same refrain, even as religion, "Sacrifice! Abnegate! Submit!" The spirit of Anarchism has lifted man from his prostrate position. He now stands erect, with his face toward the light. He has learned to see the insatiable, devouring, devastating nature of property, and he is preparing to strike the monster dead.

"Property is robbery," said the great French Anarchist Proudhon. Yes, but without risk and danger to the robber. Monopolizing the accumulated efforts of man, property has robbed him of his birth right, and has turned him loose a pauper and an outcast. Property has not even the time-worn excuse that man does not create enough to satisfy all needs. The A B C student of economics knows that the productivity of labor within the last few decades far exceeds normal demand. But what are normal demands to an abnormal institution? The only demand that property recognizes is its own gluttonous appetite for greater wealth, because wealth means power; the power to subdue, to crush, to exploit, the power to enslave, to outrage, to degrade. America is particularly boastful of her great power, her enormous national wealth. Poor America, of what avail is all her wealth, if the individuals comprising the nation are wretchedly poor? If they live in squalor, in filth, in crime, with hope and joy gone, a homeless, soilless army of human prey. . . .

Just as religion has fettered the human mind, and as property, or the monopoly of things, has subdued and stifled man's needs, so has the State enslaved his spirit, dictating every phase of conduct. "All government in essence," says Emerson, "is tyranny." It matters not whether it is government by divine right or majority rule. In every instance its aim is the absolute subordination of the individual.

Referring to the American government, the greatest American Anarchist, David Thoreau, said: "Government, what is it but a tradition, though a recent one, endeavoring to transmit itself unimpaired to posterity, but each instance losing its integrity; it has not the vitality and force of a single living man. Law never made man a whit more just; and by means of their respect for it, even the well disposed are daily made agents of injustice." . . .

Anarchism, then, really stands for the liberation of the human mind from the dominion of religion; the liberation of the human body from the dominion of property; liberation from the shackles and restraint of government. Anarchism stands for a social order based on the free grouping of individuals for the purpose of producing real social wealth; an order that will guarantee to every human being free access to the earth and full enjoyment of the necessities of life, according to individual desires, tastes, and inclinations.

Source: Essays on Anarchism. By Emma Goldman. 3rd edition revised. New York: Mother Earth Press, 1917.

Emma Goldman (1869–1940) was known as "Red Emma" and was a leading anarchist, lecturer, popularizer of the arts, and agitator for birth control, women's rights, and free speech.

Thorstein Veblen
The Engineers and the Price System

The state of industry, in America and in the other advanced industrial countries, will impose certain exacting conditions on any movement that aims to displace the Vested Interests. These conditions lie in the nature of things; that is to say, in the nature of the existing industrial system; and until they are met in some passable fashion, this industrial system can not be taken over in any effectual or enduring manner. And it is plain that whatever is found to be true in these respects for America will also hold true in much the same degree for the other countries that are dominated by the mechanical industry and the system of absentee ownership.

It may also confidently be set down at the outset that such an impartial review of the evidence as is here aimed at will make it appear that there need be no present apprehension of the Vested Interests' being unseated by any popular uprising in America, even if the popular irritation should rise very appreciably above its present pitch, and even if certain advocates of "direct action," here and there, should be so ill-advised as to make some rash gesture of revolt. The only present danger is that a boisterous campaign of repression and inquisition on the part of the Guardians of the Vested Interests may stir up some transient flutter of seditious disturbance.

To this end, then, it will be necessary to recall, in a summary way, those main facts of the industrial system and of present businesslike control of this system which come immediately into the case. By way of general premise it is to be noted that the established order of business rests on absentee ownership and is managed with an eye single to the largest obtainable net return in terms of price; that is to say, it is a system of businesslike management on a commercial footing. The underlying population is dependent on the working of this industrial system for its livelihood; and their material interest therefore centers in the output and distribution of consumable goods, not in an increasing volume of earnings for the absentee owners. Hence there is a division of interest between the business community, who do business for the absentee owners, and the underlying population, who work for a living; and in the nature of the case this division of interest between the absentee owners and the underlying population is growing wider and more evident from day to day; which engenders a certain division of sentiment and a degree of mutual distrust. With it all the underlying population are still in a sufficiently deferential frame of mind toward their absentee owners, and are quite conscientiously delicate about any abatement of the free income which their owners come in for, according to the rules of the game as it is played.

The business concerns which so have the management of industry on this plan of absentee ownership are capitalized on their business capacity, not on their industrial capacity; that is to say, they are capitalized on their capacity to produce earnings, not on their capacity to produce goods. Their capitalization has, in effect, been calculated and fixed on the highest ordinary rate of earnings previously obtained; and on pain of insolvency their businesslike managers are now required to meet fixed income-charges on this capitalization. Therefore, as a proposition of safe and sane business management, prices have to be maintained or advanced.

From this businesslike requirement of meeting these fixed overhead charges on the capitalization there result certain customary lines of waste and obstruction, which are unavoidable so long as industry is managed by businesslike methods and for businesslike ends. These ordinary lines of waste and obstruction are necessarily (and blamelessly) included in the businesslike conduct of production. They are many and various in detail, but they may for convenience be classed under four heads: (a) Unemployment of material resources, equipment and manpower, in whole or in part, deliberately or through ignorance; (b) Salesmanship (includes, e.g., needless multiplication of merchants and shops, wholesale and retail, newspaper advertising and bill-boards, sales-exhibits, sales-agents, fancy packages and labels, adulteration, multiplication of brands and proprietary articles); (c) Production (and sales-cost) of superfluities and spurious goods; (d) Systematic dislocation, sabotage and duplication, due in part to businesslike strategy, in part to businesslike ignorance of industrial requirements (includes, e.g., such things as cross-freights, monopolization of resources, withholding of facilities and information from business rivals whom it is thought wise to hinder or defeat). There is, of course, no blame, and no sense of blame or shame attaching to all this everyday waste and confusion that goes to make up the workday total of businesslike management. All of it is a legitimate and necessary part of the established order of business enterprise, within the law and within the ethics of the trade. . . .

By reason of doctrinal consistency and loyalty to tradition, the certified economists have habitually described business enterprise as a rational arrangement for administering the country's industrial system and assuring a full and equitable distribution of consumable goods to the consumers. There need be no quarrel with that view. But it is only fair to enter the reservation that, considered as an arrangement for administering the country's industrial system, business enterprise based on absentee ownership has the defects of its qualities; and these defects of this good old plan are now calling attention to themselves. Hitherto, and ever since the mechanical industry first came into the dominant place in this industrial system, the defects of this businesslike management of industry have continually been encroaching more and more on its qualities. It took its rise as a system of management by the owners of the industrial equipment, and it has in its riper years grown into a system of absentee ownership managed by quasi-responsible financial agents. Having begun as an industrial community which centered about an open market, it has matured into a community of Vested Interests whose vested right it is to keep up prices by a short supply in a closed market. There is no extravagance in saying that, by and large, this arrangement for controlling the production and distribution of food and services through the agency of absentee ownership has now come to be, in the main, a blundering muddle of defects.

Source: The Engineers and the Price System. By Thorstein Veblen. New York: B.W. Huebsch, 1921. Reprint, New York: Harcourt, Brace & World, 1963.

Thorstein Veblen (1857–1929) was an American social theorist who taught at various universities.

World War I

World War I and its aftermath led to debates within American political thought over the desirability of U.S. involvement in the world community. The major issues revolved around the role that the United States should play in the proposed postwar international order, an order that was largely the brainchild of Woodrow Wilson (1856–1924). Participation in the war had been fairly unpopular in the United States—although that changed upon the actual entry into the war—and the desire for a return to the long-term policy of noninvolvement in world affairs was strong enough to keep the United States from participating in the League of Nations.

The first selection is an address to the Senate in 1917 by President Wilson shortly before the United States joined the conflict—which began in 1914— and when U.S. policy was still to remain neutral. The second selection is from the social reformer Jane Addams (1860–1935) and is an example of the opposition to the war.

Woodrow Wilson
Address to the Senate

I have sought this opportunity to address you because I thought that I owed it to you, as the counsel associated with me in the final determination of our international obligations, to disclose to you without reserve the thought and purpose that have been taking form in my mind in regard to the duty of our Government in the days to come when it will be necessary to lay afresh and upon a new plan the foundations of peace among the nations.

It is inconceivable that the people of the United States should play no part in that great enterprise. To take part in such a service will be the opportunity for which they have sought to prepare themselves by the very principles and purposes of their polity and the approved practices of their Government ever since the days when they set up a new nation in the high and honorable hope that it might in all that it was and did show mankind the way to liberty. They cannot in honor withhold the service to which they are now about to be challenged. They do not wish to withhold it. But they owe it to themselves and to the other nations of the world to state the conditions under which they will feel free to render it.

That service is nothing less than this, to add their authority and their power to the authority and force of other nations to guarantee peace and justice throughout the world. Such a settlement cannot now be long postponed. It is right that before it comes this Government should frankly formulate the conditions upon which it would feel justified in asking our people to approve its formal and solemn adherence to a League for Peace. I am here to attempt to state those conditions.

The present war must first be ended; but we owe it to candor and to a just regard for the opinion of mankind to say that, so far as our participation in guarantees of future peace is concerned, it makes a great deal of difference in what way and upon what terms it is ended. The treaties and agreements which bring it to an end must embody terms which will create a peace that is worth guaranteeing and preserving, a peace that will win the approval of mankind, not merely a peace that will serve the several interests and immediate aims of the nations engaged. We shall have no voice in determining what those terms shall be, but we shall, I feel sure, have a voice in determining whether they shall be made lasting or not by the guarantees of a universal covenant; and our judgment upon what is fundamental and essential as a condition precedent to permanency should be spoken now, not afterwards when it may be too late.

No covenant of co-operative peace that does not include the peoples of the New World can suffice to keep the future safe against war; and yet there is only one sort of peace that the peoples of America could join in guaranteeing. The elements of that peace must be elements that engage the confidence and satisfy the principles of the American governments, elements consistent with their political faith and with the practical convictions which the peoples of America have once for all embraced and undertaken to defend.

I do not mean to say that any American government would throw any obstacle in the way of any terms of peace the governments now at war might agree upon, or seek to upset them when made, whatever they might be. I only take it for granted that mere terms of peace between the belligerents will not satisfy even the belligerents themselves. Mere agreements may not make peace secure. It will be absolutely necessary that a force be created as a guarantor of the permanency of the settlement so much greater than the force of any nation now engaged or any alliance hitherto formed or projected that no nation, no probable combination of nations could face or withstand it. If the peace presently to be made is to endure, it must be a peace made secure by the organized major force of mankind.

The terms of the immediate peace agreed upon will determine whether it is a peace for which such a guarantee can be secured. The question upon which the whole future peace and policy of the world depends is this: Is the present war a struggle for a just and secure peace, or only for a new balance of power? If it be only a struggle for a new balance of power, who will guarantee, who can guarantee the stable equilibrium of the new arrangement? Only a tranquil Europe can be a stable Europe. There must be, not a balance of power, but a community of power; not organized rivalries, but an organized common peace.

Fortunately we have received very explicit assurances on this point. The statesmen of both of the groups of nations now arrayed against one another have said, in terms that could not be misinterpreted, that it was no part of the purpose they had in mind to crush their antagonists. But the implications of these assurances may not be equally clear to all—may not be the same on both sides of the water. I think it will be serviceable if I attempt to set forth what we understand them to be.

They imply, first of all, that it must be a peace without victory. It is not pleasant to say this. I beg that I may be permitted to put my own interpretation upon it and that it may be understood that no other interpretation was in my thought. I am seeking only to face realities and to face them without soft concealments. Victory would mean peace forced upon the loser, a victor's terms imposed upon the vanquished. It would be accepted in humiliation, under duress, at an intolerable sacrifice, and would leave a sting, a resentment, a bitter memory upon which terms of peace would rest, not permanently, but only as upon quicksand. Only a peace between equals can last. Only a peace the very principle of which is equality and a common participation in a common benefit. The right state of mind, the right feeling between nations, is as necessary for a lasting peace as is the just settlement of vexed questions of territory or of racial and national allegiance.

The equality of nations upon which peace must be founded if it is to last must be an equality of rights; the guarantee exchanged must neither recognize nor imply a difference between big nations and small, between those that are powerful and those that are weak. Right must be based upon the common strength, not upon the individual strength, of the nations upon whose concert peace will depend. Equality of territory or of resources there of course cannot be; nor any other sort of equality not gained in the ordinary peaceful and legitimate development of the peoples themselves. But no one asks or expects anything more than an equality of rights. Mankind is looking now for freedom of life, not for equipoises of power.

And there is a deeper thing involved than even equality of right among organized nations. No peace can last, or ought to last, which does not recognize and accept the principle that governments derive all their just powers from the consent of the governed, and that no right anywhere exists to hand peoples about from sovereignty to sovereignty as if they were property. . . .

I speak of this, not because of any desire to exalt an abstract political principle which has always been held very dear by those who have sought to build up liberty in America, but for the same reason that I have spoken of the other conditions of peace which seem to me clearly indispensable—because I wish frankly to uncover reality. Any peace which does not recognize and accept this principle will inevitably be upset. It will not rest upon the affections or the convictions of mankind. The ferment of spirit of whole populations will fight subtly and constantly against it, and all the world will sympathize. The world can be at peace only if its life is stable, and there can be no stability where the will is in rebellion, where there is not tranquillity of spirit and a sense of justice, of freedom, and of right. . . .

I am proposing, as it were, that the nations should with one accord adopt the doctrine . . . that no nation should seek to extend its polity over any other nation or people, but that every people should be left free to determine its own polity, its own way of development, unhindered, unthreatened, unafraid, the little along with the great and powerful.

I am proposing that all nations henceforth avoid entangling alliances which would draw them into competitions of power; catch them in a net of intrigue and selfish rivalry, and disturb their own affairs with influences intruded from without. There is no entangling alliance in a concert of power. When all unite to act in the same sense and with the same purpose all act in the common interest and are free to live their own lives under a common protection.

I am proposing government by the consent of the governed; that freedom of the seas which in international conference after conference representatives of the United States have urged with the eloquence of those who are the convinced disciples of liberty; and that moderation of armaments which makes of armies and navies a power for order merely, not an instrument of aggression or of selfish violence.

These are American principles, American policies. We could stand for no others. And they are also the principles and policies of forward looking men and women everywhere, of every modern nation, of every enlightened community. They are the principles of mankind and must prevail.

Source: Address to the Senate, January 22, 1917. *The Public Papers of Woodrow Wilson.* Edited by Ray Stannard Baker and William I. Dodd, 4:407–14. New York: Harper & Brothers, 1926.

Woodrow Wilson (1856–1924) was the twenty-eighth president of the United States. He had been a professor of jurisprudence and political economy at Princeton University and president of Princeton. He was instrumental in founding the League of Nations.

Jane Addams
Women, War, and Babies

Many women throughout the world have set their faces unalterably against war. This is our reason for organization against war. I head a movement planned to unite womanhood, in all parts of the world, in a great protest against Europe's war. It is called the Women's Peace Party and is international in scope. It began its existence at Washington, and is increasing in membership with astonishing rapidity.

As women we are the custodians of the life of the ages and we will not longer consent to its reckless destruction. We are particularly charged with the future of childhood, the care of the helpless and the unfortunate, and we will not longer endure without protest that added burden of maimed and invalid men and poverty-stricken women and orphans which war places on us.

We have builded by the patient drudgery of the past the basic foundations of the home and of peaceful industry; we will not longer endure that hoary evil which in an hour destroys or tolerate that denial of the sovereignty of reason and justice by which war and all that makes for war today render impotent the idealism of the race.

Therefore we demand that our right to be consulted in the settlement of questions concerning not alone the life of individuals but of nations be recognized and respected, that women be given a share in deciding between war and peace.

Some of the objects we are working on to obtain, are limitations of armaments and the nationalization of their manufacture; organized opposition to militarism in our own country and education of youth in the ideals of peace; democratic control of foreign policies; the further humanizing of Governments by the extension of the franchise to women; "concert of nations" to supercede "balance of power;" action toward the gradual organization of the world to substitute law for war.

We also believe in the substitution of an international police for rival armies and navies; removal of the economic causes of war; the appointment by our Government of a commission of men and women, with an adequate appropriation, to promote international peace.

At the present moment women in Europe are being told: "Bring children into the world for the benefit of the nation; for the strengthening of future battle lines; forget everything that you have been taught to hold dear; forget your long struggle to establish the responsibilities of fatherhood; forget all but the appetite of war for human flesh. It must be satisfied and you must be the ones to feed it, cost what it may.

This war is destroying the home unit in the most highly civilized countries of the world to an extent which is not less than appalling. Could there be a more definite and dreadful illustration of the tendencies of war to break down and destroy the family unit? All such consequences of war mitigate against the age long efforts of woman to establish the paternity of her child and the father's responsibility for it.

In the interest of this effort the State has made marriage a matter of license and record, and the Church has surrounded it by every possible sanctity. Under the pressure of war, however, both of these institutions have in a large measure withdrawn their protection.

All that women have held dear, all that the Church has worked for and the State has ordered, has been swept away in a breath—the hot breath of war—leaving woman in her primitive, pitiable state of the necessity of self-defense. So long as a State, through the exigencies of war, is obliged to place military authority above all civil rights, women can have within it no worthy place, no opportunity for their development, and they cannot hope for authority in its councils.

Thousands of them in Europe, as in the United States had become so thoroughly imbued with the idea that the recognition of the sacredness of human life had at last become established, throughout the world, that the news of this war to them came as an incredible shock. Women are entitled in all justice to some consideration in this matter of war making, if only because they have necessarily been paramount in the nurture of that human life which is now being so lavishly spent.

The advanced nations know very accurately, and we have begun to know in America, how many children are needlessly lost in the first years of infancy. Measures inaugurated for the prevention of infant mortality were slowly spreading from one country to another. All that effort has been scattered to the winds by the war. No one is pretending to count the babies who are dying throughout the villages and countrysides of the warring nations.

Source: Harper's Weekly 61 (July 31, 1919): 101.

Jane Addams (1860–1935) was a social settlement worker and peace advocate. She founded Hull House in Chicago and was its resident head from 1889 to 1935.

Minorities

AFRICAN AMERICANS

The first part of the century was a time of great importance in African-American culture. W. E. B. Du Bois (1868–1963) became a major spokesperson for Blacks. Marcus Garvey (1887–1940), believing that Blacks could gain nothing from associating with whites, began an important movement for Black pride, self-reliance, and autonomous economic development. Du Bois's "Talented Tenth" refers to those African Americans who could gain a college education and would thus be able to lead other African Americans in improving their lot. Du Bois was an opponent of Booker T. Washington (1856–1915) (see his "Atlanta Exposition Address" in the previous chapter), who argued that while it is important to educate African Americans, their education should be limited to the industrial arts or manual training so as not to antagonize whites.

W. E. B. Du Bois
The Talented Tenth

The Negro race, like all races, is going to be saved by its exceptional men. The problem of education, then, among Negroes must first of all deal with the Talented Tenth; it is the problem of developing the Best of this race that they may guide the Mass away from the contamination and death of the Worst, in their own and other races. Now the training of men is a difficult and intricate task. Its technique is a matter for educational experts, but its object is for the vision of seers. If we make money the object of man-training, we shall develop moneymakers but not necessarily men; if we make technical skill the object of education, we may possess artisans but not, in nature, men. Men we shall have only as we make manhood the object of the work of the schools—intelligence, broad sympathy, knowledge of the world that was and is, and of the relation of men to it—this is the curriculum of that Higher Education which must underlie true life. On this foundation we may build bread winning, skill of hand and quickness of brain, with never a fear lest the child and man mistake the means of living for the object of life. . . .

Modern industry has taken great strides since the war, and the teaching of trades is no longer a simple matter. Machinery and long processes of work have greatly changed the work of the carpenter, the iron-worker and the shoemaker. A really efficient workman must be to-day an intelligent man who has had good technical training in addition to thorough common school, and perhaps even higher training. To meet this situation the industrial schools began a further development; they established distinct Trade Schools for the thorough training of better class artisans, and at the same time they sought to preserve for the purposes of general education, such of the simpler processes of elementary trade learning as were best suited therefor. In this differentiation of the Trade School and manual training, the best of the industrial schools simply followed the plain trend of the present educational epoch. A prominent educator tells us that, in Sweden, "In the beginning the economic conception was generally adopted, and everywhere manual training was looked upon as a means of preparing the children of the common people to earn their living. But gradually it came to be recognized that manual training has a more elevated purpose, and one, indeed, more useful in the deeper meaning of the term. It came to be considered as an educative process for the complete moral, physical and intellectual development of the child."

Thus . . . in the manning of trade schools and manual training schools we are thrown back upon the higher training as its source and chief support. There was a time when any aged and worn out carpenter could teach in a trade school. But not so to-day. Indeed the demand for college-bred men by a school like Tuskegee, ought to make Mr. Booker T. Washington the firmest friend of higher training. Here he has as helpers the son of a Negro senator, trained in Greek and the humanities, and graduated at Harvard; the son of a Negro congressman and lawyer, trained in Latin and mathematics, and graduated at Oberlin; he has as his wife, a woman who read Virgil and Homer in the same class room with me; he has as college chaplain, a classical graduate of Atlanta University; as teacher of science, a graduate of Fisk; as teacher of history, a graduate of Smith, — indeed some thirty of his chief teachers are college graduates, and instead of studying French grammars in the midst of weeds, or buying pianos for dirty cabins, they are at Mr. Washington's right hand helping him in a noble work. And yet one of the effects of Mr. Washington's propaganda has been to throw doubt upon the expediency of such training for Negroes, as these persons have had.

Men of America, the problem is plain before you. Here is a race transplanted through the criminal foolishness of your fathers. Whether you like it or not the millions are here, and here they will remain. If you do not lift them up, they will pull you down. Education and work are the levers to uplift a people. Work alone will not do it unless inspired by the right ideals and guided by intelligence. Education must not simply teach work—it must teach Life. The Talented Tenth of the Negro race must be made leaders of thought and missionaries of culture among their people. No others can do this work and negro colleges must train men for it. The Negro race, like all other races, is going to be saved by its exceptional men.

Source: *The Negro Problem: A Series of Articles by Representative American Negroes of To-Day.* New York: James Pott Co., 1903.

W. E. B. Du Bois (1868–1963) was a historian, sociologist, and reformer who helped to found the National Association for the Advancement of Colored People (NAACP).

Marcus Garvey
Declaration of Rights of the Negro Peoples of the World

Drafted and adopted at Convention held in New York, 1920, over which Marcus Garvey presided as Chairman, and at which he was elected Provisional President of Africa.

(Preamble)

"Be it Resolved, That the Negro people of the world, through their chosen representatives in convention assembled in Liberty Hall, in the City of New York and United States of America, from August 1 to August 31, in the year of our Lord, one thousand nine hundred and twenty, protest against the wrongs and injustices they are suffering at the hands of their white brethren, and state what they deem their fair and just rights, as well as the treatment they propose to demand of all men in the future."

We complain:

I. "That nowhere in the world, with few exceptions, are black men accorded equal treatment with white men, although in the same situation and circumstances, but, on the contrary, are discriminated against and denied the common rights due to human beings for no other reason than their race and color."

"We are not willingly accepted as guests in the public hotels and inns of the world for no other reason than our race and color."

II. "In certain parts of the United States of America our race is denied the right of public trial accorded to other races when accused of crime, but are lynched and burned by mobs, and such brutal and inhuman treatment is even practised upon our women."

III. "That European nations have parcelled out among them and taken possession of nearly all of the continent of Africa, and the natives are compelled to surrender their lands to aliens and are treated in most instances like slaves."

IV. "In the southern portion of the United States of America, although citizens under the Federal Constitution, and in some states almost equal to the whites in population and are qualified land owners and taxpayers, we are, nevertheless, denied all voice in the making and administration of the laws and are taxed without representation by the state governments, and at the same time compelled to do military service in defense of the country."

V. "On the public conveyances and common carriers in the Southern portion of the United States we are jim-crowed and compelled to accept separate and inferior accommodations and made to pay the same fare charged for first-class accommodations, and our families are often humiliated and insulted by drunken white men who habitually pass through the jim-crow cars going to the smoking car."

VI. "The physicians of our race are denied the right to attend their patients while in the public hospitals of the cities and states where they reside in certain parts of the United States."

"Our children are forced to attend inferior separate schools for shorter terms than white children, and the public school funds are unequally divided between the white and colored schools."

VII. "We are discriminated against and denied an equal chance to earn wages for the support of our families, and in many instances are refused admission into labor unions, and nearly everywhere are paid smaller wages than white men."

VIII. "In Civil Service and departmental offices we are everywhere discriminated against and made to feel that to be a black man in Europe, America and the West Indies is equivalent to being an outcast and a leper among the races of men, no matter what the character and attainments of the black man may be."

IX. "In the British and other West Indian Islands and colonies, Negroes are secretly and cunningly discriminated against, and denied those fuller rights of governments to which white citizens are appointed, nominated and elected."

X. "That our people in those parts are forced to work for lower wages than the average standard of white men and are kept in conditions repugnant to good civilized tastes and customs."

XI. "That the many acts of injustices against members of our race before the courts of law in the respective islands and colonies are of such nature, as to create disgust and disrespect for the white man's sense of justice."

XII. "Against all such inhuman, unchristian and uncivilized treatment we here and now emphatically protest, and invoke the condemnation of all mankind."

"In order to encourage our race all over the world and to stimulate it to a higher and grander destiny, we demand and insist on the following Declaration of Rights:

1. "Be it known to all men that whereas, all men are created equal and entitled to the rights of life, liberty and the pursuit of happiness, and because of this we, the duly elected representatives of the Negro peoples of the world, invoking the aid of the just and Almighty God do declare all men women and children of our blood throughout the world free citizens, and do claim them as free citizens of Africa, the Motherland of all Negroes."

2. "That we believe in the supreme authority of our race in all things racial; that all things are created and given to man as a common possession; that there should be an equitable distribution and apportionment of all such things, and in consideration of the fact that as a race we are now deprived of those things that are morally and legally ours, we believe it right that all such things should be acquired and held by whatsoever means possible.

3. "That we believe the Negro, like any other race, should be governed by the ethics of civilization, and therefore, should not be deprived of any of those rights or privileges common to other human beings."

4. "We declare that Negroes, wheresoever they form a community among themselves, should be given the right to elect their own representatives to represent them in legislatures, courts of law, or such institutions as may exercise control over that particular community."

5. "We assert that the Negro is entitled to even-handed justice before all courts of law and equity in whatever country he may be found, and when this is denied him on account of his race or color such denial is an insult to the race as a whole and should be resented by the entire body of Negroes."

6. "We declare it unfair and prejudicial to the rights of Negroes in communities where they exist in considerable numbers to be tried by a judge and jury composed entirely of an alien race, but in all such cases members of our race are entitled to representation on the jury."

7. "We believe that any law or practice that tends to deprive any African of his land or the privileges of free citizenship within his country is unjust and immoral, and no native should respect any such law or practice."

8. "We declare taxation without representation unjust and tyrannous, and there should be no obligation on the part of the Negro to obey the levy of a tax by any law-making body from which he is excluded and denied representation on account of his race and color."

9. "We believe that any law especially directed against the Negro to his detriment and singling him out because of his race or color is unfair and immoral, and should not be respected."

10. "We believe all men entitled to common human respect, and that our race

should in no way tolerate any insults that may be interpreted to mean disrespect to our color."

11. "We deprecate the use of the term 'nigger' as applied to Negroes, and demand that the word 'Negro' be written with a capital 'N'."

12. "We believe that the Negro should adopt every means to protect himself against barbarous practices inflicted upon him because of color."

13. "We believe in the freedom of Africa for the Negro people of the world, and by the principle of Europe for the Europeans and Asia for the Asiatic; we also demand Africa for the Africans at home and abroad."

14. "We believe in the inherent right of the Negro to possess himself of Africa, and that his possession of same shall not be regarded as an infringement on any claim or purchase made by any race or nation."

15. "We strongly condemn the cupidity of those nations of the world who, by open aggression or secret schemes, have seized the territories and inexhaustible natural wealth of Africa, and we place on record our most solemn determination to reclaim the treasures and possession of the vast continent of our forefathers."

16. "We believe all men should live in peace one with the other, but when races and nations provoke the ire of other races and nations by attempting to infringe upon their rights, war becomes inevitable, and the attempt in any way to free one's self or protect one's self or protect one's rights or heritage becomes justifiable."

17. "Whereas, the lynching, by burning, hanging or any other means, of human beings is a barbarous practice, and a shame and disgrace to civilization, we therefore declare any country guilty of such atrocities outside the pale of civilization."

18. "We protest against the atrocious crime of whipping, flogging and overworking of the native tribes of Africa and Negroes everywhere. These are methods that should be abolished, and all means should be taken to prevent a continuance of such brutal practices."

19. "We protest the atrocious practice of shaving the heads of Africans, especially of African women or individuals of Negro blood, when placed in prison as a punishment for crime by an alien race."

20. "We protest against segregated districts, separate public conveyance, industrial discrimination, lynching and limitations of political privileges of any Negro citizen in any part of the world on account of race, color or creed, and will exert our full influence and power against all such."

21. "We protest against any punishment inflicted upon a Negro with severity, as against lighter punishment inflicted upon another of an alien race for like offense, as an act of prejudice and injustice, and should be resented by the entire race."

22. "We protest against the system of education in any country where Negroes are denied the same privileges and advantages as other races."

23. "We declare it inhuman and unfair to boycott Negroes from industries and labor in any part of the world."

24. "We believe in the doctrine of the freedom of the press, and we therefore emphatically protest against the suppression of Negro newspapers and periodicals in various parts of the world, and call upon Negroes everywhere to employ all available means to prevent such suppression."

25. "We further demand free speech universally for all men."

26. "We hereby protest against the publication of scandalous and inflammatory articles by an alien press tending to create racial strife and the exhibition of picture films showing the Negroes a cannibal."

27. "We believe in the self-determination of all peoples."

28. "We declare for the freedom of religious worship."

29. "With the help of Almighty God, we declare ourselves the sworn protectors of the honor and virtue of our women and children, and pledge our lives for their protection and defense everywhere, and under all circumstances from wrongs and outrages."

30. "We demand the right of unlimited and unprejudiced education for ourselves and our posterity forever."

31. "We declare that the teaching in any school by alien teachers to our boys and girls, that the alien race is superior to the Negro race, is an insult to the Negro people of the world."

32. "Where Negroes form a part of the citizenry of any country, and pass the civil service examination of such country, we declare them entitled to the same consideration as other citizens as to appointments in such civil service."

33. "We vigorously protest against the increasingly unfair and unjust treatment accorded Negro travelers on land and sea by the agents and employees of railroad and steamship companies and insist that for equal fare we receive equal privileges with travelers of other races."

34. "We declare it unjust for any country, State or nation to enact laws tending to hinder and obstruct the free immigration of Negroes on account of their race and color."

35. "That the right of the Negro to travel unmolested throughout the world be not abridged by any person or persons, and all Negroes are called upon to give aid to a fellow Negro when thus molested."

36. "We declare that all Negroes are entitled to the same right to travel over the world as other men."

37. "We hereby demand that the governments of the world recognize our leader and his representatives chosen by the race to look after the welfare of our people under such governments."

38. "We demand complete control of our social institutions without inference by any alien race or races."

39. "That the colors, Red, Black and Green, be the colors of the Negro race."

40. "Resolved, That the anthem 'Ethiopia, Thou Land of Our Fathers,' etc., shall be the anthem of the Negro race." . . .

41. "We believe that any limited liberty which deprives one of the complete rights and prerogatives of full citizenship is but a modified form of slavery."

42. "We declare it an injustice to our people and a serious impediment to the health of the race to deny to competent licensed Negro physicians the right to practise in the public hospitals of the communities in which they reside, for no other reason than their race and color."

43. "We call upon the various governments of the world to accept and acknowledge Negro representatives who shall be sent to the said government to represent the general welfare of the Negro peoples of the world."

44. "We deplore and protest against the practice of confining juvenile prisoners in prisons with adults, and we recommend that such youthful prisoners be taught gainful trades under humane supervision."

45. "Be it further resolved, that we as a race of people declare the League of Nations null and void as far as the Negro is concerned, in that it seeks to deprive Negroes of their liberty."

46. "We demand of all men to do unto us as we would do unto them, in the name of justice; and we cheerfully accord to all men all the rights we claim herein for ourselves."

47. "We declare that no Negro shall engage himself in battle for an alien race without first obtaining the consent of the leader of the Negro people of the world, except in a matter of national self-defense."

48. "We protest against the practice of drafting Negroes and sending them to war with alien forces without proper training, and demand in all cases that Negro soldiers be given the same training as the aliens."

49. "We demand that instructions given Negro children in schools include the subject of 'Negro History,' to their benefit."

50. "We demand a free and unfettered commercial intercourse with all the Negro people of the world."

51. "We declare for the absolute freedom of the seas for all peoples."

52. "We demand that our duly accredited representatives be given proper recognition in all leagues, conferences, conventions or courts of international arbitration wherever human rights are discussed."

53. "We proclaim the 31st day of August of each year to be an international holiday to be observed by all Negroes."

54. "We want all men to know we shall maintain and contend for the freedom

and equality of every man, woman and child of our race, with our lives, our fortunes and our sacred honor."

These rights we believe to be justly ours and proper for the protection of the Negro race at large, and because of this belief we, on behalf of the four hundred million Negroes of the world, do pledge herein the sacred blood of the race in defense, and we hereby subscribe our names as a guarantee of the truthfulness and faithfulness hereof in the presence of Almighty God, on the 13th day of August, in the year of our Lord one thousand nine hundred and twenty.

Source: Philosophy and Opinions of Marcus Garvey. Edited by Amy Jacques Garvey. Volume 2. New York: Arno Press and New York Times, 1969.

Marcus Garvey (1887–1940) was the founder of the Universal Negro Improvement Association (UNIA). He was an early Black Nationalist.

INDIANS

The first part of the twentieth century was a low point for Indians in America. In the selection here, Lame Deer (1900–1970) remembers his childhood on a reservation in South Dakota.

Lame Deer
Memories

There were twelve of us, but they are all dead now, except one sister. Most of them didn't even grow up. My big brother, Tom, and his wife were killed by the flu in 1917. I lost my own little boy thirty-five years ago. I was a hundred miles away, caught in a blizzard. A doctor couldn't be found for him soon enough. I was told it was the measles. Last year I lost another baby boy, a foster child. This time they told me it was due to some intestinal trouble. So in a lifetime we haven't made much progress. We medicine men try to doctor our sick, but we suffer from many new white man's diseases, which come from the white man's food and white man's living, and we have no herbs for that.

My big sister was the oldest of us all. When she died in 1914 my folks took it so hard that our life was changed. In honor of her memory they gave away most of their possessions, even beds and mattresses, even the things without which the family would find it hard to go on. My mother died of tuberculosis in 1920, when I was seventeen years old, and that was our family's "last stand." On her last day I felt that her body was already gone; only her soul was still there. I was holding her hand and she was looking at me. Her eyes were big and sad, as if she knew that I was in for a hard time. She said, "*Onsika, onsika*—pitiful, pitiful," These were her last words. She wasn't sorry for herself; she was sorry for me. I went up on a hill by myself and cried.

When grandfather Crazy Heart died they killed his two ponies, heads toward the east and tails to the west. They had told each horse, "Grandson, your owner loved you. He has need of you where he's going now." Grandfather knew for sure where he was going, and so did the people who buried him according to our old custom. . . .

But in 1920 they wouldn't even allow us to be dead in our own way. We had to be buried in the Christian fashion. It was as if they wanted to take my mother to a white boarding school way up there. For four days I felt my mother's *nagi,* her presence, her soul, near me. I felt that some of her goodness was staying with me. The priest talked about eternity. I told him we Indians did not believe in a forever and forever. We say that only the rocks and the mountains last, but even they will disappear. There's a new day coming, but no forever, I told him. "When my time comes, I want to go where my ancestors have gone." The priest said, "That may be hell." I told him that I'd rather be frying with a Sioux grandmother or uncle than sit on a cloud playing harp with a pale-faced stranger. I told him, "That Christian name, John, don't call me that when I'm gone. Call me Tahca Ushte— Lame Deer."

With the death of my mother one world crumbled for me. It coincided with a new rule the Government made about grazing pay and allotments. Barbed-wire fences closed in on us. My dad said, "We might just as well give up." He went back to Standing Rock, where he was from. He left my sister about sixty horses, forty scrub cows and one bull. I had about sixty head of broken saddle horses and fifty cows. My dad turned me loose. "Hey, I give you these horses; do as you please. If you want to live like a white man, go and buy a car till you are broke and walk on foot." I guess Dad knew what was in my mind.

I started trading my stock for a Model-T Ford and bought things that were in style for the rodeo—fancy boots, silver spurs, gaudy horse-trappings, a big hat. I followed the rodeo circuit, but I wasn't too interested in competing as a rider. It was just an excuse to travel to different reservations. My life was changed and I myself was changing. I hardly recognized myself anymore. I was a wanderer, a hippie Indian. I knew nothing then. Right or wrong were just words. My life was a find-out. If somebody said, "That's bad," I still wanted to experience it. Maybe it would turn out to be good. I wasn't drinking then but soon would be. My horses and cows were gone. Instead I was the owner of a half-dozen wrecked ja-lopies. Yet I felt the spirits. Always at night they came down to me. I could hear them, something like the whistling from the hearing aid that I am wearing now. I could feel their touch like a feather on a sore spot. I always burned a little sweet grass for them. Though I lived like a hobo, I was visiting many old medicine men, trying to learn their ways.

I didn't need a house then or a pasture. Somewhere there would be a cave, a crack in the rocks, where I could hole up during a rain. I wanted the plants and the stones to tell me their secrets. I talked to them. I roamed. I was like a part of the earth. Everything had been taken from me except myself. Now and then, in some place or other, I looked at my face in a mirror to remind myself who I was. Poverty, hardship, laughter, shame, adventure—I wanted to experience them all. At times I felt like one of those modern declawed cats, like a lone coyote with traps, poisoned meat, and a ranger's gun waiting for him, but this did not worry me. I was neither sad nor happy. I just was.

I knew an old Indian at this time who was being forced to leave his tent and to go live in a new house. They told him that he would be more comfortable there and that they had to burn up his old tent because it was verminous and unsanitary. He looked thin and feeble, but he put up a terrific fight. They had a hard time dragging him. He was cursing them all the time: "I don't want no son-of-bitch house. I don't want to live in a box. Throw out the goddam refrigerator, drink him up! Throw out the chair, saw off the damn legs, sit on the ground. Throw out that thing to piss in. I won't use it. Dump the son-of-a-bitch goldfish in there. Kill the damn cow, eat him up. Tomorrow is another day. There's no tomorrow in this goddam box!"

Source: Lame Deer: Seeker of Visions. By John Fire/Lame Deer and Richard Erdoes. New York: Simon & Schuster, 1972.

John Fire Lame Deer (1900–1970) was an Oglala Sioux medicine man.

CHAPTER 10

The Depression and the New Deal, 1929–1945

✳ ✳ ✳

The period from the stock market crash of 1929 through World War II was dominated by a single issue—the economy and the appropriate response to it. But there was no agreement on what had happened or why it happened, let alone what to do about it.

Theories abound on how to characterize the New Deal. Conservatives often consider it to have been an experiment in socialism; liberals used to identify their policies with it; and socialists consider it a device to protect capitalism. In addition to its main provisions—social security, unemployment insurance, price supports for agriculture, temporary job schemes, and regulation of business—the greatest effect of the New Deal was to shift power from the states to the national government. This happened because a national crisis was met with national programs with national funding and quite limited national control. The greatest national controls over programs came after World War II.

Amendments

The Twentieth Amendment is primarily a technical amendment changing details of the terms of the executive and legislative branches and clarifying issues regarding the procedures to be followed on the death of a president-elect before taking office and other eventualities, none of which have ever occurred.

The Twenty-first Amendment is the repeal of the Eighteenth Amendment. It is important because it shows that there are such things as unenforceable laws. Although the prohibition movement had been strong enough politically to pass the Eighteenth Amendment, prohibition was not acceptable to enough people to make it workable. This situation may be an example of Madisonian factions at work, although it is not clear which was a majority faction — if there ever was one — or if the majority simply changed.

Amendment XX

February 6, 1933

Section 1. The terms of the President and Vice President shall end at noon on the twentieth day of January, and the terms of Senators and Representatives at noon on the third day of January, of the years in which such terms would have ended if this article had not been ratified; and the terms of their successors shall then begin.

Section 2. The Congress shall assemble at least once in every year, and such meeting shall begin at noon on the third day of January, unless they shall by law appoint a different day.

Section 3. If, at the time fixed for the beginning of the term of the President, the President elect shall have died, the Vice President elect shall become President. If a President shall not have been chosen before the time fixed for the beginning of his term, or if the President elect shall have failed to qualify, then the Vice President elect shall act as President until a President shall have qualified; and the Congress may by law provide for the case wherein neither a President elect nor a Vice President elect shall have qualified, declaring who shall then act as President, or the manner in which one who is to act shall be selected and such person shall act accordingly until a President or Vice President shall have qualified.

Section 4. The Congress may by law provide for the case of the death of any of the persons from whom the House of Representatives may choose a President whenever the right of choice shall have devolved upon them, and for the case of the death of any of the persons from whom the Senate may choose a Vice President whenever the right of choice shall have devolved upon them.

Section 5. Sections 1 and 2 shall take effect on the fifteenth day of October following the ratification of this article.

Section 6. This article shall be inoperative unless it shall have been ratified as an amendment to the Constitution by the legislatures of three fourths of the several States within seven years from the date of its submission.

Amendment XXI

December 5, 1933

Section 1. The eighteenth article of amendment to the Constitution of the United States is hereby repealed.

Section 2. The transportation or importation into any State, Territory, or possession of the United States for delivery or use therein of intoxicating liquors, in violation of the laws thereof, is hereby prohibited.

Section 3. This article shall be inoperative unless it shall have been ratified as an amendment to the Constitution, within seven years from the date of the submission hereof to the States by the Congress.

The Great Depression

The Great Depression shook the confidence of Americans in their country. The depth of the poverty and the intractable nature of the problems led Americans to explore political extremes on both ends of the political spectrum that they had not taken very seriously before.

Father Charles E. Coughlin (1891–1979) was a Roman Catholic priest who, during the early days of the Great Depression, became one of the first of a long series of popular radio and then television preachers. Father Coughlin was a powerful political force in the United States for a fairly brief period. Frequently called a fascist, he was probably more accurately labeled a populist. His early sermons were directed at the problems caused by the Depression. Later sermons became more strident and anti-Semitic, and he opposed entering the war against Germany. After a struggle within the church, he was removed from his duties. The selection here is from a political party he led.

Norman Thomas (1884–1968) was the most important socialist in the United States from the era of the Depression until his death. He ran for president a number of times, but he was most important as a reasoned advocate for the socialist position. He did not represent the most extreme positions taken during the Depression; he made socialism almost respectable.

Charles E. Coughlin
1936 Platform of the Unionist Party

1. America shall be self-contained and self-sustained—no foreign entanglements, be they political, financial or military.

2. Congress and Congress alone shall coin, issue and regulate all the money and credit in the United States through a central bank of issue.

3. Immediately following the establishment of the central bank of issue, Congress shall provide for the retirement of all tax-exempt, interest-bearing bonds and certificates of indebtedness of the Federal Government, and shall refinance all the present agricultural mortgage indebtedness for the farmer and all the home mortgage indebtedness for the city owner by the use of its money and credit which it now gives to the control of private bankers.

4. Congress shall legislate that there will be an assurance of a living wage for all laborers capable of working and willing to work.

5. Congress shall legislate that there will be an assurance of production at a profit for the farmer.

6. Congress shall legislate that there will be assurance of reasonable and decent security for the aged, who, through no fault of their own, have been victimized and exploited by an unjust economic system which has so concentrated wealth in the hands of a few that it has impoverished great masses of our people.

7. Congress shall legislate that American agricultural, industrial and commercial markets will be protected from manipulation of foreign monies and from all raw material and processed goods produced abroad at less than a living wage.

8. Congress shall establish an adequate and perfect defense for our country from foreign aggression either by air, by land, or by sea, but with the understanding that our naval, air and military forces must not be used under any consideration in foreign fields or in foreign waters whether alone or in conjunction with any foreign power. If there must be conscription, there shall be conscription of wealth as well as of men.

9. Congress shall so legislate that all federal offices and positions of every nature shall be distributed through civil service qualifications and not through a system of party spoils and corrupt patronage.

10. Congress shall restore representative government to the people of the United States to preserve the sovereignty of the individual States of the United States by the ruthless eradication of bureaucracies.

11. Congress shall organize and institute federal works for the conservation of public lands, waters and forests, thereby creating billions of dollars of wealth, millions of jobs at the prevailing wage, and thousands of homes.

12. Congress shall protect small industry and private enterprise by controlling and decentralizing the economic domination of monopolies to the end that these small industries and enterprises may not only survive and prosper but that they may be multiplied.

13. Congress shall protect private property from confiscation through unnecessary taxation with the understanding that the human rights of the masses take precedence over the financial rights of the classes.

14. Congress shall set a limitation upon the net income of any individual in any one year and a limitation of the amount that such an individual may receive

as a gift or as an inheritance, which limitation shall be executed through taxation.

15. Congress shall re-establish conditions so that the youths of the nation as they emerge from schools and colleges, will have the opportunity to earn a decent living while in the process of perfecting themselves in a trade or profession.

Source: National Party Platforms 1840–1968. Compiled by Kirk H. Porter and Donald Bruce Johnson. Urbana: University of Illinois Press, 1970.

Norman Thomas
A Socialist Philosophy

Here is a world relentlessly drifting by the inherent necessities of a machine age to some kind of collectivism, but to a collectivism under capitalistic nationalism so imperfect, unintelligent and generally chaotic, so cumbered with false standards and motives and inadequate ideals that it is far more likely to carry us to war than to give us bread and peace and freedom. It is a world wherein the evolution of a new capitalism is so precarious and its nature so unsatisfactory that it offers no hope of salvation. Men who want consciously to control the development of collectivism and the management of an interdependent world must to-day choose between communism and some form of socialism. Neither offers automatic salvation but only the conditions for a better ordering of human affairs. The hope of communism is spreading in a world of poor and exploited workers. But it is so bound up with war, dictatorship, the definite mobilization of the crowd mind about a dogmatic creed, that it cannot claim in any near future to offer peace or freedom, whatever it may do better to supply the masses with bread and economic justice.

Before we accept the conclusion that the whole world must submit to a discipline similar to that through which Russia is passing, it is well to examine not merely the general questions of war or democracy as we have done but more closely the positive question of what socialism offers or may offer.

Here again we must face the fact that socialism offers no salvation by faith or by panacea. We have acknowledged that the record of parliamentary governments by socialist parties in Europe is no record of thrilling achievement. For this there are explanations in the extraordinary difficulties that the German Social Democracy or the British Labor Party has faced. But it is the business of socialism to surmount difficulties, not to explain that they exist. . . .

The operation of our complex machinery for the common good rather than for private throws into strong relief the rôle of the consumer. We work to live; we do not or should not live to work. Man is not merely a producing machine. He is not at his noblest even as a high-powered salesman. This observation is important when so much necessary work is dull, repetitive and monotonous. Overemphasis on man's rôle as a producer is dangerously to put the cart before the horse. . . .

In time the reëducation of men in other motives than the acquisitive, the perfection of psychological and vocational guidance, the general lightening of the amount of the necessary disagreeable and monotonous work in the world, the efficient forecasting of the number of workers likely to be needed in certain fields, and the increase of the social income, may make possible equality of pay with far less tyranny than the blundering, inequitable wage system under capitalism imposes. . . . Equality or virtual equality of income lies at the end, not the beginning, of the road of socialization and reëducation. It cannot, therefore, be made the cardinal principle of a socialist philosophy. What socialism will do will be to increase such general social income as parks, schools, health services, etc., eliminate parasitism and accelerate processes now in operation to bring about equality of pay first within certain professions and trades and then between them. It will educate men in other rewards than the pecuniary for unusual competence and especial service but it can afford if necessary to give material rewards in moderation so long as it gives with them no power to found an economic dynasty.

Source: America's Way Out: A Program for Democracy. By Norman Thomas. New York: Macmillan, 1931.

Norman Thomas (1884–1968) was the leading American socialist politician of the second quarter of the twentieth century. He was a candidate for president in 1928, 1932, 1936, 1940, 1944, and 1948.

The New Deal

FRANKLIN DELANO ROOSEVELT

Franklin Delano Roosevelt (1882–1945) was the central figure of the New Deal. He was a consummate politician who was able to express his concern for and identification with the serious problems of poverty the country experienced during the Depression even though he came from an extremely wealthy, patrician background.

Roosevelt brought together in Washington creative experts from a number of fields who, faced with the crisis of the Depression, were willing to reconsider the way American government did business. This reconsideration led to the establishment of a number of national programs directed both at alleviating the immediate problems and at trying to prevent them from developing again. The re-

sult was the beginnings of a shift of power to the national level and away from the states. This happened for two reasons. First, the states had no money to spend and the national programs came with at least some national funding. Some states were better off than others, and it was felt that poverty should not have to be born disproportionately by people depending on where they lived. Second, many people argued that it was necessary to establish national norms rather than allowing the individual states to establish their own. One concern was that the South would spend no money to help African Americans, but this was just one example of a broader problem. It was believed that the state governments were in the hands of people who reflected narrow interests that they would choose to benefit.

Franklin Delano Roosevelt
First Inaugural Address

I am certain that my fellow Americans expect that on my induction into the Presidency I will address them with a candor and a decision which the present situation of our nation impels. This is pre-eminently the time to speak the truth, the whole truth, frankly and boldly. Nor need we shrink from honestly facing conditions in our country today. This great nation will endure as it has endured, will revive and will prosper. So, first of all, let me assert my firm belief that the only thing we have to fear is fear itself—nameless, unreasoning, unjustified terror which paralyzes needed efforts to convert retreat into advance. In every dark hour of our national life a leadership of frankness and vigor has met with that understanding and support of the people themselves which is essential to victory. I am convinced that you will again give that support to leadership in these critical days.

In such a spirit on my part and on yours we face our common difficulties. They concern, thank God, only material things. Values have shrunken to fantastic levels; taxes have risen; our ability to pay has fallen; government of all kinds is faced by serious curtailment of income; the means of exchange are frozen in the currents of trade; the withered leaves of industrial enterprise lie on every side; farmers find no markets for their produce; the savings of many years in thousands of families are gone.

More important, a host of unemployed citizens face the grim problem of existence, and an equally great number toil with little return. Only a foolish optimist can deny the dark realities of the moment.

Yet our distress comes from no failure of substance. We are stricken by no plague of locusts. Compared with the perils which our forefathers conquered because they believed and were not afraid, we still have much to be thankful for. Nature still offers her bounty and human efforts have multiplied it. Plenty is at our doorstep, but a generous use of it languishes in the very sight of the supply. Primarily, this is because the rulers of the exchange of mankind's goods have failed through their own stubbornness and their own incompetence, have admitted their failure, and abdicated. Practices of the unscrupulous money changers stand indicted in the court of public opinion, rejected by the hearts and minds of men.

True, they have tried, but their efforts have been cast in the pattern of an outworn tradition. Faced by failure of credit they have proposed only the lending of more money. Stripped of the lure of profit by which to induce our people to follow their false leadership, they have resorted to exhortations, pleading tearfully for restored confidence. They know only the rules of a generation of self-seekers. They have no vision, and when there is no vision the people perish.

The money changers have fled from their high seats in the temple of our civilization. We may now restore that temple to the ancient truths. The measure of the restoration lies in the extent to which we apply social values more noble than mere monetary profit.

Happiness lies not in the mere possession of money; it lies in the joy of achievement, in the thrill of creative effort. The joy and moral stimulation of work no longer must be forgotten in the mad chase of evanescent profits. These dark days will be worth all they cost us if they teach us that our true destiny is not to be ministered unto but to minister to ourselves and to our fellow-men.

Recognition of the falsity of material wealth as the standard of success goes hand in hand with the abandonment of the false belief that public office and high political position are to be valued only by the standards of pride of place and personal profit; and there must be an end to a conduct in banking and in business which too often has given to a sacred trust the likeness of callous and selfish wrongdoing.

Small wonder that confidence languishes, for it thrives only on honesty, on honor, on the sacredness of obligations, on faithful protection, on unselfish performance; without them it cannot live.

Restoration calls, however, not for changes in ethics alone. This Nation asks for action, and action now.

Our greatest primary task is to put people to work. This is no unsolvable problem if we face it wisely and courageously. It can be accomplished in part by direct recruiting by the Government itself, treating the task as we would treat the emergency of a war, but at the same time, through this employment, accomplishing greatly needed projects to stimulate and reorganize the use of our natural resources.

Hand in hand with this, we must frankly recognize the overbalance of population in our industrial centers and, by engaging on a national scale in a redistribution, endeavor to provide a better use of the land for those best fitted for the land. The task can be helped by definite efforts to raise the values of agricultural products and with this the power to purchase the output of our cities. It can be helped by preventing realistically the tragedy of the growing loss through foreclosure of our small homes and our farms. It can be helped by insistence that the Federal, State and local governments act forthwith on the demand that their cost be drastically reduced. It can be helped by the unifying of relief activities which today are often scattered, uneconomical and unequal. It can be helped by national planning for and supervision of all forms of transportation and of communications and other utilities which have a definitely public character. There are many ways in which it can be helped, but it can never be helped merely by talking about it. We must act, and act quickly.

Finally, in our progress toward a resumption of work we require two safeguards against a return of the evils of the old order: there must be a strict supervision of all banking and credits and investments, there must be an end to speculation with other people's money; and there must be provision for an adequate but sound currency. . . .

If I read the temper of our people correctly, we now realize as we have never realized before, our interdependence on each other; that we cannot merely take, but we must give as well; that if we are to go forward, we must move as a trained and loyal army willing to sacrifice for the good of a common discipline, because without such discipline, no progress is made, no leadership becomes effective. We are, I know, ready and willing to submit our lives and property to such discipline, because it makes possible a leadership which aims at a larger good. This I propose to offer, pledging that the larger purposes will bind upon us all as a sacred obligation with a unity of duty hitherto evoked only in time of armed strife.

With this pledge taken, I assume unhesitatingly the leadership of this great army of our people, dedicated to a disciplined attack upon our common problems.

Action in this image and to this end is feasible under the form of government which we have inherited from our ancestors. Our Constitution is so simple and practical that it is possible always to meet extraordinary needs by changes in emphasis and arrangement without loss of essential form. That is why our constitutional system has proved itself the most superbly enduring political mechanism the modern world has produced. It has met every stress of vast expansion of territory, of foreign wars, of bitter internal strife, of world relations.

It is to be hoped that the normal balance of Executive and legislative authority may be wholly adequate to meet the unprecedented task before us. But it may be that an unprecedented demand and need for undelayed action may call for temporary departure from that normal balance of public procedure.

I am prepared under my constitutional duty to recommend the measures that a stricken Nation in the midst of a stricken world may require.

These measures, or such other measures as the Congress may build out of its experience and wisdom, I shall seek, within my constitutional authority, to bring to speedy adoption.

But in the event that the Congress shall fail to take one of these two courses, and in the event that the national emergency is still critical, I shall not evade the clear course of duty that will then confront me. I shall ask the Congress for the one remaining instrument to meet the crisis—broad Executive power to wage a war against the emergency as great as the power that would be given to me if we were in fact invaded by a foreign foe.

Source: The Public Papers and Addresses of Franklin D. Roosevelt. Edited by Samuel I. Rosenman, 2:11–15. New York: Random House, 1938.

Franklin Delano Roosevelt
Message to the Congress on the State of the Union.
January 11, 1944

This Nation in the past two years has become an active partner in the world's greatest war against human slavery.

We have joined with like-minded people in order to defend ourselves in a world that has been gravely threatened with gangster rule.

But I do not think that any of us Americans can be content with mere survival. Sacrifices that we and our allies are making impose upon us all a sacred obligation to see to it that out of this war and our children will gain something better than mere survival.

We are united in determination that this war shall not be followed by another interim which leads to new disaster—that we shall not repeat the tragic errors of ostrich isolationism—that we shall not repeat the excesses of the wild twenties when this Nation went for a joy ride on a roller coaster which ended in a tragic crash.

The one supreme objective for the future, can be summed up in one word: Security. . . .

And that means not only physical security which provides safety from attacks by aggressors. It means also economic security, social security, moral security—in a family of Nations. . . .

The best interests of each Nation, large and small, demand that all freedom-loving Nations shall join together in a just and durable system of peace. In the present world situation, evidenced by the actions of Germany, Italy, and Japan, unquestioned military control over disturbers of the peace is as necessary among Nations as it is among citizens in a community. And an equally basic essential to peace is a decent standard of living for all individual men and women and children in all Nations. Freedom from fear is eternally linked with freedom from want.

There are people who burrow through our Nation like unseeing moles, and attempt to spread the suspicion that if other Nations are encouraged to raise their standards of living, our own American standard of living must of necessity be depressed.

The fact is the very contrary. It has been shown time and again that if the standard of living of any country goes up, so does its purchasing power—and that such a rise encourages a better standard of living in neighboring countries with whom it trades. That is just plain common sense.

The overwhelming majority of our people have met the demands of this war with magnificent courage and understanding. They have accepted inconveniences; they have accepted hardships; they have accepted tragic sacrifices. And they are ready and eager to make whatever further contributions are needed to win the war as quickly as possible—if only they are given the chance to know what is required of them.

However, while the majority goes on about its great work without complaint, a noisy minority maintains an uproar of demands for special favors for special groups. There are pests who swarm through the lobbies of the Congress and the cocktail bars of Washington, representing these special groups as opposed to the basic interests of the Nation as a whole. They have come to look upon the war primarily as a chance to make profits for themselves at the expense of their neighbors—profits in money or in terms of political or social preferment. . . .

In order to concentrate all our energies and resources on winning the war, and to maintain a fair and stable economy at home, I recommend that the Congress adopt:

(1) A realistic tax law—which will tax all unreasonable profits, both individual and corporate, and reduce the ultimate cost of the war to our sons and daughters. The tax bill now under consideration by the Congress does not begin to meet this test.

(2) A continuation of the law for the renegotiation of war contracts—which will prevent exorbitant profits and assure fair prices to the Government. For two long years I have pleaded with the Congress to take undue profits out of war.

(3) A cost of food law—which will enable the Government (a) to place a reasonable floor under the prices the farmer may expect for his production; and (b) to place a ceiling on the prices a consumer will have to pay for the food he buys.

This should apply to necessities only; and will require public funds to carry out. It will cost in appropriations about one percent of the present annual cost of the war.

(4) Early reenactment of the stabilization statute of October, 1942. This expires June 30, 1944, and if it is not extended well in advance, the country might just as well expect price chaos by summer.

We cannot have stabilization by wishful thinking. We must take positive action to maintain the integrity of the American dollar.

(5) A national service law—which, for the duration of the war, will prevent strikes, and, with certain appropriate exception, will make available for war production or for any other essential services every able-bodied adult in this Nation.

These five measures together form a just and equitable whole. I would not recommend a national service law unless the other laws were passed to keep down the cost of living, to share equitably the burdens of taxation, to hold the stabilization line, and to prevent undue profits. . . .

It is our duty now to begin to lay the plans and determine the strategy for the winning of a lasting peace and the establishment of an American standard of living higher than ever before known. We cannot be content, no matter how high that general standard of living may be, if some fraction of our people—whether it be one-third or one-fifth or one-tenth-is ill-fed, ill-clothed, ill-housed, and insecure.

This Republic had its beginning, and grew to its present strength, under the protection of certain inalienable political rights—among them the right of free speech, free press, free worship, trial by jury, freedom from unreasonable searches and seizures. They were our rights to life and liberty.

As our Nation has grown in size and stature, however—as our industrial economy expanded-these political rights proved inadequate to assure us equality in the pursuit of happiness.

We have come to a clear realization of the fact that true individual freedom cannot exist without economic security and independence. "Necessitous men are not free men." People who are hungry and out of a job are the stuff of which dictatorships are made.

In our day these economic truths have become accepted as self-evident. We have accepted, so to speak, a second Bill of Rights under which a new basis of security and prosperity can be established for all—regardless of station, race, or creed. Among these are:

> The right to a useful and remunerative job in the industries or shops or farms or mines of the Nation;

The right to earn enough to provide adequate food and clothing and recreation;

The right of every farmer to raise and sell his products at a return which will give him and his family a decent living;

The right of every businessman, large and small, to trade in an atmosphere of freedom from unfair competition and domination by monopolies at home or abroad;

The right of every family to a decent home;

The right of adequate medical care and the opportunity to achieve and enjoy good health;

The right to adequate protection from the economic fears of old age, sickness, accident, and unemployment;

The right to a good education.

All of these rights spell security. And after this war is won we must be prepared to move forward, in the implementation of these rights, to new goals of human happiness and well-being. America's own rightful place in the world depends in large part upon how fully these and similar rights have been carried into practice for our citizens. For unless there is security here at home there cannot be lasting peace in the world.

Source: The Public Papers and Addresses of Franklin D. Roosevelt. Edited by Samuel I. Rosenman, 13:32–41. New York: Random House, 1950.

Franklin Delano Roosevelt (1882–1945) was the thirty-second president of the United States.

OTHER NEW DEAL SUPPORTERS AND ACTS

The selections that follow reflect both various supporters of the New Deal and one of the central laws passed during the period. One of the most important American political thinkers of the twentieth century was primarily a journalist. Walter Lippman (1889–1974) wrote a number of significant political works beginning before World War I and ending well after World War II. He was well known as an advisor to many U.S. presidents, although President Lyndon Johnson, who had originally welcomed him to the White House, rejected him after Lippman criticized Johnson's handling of the war in Vietnam. As a general proposition, Lippman was most radical in his earliest writings and gradually changed, though he never became a conservative. *A Preface to Politics* (1914) was an argument for something quite close to democratic socialism. *The Good Society* (1936) was an argument in support of what he saw as the central tenets of Western democracy, particularly that each person should be treated as an end in himself or herself rather than a means to some other end. He worried that the

modern division of labor and world markets was making such an understanding of the human being less possible. In the selection reprinted here he argues for government responsibility for the well-being of the people.

The Wagner Act was the main New Deal law concerning labor relations.

Walter Lippman
The New Imperative

It has, I think, been clearly established that government must henceforth hold itself consciously responsible for the maintenance of the standard of life prevailing among the people. This is, I believe, a new imperative which takes its place alongside the older imperatives to defend the nation against attack and to preserve domestic peace. If this is true, it is important. If it is true, it is desirable to grasp it as a general idea apart from the bewildering details of the particular measures in which for the moment it happens to be embodied. Thus, for example, opinions differ about the immediate objectives of foreign policy and even more about such instruments of policy as treaties, battleships, cruisers and submarines. But all debate about these matters starts from the common premise that it is a duty of government to defend the safety of the nation. In respect to domestic peace there is no dispute that government must maintain law and order however much men may differ about particular laws or about how to organize the police and the judiciary. But in this new and unexplored realm the basic idea has not yet been accepted into the tradition of government. It is entangled with superficial differences about highly debatable particular measures. Yet experience in the post-war era has shown, I am convinced, that the ability to protect the popular standard of life is an indispensable condition of the survival of political institutions. . . .

It has been said that to place upon government responsibility for the defense of the popular standard of life is to ask of it more than it can do: the rulers of men are not wise enough or brave enough or disinterested enough to fulfill this new imperative. That may be. My thesis is that they have to attempt it whether or not they succeed. We have on the one hand an economic order incapable of maintaining itself by individual adjustments alone; we have on the other hand the political power of the masses of the people. When an intricate capitalism is combined with popular sovereignty the people will turn to the state for help whenever capitalism is unable to satisfy their habitual expectations. The skeptics may be right in saying that no government can satisfy those expectations. But the democracy will not believe them and it will follow leaders who at least promise to try.

Delivered as the Phi Beta Kappa oration in Sanders Theater, Harvard University, June 21, 1935.

Source: The New Imperative. By Walter Lippmann. New York: Macmillan, 1935.

Walter Lippmann (1889–1974) was the premiere American journalist of the middle of the twentieth century. He wrote many books and became a popular political thinker and advisor to many presidents.

The National Labor Relations Act (The Wagner Act)

Be it enacted by the Senate and House of Representatives of the United States of America in Congress assembled,

FINDINGS AND POLICY

Section 1. The denial by employers of the right of employees to organize and the refusal by employers to accept the procedure of collective bargaining lead to strikes and other forms of industrial strife or unrest, which have the intent or the necessary effect of burdening or obstructing commerce by (a) impairing the efficiency, safety, or operation of the instrumentalities of commerce; (b) occurring in the current of commerce; (c) materially affecting, restraining, or controlling the flow of raw materials or manufactured or processed goods from or into the channels of commerce, or the prices of such materials or goods in commerce; or (d) causing diminution of employment and wages in such volume as substantially to impair or disrupt the market for goods flowing from or into the channels of commerce.

The inequality of bargaining power between employees who do not possess full freedom of association or actual liberty of contract, and employers who are organized in the corporate or other forms of ownership association substantially burdens and affects the flow of commerce, and tends to aggravate recurrent business depressions, by depressing wage rates and the purchasing power of wage earners in industry and by preventing the stabilization of competitive wage rates and working conditions within and between industries.

Experience has proved that protection by law of the right of employees to organize and bargain collectively safeguards commerce from injury, impairment, or interruption, and promotes the flow of commerce by removing certain recognized sources of industrial strife and unrest, by encouraging practices fundamental to the friendly adjustment of industrial disputes arising out of differences as to wages, hours, or other working conditions, and by restoring equality of bargaining power between employers and employees.

It is hereby declared to be the policy of the United States to eliminate the causes of certain substantial obstructions to the free flow of commerce and to mitigate and eliminate these obstructions when they have occurred by encouraging the practice and procedure of collective bargaining and by protecting the exercise by workers, of full freedom of association, self-organization, and designation of representatives of their own choosing, for the purpose of negotiating the terms and conditions of their employment or other mutual aid or protection. . . .

RIGHTS OF EMPLOYEES

Sec. 7. Employees shall have the right to self-organization, to form, join, or assist labor organizations, to bargain collectively through representatives of their own choosing, and to engage in concerted activities, for the purpose of collective bargaining or other mutual aid or protection.

Sec. 8. It shall be an unfair labor practice for an employer—

(1) To interfere with, restrain, or coerce employees in the exercise of the rights guaranteed in section 7.

(2) To dominate or interfere with the formation or administration of any labor organization or contribute financial or other support to it: *Provided*, That subject to rules and regulations made and published by the Board . . . an employer shall not be prohibited from permitting employees to confer with him during working hours without loss of time or pay.

(3) By discrimination in regard to hire or tenure of employment or any term or condition of employment to encourage or discourage membership in any labor organization: *Provided*, That nothing in this Act, or in the National Industrial Recovery Act (U.S.C., Supp. VII, title 15, secs. 701–712), as amended from time to time, or in any code or agreement approved or prescribed thereunder, or in any other statute of the United States, shall preclude an employer from making an agreement with a labor organization (not established, maintained, or assisted by any action defined in this Act as an unfair labor practice) to require as a condition of employment membership therein, if such labor organization is the representative of the employees . . . in the appropriate collective bargaining unit covered by such agreement when made.

(4) To discharge or otherwise discriminate against an employee because he has filed charges or given testimony under this Act.

(5) To refuse to bargain collectively with the representatives of his employees. . . .

Source: 49 Stat. 449 (1935).

The New Deal had its opponents on both the left and the right. Herbert Hoover (1874–1964), the president defeated by Roosevelt, argues that the New Deal was not really necessary. The Communist Party argues that it doesn't go nearly far enough and is merely a façade for the protection of capitalism.

Herbert Hoover
We May Sum Up

The issue of civilization today is whether Liberty can survive the wounds it has received in these recent years.

After the war Liberalism came into a vast ascendency. The arms of democracy had been victorious over the legions of despotism. Those dismembered nations hastened with high hopes to adopt the forms and endeavored to develop the spirit of individual Liberty. Then came the dreadful aftermaths—the realization of losses from the gigantic destruction, the rise of bitter nationalism with all its barriers and snatching for advantage, the attempts by inflations to shift and postpone the debt burdens of the day, the vicious speculation and exploitation to which inflation gives opportunity, the dislocations from rapid advances of scientific discovery and labor saving devices, and the final plunge into the liquidation by the great depression. The human misery that has flowed from it all has discredited the social systems of all nations, no matter how great their concept of liberty, justice, and peace. . . .

What I am interested in in this inquiry is something that transcends the transitory actions, as important as they are, something far more pregnant with disaster to all that America has been to its people and to the world. No nation can introduce a new social philosophy or a new culture alien to its growth without moral and spiritual chaos. I am anxious for the future of freedom and liberty of men. That America has stood for; that has created her greatness; that is all the future holds that is worth while.

The unit of American life is the family and the home. Through it vibrates every hope of the future. It is the economic unit as well as the moral and spiritual unit. But it is more than this. It is beginning of self-government. It is the throne of our highest ideals. It is the center of the spiritual energy of our people.

The purpose of American life is the constant betterment of all these homes. If we sustain that purpose every individual may have the vision of decent and improving life. That vision is the urge of America. It creates the buoyant spirit of our country. The inspiring hope of every real American is for an enlarged opportunity for his children. The obligation of our generation to them is to pass on the heritage of Liberty which was entrusted to us. To secure the blessings of Liberty to ourselves and to our posterity was the purpose in sacrifice of our fathers. We have no right to load upon our children unnecessary debts from our follies or to force them to meet life in regimented forms which limit their self-expression, their opportunities, their achievements. St. Paul said nearly two thousand years ago, "Ye have been called unto liberty."

Our American System and its great purpose are builded upon the positive conception that "men are endowed by their Creator with certain unalienable Rights, that among these are Life, Liberty, and the pursuit of Happiness"; that the purpose and structure of government is to protect these rights; that upon them the government itself shall not encroach. From these liberties has come that unloosing of creative instincts and aspirations which have builded this, the greatest nation of all time.

The Bill of Rights—our forefathers' listing of unalienable liberties and personal securities—was written a century and a half ago. We have had need to work out both practical application of these liberties and the machinery for maintaining them in the changing scene of the years. We have seen some of them fade from memory, such as the protection from quartering of troops. We have had to add some new rights to assure freedom from slavery and to give universal franchise. We have had to keep the balance as between some of them and to see that some—chiefly property rights—are not used to override other rights. We have steadily developed from the spirit of freedom high standards and ideals of human relationship, a great system of advancement of mankind. We have at times failed to live up to our ideals, but that they shall continue to shine brightly is the important thing. . . .

Today forces have come into action from ignorance, panic, or design which, either by subtle encroachment or by the breaking down of their safeguards, do endanger their primary purpose. These liberties are of urgent practical importance. The very employment upon which millions depend for their bread is today delayed because of the disturbance of confidence in their security. . . .

No country or no society can be conducted by partly acknowledging the securities of Liberty and partly denying them, nor by recognizing some of them and denying others. That is part democracy and part tyranny. At once there are conflicts and interferences which not only damage the whole economic mechanism but drive unceasingly for more and more dictation.

Even partial regimentation cannot be made to work and still maintain live democratic institutions. Representative government will sooner or later be at conflict with it along the whole front, both in the incidentals of daily working and in the whole field of free choice by the people. If it be continued the Congress must further surrender its checks and balances on administration and its free criticism since these, with intensified duties to its constituents, create interferences that will make efficient administration of this regimented machine impossible. . . .

It is not that the proposals or philosophies or tendencies of National Regimentation are new discoveries to humanity, which offer the bright hope of new invention or new genius in human leadership. They have the common characteristic of these other philosophies of society and of those of the Middle Ages—that the liberties of men flow only from the state; that men are subjective to the state; that men shall be regimented, not free men. Herein is the flat conflict with true Liberalism. It is all old, very, very old, the idea that the good of men arises from the direction of centralized executive power, whether it be exercised through bureaucracies, mild dictatorships or despotisms, monarchies or autocracies. For Liberty is the emancipation of men from power and servitude and the substitution of freedom for force of government.

Liberty comes alone and lives alone where the hard-won rights of men are held unalienable, where governments themselves may not infringe, where governments are indeed but the mechanisms to protect and sustain these liberties from encroachment. It was this for which our fathers died, it was this heritage they gave to us. It was not the provisions with regard to interstate commerce or the determination of weights and measures or coinage, for which the Constitution was devised—it was the guarantees that men possessed fundamental liberties apart from the state, that they were not the pawns but the masters of the state. It has not been for the aid and comfort of any form of economic domination that our liberties have been hallowed by sacrifice. It has not been for the comfort of machinery that we have builded and extended these liberties, but for the independence and comfort of homes.

Those who proclaim that in a Machine Age there is created an irreconcilable conflict in which liberty cannot survive should not forget the battles of liberty over the centuries, for let it be remembered that in the end both big business and machinery will vanish before freedom if that be necessary. But it is not necessary. It is not because Liberty is unworkable, but because we have not worked it conscientiously or have forgotten its true meaning that we often get the notion of the irreconcilable conflict with the Machine Age.

We cannot extend the mastery of government over the daily life of a people without somewhere making it master of people's souls and thoughts. That is going on today. It is part of all regimentation.

Even if the government conduct of business could give us the maximum of efficiency instead of least efficiency, it would be purchased at the cost of freedom. It would increase rather than decrease abuse and corruption, stifle initiative and invention, undermine the development of leadership, cripple the mental and spiritual energies of our people, extinguish equality of opportunity, and dry up the spirit of liberty and the forces which make progress.

It is a false Liberalism that interprets itself into government dictation, or operation of commerce, industry and agriculture. Every move in that direction poisons the very springs of true Liberalism. It poisons political equality, free thought, free press, and equality of opportunity. It is the road not to liberty but to less liberty. True Liberalism is found not in striving to spread bureaucracy, but in striving to set bounds to it. Liberalism is a force proceeding from the deep realization that economic freedom cannot be sacrificed if political freedom is to be preserved. True Liberalism seeks all legitimate freedom first in the confident belief that without such freedom the pursuit of other blessings is in vain.

The nation seeks for solution of its many difficulties. These solutions can come alone through the constructive forces from the system built upon Liberty. They cannot be achieved by the destructive forces of Regimentation. The purification of Liberty from abuses, the restoration of confidence in the rights of men, the release of the dynamic forces of initiative and enterprise are alone the methods by which these solutions can be found and the purpose of American life assured.

Source: *The Challenge to Liberty.* By Herbert Hoover, 189–205. New York: Charles Scribner's Sons, 1934.

Herbert Hoover (1874–1964) was the thirty-first president of the United States. He had previously been a mining engineer.

Manifesto of the Communist Party of the United States

The crisis of the capitalist system is becoming more and more a catastrophe for the workers and toiling masses. Growing millions of the exploited population are faced with increased difficulties in finding the barest means of livelihood. Unemployment relief is being drastically cut and in many cases abolished altogether. Real wages are being reduced further every month, and labor is being speeded up to an inhuman degree.

The vast majority of the poor farmers are slowly but surely being squeezed off the land and thrown on the "free" labor market to compete with the workers. The oppressed Negro people are loaded down with the heaviest economic burdens, especially of unemployment, denied even the crumbs of relief given to the starving white masses, and further subjected to bestial lynch law and Jim-Crowism. Women workers and housewives are especially sufferers from the crisis, and from the fascist movements to drive them out of industry. Millions of young workers are thrown upon the streets by the closing of schools and simultaneously are denied any chance to earn their living in the industries.

What the New Deal Has Given Workers

The suffering masses have been told to look to Washington for their salvation. Mr. Roosevelt and his New Deal have been decked out with the rainbow promises of returning prosperity. But the bitter truth is rapidly being learned that Roosevelt and his New Deal represent the Wall Street bankers and big corporations—finance capital—just the same as Hoover before him, but carrying out even fiercer attacks against the living standards of the masses of the people. Under Roosevelt and the New Deal policies, the public treasury has been turned into a huge trough where the big capitalists eat their fill. Over ten billion dollars have been handed out to the banks and corporations, billions have been squeezed out of the workers and farmers by inflation and by all sorts of new taxes upon the masses. Under the Roosevelt regime, the main burden of taxation has been shifted away from the big capitalists onto the impoverished masses. . . .

The policies of the government in Washington have one purpose, to make the workers and farmers and middle classes pay the costs of the crisis, to preserve the profits of the big capitalists at all costs, to establish fascism at home and to wage imperialist war abroad. . . .

What a Workers' Government Would Do

The first acts of . . . a revolutionary workers' government would be to open up the warehouses and distribute among all the working people the enormous unused surplus stores of food and clothing.

It would open up the tremendous accumulation of unused buildings—now withheld for private profit—for the benefit of tens of millions who now wander homeless in the streets or crouch in cellars or slums.

Such a government would immediately provide an endless flow of commodities to replace the stores thus used up by opening all the factories, mills and mines, and giving every person a job at constantly increasing wages.

All former claims to ownership of the means of production, including stocks, bonds, etc., would be relegated to the museum, with special provisions to protect small savings. No public funds would be paid out to anyone except for services rendered to the community.

Unemployment and social insurance would immediately be provided for all, to cover all loss of work due to cause outside the control of the workers, whether by closing of factories, by sickness, old age, maternity, or otherwise, at full wages without special costs to the workers.

Such a government would immediately begin to reorganize the present anarchic system of production along socialist lines. It would eliminate the untold waste of capitalism; it would bring to full use the tremendous achievements of science, which have been pushed aside by the capitalist rulers from consideration of private profit. Such a socialist reorganization of industry would almost immediately double the existing productive forces of the country. Such a revolutionary government would secure to the farmers the possession of their land and provide them with the necessary means for a comfortable living; it would make it possible for the farming population to unite their forces in a co-operative socialist agriculture, and thus bring to the farming population all the advantages of modern civilization, and would multiply manifold the productive capacities of American agriculture. It would proceed at once to the complete liberation of the Negro people from all oppression, secure the right of self-determination of the Black Belt, and would secure unconditional economic, political and social equality.

With the establishment of a socialist system in America, there will be such a flood of wealth available for the country as can hardly be imagined. Productive labor, instead of being a burden, will become a desirable privilege for every citizen of the new society. The wealth of such a society will immediately become so great that, without any special burdens, tremendous surpluses will be available for use as free gifts to the economically backward nations, in the first place, to those which have suffered from the imperialist exploitation of American capitalism—Cuba, Latin American, the Philippines, China—to enable these peoples also to build a socialist society in the shortest possible time.

Source: What Is Communism? By Earl Browder. New York: Vanguard Press, 1936.

African Americans

Ralph J. Bunche (1904–71), an African-American diplomat who was awarded the Nobel Peace Prize, here presents an argument encouraging African Americans to organize themselves to be more involved in the political process.

Ralph J. Bunche
Tactics and Programs of Minority Groups

J. S. Mill in his fine treatise on *Representative Government* expressed the belief that it is virtually impossible to build up a democracy out of the intermingling of racially differentiated groups of men. It may be that historical experience has indicated the error of Mill's thesis insofar as different "racial" groups among the white peoples of the world are concerned, but there is apparently much evidence to substantiate it when related to the intermixture of white and black populations in the same society. Throughout the world today, wherever whites and blacks are present in any significant numbers in the same community, democracy becomes the tool of the dominant elements in the white population in their ruthless determination to keep the blacks suppressed. This is true, whether the blacks constitute the overwhelming majority of the population, as in South Africa and Algeria, or the minority, as in the United States.

The responsibility, however, rests not with the institution of democracy, *per se,* nor in the readily accepted belief that black and white simply cannot mix amicably on a common political and economic basis. Recent world history points out too clearly that modern democracy, conceived in the womb of middle-class revolutions, was early put to work in support of those ruling middle-class interests of capitalistic society which fathered it. It has remained their loyal child and has rendered profitable service for them. But when in modern European countries it came to be vigorously wooed by those mass interests of society whose lot under modern industrialism has been that of cruel oppression, democracy was quickly discredited and disowned, and fascism became the favored child of Big-Business-controlled governments. The significant fact is that democracy, while never offered in any large measure to the black populations of the world, has been extended to the great masses of the working-class population only so long as it was employed by them as a harmless device involving no real threat to the increasing control of the society by the ruling classes.

Minority populations, and particularly racial minorities, striving to exist in any theoretically democratic modern society, are compelled to struggle strenuously for even a moderate participation in the democratic game. Minority groups are always with us. They may be national minorities, *i.e.,* distinct ethnic groups with an individual national and cultural character living within a state which is dominated by some other nationality, as in German and Polish Upper Silesia; or they may come under the looser definition of minorities employed by the League of Nations, including any people in any state differing from the majority population in either race, language or religion, such as the Negro in the United States. But whatever the nature of the minority group, its special problems may always be translated in terms of political, economic, and social disadvantages. Group antagonisms develop, which are fed by mythical beliefs and attitudes of scorn, derision, hate and discrimination. These serve as effective social barriers and fix the social, and hence, the political and economic status of the minority population. The mental images or verbal characterizations generally accepted as descriptive of the members of the particular racial group . . . give rise to stereotypes which are of the greatest significance in race relations. These race distinctions, along with similar class and caste distinctions, are so thoroughly rooted in our social consciousness as to command serious attention in any consideration of programs whose objective is equitable treatment for minority racial groups.

Many are the non-scientific solutions for the problem of black-white race relations that have been offered. Racial equality and tolerance have been pled for far and wide. But these solutions ignore the seemingly basic fact that whenever two groups of peoples in daily contact with each other, and having readily identifiable cultural or racial differentiations, are likewise forced into economic competition, group antagonisms must inevitably prevail.

The Negro As a Minority Group in the U.S.

The Negro group in the United States is characterized by the conditions of easy racial identification and severe economic competition with the dominant white population. In addition, the position of the Negro in this country is conditioned by the historical fact of his ancestral slavery. All of the present-day relations between the disadvantaged Negro group and the majority white group are influenced by this master-slave heritage, and the traditional competition between poor-white and Negro masses. The stamp of racial and social inferiority placed upon the Negro, the detached, condescending paternalism of the "better elements" of the Southern white population, the "missionary" enterprise of Northern philanthropy, the bitter antipathies between black and white laboring masses, "Uncle Tomism" in both its cruder and more polished modern forms, and the inferiority complex of the Negro group itself, may be directly traced to these historical roots.

The factors of race and the slavery tradition do not fully explain the perpetuation of the "race problem," however. Much of what is called prejudice against the Negro can be explained in economic terms, and in the peculiar culture of the Southern states, with their large "poor-white" populations. The determination of the ruling class of large land-holders in the South to perpetuate in law and custom the doctrine of the racial inferiority of the Negro was made possible only because this numerically preponderant poor-white population feared the economic competition and the social and political power of the large black population. The cultural, political and economic degradation of the Negro also gave the poor-whites their sole chance for "status." . . .

In reality the Negro population in the United States is a minority group only in the narrowly racial sense. In every other respect it is subject to the same divisive influences impinging upon the life of every other group in the nation. Economically, the Negro, in the vast majority, is identified with the peasant and proletarian classes of the country, which are certainly not in the minority. Politically, the Negro, until recent years under the spell of the "Lincolnian Legend," was almost completely identified with the Republican Party. He was aligned, therefore, with what constituted with monotonous regularity the majority political group. The Negro thus has been subjected to the same sectional, political and economic forces which have influenced the white population, with admitted additional aggravation due solely to the race equation.

Negro leadership, however, has traditionally put its stress on the element of race; it has attributed the plight of the Negro to a peculiar racial condition. Leaders and organizations alike have had but one end in view—the elimination of "discrimination against the race." This attitude has been reflected in the tactics which they have employed to correct abuses suffered by their group. They have not realized that so long as this basic conflict in the economic interests of the white and black groups persists, and it is a perfectly natural phenomenon in a modern industrial society, neither prayer, nor logic, nor emotional or legal appeal can make much headway against the stereotyped racial attitudes and beliefs of the masses of the dominant population. The significance of this to the programs of the corrective and reform organizations working on behalf of the group should be obvious. The most that such organizations can hope to do is to devote themselves to the correction of the more flagrant specific cases of abuse, which because of their extreme nature may exceed even a prejudiced popular approval; and to a campaign of public enlightenment concerning the merits of the group they represent and the necessity for the establishment of a general community of interest among all groups in the population.

Source: "A Critical Analysis of the Tactics and Programs of Minority Groups." By Ralph Bunche. *Journal of Negro Education* 4, no. 3 (July 1935).

Ralph J. Bunche (1904–71) was an African-American diplomat. He was awarded the Nobel Peace Prize in 1950 for his work as a United Nations mediator in Palestine.

The Postwar Years,
1945–1965

✵ ✵ ✵

The end of World War II brought with it a new set of problems as well as the revival of old issues and conflicts, particularly the concerns of African Americans and women. These concerns revived in a period where right and left were deeply divided. Parts of the period were dominated by a virulent anti-Communism that deeply shook the nation and continued in somewhat diminished form until the recent changes in Eastern Europe, and still exists for some groups. At the same time, this was the period that presaged a significant liberal advance. Thus, a period known for its apathy was also a period in which the seeds were sown for the turmoil of the period we call the Sixties.

With regard to political rights, the Supreme Court ruled in *Baker* v. *Carr* (569 U.S. 186 [1962]) that the Fourteenth Amendment demands substantially equal legislative representation for all citizens. In criminal justice, the Supreme Court ruled in *Gideon* v. *Wainright* (372 U.S. 335 [1963]) that poverty should not be a bar to the right of counsel. In these and other cases, the Supreme Court ruled that the Fourteenth Amendment required the states to grant the rights guaranteed in the Bill of Rights and spelled out the content of some of those rights.

Desegregation and the Civil Rights Movement

A major source of the changes in civil rights was the willingness of the Supreme Court, beginning in 1954, to apply the Fourteenth Amendment to individual rights. *Brown* v. *Board of Education of Topeka* (347 U.S. 483 [1954]) overturned the long-standing doctrine of *Plessy* v. *Ferguson* (163 U.S. 537 [1896]) that "separate but equal" facilities were allowable, arguing that separate was inherently unequal.

This decision provided the impetus for the Civil Rights Movement. The selections that follow include a Southern rejection of *Brown*, one of the most important speeches of Martin Luther King, Jr. (1929–68), a speech by Malcolm X (1925–1965) — both of whom were assassinated — and a policy statement from the Congress on Racial Equality (CORE).

Brown et al. v. Board of Education of Topeka et al.

Decided May 17, 1954

Mr. Chief Justice WARREN delivered the opinion of the Court.

The plaintiffs contend that segregated public schools are not "equal" and cannot be made "equal," and that hence they are deprived of the equal protection of the laws.

In the first cases in this Court construing the Fourteenth Amendment, decided shortly after its adoption, the Court interpreted it as proscribing all state-imposed discriminations against the Negro race. The doctrine of "separate but equal" did not make its appearance in this Court until 1896 in the case of Plessy v. Ferguson (163 U.S. 537) involving not education but transportation. American courts have since labored with the doctrine for over half a century. In this Court, there have been six cases involving the "separate but equal" doctrine in the field of public education. In Cumming v. Board of Education of Richmond County, 175 U.S. 528, 20 S.Ct. 197, 44 L.Ed. 262, and Gong Lum v. Rice, 275 U.S. 78, 48 S.Ct. 91, 72 L.Ed. 172, the validity of the doctrine itself was not challenged. In more recent cases, all on the graduate school level, inequality was found in that specific benefits enjoyed by white students were denied to Negro students of the same educational qualifications. State of Missouri ex rel. Gaines v. Canada, 305 U.S. 337, 59 S.Ct. 232, 83 L.Ed. 208; Sipuel v. Board of Regents of University of Oklahoma, 332 U.S. 631, 68 S.Ct. 299, 92 L.Ed. 247; Sweatt v. Painter, 339 U.S. 629, 70 S.Ct. 848, 94 L.Ed. 1114; McLaurin v. Oklahoma State Regents, 339 U.S. 637, 70 S.Ct. 851, 94 L.Ed. 1149. In none of these cases was it necessary to re-examine the doctrine to grant relief to the Negro plaintiff. And in Sweatt v. Painter, supra, the Court expressly reserved decision on the question whether Plessy v. Ferguson should be held inapplicable to public education.

In the instant cases, that question is directly presented. Here, unlike Sweatt v. Painter, there are findings below that the Negro and white schools involved have been equalized, or are being equalized, with respect to buildings, curricula, qualifications and salaries of teachers, and other "tangible" factors. Our decision, therefore, cannot turn on merely a comparison of these tangible factors in the Negro and white schools involved in each of the cases. We must look instead to the effect of segregation itself on public education.

[1] In approaching this problem, we cannot turn the clock back to 1868 when the Amendment was adopted, or even to 1896 when Plessy v. Ferguson was written. We must consider public education in the light of its full development and its present place in American life throughout the Nation. Only in this way can it be determined if segregation in public schools deprives these plaintiffs of the equal protection of the laws.

[2] Today, education is perhaps the most important function of state and local governments. Compulsory school attendance laws and the great expenditures for education both demonstrate our recognition of the importance of education to our democratic society. It is required in the performance of our most basic public responsibilities, even service in the armed forces. It is the very foundation of good citizenship. Today it is a principal instrument in awakening the child to cultural values, in preparing him for later professional training, and in helping him to adjust normally to his environment. In these days, it is doubtful that any child may reasonably be expected to succeed in life if he is denied the opportunity of an education. Such an opportunity, where the state has undertaken to provide it, is a right which must be made available to all on equal terms.

[3] We come then to the question presented: Does segregation of children in public schools solely on the basis of race, even though the physical facilities and other "tangible" factors may be equal, deprive the children of the minority group of equal educational opportunities? We believe that it does.

In Sweatt v. Painter, supra [339 U.S. 629, 70 S.Ct. 850], in finding that a segregated law school for Negroes could not provide them equal educational opportunities, this Court relied in large part on "those qualities which are incapable of objective measurement but which make for greatness in a law school." In McLaurin v. Oklahoma State Regents, supra [339 U.S. 637, 70 S.Ct. 853], the Court, in requiring that a Negro admitted to a white graduate school be treated like all other students, again resorted to intangible considerations: ". . . his ability to study, to engage in discussions and exchange views with other students, and, in general, to learn his profession." Such considerations apply with added force to children in grade and high schools. To separate them from others of similar age and qualifications solely because of their race generates a feeling of inferiority as to their status in the community that may affect their hearts and minds in a way unlikely ever to be undone. The effect of this separation on their educational opportunities was well stated by a finding in the Kansas case by a court which nevertheless felt compelled to rule against the Negro plaintiffs:

> "Segregation of white and colored children in public schools has a detrimental effect upon the colored children. The impact is greater when it has the sanction of the law; for the policy of separating the races is usually interpreted as denoting the inferiority of the negro group. A sense of inferiority

affects the motivation of a child to learn. Segregation with the sanction of law, therefore, has a tendency to [retard] the educational and mental development of Negro children and to deprive them of some of the benefits they would receive in a racial[ly] integrated school system."

Whatever may have been the extent of psychological knowledge at the time of Plessy v. Ferguson, this finding is amply supported by modern authority. Any language in Plessy v. Ferguson contrary to this finding is rejected.

[4] We conclude that in the field of public education the doctrine of "separate but equal" has no place. Separate educational facilities are inherently unequal. Therefore, we hold that the plaintiffs and others similarly situated for whom the actions have been brought are, by reason of the segregation complained of, deprived of the equal protection of the laws guaranteed by the Fourteenth Amendment.

Source: 347 U.S. 483.

The Southern Manifesto
Declaration of Constitutional Principles

The unwarranted decision of the Supreme Court in the public school cases is now bearing the fruit always produced when men substitute naked power for established law.

The Founding fathers gave us a Constitution of checks and balances because they realized the inescapable lesson of history that no man or group of men can be safely entrusted with unlimited power. They framed this Constitution with its provisions for change by amendment in order to secure the fundamentals of government against the dangers of temporary popular passion or the personal predilections of public officeholders.

We regard the decision of the Supreme Court in the school cases as a clear abuse of judicial power. It climaxes a trend in the Federal judiciary undertaking to legislate, in derogation of the authority of Congress, and to encroach upon the reserved rights of the States and the people.

The original Constitution does not mention education. Neither does the 14th amendment nor any other amendment. The debates preceding the submission of the 14th amendment clearly show that there was no intent that it should affect the systems of education maintained by the States.

The very Congress which proposed the amendment subsequently provided for segregated schools in the District of Columbia.

When the amendment was adopted, in 1868, there were 37 States of the Union. Every one of the 26 States that had any substantial racial differences among its people either approved the operation of segregated schools already in existence or subsequently established such schools by action of the same lawmaking body which considered the 14th amendment.

As admitted by the Supreme Court in the public school case *(Brown v. Board of Education)*, the doctrine of separate but equal schools "apparently originated in *Roberts* v. *City of Boston* (1849), upholding school segregation against attack as being violative of a State constitutional guarantee of equality." This constitutional doctrine began in the North—not in the South, and it was followed not only in Massachusetts, but in Connecticut, New York, Illinois, Indiana, Michigan, Minnesota, New Jersey, Ohio, Pennsylvania, and other northern States until they, exercising their rights as States through the constitutional process of local self-government, changed their school systems.

In the case of *Plessy* v. *Ferguson,* in 1896, the Supreme Court expressly declared that under the 14th amendment no person was denied any of his rights if the States provided separate but equal public facilities. This decision has been followed in many other cases. It is notable that the Supreme Court, speaking through Chief Justice Taft, a former President of the United States, unanimously declared, in 1927, in *Lum* v. *Rice,* that the "separate but equal" principle is "within the discretion of the State in regulating its public schools and does not conflict with the 14th amendment."

This interpretation, restated time and again, became a part of the life of the people of many of the States and confirmed their habits, customs, traditions, and way of life. It is founded on elemental humanity and commonsense, for parents should not be deprived by Government of the right to direct the lives of and education of their own children.

Though there has been no constitutional amendment or act of Congress changing this established legal principle almost a century old, the Supreme Court of the United States, with no legal basis for such action, undertook to exercise their naked judicial power and substituted their personal political and social ideas for the established law of the land.

This unwarranted exercise of power by the Court, contrary to the Constitution, is creating chaos and confusion in the States principally affected. It is destroying the amicable relations between the white and Negro races that have been created through 90 years of patient effort by the good people of both races. It has planted hatred and suspicion where there has been heretofore friendship and understanding.

Without regard to the consent of the governed, outside agitators are threatening immediate and revolutionary changes in our public-school systems. If done, this is certain to destroy the system of public education in some of the States.

With the gravest concern for the explosive and dangerous condition created by this decision and inflamed by outside meddlers:

We reaffirm our reliance on the Constitution as the fundamental law of the land.

We decry the Supreme Court's encroachments on rights reserved to the States and to the people, contrary to established law and to the Constitution.

We commend the motives of those States which have declared the intention to resist forced integration by any lawful means.

We appeal to the States and people who are not directly affected by these decisions to consider the constitutional principles involved against the time when they, too, on issues vital to them, may be the victims of judicial encroachment.

Even though we constitute a minority in the present Congress, we have full faith that a majority of the American people believe in the dual system of Government which has enabled us to achieve our greatness and will in time demand that the reserved rights of the State and of the people be made secure against judicial usurpation.

We pledge ourselves to use all lawful means to bring about a reversal of this decision which is contrary to the Constitution and to prevent the use of force in its implementation. In this trying period, as we all seek to right this wrong, we appeal to our people not to be provoked by the agitators and troublemakers invading our States and to scrupulously refrain from disorders and lawless acts.

Source: Congressional Record, 84th Congress, 2nd session (1956): 4515–16.

Martin Luther King, Jr.
I Have a Dream

Five score years ago, a great American, in whose symbolic shadow we stand, signed the Emancipation Proclamation. This momentous decree came as a great beacon light of hope to millions of Negro slaves who had been seared in the flames of withering injustice. It came as a joyous daybreak to end the long night of captivity.

But one hundred years later, we must face the tragic fact that the Negro is still not free. One hundred years later, the life of the Negro is still sadly crippled by the manacles of segregation and the chains of discrimination. One hundred years later, the Negro lives on a lonely island of poverty in the midst of a vast ocean of material prosperity. One hundred years later the Negro is still languished in the corners of American society and finds himself an exile in his own land. So we have come here today to dramatize an appalling condition.

In a sense we have come to our nation's Capital to cash a check. When the architects of our republic wrote the magnificent words of the Constitution and the

Declaration Independence, they were signing a promissory note to which every American was to fall heir. This note was a promise that all men would be guaranteed the unalienable rights of life, liberty, and the pursuit of happiness.

It is obvious today that America has defaulted on this promissory note insofar as her citizens of color are concerned. Instead of honoring this sacred obligation, America has given the Negro people a bad check; a check which has come back marked "insufficient funds." But we refuse to believe that the bank of justice is bankrupt. We refuse to believe that there are insufficient funds in the great vaults of opportunity of this nation. So we have come to cash this check—a check that will give us upon demand the riches of freedom and the security of justice. We have also come to this hallowed spot to remind America of the fierce urgency of *now*. This is no time to engage in the luxury of cooling off or to take the tranquilizing drug of gradualism. *Now* is the time to make real the promises of Democracy. *Now* is the time to rise form the dark and desolate valley of segregation to the sunlit path of racial justice. *Now* is the time to open the doors of opportunity to all of God's children. *Now* is the time to lift our nation from the quicksands of racial injustice to the solid rock of brotherhood.

It would be fatal for the nation to overlook the urgency of the moment and to underestimate the determination of the Negro. This sweltering summer of the Negro's legitimate discontent will not pass until there is an invigorating autumn of freedom and equality. 1963 is not an end, but a beginning. Those who hope that the Negro needed to blow off steam and will now be content will have a rude awakening if the Nation returns to business as usual. There will be neither rest nor tranquility in America until the Negro is granted his citizenship rights. The whirlwinds of revolt will continue to shake the foundations of our Nation until the bright day of justice emerges.

But there is something that I must say to my people who stand on the warm threshold which leads into the palace of justice. In the process of gaining our rightful place we must not be guilty of wrongful deeds. Let us not seek to satisfy our thirst for freedom by drinking from the cup of bitterness and hatred. We must forever conduct our struggle on the high plane of dignity and discipline. We must not allow our creative protest to degenerate into physical violence. Again and again we must rise to the majestic heights of meeting physical force with soul force. The marvelous new militancy which has engulfed the Negro community must not lead us to a distrust of all white people, for many of our white brothers, as evidenced by their presence here today, have come to realize that their destiny is tied up with our destiny and their freedom is inextricably bound to our freedom. We cannot walk alone.

And as we walk, we must make the pledge that we shall march ahead. We cannot turn back. There are those who are asking the devotees of civil rights, "When will you be satisfied?" We can never be satisfied as long as the Negro is the victim of the unspeakable horrors of police brutality. We can never be satisfied as long as our bodies, heavy with the fatigue of travel, cannot gain lodging in the motels of the highways and the hotels of the cities. We cannot be satisfied as long as the Negro's basic mobility is from a smaller ghetto to a larger one. We can never be satisfied as long as a Negro in Mississippi cannot vote and a Negro in New York believes he has nothing for which to vote. No, no we are not satisfied, and we will not be satisfied until justice rolls down like waters and righteousness like a mighty stream.

I am not unmindful that some of you have come here out of great trials and tribulations. Some of you have come fresh from narrow jail cells. Some of you have come from areas where your quest for freedom left you battered by the storms of persecution and staggered by the winds of police brutality. You have been the veterans of creative suffering. Continue to work with the faith that unearned suffering is redemptive.

Go back to Mississippi, go back to Alabama, go back to South Carolina, go back to Georgia, go back to Louisiana, go back to the slums and ghettos of our modern cities, knowing that somehow this situation can and will be changed. Let us not wallow in the valley of despair.

I say to you today, my friends, that in spite of the difficulties and frustrations of the moment I still have a dream. It is a dream deeply rooted in the American dream.

I have a dream that one day this nation will rise up and live out the true meaning of its creed: "We hold these truths to be self-evident; that all men are created equal."

I have a dream that one day on the red hills of Georgia the sons of former slaves and the sons of former slaveowners will be able to sit down together at the table of brotherhood.

I have a dream that one day even the state of Mississippi, a desert state sweltering with the heat of injustice and oppression, will be transformed into an oasis of freedom and justice.

I have a dream that my four little children will one day live in a nation where they will not be judged by the color of their skin but by the content of their character.

I have a dream today.

I have a dream that one day the state of Alabama, whose governor's lips are presently dripping with the words of interposition and nullification, will be transformed into a situation where little black boys and black girls will be able to join hands with little white boys and white girls and walk together as sisters and brothers.

I have a dream today.

I have a dream that one day every valley shall be exalted, every hill and mountain shall be made low, the rough places will be made plains, and the crooked places will be made straight, and the glory of the Lord shall be revealed, and all flesh shall see it together.

This is our hope. This is the faith with which I return to the South. With this faith we will be able to hew out of the mountain of despair a stone of hope. With this faith we will be able to transform the jangling discords of our nation into a beautiful symphony of brotherhood. With this faith we will be able to work together, to pray together, to struggle together, to go to jail together, to stand up for freedom together, knowing that we will be free one day.

This will be the day when all of God's children will be able to sing with new meaning "My country 'tis of thee, sweet land of liberty, of thee I sing. Land where my fathers died, land of the pilgrim's pride, from every mountainside, let freedom ring."

And if America is to be a great nation this must become true. So let freedom ring from the prodigious hilltops of New Hampshire. Let freedom ring form the mighty mountains of New York. Let freedom ring from the heightening Alleghenies of Pennsylvania!

Let freedom ring from the snowcapped Rockies of Colorado!

Let freedom ring from the curvacious peaks of California!

But not only that; let freedom ring from Stone Mountain of Georgia!

Let freedom ring from Lookout Mountain of Tennessee!

Let freedom ring from every hill and mole hill of Mississippi. From every mountainside, let freedom ring.

When we let freedom ring, when we let it ring from every village and every hamlet, from every state and every city, we will be able to speed up that day when all of God's children, black men and white men, Jews and Gentiles, Protestants and Catholics, will be able to join hands and sing in the words of the old Negro spiritual, "Free at last! free at last! thank God almighty, we are free at last!"

Source: "Address at the March on Washington, 1963." By Martin Luther King, Jr. *Southern Christian Leadership Conference Newsletter* 1, no. 12 (September 1963): 5, 8.

Martin Luther King, Jr. (1929–68), was a U.S. civil rights leader until his assassination. He was awarded the Noble Peace Prize in 1964.

Malcolm X
The Ballot or the Bullet

Mr. Moderator, Brother Lomax, brothers and sisters, friends and enemies: I just can't believe everyone in here is a friend and I don't want to leave anybody out. The question tonight, as I understand it, is "The Negro Revolt, and Where Do We Go From Here?" or "What Next?" In my little humble way of understanding it, it points toward either the ballot or the bullet.

Although I'm still a Muslim, I'm not here tonight to discuss my religion. I'm not here to try and change your religion. I'm not here to argue or discuss anything that we differ about, because it's time for us to submerge our differences and realize that it is best for us to first see that we have the same problem, a common problem—a problem that will make you catch hell whether you're a Baptist, or a Methodist, or a Muslim, or a nationalist. Whether you're educated or illiterate, whether you live on the boulevard or in the alley, you're going to catch hell just like I am. We're all in the same boat and we all are going to catch the same hell from the same man. He just happens to be a white man. All of us have suffered here, in this country, political oppression at the hands of the white man, economic exploitation at the hands of the white man, and social degradation at the hands of the white man.

Now in speaking like this, it doesn't mean that we're anti-white, but it does mean we're anti-exploitation, we're anti-degradation, we're anti-oppression. And if the white man doesn't want us to be anti-him, let him stop oppressing and exploiting and degrading us. Whether we are Christians or Muslims or nationalists or agnostics or atheists, we must first learn to forget our differences. If we have differences, let us differ in the closet; when we come out in front, let us not have anything to argue about until we get finished arguing with the man. . . .

If we don't do something real soon, I think you'll have to agree that we're going to be forced either to use the ballot or the bullet. It's one or the other in 1964. It isn't that time is running out—time has run out! 1964 threatens to be the most explosive year America has ever witnessed. The most explosive year. Why? It's also a political year. It's the year when all of the white politicians will be back in the so-called Negro community jiving you and me for some votes. The year when all of the white political crooks will be right back in your and my community with their false promises, building up our hopes for a letdown, with their trickery and their treachery, with their dissatisfactions, it can only lead to one thing, an explosion; and now we have the type of black man on the scene in America today . . . who just doesn't intend to turn the other cheek any longer.

Don't let anybody tell you anything about the odds are against you. If they draft you, they send you to Korea and make you face 800 million Chinese. If you can be brave over there, you can be brave right here. These odds aren't as great as those odds. And if you fight here, you will at least know what you're fighting for.

I'm not a politician, not even student of politics; in fact, I'm not a student of much of anything. I'm not a Democrat, I'm not a Republican, and I don't even consider myself an American. If you and I were Americans, there'd be no problem. Those Hunkies that just got off the boat, they're already Americans; Polacks are already Americans; the Italian refugees are already Americans. Everything that came out of Europe, every blue-eyed thing, is already an American. And as long as you and I have been over here, we aren't Americans yet.

Well, I am one who doesn't believe in deluding myself. I'm not going to sit at your table and watch you eat, with nothing on my plate, and call myself a diner. Sitting at the table doesn't make you a diner, unless you eat some of what's on that plate. Being here in America doesn't make you an American. Being born here in America doesn't make you an American. Why, if birth made you American, you wouldn't need any legislation, you wouldn't need any amendments to the Constitution, you wouldn't be faced with civil-rights filibustering in Washington, D.C., right now. They don't have to pass civil-rights legislation to make a Polack an American.

No, I'm not an American. I'm one of the 22 million black people who are the victims of Americanism. One of the 22 million black people who are the victims of democracy, nothing but disguised hypocrisy. So, I'm not standing here speaking to you as an American, or a patriot, or a flag-saluter, or a flag-waver — no, not I. I'm speaking as a victim of this American system. And I see America through the eyes of the victim. I don't see any American dream; I see an American nightmare.

The political philosophy of black nationalism means that the black man should control the politics and the politicians in his own community; no more. The black man in the black community has to be re-educated into the science of politics so he will know what politics is supposed to bring him in return. Don't be throwing out any ballots. A ballot is like a bullet. You don't throw your ballots until you see a target, and if that target is not within your reach, keep your ballot in your pocket. The political philosophy of black nationalism is being taught in the Christian church. It's being taught in the NAACP. It's being taught in CORE meetings. It's being taught in SNCC [Student Nonviolent Coordinating Committee] meetings. It's being taught in Muslim meetings. It's being taught where nothing but atheists and agnostics come together. It's being taught everywhere. Black people are fed up with the dillydallying, pussyfooting, compromising approach that we've been using toward getting our freedom. We want freedom *now*, but we're not going to get it saying "We Shall Overcome." We've got to fight until we overcome.

The economic philosophy of black nationalism is pure and simple. It only means that we should control the economy of our community. Why should white people be running all the stores in our community? Why should white people be running the banks of our community? Why should the economy of our community be in the hands of the white man? Why? If a black man can't move his store into a white community, you tell me why a white man should move his store into a black community. The philosophy of black nationalism involves a re-education program in the black community in regards to economics. Our people have to be made to see that any time you take your dollar out of your community and spend it in a community where you don't live, the community where you live will get poorer and poorer, and the community where you spend your money will get richer and richer. Then you wonder why where you live is always a ghetto or a slum area. And where you and I are concerned, not only do we lose it when we spend it out of the community, but the white man has got all our stores in the community tied up; so that though we spend it in the community, at sundown the man who runs the store takes it over across town somewhere. He's got us in a vise.

So the economic philosophy of black nationalism means in every church, in every civic organization, in every fraternal order, it's time now for our people to become conscious of the importance of controlling the economy of our community. If we own the stores, if we operate the businesses, if we try and establish some industry in our own community, then we're developing to the position where we are creating employment for our own kind. Once you gain control of the economy of your own community, then you don't have to picket and boycott and beg some cracker downtown for a job in his business.

The social philosophy of black nationalism only means that we have to get together and remove the evils, the vices, alcoholism, drug addiction, and other evils that are destroying the moral fiber of our community. We ourselves have to lift the level of our community, the standard of our community to a higher level, make our own society beautiful so that we will be satisfied in our own social circles and won't be running around here trying to knock our way into a social circle where we're not wanted.

Source: Malcolm X Speaks. New York: Merit Publishers, 1965.

Malcolm X (1925–65), born Malcolm Little, was an early follower of the Black Muslims who became a leader within the movement. He later established a variant movement that began to move away from the extreme anti-white position of the Black Muslims and adopted the Islamic faith that Malcolm X had found in the Middle East. He was assassinated by members of the Black Muslims.

CORE: "An Alternate to Bitterness and Mere Sentiment"

CORE sees discrimination as a problem for all Americans. Not just Negroes suffer from it and not just Negroes will profit when it is eliminated. Furthermore, Negroes alone cannot eliminate it. Equality cannot be seized any more than it can be given. It must be a shared experience.

CORE is an inter-racial group. Membership involves no religious affiliation. It is open to anybody who opposes racial discrimination, who wants to fight it and who will adhere to CORE's rules. The only people not welcome in CORE are "those Americans whose loyalty is primarily to a foreign power and those whose tactics and beliefs are contrary to democracy and human values." CORE has only one enemy: discrimination, and only one function: to fight that enemy.

A great deal has been achieved for civil rights through the courts, and legal action has an important place in the civil rights movements. But legal action is necessarily limited to lawyers. CORE's techniques enable large numbers of ordinary people to participate in campaigns to end discrimination.

Direct action has a value that goes beyond its visible accomplishments. To those who are the target of discrimination, it provides an alternative to bitterness or resignation and, to others, an alternative to mere expressions of sentiment. In the past, Negroes often found themselves in positions of disadvantage which they had no power to escape from or even to oppose. This inability to challenge second-class citizenship, with all of its humiliations, tended to undermine self-respect. CORE's methods now provide a meaningful and socially useful outlet.

Source: All about CORE. [New York:] Congress of Racial Equality, 1963.

Amendments

Three significant amendments to the Constitution were passed between 1951 and 1964. The Twenty-second Amendment limited the president to two terms, a limit that had been the custom from the time of George Washington until World War II, when Franklin Delano Roosevelt was elected to a third and fourth term.

The Twenty-third Amendment allows the District of Columbia to participate in the election of the president and vice president. The District of Columbia is a creation of Congress, all of its laws have to be approved by Congress, and its representation in Congress is limited to observers. This amendment enfranchised District of Columbia residents in national elections for the first time.

The Twenty-fourth Amendment is the main amendment to be produced by the Civil Rights Movement. This amendment prohibits the practice of poll taxing, which states had been using to keep African Americans from voting.

Amendment XXII

March 1, 1951

Section 1. No person shall be elected to the office of the President more than twice, and no person who has held the office of President, or acted as President, for more than two years of a term to which some other person was elected President shall be elected to the office of the President more than once. But this Article shall not apply to any person holding the office of President when this Article was proposed by the Congress, and shall not prevent any person who may be holding the office of President, or acting as President, during the term within which this Article becomes operative from holding the office of President or acting as President during the remainder of such term.

Section 2. This Article shall be inoperative unless it shall have been ratified as an amendment to the Constitution by the Legislatures of three fourths of the several States within seven years from the date of its submission to the States by the Congress.

Amendment XXIII

May 29, 1961

Section 1. The District constituting the seat of Government of the United States shall appoint in such manner as the Congress may direct:

A number of electors of President and Vice-President equal to the whole number of Senators and Representatives in Congress to which the District would be entitled if it were a State, but in no event more than the least populous State; they shall be in addition to those appointed by the States, but they shall be considered, for the purposes of the election of President and Vice-President, to be electors appointed by a State; and they shall meet in the District and perform such duties as provided by the twelfth article of amendment.

Section 2. The Congress shall have power to enforce this article by appropriate legislation.

Amendment XXIV

January 23, 1964

Section 1. The right of citizens of the United States to vote in any primary or other election for President or Vice-President, for electors for President or Vice-

President, or for Senator or Representative in Congress, shall not be denied or abridged by the United States or any State by reason of failure to pay any poll tax or other tax.

Section 2. The Congress shall have power to enforce this article by appropriate legislation.

The McCarthy Era and Its Aftermath

Senator Joseph McCarthy (1908–57) of Wisconsin started an anti-Communist Red Scare when he announced that he had a list of active Communists in government employment. The list was fake. His campaign reached all areas of American life. Many government employees lost their jobs, as did academics and many workers at all levels of the film industry in Hollywood.

McCarthy overreached himself when he took on the Army and nationally televised hearings showed him at his worst. This was the first significant use of television in shaping political debate in the United States. After the hearings McCarthy was censured by the Senate; he died shortly thereafter.

But McCarthy had precursors going back to the anti-anarchist Red Scare of the 1920s and a long American tradition of opposition to socialism behind him. McCarthy made anti-Communism a central tenet of the radical right that continued until the collapse of Communism and can still be found today.

Developing out of the anti-Communism of the McCarthy era, a number of groups and individuals emerged in the late 1950s and early 1960s to become important actors in American political thought. Some of these groups grew in strength throughout the 1970s and 1980s. The John Birch Society was the closest to McCarthy's approach because it was almost entirely concerned with anti-Communism. It had a conspiracy theory of history that seemed to give the Communists almost supernatural powers. They intended to use the same tactics against the Communists that they believed the Communists were using against the United States.

A more long-lasting influence was Ayn Rand (1905–82) and Objectivism. Rand restated Herbert Spencer (1820–1903) and Social Darwinism in the more palatable form of her novels, particularly *Atlas Shrugged* (1957). Rand was immensely influential on the rising generation of conservatives. Some of her followers became anarcho-capitalists, while others first became activists in the 1964 presidential campaign of Barry Goldwater (1909-) and then supporters of Ronald Reagan (1911-) in his gubernatorial and presidential campaigns and during his eight years in Washington.

The selections here include the major anti-Communist legislation and a statement from the John Birch Society.

The Communist Control Act of 1954

Be it enacted by the Senate and House of Representatives of the United States of America in Congress assembled, that this Act may be cited as the "Communist Control Act of 1954."

FINDINGS OF FACT

Sec. 2. The Congress hereby finds and declares that the Communist Party of the United States, although purportedly a political party, is in fact an instrumentality of a conspiracy to overthrow the Government of the United States. It constitutes an authoritarian dictatorship within a republic, demanding for itself the rights and privileges accorded to political parties, but denying to all others the liberties guaranteed by the Constitution. Unlike political parties, which evolve their policies and programs through public means, by the reconciliation of a wide variety of individual views, and submit those policies and programs to the electorate at large for approval or disapproval, the policies and programs of the Communist Party are secretly prescribed for it by the foreign leaders of the world Communist movement. Its members have no part in determining its goals, and are not permitted to voice dissent to party objectives. Unlike members of political parties, members of the Communist Party are recruited for indoctrination with respect to its objectives and methods, and are organized, instructed, and disciplined to carry into action slavishly the assignments given them by their hierarchical chieftains. Unlike political parties, the Communist Party acknowledges no constitutional or statutory limitations upon its conduct or upon that of its members. The Communist Party is relatively small numerically, and gives scant indication of capacity ever to attain its ends by lawful political means. The peril inherent in its operation arises not from its numbers, but from its failure to acknowledge any limitation as to the nature of its activities, and its dedication to the proposition that the present constitutional Government of the United States ultimately must be brought to ruin by any available means, including resort to force and violence. Holding that doctrine, its role as the agency of a hostile foreign power renders its existence a clear present and continuing danger to the security to the United States. It is the means whereby individuals are seduced into the service of the world Communist movement, trained to do its bidding, and directed and controlled in the conspiratorial performance of their revolutionary services. Therefore, the Communist Party should be outlawed.

PROSCRIBED ORGANIZATIONS

Sec. 3. The Communist Party of the United States, or any successors of such party regardless of the assumed name, whose object or purpose is to overthrow the Government of the United States, or the government of any State, Territory, District, or possession thereof, or the government of any political subdivision therein by force and violence, are not entitled to any of the rights, privileges, and immunities attendant upon legal bodies created under the jurisdiction of the laws of the United States or any political subdivision thereof; and whatever rights, privileges, and immunities which have heretofore been granted to said party or any subsidiary organization by reason of the laws of the United States or any political subdivision thereof, are hereby terminated: *Provided, however,* That nothing in this section shall be construed as amending the Internal Security Act of 1950, as amended.

Sec. 4. Whoever knowingly and willfully becomes or remains a member of (1) the Communist Party, or (2) any other organization having for one of its purposes or objectives the establishment, control, conduct, seizure, or overthrow of the Government of the United States, or the government of any State or political subdivision thereof, by the use of force or violence, with knowledge of the purpose or objective of such organization shall be subject to all the provisions and penalties of the Internal Security Act of 1950, as amended, as a member of a "Communist-action" organization.

(b) For the purposes of this section, the term "Communist Party" means the organization now known as the Communist Party of the United States of America, the Communist Party of any State or subdivision thereof, and any unit or subdivision of any such organization, whether or not any change is hereafter made in the name thereof.

Sec. 5. In determining membership of participation in the Communist Party or any other organization defined in this Act, or knowledge of the purpose or objective of such party or organization, the jury, under instructions from the court, shall consider evidence, if presented, as to whether the accused person:

(1) Has been listed to his knowledge as a member in any book or any of the lists, records, correspondence, or any other document of the organization;

(2) Has made financial contribution to the organization in dues, assessments, loans, or in any other form;

(3) Has made himself subject to the discipline of the organization in any form whatsoever;

(4) Has executed orders, plans, or directives of any kind of the organization;

(5) Has acted as an agent, courier, messenger, correspondent, organizer, or in any capacity in behalf of the organization;

(6) Has conferred with officers or other members of the organization in behalf of any plan or enterprise of the organization;

(7) Has been accepted to his knowledge as an officer or member of the organization or as to be called upon for services by other officers or members of the organization;

(8) Has written, spoken or in any other way communicated by signal, semaphore, sign, or in any other form of communication orders, directives, or plans of the organization;

(9) Has prepared documents, pamphlets, leaflets, books, or any other type of publication in behalf of the objectives and purposes of the organization;

(10) Has mailed, shipped, circulated, distributed, delivered, or in any other way sent or delivered to others material or propaganda of any kind in behalf of the organization;

(11) Has advised, counseled or in any other way imparted information, suggestions, recommendations to officers or members of the organization or to anyone else in behalf of the objectives of the organization;

(12) Has indicated by word, action, conduct, writing or in any other way a willingness to carry out in any manner and to any degree the plans, designs, objectives, or purposes of the organizations;

(13) Has in any other way participated in the activities, planning, actions, objectives, or purposes of the organization;

(14) The enumeration of the above subjects of evidence on membership or participation in the Communist Party or any other organization as above defined, shall not limit the inquiry into and consideration of any other subject of evidence on membership and participation as herein stated.

Source: 68 Stat. 775 (1954).

Beliefs and Principles of the John Birch Society

I

With very few exceptions the members of the John Birch Society are deeply religious people. A member's particular faith is entirely his own affair. Our hope is to make better Catholics, better Protestants, better Jews — or better Moslems — out of those who belong to the society. Our never-ending concern is with morality, integrity, and purpose. Regardless of the differences between us in creed and dogma, we all believe that man is endowed by a Divine Creator with an innate desire and conscious purpose to improve both his world and himself. We believe that the direction which constitutes improvement is clearly visible and identifiable throughout man's known history, and that this God-given upward reach in the heart of man is a composite conscience to which we all must listen.

II

We believe that the Communists seek to drive their slaves and themselves along exactly the opposite and downward direction, to the Satanic debasement of both man and his universe. We believe that communism is as utterly incompatible with all religion as it is contemptuous of all morality and destructive of all freedom. It is intrinsically evil. It must be opposed, therefore, with equal firmness, on religious grounds, moral grounds, and political grounds. We believe that the continued coexistence of communism and a Christian-style civilization on one planet is impossible. The struggle between them must end with one completely triumphant and the other completely destroyed. We intend to do our part, therefore, to halt, weaken, rout, and eventually to bury, the whole international Communist conspiracy.

III

We believe that means are as important as ends in any civilized society. Of all the falsehoods that have been so widely and deliberately circulated about us, none is so viciously untrue as the charge that we are willing to condone foul means for the sake of achieving praiseworthy ends. We think that communism as a way of life, for instance, is completely wrong; but our ultimate quarrel with the Communists is that they insist on imposing that way of life on the rest of us by murder, treason, and cruelty rather than by persuasion. Even if our own use of force ever becomes necessary and morally acceptable because it is in self-defense, we must never lose sight of the legal, traditional, and humanitarian considerations of a compassionate civilization. The Communists recognize no such compulsions, but this very ingredient of amoral brutishness will help to destroy them in the end.

IV

We believe in patriotism. Most of us will gladly concede that a parliament of nations, designed for the purpose of increasing the freedom and ease with which individuals, ideals, and goods might cross national boundaries, would be desirable. And we hope that in some future decade we may help to bring about such a step of progress in man's pursuit of peace, prosperity, and happiness. But we feel that the present United Nations was designed by its founders for the exactly opposite purpose of increasing the rigidity of Government controls over the lives and affairs of individual men. We believe it has become, as it was intended to become, a major instrumentality for the establishment of a one-world Communist tyranny over the population of the whole earth. One of our most immediate objectives, therefore, is to get the United States out of the United Nations, and the United Nations out of the United States. We seek thus to save our own country from the gradual and piecemeal surrender of its sovereignty to this Communist-controlled supergovernment, and to stop giving our support to the steady enslavement of other people through the machinations of this Communist agency.

V

We believe that a constitutional Republic, such as our founding Fathers gave us, is probably the best of all forms of government. We believe that a democracy, which they tried hard to obviate, and into which the liberals have been trying for 50 years to convert our Republic, is one of the worst of all forms of government. We call attention to the fact that up to 1928 the U.S. Army Training Manual still gave our men in uniform the following quite accurate definition, which would have been thoroughly approved by the Constitutional Convention that established our Republic. 'Democracy: A Government of the masses. Authority derived through mass meeting or any form of direct expression results in mobocracy. Attitude toward property is communistic—negating property rights. Attitude towards law is that the will of the majority shall regulate, whether it be based upon deliberation or governed by passion, prejudice, and impulse, without restraint or regard to consequences. Results in demagogism, license, agitation, discontent, anarchy.' It is because all history proves this to be true that we repeat so emphatically : 'This is a Republic, not a democracy; let's keep it that way.'

VI

We are opposed to collectivism as a political and economic system, even when it does not have the police-state features of communism. We are opposed to it no matter whether the collectivism be called socialism or the welfare state or the New Deal or the Fair Deal or the new Frontier, or advanced under some other semantic disguise. And we are opposed to it no matter what may be the framework or form of government under which collectivism is imposed. We believe that increasing the size of government, increasing the centralization of government, and increasing the functions of government all act as brakes on material progress and as destroyers of personal freedom.

VII

We believe that even where the size and functions of government are properly limited, as much of the power and duties of governmental units as possible, as close to the people served by such units as possible. For the tendencies of any government body to waste, expansion, and despotism all increase with the distance of that body from the people governed; the more closely any governing body can be kept under observation by those who pay its bills and provide its delegated authority, the more honestly responsible it will be. And the diffusion of governmental power and functions is one of the greatest safeguards against tyranny man has yet devised. For this reason it is extremely important in our case to keep our township, city, County and State governments from being bribed and coerced into coming under one direct chain of control from Washington.

VIII

We believe that for any people eternal vigilance is the price of liberty far more as against the insidious encroachment of internal tyranny than against the danger of subjugation from the outside or from the prospect of any sharp and decisive revolution. In a republic we must constantly seek to elect and to keep in power a government we can trust, manned by the people we can trust, maintaining a currency we can trust, and working for purposes we can trust (none of which we have today). We think it is even more important for the government to obey the laws than for the people to do so. But for 30 years we have had a steady stream of governments which increasingly have regarded our laws and even our Constitution as mere pieces of paper, which should not be allowed to stand in the way of what they, in their omniscient benevolence, considered to be 'for the greatest good of the greatest number.' (Or in their power-seeking plans pretended so to believe.) We want a restoration of a "government of laws, and not of men" in this country; and if a few impeachments are necessary to bring that about, then we are all for the impeachments.

IX

We believe that in a general way history repeats itself. For any combination of causes, similar to an earlier combination of causes, will lead as a rule to a combination of results somewhat similar to the one produced before. And history is simply a series of causes which produced results, and so on around cycles as clearly discernible as any of the dozens that take place elsewhere in the physical and biological sciences. But we believe that the most important history consists not of the repetitions but of the changes in these recurring links in the series. For the changes mark the extent to which man has either been able to improve himself and his environment, or has allowed both to deteriorate, since the last time around. We think that this true history is largely determined by ambitious individuals (both good and evil) and by small minorities who really know what they want. And in the John Birch Society our sense of gratitude and responsibility (to God and to the noble men of the past), for what we have inherited makes us determined to exert our influence, labor, and sacrifice for changes which we think will constitute improvement.

X

In summary, we are striving, by all honorable means at our disposal and to the limits of our energies and abilities, to bring about less government, more responsibility, and a better world. Because the Communists seek, always and everywhere, to bring about more government, less individual responsibility, and a completely amoral world, we would have to oppose them at every turn, even on the philosophical level. Because they are seeking through a gigantically organized conspiracy to destroy all opposition, we must fight them even more aggressively on the plane of action. But our struggle with the Communists, while the most urgent and important task before us today, is basically only incidental to our more important long-range and constructive purposes. For that very reason we are likely to be more effective against the Communists than if we were merely an ad hoc group seeking to expose and destroy so huge and powerful a gang of criminals. In organization, dedication, and purpose we offer a new form of opposition to the Communists which they have not faced in any other country. We have tried to raise a standard to which the wise and the honest can repair. We welcome all honorable allies in this present unceasing war. And we hope that once they and we and millions like us have won a decisive victory at last, many of these same allies will join us in our long look toward the future.

Source: Congressional Record, 87th Congress, 2nd session, June 12, 1962.

The Beginnings of the Second Wave of Feminism

Feminism began its resurgence during the early 1960s. The movement was fed by the publication in France of *Le Deuxième sexe* (1949) by Simone de Beauvoir (1908–86) and its publication in English as *The Second Sex* (1952), followed by the publication of *The Feminine Mystique* (1963) by Betty Friedan (1921-). Both books look at the way women are socialized to believe themselves inferior to men. The growing understanding of this phenomenon led to the development of the wide-ranging women's movement that now exists. Friedan suggests ways of overcoming this socialization.

Betty Friedan
A New Life Plan for Women

It . . . is time to stop giving lip service to the idea that there are no battles left to be fought for women in America, that women's fights have already been won. It is ridiculous to tell girls to keep quiet when they enter a new field, or an old one, so the men will not notice they are there. In almost every professional field, in business and in the arts and sciences, women are still treated as second-class citizens. It would be a great service to tell girls who plan to work in society to expect this subtle, uncomfortable discrimination—tell them not to be quiet, and hope it will go away, but fight it. A girl should not expect special privileges because of her sex, but neither should she "adjust" to prejudice and discrimination.

She must learn to compete then, not as a woman, but as a human being. Not until a great many women move out of the fringes into the mainstream will society itself provide the arrangements for their new life plan. But every girl who manages to stick it out through law school or medical school, who finishes her M.A. or Ph.D. and goes on to use it, helps others move on. Every woman who fights the remaining barriers to full equality which are masked by the feminine mystique makes it easier for the next woman. . . . Even in politics, women must make their contribution not as "housewives" but as citizens. It is, perhaps, a step in the right direction when a woman protests nuclear testing under the banner of "Women Strike for Peace." But why does the professional illustrator who heads the movement say she is "just a housewife," and her followers insist that once the testing stops, they will stay happily at home with their children? Even in the city strongholds of the big political party machines, women can—and are beginning to—change the insidious unwritten rules which let them do the political housework while the men make the decisions. When enough women make life plans geared to their real abilities, and speak out for maternity leaves or even maternity sabbaticals, professionally run nurseries, and the other changes in the rules that may be necessary, they will not have to sacrifice the right to honorable competition and contribution any more than they will have to sacrifice marriage and motherhood. It is wrong to keep spelling out unnecessary choices that make women unconsciously resist either commitment or motherhood—and that hold back recognition of the needed social changes. It is not a question of women having their cake and eating it, too. A woman is handicapped by her sex, and handicaps society, either by slavishly copying the pattern of man's advance in the professions, or by refusing to compete with man at all. But with the vision to make a new life plan of her own, she can fulfill a commitment to profession and politics, and to marriage and motherhood with equal seriousness.

Women who have done this, in spite of the dire warnings of the feminine mystique, are in a sense "mutations," the image of what the American woman can be. When they did not or could not work full time for a living, they spent part-time hours on work which truly interested them. Because time was of the essence, they often skipped the time-wasting, self-serving details of both housewifery and professional busywork.

Whether they knew it or not, they were following a life plan. They had their babies before or after internship, between fellowships. If good full-time help was not available in the children's early years, they gave up their jobs and took a part-time post that may not have paid handsomely, but kept them moving ahead in their profession. The teachers innovated in PTA, and substituted; the doctors took clinical or research jobs close to home; the editors and writers started freelancing. Even if the money they made was not needed for groceries or household help (and usually it was), they earned tangible proof of their ability to contribute.

They did not consider themselves "lucky" to be housewives; they competed in society. They knew that marriage and motherhood are an essential part of life, but not the whole of it.

These "mutations" suffered—and surmounted—the "cultural discontinuity in role conditioning," the "role crisis" and the identity crisis. They had problems, of course, tough ones—juggling their pregnancies, finding nurses and house-keepers, having to give up good assignments when their husbands were trans-ferred. They also had to take a lot of hostility from other women—and many had to live with the active resentment of their husbands. And, because of the mystique, many suffered unnecessary pains of guilt. It took, and still takes, ex-traordinary strength of purpose for women to pursue their own life plans when society does not expect it of them. However, unlike the trapped housewives whose problems multiply with the years, these women solved their problems and moved on. They resisted the mass persuasions and manipulations, and did not give up their own, often painful, values of the comforts of conformity. They did not retreat into privatism, but met the challenges of the real world. And they know quite surely now who they are.

Source: The Feminine Mystique. By Betty Friedan, 360–64. New York: Dell, 1963.

Betty Friedan (1921-) is a feminist author and lecturer.

Conservatism

Modern American conservatism developed in the postwar period as a counter to both the radical right and New Deal liberalism. For the immediate postwar pe-riod conservatives stressed what might be called fiscal conservatism while ac-cepting many of the reforms of the New Deal era. Later, conservatives actually expanded some of the New Deal programs. For example, Social Security grew more rapidly under Republican presidents (mostly under Richard Nixon [1913–94]) than under Democratic ones.

The most right wing of the conservatives galvanized around Barry Goldwater (1909-) and began to raise broader questions of social policy in addition to questions about fiscal policy. Also, the radical right pressured the conservatives to become more militantly anti-Communist, and a conservative position in for-eign policy developed that took an approach focused solely on the national in-terest as opposed to broader issues of human rights or regard for the interests of other countries.

The selection that follows is an extract from Milton Friedman's important book *Capitalism and Freedom* (1963). Friedman (1912-) argues that freedom is only possible under capitalism. Note that he uses the word "liberal" to describe his position. This illustrates the way that ideological words change over time.

The word "liberal" at the turn of the century in the United States described the free market capitalist position. It is still used in much that way in the United Kingdom. Also included is Goldwater's acceptance speech for the 1964 Republican nomination for president.

Milton Friedman
Capitalism and Freedom
The Relation between Economic Freedom and Political Freedom

It is widely believed that politics and economics are separate and largely unconnected; that individual freedom is a political problem and material welfare an economic problem; and that any kind of political arrangements can be combined with any kind of economic arrangements. The chief contemporary manifestation of this idea is the advocacy of "democratic socialism" by many who condemn out of hand the restrictions on individual freedom imposed by "totalitarian socialism" in Russia, and who are persuaded that it is possible for a country to adopt the essential features of Russian economic arrangements and yet to ensure individual freedom through political arrangements. The thesis of this chapter is that such a view is a delusion, that there is an intimate connection between economics and politics, that only certain combinations of political and economic arrangements are possible, and that in particular, a society which is socialist cannot also be democratic, in the sense of guaranteeing individual freedom.

Economic arrangements play a dual role in the promotion of a free society. On the one hand, freedom in economic arrangements is itself a component of freedom broadly understood, so economic freedom is an end in itself. In the second place, economic freedom is also an indispensable means toward the achievement of political freedom.

The first of these roles of economic freedom needs special emphasis because intellectuals in particular have a strong bias against regarding this aspect of freedom as important. They tend to express contempt for what they regard as material aspects of life, and to regard their own pursuit of allegedly higher values as on a different plane of significance and as deserving of special attention. For most citizens of the country, however, if not for the intellectual, the direct importance of economic freedom is at least comparable in significance to the indirect importance of economic freedom as a means to political freedom.

The citizen of Great Britain, who after World War II was not permitted to spend his vacation in the United States because of exchange control, was being deprived of an essential freedom no less than the citizen of the United States, who was denied the opportunity to spend his vacation in Russia because of his political views. The one was ostensibly an economic limitation on freedom and the other a political limitation, yet there is no essential difference between the two.

The citizen of the United States who is compelled by law to devote something like 10 per cent of his income to the purchase of a particular kind of retirement contract, administered by the government, is being deprived of a corresponding part of his personal freedom. How strongly this deprivation may be felt and its closeness to the deprivation of religious freedom, which all would regard as "civil" or "political" rather than "economic", were dramatized by an episode involving a group of farmers of the Amish sect. On grounds of principle, this group regarded compulsory federal old age programs as an infringement of their personal individual freedom and refused to pay taxes or accept benefits. As a result, some of their livestock were sold by auction in order to satisfy claims for social security levies. True, the number of citizens who regard compulsory old age insurance as a deprivation of freedom may be few, but the believer in freedom has never counted noses.

A citizen of the United States who under the laws of various states is not free to follow the occupation of his own choosing unless he can get a license for it, is likewise being deprived of an essential part of his freedom. So is the man who would like to exchange some of his goods with, say, a Swiss for a watch but is prevented from doing so by a quota. So also is the Californian who was thrown into jail for selling Alka Seltzer at a price below that set by the manufacturer under so-called "fair trade" laws. So also is the farmer who cannot grow the amount of wheat he wants. And so on. Clearly, economic freedom, in and of itself, is an extremely important part of total freedom.

Viewed as a means to the end of political freedom, economic arrangements are important because of their effect on the concentration or dispersion of power. The kind of economic organization that provides economic freedom directly, namely, competitive capitalism, also promotes political freedom because it separates economic power from political power and in this way enables the one to offset the other.

Historical evidence speaks with a single voice on the relation between political freedom and a free market. I know of no example in time or place of a society that has been marked by a large measure of political freedom, and that has not also used something comparable to a free market to organize the bulk of economic activity.

Source: Capitalism and Freedom. By Milton Friedman with the assistance of Rose D. Friedman. Chicago: University of Chicago Press, 1962.

Milton Friedman (1912-) won the Nobel Prize in Economics for his work in monetary theory. The best-known conservative economist in the United States, he taught economics at the University of Chicago for many years.

Barry Goldwater

Acceptance Speech at the 1964 Republican National Convention

We see, in private property and an economy based upon and fostering private property, the one way to make government a durable ally of the whole man, rather than his determined enemy. We see, in the sanctity of private property, the only durable foundation for Constitutional government in a free society.

And beyond that, we see and cherish diversity of ways, diversity of thoughts, of motives and accomplishments. We do no seek to live anyone's life for him— we seek only to secure his rights, guarantee him opportunity to strive, with government performing only those needed and Constitutionally-sanctioned tasks which cannot otherwise be performed.

We seek a government that attends to its inherent responsibilities of maintaining a stable monetary and fiscal climate—encouraging a free and competitive economy, and enforcing law and order.

Thus do we seek inventiveness, diversity, and creative difference within a stable order. For we Republicans define government's role, where needed, at *many* levels, preferably the one *closest* to the people involved.

Our towns and our cities, then our counties and states, then our regional compacts—and *only then* the national government! *That* is the ladder of liberty built by decentralized power. On it, also, we must have balance *between* branches of government at *every* level.

Balance, diversity, creative difference   *these* are the elements of the Republican equation. Republicans agree on these elements and they heartily agree to disagree on many, many of their applications.

This is a party for free men—*not* for blind followers and *not* for conformists.

In 1858, Lincoln said of the Republican Party that it was composed of "strange, discordant, and even hostile elements." Yet all of the elements agreed on one paramount objective—to arrest the progress of slavery and place it in the course of ultimate extinction.

Today as then, but more urgently and more broadly than then, the task of preserving and enlarging freedom at home, and of safeguarding it from the forces of tyranny abroad, is great enough to challenge *all* our resources and to require *all* our strength.

Any who join us in all sincerity, we welcome, Those who do not care for our cause we do not expect to enter our ranks in any case.

And let our Republicanism, so focused and so dedicated, not be made fuzzy and futile by unthinking labels.

Extremism in the defense of liberty is no vice. Moderation in the pursuit of justice is no virtue.

The beauty of the very system we Republicans are pledged to restore and revitalize, the beauty of this Federal system of ours, is in its reconciliation of diversity with unity. We must not see malice in honest differences of opinion, no matter how great, so long as they are not inconsistent with the pledges we have given to each other in and through the Constitution.

Our Republican cause is not to level out the world or make its people conform in computer-regimented sameness.

Our Republican cause is to free our people and light the way for liberty throughout the world.

Ours is a very human cause for very *humane* goals.

Source: *Where I Stand.* By Senator Barry Goldwater, 9–17. New York: McGraw-Hill, 1964.

Barry Goldwater (1909-) was a U.S. senator from Arizona (1952–64, 1969–87). He was the Republican candidate for president in 1964.

Reapportionment

One of the most important political issues at the very beginning of the Sixties might appear to be a technical matter, but in fact it reflected an early manifestation of the concern with equality that became a focus of the period. Reapportionment is the process mandated by the Constitution by which federal electoral districts are adjusted after each census to reflect population changes. But at both federal and state levels, this had been carried out in a way that protected rural interests against urban interests, and in favor of whites rather than African Americans. In *Reynolds* v. *Sims*, the Supreme Court mandated that the process be undertaken and undertaken fairly at both federal and state levels, the requirement for state action being based on the constitutional guarantee of a republican government in the states.

Reynolds v. *Sims*

Legislators represent people, not trees or acres. Legislators are elected by voters, not farms or cities or economic interests. As long as ours is a representative form of government, and our legislatures are those instruments of government elected directly by and directly representative of the people, the right to elect legislators in a free and unimpaired fashion is a bedrock of our political system. It could hardly be gain-said that a constitutional claim had been asserted by an allegation that certain otherwise qualified voters had been entirely prohibited from voting for members of their state legislature. And, if a State should provide that the votes of citizens in one part of the State should be given two times, or five times, or 10 times the weight of votes of citizens in another part of the State, it could hardly be contended that the right to vote of those residing in the disfavored areas had not been effectively diluted. It would appear extraordinary to suggest that a State could be constitutionally permitted to enact a law providing that certain of the State's voters could vote two, five, or 10 times for their legislative representatives, while voters living elsewhere could vote only once. And it is inconceivable that a state law to the effect that, in counting votes for legislators, the votes of citizens in one part of the State would be multiplied by two, five, or 10 while the votes of persons in another areas would be counted only at face value, could be constitutionally sustainable. Of course, the effect of legislating districting schemes which give the same number of representatives to unequal numbers of constituents is identical. Overweighting and overvaluation of the votes of those living here has the certain effect of dilution and undervaluation of the votes of those living there. The resulting discrimination against those individual voters living in disfavored areas is easily demonstrable mathematically. Their right to vote is simply not the same right to vote as that of those living in a favored part of the State. Two, five, or 10 of them must vote before the effect of their voting is equivalent to that of their favored neighbor. Weighting the votes of citizens differently, by any method or means, merely because of where they happen to reside, hardly seems justifiable. One must be ever aware that the Constitution forbids "sophisticated as well as simple-minded modes of discrimination."

Source: 377 U.S. (1964) 562.

CHAPTER 12

The Sixties and Beyond

✳ ✳ ✳

The Sixties is a label we use for the period from about 1965 to 1975. It was a time of great ferment in American political thought. Civil rights, the Vietnam War, and the growth of a new women's movement dominated the period. We think of it as the period of the left in American political thought, and it was. But the right was also alive and well. As a result, the Sixties gave birth to an ideological polarization that still affects the United States.

The roots of the Sixties are found in the Civil Rights Movement that developed after *Brown* v. *Board of Education* (1954), on the one hand, and a rejection of what was seen as the superficiality and materialism of contemporary American culture, exemplified initially by the Beatniks, on the other. The Civil Rights Movement gave rise to all the political movements of the Sixties and beyond — the antiwar movement, feminism, the gay movement, the movement for North American Indian rights, environmentalism, and so forth; the rejection of contemporary culture gave rise to the hippies, the communal movement, and the drug culture.

The fact that some people active in Sixties political movements are now active in movements identified with the right illustrates that there is a continuity of concern with the size and power of government common to both left and right, despite very obvious differences between their desired outcomes. The fundamental issues are similar to those that fueled Shays's Rebellion (1786–87), whose leaders wanted political power held at the local level because they believed that the corrupting nature of power needed to be kept in immediate check by citizens who knew the officeholders well. This is little different from the Sixties demand for "Power to the People" or the contemporary attacks on central government in the name of local control. The differences stem from the belief in the Sixties that decentralization would further an egalitarian agenda and the belief today that it would further a libertarian one. Throughout the entire period, the opposition to the New Left was based on the widely held belief, stretching back to the Depression and New Deal, that there are national problems that require national solutions coupled with the related belief that only a national government will be both willing and able to protect the interests of minorities from the majority, particularly local and regional majorities.

Beatniks

The late 1950s and early 1960s, a period then known for its apathy, was the breeding ground for the radicalism of the Sixties. Some people sought refuge in a search for new thrills and pleasure, while others found solace in Oriental religions, particularly Zen Buddhism.

The search for pleasure combined with Zen and existentialism to produce the Beatniks, who were the first dropouts and the immediate forebears of the hippies and the communal movement. The word *Beat* had its root in *beatific*, with its implications of rapture and its ties to religion, but the Beats were also intent on shocking the American public into a recognition that much was wrong in the country. *Howl* (1956) by Allen Ginsberg (1926–1997) is an example of this aspect of the Beats. *The Dharma Bums* (1958) by Jack Kerouac (1922–69) reflected the Beats' interest in Zen Buddhism. The Beat movement waned, but its ideas were picked up by the hippies, who gave them new and even more vital expression.

Amendments

Two amendments to the Constitution were passed in this period. The Twenty-fifth Amendment was the result of growing concern over the possible incapacity of the president. Historians have shown that Woodrow Wilson (1856–1924) had suffered a stroke that left him incapable of fulfilling his duties and that this had been covered up. More recently, Dwight Eisenhower (1890–1969) had a heart attack during his term, Lyndon Johnson (1908–73) had surgery, and Ronald Reagan (1911-) had surgery after an attempted assassination.

The Twenty-sixth Amendment was the result of a long battle brought on by the fact that thousands of people between the ages of eighteen and twenty-one were dying in Vietnam but did not have the right to vote.

Amendment XXV

February 10, 1967

Section 1. In case of the removal of the President from office or of his death or resignation, the Vice-President shall become President.

Section 2. Whenever there is a vacancy in the office of the Vice-President, the President shall nominate a Vice-President who shall take office upon confirmation by a majority vote of both Houses of Congress.

Section 3. Whenever the President transmits to the President pro tempore of the Senate and the Speaker of the House of Representatives his written declaration that he is unable to discharge the powers and duties of his office, and until he transmits to them a written declaration to the contrary, such powers and duties shall be discharged by the Vice-President as Acting President.

Section 4. Whenever the Vice-President and majority of either the principal officers of the executive departments or of such other body as Congress may by law provide, transmit to the President pro tempore of the Senate and the Speaker of the House of Representatives their written declaration that the President is unable to discharge the powers and duties of his office, the Vice President shall immediately assume the powers and duties of the office as Acting President.

Thereafter, when the President transmits to the President pro tempore of the Senate and the Speaker of the House of Representatives his written declaration that no inability exists, he shall resume the powers and duties of his office unless the Vice-President and a majority of either the principal officers of the executive department or of such other body as Congress may by law provide, transmit within four days to the President pro tempore of the Senate and the Speaker of the House of Representatives their written declaration that the President is unable to discharge the powers and duties of his office. Thereupon Congress shall decide the issue, assembling within forty-eight hours for that purpose if not in session. If the Congress, within twenty-one days after receipt of the latter written declaration, or, if Congress is not in session, within twenty-one days after Congress is required to assemble, determines by two-thirds vote of both Houses that the President is unable to discharge the powers and duties of his office, the Vice-President shall continue to discharge the same as Acting President; otherwise, the President shall resume the powers and duties of his office.

Amendment XXVI

July 5, 1971

Section 1. The right of citizens of the United States, who are eighteen years of age or older, to vote shall not be denied or abridged by the United States or by any State on account of age.

Section 2. The Congress shall have power to enforce this article by appropriate legislation.

The Antiwar Movement

The movement against the war in Vietnam brought about great stress within American society, from deep divisions within families to verbal and physical conflict across the country. The sides simply did not comprehend the position taken by their opponents. A famous document of the antiwar movement that tried to explain the position from the point of view of a family initially divided and then brought together by a son's antiwar activity was Charlotte E. Keyes's "Suppose They Gave a War and No One Came" (*McCall's*, October 1966). In this essay Keyes traced her son's gradually heightened antiwar activity and the family's difficulties understanding his position until, finally, they become convinced, supporting, and proud.

The New Left

Inspired by the Civil Rights Movement and worried about the war in Vietnam, a student movement developed on campuses in the northern United States.[1] Major student movements have been common in Europe, Latin America, and Asia, but the United States has not had many significant student movements. The Sixties student movements matured into the New Left, which rejected the internecine fighting and authoritarianism of what it thought of as the Old Left.

The U.S. student movement began as a broad-based, far-reaching movement concerned with equality, free speech, and participatory democracy, and it took a strong position against the war in Vietnam. The student movement became national in scope, but it also addressed issues on individual campuses. "The Movement," as it came to be called, argued for "Power to the People" in all settings, be they communities, schools, universities, or nations. Opposition was widespread both to the peaceful protests and to the violent activities that some of the antiwar groups sponsored.

During the Sixties the United States experienced a brief and, in comparison to a number of European countries, very mild period of violent political activity. In 1969 Students for a Democratic Society split into the Worker-Student Alliance and Revolutionary Youth Movement factions, a repetition of the internecine divisions of the Old Left. The Weather Underground (originally Weatherman, taken from Bob Dylan's line "You don't need a weatherman to know which way the wind blows") was founded in a further split from the Revolutionary Youth Movement. The Weather Underground saw itself as the vanguard of a revolutionary working class dedicated to overthrowing American imperialism abroad and eliminating the colonization of Black America internally. They set off bombs around the United States and participated in a number of other armed actions. Members of the Weather Underground were killed in an accidental explosion in a New York City apartment, and they, together with white students killed by the National Guard at Kent State University, Black students killed at Jackson State University, and a number of Black Panthers killed in encounters with the police, became martyrs to the New Left cause.

The U.S. student movement began to dwindle with the end of the war in Vietnam and the end of the draft. It was also affected by the growth of the women's movement and changes in the Civil Rights Movement. Blatant inequalities within the New Left affecting both African Americans and women eventually led both groups to reject the white male leadership of the New Left.

The best-known and most important document from the position of those supporting participatory democracy is the Port Huron Statement. It was drafted by members of Students for a Democratic Society (SDS) and provided the basis for the importance of SDS in the coming movement for social change.

Port Huron Statement

Human relationships should involve fraternity and honesty. Human interdependence is contemporary fact; human brotherhood must be willed, however, as a condition of future survival and as the most appropriate form of social relations. Personal links between man and man are needed, especially to go beyond the partial and fragmentary bonds of function that bind men only as worker to worker, employer to employee, teacher to student, American to Russian.

Loneliness, estrangement, isolation describe the vast distance between man and man today. These dominant tendencies cannot be overcome by better personnel management, nor by improved gadgets, but only when a love of man overcomes the idolatrous worship of things by man. As the individualism we affirm is not egoism, the selflessness we affirm is not self-elimination. On the contrary, we believe in generosity of a kind that imprints one's unique individual qualities in the relation to other men, and to all human activity. Further, to dislike isolation is not to favor the abolition of privacy; the latter differs from isolation in that it occurs or is abolished according to individual will.

We would replace power rooted in possession, privilege, or circumstance by power and uniqueness rooted in love, reflectiveness, reason, and creativity. As a *social system* we seek the establishment of a democracy of individual participation, governed by two central aims: that the individual share in those social decisions determining the quality and direction of his life; that society be organized to encourage independence in men and provide the media for their common participation.

In a participatory democracy, the political life would be based in several root principles:

> that decision-making of basic social consequence be carried on by public groupings;
> that politics be seen positively, as the art of collectively creating an acceptable pattern of social relations;
> that politics has the function of bringing people out of isolation and into community, thus being a necessary, though not sufficient, means of finding meaning in personal life;
> that the political order should serve to clarify problems in a way instrumental to their solution; it should provide outlets for the expression of personal grievance and aspiration; opposing views should be organized so as to illuminate choices and facilitate the attainment of goals; channels should be commonly available to relate men to knowledge and to power so that private problems—from bad recreation facilities to personal alienation—are formulated as general issues.

The economic sphere would have as its basis the principles:

> that work should involve incentives worthier than money or survival. It should be educative, not stultifying; creative, not mechanical; self-directed, not manipulated, encouraging independence, a respect for others, a sense of dignity and a willingness to accept social responsibility, since it is this experience that has crucial influence on habits, perceptions and individual ethics;
> that the economic experience is so personally decisive that the individual must share in its full determination;
> that the economy itself is of such social importance that its major resources and means of production should be open to democratic participation and subject to democratic social regulation.

Like the political and economic ones, major social institutions—cultural, educational, rehabilitative, and others—should be generally organized with the well-being and dignity of man as the essential measure of success.

In social change or interchange, we find violence to be abhorrent because it requires generally the transformation of the target, be it a human being or a community of people, into a depersonalized object of hate. It is imperative that the means of violence be abolished and the institutions—local, national, international—that encourage nonviolence as a condition of conflict be developed.

These are our central values, in skeletal form. It remains vital to understand their denial or attainment in the context of the modern world.

Source: Students for a Democratic Society, *Port Huron Statement* (1962).

The Communal Movement

During the Sixties many people chose a lifestyle that has a long history in the United States, but which many people erroneously thought had disappeared.[2] Life in an intentional community (called communes, communitarian experiments, and utopian societies, among other things) reflected the desire of many people to create the improved future society now rather than to wait for the hoped-for revolution. Others believed that no revolution would be forthcoming; therefore, it only made sense to withdraw from the corrupt contemporary society to build a new and better way of living. Yet others saw the communes, particularly those in the cities, as a tool of revolution, safe houses into which it was possible to disappear to avoid the attentions of the police or a place to rest and recover after periods of intense action. Thus, intentional communities varied according to the purposes they served.

The major divisions among the communities were urban versus rural, religious versus secular, permanent versus temporary, and activist versus dropout. The ones that were most likely to survive, and many have, were rural, religious, permanent, and dropout, although a few urban and a number of secular communities still exist that were founded in the Sixties or earlier. None of the current members would describe themselves as dropouts. They have created a satisfying life separate from the society they rejected.

The Civil Rights Movement

The Sixties increasing radicalism within the Civil Rights Movement, along with the growing national recognition that the country did, indeed, have a problem. Radical African Americans and their supporters argued that the United States was racist to the core and incapable of reform. They compared the United States to colonial regimes in Africa and Asia because they saw the segregation of the South and the ghettoes of the North as forms of internal colonialism, and they argued that colonial regimes could only be changed through revolution. But as with so many other radicals, they found that relatively few of the oppressed were ready to follow them into the uncertainties of armed revolt. Thus, three other modes of response developed—the raising of Black consciousness, the development of Black Power, and Black nationalism or separatism.

Black consciousness. One of the most important slogans to come out of the period was "Black is Beautiful." In American culture black has often been the symbol of evil and ugliness. The notion that "Black is Beautiful" was an important step toward a feeling of self-worth. To be taught that skin color is a mark of inferiority degrades a person. As long as whiteness remained the goal, the African American suffered the worst kind of alienation—hatred of self. Black consciousness and the positive valuation of blackness was an important part of the personal reevaluation that African Americans had to go through before serious change could take place in this country. Today Afrocentrism and the label "African American" play somewhat the same role by allowing African Americans to identify themselves with the rich cultures of Africa that are part of their heritage.

Black power. The idea behind Black Power is the notion that people should control their own destinies. People should have effective political and economic control within their own community. This means that the community should control the educational system, including the content of the education, and that communities should contain businesses, banks, and credit unions run by and for the people of the community. Police should be from the community, and people from the community should be on police boards. And, of course, there should be community political representation. These are all fairly standard American demands, but when "community" was replaced by the word "Black" or "African-American" the stance became radical and objectionable to many whites.

Black nationalism. The tenth point of the Black Panther Party Platform reads "We want land, bread, housing, education, clothing, justice and peace." For a time the Nation of Islam successfully established communities within American cities that were effectively separate from the rest of society, but there have been few other successful attempts at separatism and, of course, no separate nation.

Stokely Carmichael and Charles V. Hamilton
Black Power

Whether one is talking about the fantastic changes taking place in Africa, Asia or the black communities of America, it is necessary to realize that the current, turbulent period in history is characterized by the demands of previously oppressed peoples to be free of their oppression. Those demands will not be quieted by guns or soft talk; those demands have a logic of their own—a logic frequently misunderstood by the oppressors.

Black and colored peoples are saying in a clear voice that they intend to determine for themselves the kinds of political, social and economic systems they will live under. Of necessity, this means that the existing systems of the dominant, oppressive group—the entire spectrum of values, beliefs, traditions and institutions—will have to be challenged and changed. It is not to be expected that this fundamental scrutiny will be led by those who benefit or even have expectations of benefit from the status quo.

We are calling at this time for new political forms which will be the link between broadened participation (now occurring) and legitimate government. These forms will provide a means whereby a newly politicized people can get what they need from the government. It is not enough to add more and more people to the voter rolls and then send them into the old "do-nothing," compromise-oriented political parties. Those new voters will only become frustrated and alienated. This country can continue to appropriate money for programs to be run by the same kinds of insensitive people with paternalistic, Anglo-conformity attitudes and the programs will continue to fail. They should fail, because they do not have the confidence and trust of the masses. In order to gain that confidence and trust, the people must be much more involved in the formulation and implementation of policy. Black people are indeed saying: "Mr Charlie, we'd rather do it ourselves." And in doing it themselves, they will be developing the *habit* of participation, the *consciousness* of ability to achieve, and the experience and wisdom to govern. Only this can ultimately create a viable body politic. It is not enough that shiny new school buildings be built in the ghettos, if the black people whose children attend them basically feel no attachment to those schools. Learning will not take place.

Source: Black Power: The Politics of Liberation in America. By Stokely Carmichael and Charles V. Hamilton. New York: Vintage Books, 1967.

Stokely Carmichael (1941-) is now known as Kwame Touré and lives in Africa. In the United States he was a civil rights activist and organizer. He was one of the leaders of the Student Nonviolent Coordinating Committee (SNCC), later renamed the Student National Coordinating Committee when it changed tactics.

Charles V. Hamilton (1929-) is Wallace S. Sayre Professor of Government at Columbia University and one of the most prominent African-American academics in the United States.

October 1966 Black Panther Party Platform and Program What We Want What We Believe

1. *We want freedom. We want power to* determine the destiny *of our Black Community.* . . .

2. *We want* full employment *for our people.* . . .

3. *We want an* end to the robbery *by the white man of our Black Community.* . . .

4. *We want decent housing, fit for shelter of human beings.* . . .

5. *We want education for our people that exposes the true nature of this decadent American society.* . . .

6. *We want all black men to be exempt from military service.* . . .

7. *We want an immediate end to* POLICE BRUTALITY *and* MURDER *of black people.* . . .

8. *We want freedom for all black men held in federal, state, county and city prisons and jails.* . . .

9. *We want all black people when brought to trial to be tried in court by a jury of their peer group or people from their black communities, as defined by the Constitution of the United States.* . . .

10. *We want land, bread, housing, education, clothing, justice and peace. And as our major political objective, a United Nations supervised plebiscite to be held throughout the black colony in which only black colonial subjects will be allowed to participate, for the purpose of determining the will of black people as to their national destiny.* . . .

Source: *The Black Panthers Speak.* Edited by Philip S. Foner. Philadelphia: J. B. Lippincott, 1970.

Anarchism

The rejection of the dominant modes of life in America led to a resurgence of the long anarchist tradition in American political thought, but it also demonstrated the deep divide within American anarchism between anarcho-capitalism and community-based anarchism. The mentor for most anarcho-capitalists was Ayn Rand (born Alissa Rosenbaum; 1905–82), whose novel *Atlas Shrugged* (1957) was an essential text in the contemporary redevelopment of anarcho-capitalism. A more philosophical defense was developed by Robert Nozick (1938-) in *Anarchy, State, and Utopia* (1974), which was immensely influential on business and government leaders.

In the period from the Sixties to the present, the most respected spokesperson for community-based anarchism has been Murray Bookchin (1921-), who is also a major figure in the environmental movement. Bookchin's *Post-Scarcity Anarchism* (1971) was the most important contribution to anarchist thought of the period. Most recently he has been involved in a debate with environmental groups such as Earth First!, founded by Dave Foreman (1946-), who treat humans as a problem within the environment rather than a part of it.

Feminism

Feminism has both made great strides and suffered significant setbacks in the recent past. The defeat of the Equal Rights Amendment convinced many that America was not ready for even modest change, and the continuing conflict over abortion has deeply divided the country. At the same time, women are accepted in many more roles than ever before in the United States, and feminist political theory has developed significantly on a number of different fronts. What follows is the Equal Rights Amendment in its entirety.

Equal Rights Amendment

Section 1. Equality of Rights under the law shall not be denied by the United States or by any State on account of sex.
Section 2. The Congress shall have the power to enforce, by appropriate legislation, the provisions of this article.
Section 3. This amendment shall take effect two years after the ratification.

*　*　*

With the defeat of the amendment, the feminist movement lost some of its momentum. Although more explicitly feminist political theory is being published today than at any time in the past and more women occupy positions of power and authority in all aspects of American life, there is uncertainty about which way the movement should proceed. One particular concern has been the position of African-American and other minority women in American society. Minority groups have often accused the women's movement of being a white women's movement—and even a middle-class white women's movement—and it is clear that the advances made by women in the last decades have had the least impact on minority women.

Indians

The Sixties saw the beginnings of a reassertion of Indian rights, as evidenced by the following selection, which refers to both old and new grievances against the government of the United States. This selection also makes it clear that the Indians are reasserting their rights under treaties signed by the U.S. government and the Indian tribes as sovereign nations not bound by U.S. law.

Declaration of Continuing Independence of the First International Indian Treaty Council at Standing Rock Sioux Indian Country

Preamble

The United States of America has continually violated the independent Native Peoples of this continent by Executive action, Legislative fiat, and Judicial decision. By its actions, the U.S. has denied all Native People their International Treaty Rights, treaty lands, and basic human rights of freedom and sovereignty. This same U.S. Government which fought to throw off the yoke of oppression and gain its own independence has now reversed its role and become the oppressor of sovereign Native People.

Might does not make right. Sovereign people of varying cultures have the absolute right to live in harmony with Mother Earth so long as they do not infringe upon this same right of other peoples. The denial of this right to any sovereign people, such as the Native American Indian Nations, must be challenged by **truth** and **action**. World concern must focus on all colonial governments to the end that sovereign people everywhere shall live as they choose, in peace with dignity and freedom.

The International Indian Treaty Conference hereby adopts this Declaration of Continuing Independence of the Sovereign Native American Indian Nations. In the course of these human events, we call upon the people of the world to support this struggle for our sovereign rights and our treaty rights. We pledge our assistance to all other sovereign people who seek their own independence.

The first International Treaty Council of the Western Hemisphere was formed on the land of the Standing Rock Sioux Tribe on June 8–16, 1974. The delegates, meeting under the guidance of the Great Spirit, represented 97 Indian tribes and nations from across North and South America.

We, the sovereign Native Peoples recognize that all lands belonging to the various Native Nations are clearly defined by the sacred treaties solemnly entered into between the Native Nations and the government of the United States of America.

We, the sovereign Native Peoples charge the United States of America with gross violations of our International Treaties. Two of the thousands of violations that can be cited are the "wrongfully taking" of the Black Hills from the Great Sioux Nation under the Fort Laramie Treaty of 1868. The second violation was the forced march of the Cherokee People from the ancestral lands in the State of Georgia to the then "Indian Territory" of Oklahoma after the Supreme Court of the United States rules the Cherokee treaty rights inviolate. The treaty violations, known as "The Trail of Tears," brought death to 2/3 of the Cherokee Nation during the forced march.

The Council further realizes that securing United States recognition of treaties signed with Native Nations requires a committed and unified struggle, using every available legal and political resource. Treaties between sovereign nations explicitly entails agreements which represent "the supreme law of the land" binding each party to an inviolate international relationship.

We acknowledge the historical fact that Independence of the People of our sacred Mother Earth have always been over sovereignty of land. These historical freedom efforts have always involved the highest human sacrifice.

We recognize that all Native Nations wish to avoid violence, but we also recognize that the United States Government has always used force and violence to deny Native Peoples basic human and treaty rights.

We adopt this Declaration of Continuing Independence, recognizing that struggle lies ahead, a struggle certain to be won, and that the human and treaty rights of all Native Nations will be honored. In this understanding, the International Indian Treaty Council declares:

We the representatives of sovereign Native Nations unite in forming a council to be know as the International Indian Treaty Council to implement these declarations.

The International Indian Treaty Council will establish offices in Washington, D.C., and New York City to approach the international forces necessary to obtain the recognition of our treaties. These offices will establish an initial system of communications among Native Nations to disseminate information, getting a general consensus concerning issues, developments, and any legislative attempts affecting Native Nations by the United States of America.

The International Indian Treaty Council recognizes the sovereignty of all Native Nations and will stand in unity to support our Native and international brothers and sisters in their respective and collective struggles concerning international treaties and agreements violated by the United States and other governments.

All treaties between the Sovereign Native Nations and the United States Government must be interpreted according to the traditional and spiritual ways of the signatory Native Nations.

We declare our recognition of the Provisional Government of the Independent Oglala Nation, established by the Traditional Chiefs and Headmen under the provisions of the 1868 Ft. Laramie Treaty with the Great Sioux Nation at Wounded Knee Mar 11, 1973.

We condemn the United States of America for its gross violation of the 1868 Fort Laramie Treaty in militarily surrounding, killing and starving the citizens of the Independent Oglala Nation into exile.

We demand the United States of American recognize the sovereignty of the Independent Oglala Nation and immediately stop all present and future criminal prosecutions of sovereign Native Peoples. We call upon the conscionable nations of the world to join us in charging and prosecuting the United States of America for its genocidal practices against the Sovereign Native Nations, most recently illustrated by Wounded Knee, 1973, and the continued refusal by the United States of America to sign the United Nations 1948 Treaty on Genocide.

We reject all executive orders, legislative acts and judicial decisions related to Native Nations since 1871, when the United States unilaterally suspended treaty-making relations with Native Nations. This includes, but is not limited to, the Major Crimes Act, the General Allotment Act, the Citizenship Act of 1924, the Indian Reorganization Act of 1934, the Indian Claims Commission Act, Public Law 280, and the Termination Act. All treaties between Native Nations and the United States made prior to 1871 shall be recognized without further need of interpretation.

We hereby ally ourselves with the colonized Puerto Rican People in their struggle for Independence from the same United States of America.

We recognize that there is only one color of Mankind in the world who are not represented in the United Nations. And that is the indigenous Redman of the Western Hemisphere. We recognize this lack of representation in the United Nations comes from the genocidal policies of the colonial power of the United States.

The International Indian Treaty Council established by this conference is directed to make application to the United Nations for recognition and membership of the sovereign Native Nations. We pledge our support to any similar application by any aboriginal people.

This conference directs the Treaty Council to open negotiations with the Government of the United States through its Department of State. We seek these negotiations in order to establish diplomatic relations with the United States. When these diplomatic relations have been established, the first order of business shall be to deal with U.S. violations of treaties with the Native Indian Nations, and violations of the rights of those native Indian Nations who have refused to sign treaties with the United States.

We, the People of the International Indian Treaty Council, following the guidance of our elders through instructions from the Great Spirit, and out of respect for our sacred Mother Earth, all her children and those yet unborn, offer our lives for our International Treaty Rights.

June, 16, 1974

Source: Akwesasne Notes 6 (1974).

The Green Movement

The most innovative recent development in political theory has been in environmentalism, which is asking new questions about the relationship between humanity and the world we inhabit. These questions focus on the rights of nature versus the rights of human beings and, less radically, on what is due future generations. The selection that follows is a general statement by Murray Bookchin.

Murray Bookchin
An Ecological Society

Today, we have a magnificent repertoire of new ideas, plans, technological designs, and working data that can give us a graphic picture of an ecological community and a participatory democracy. Valuable as these materials may be in demonstrating that we can finally build sustainable communities based on renewable resources, they should not be seen simply as new systems of engineering society into a balanced relationship with a given natural environment.

They also have far-reaching *ethical implications* that can only be ignored by fostering an eco-technocratic mentality toward so-called appropriate technologies, a term that is too ambiguous to be used in a larger ecological context of ideas.

An ecological society, structured around a confederal Commune of communes, each of which is shaped to conform with the ecosystem and bioregion in which it is located, would deploy this ensemble of technologies in an artistic way. It would make use of local resources, many of which have been abandoned because of mass production techniques. . . .

It is not too fanciful to suppose that an ecological society would ultimately consist of moderately sized municipalities, each a commune of smaller household communes or private dwellings that would be delicately attuned to the natural ecosystem in which it is located. The wisdom of living communally or individually is an issue that can only be left to decisions made by future generations, individual by individual, just as it is made today.

Source: Remaking Society. By Murray Bookchin. Montreal: Black Rose, 1989.

Murray Bookchin (1921-) is a major anarchist theorist who has recently been a major contributor to environmentalism in the United States.

Neo-Luddites

In the early nineteenth century a number of workers destroyed textile machinery because they believed that use of the machinery would take away their jobs. They were named Luddites after Ned Lud or Ludd, a workman who had broken up stocking frames in 1779. Today there are groups of people who are being called neo-Luddites because they oppose the effects of the modern economic and industrial system on the lives of individuals and the environment. Although the overwhelming majority of these people are nonviolent, undoubtedly the best known is the so-called Unabomber, who set off a number of bombs around the United States that targeted people in industry and academia. The introduction to the Unabomber Manifesto follows.

Unabomber's Manifesto
INTRODUCTION

1. The Industrial Revolution and its consequences have been a disaster for the human race. They have greatly increased the life-expectancy of those of us who live in "advanced" countries, but they have destabilized society, have made life unfulfilling, have subjected human beings to indignities, have led to widespread psychological suffering (in the Third World to physical suffering as well) and have inflicted severe damage on the natural world. The continued development of technology will worsen the situation. It will certainly subject human beings to greater indignities and inflict greater damage on the natural world, it will probably lead to greater social disruption and psychological suffering, and it may lead to increased physical suffering even in "advanced" countries.

2. The industrial-technological system may survive or it may break down. If it survives, it MAY eventually achieve a low level of physical and psychological suffering, but only after passing through a long and very painful period of adjustment and only at the cost of permanently reducing human beings and many other living organisms to engineered products and mere cogs in the social machine. Furthermore, if the system survives, the consequences will be inevitable: There is no way of reforming or modifying the system so as to prevent it from depriving people of dignity and autonomy.

3. If the system breaks down the consequences will still be very painful. But the bigger the system grows the more disastrous the results of its breakdown will be, so if it is to break down it had best break down sooner rather than later.

4. We therefore advocate a revolution against the industrial system. This revolution may or may not make use of violence: it may be sudden or it may be a relatively gradual process spanning a few decades. We can't predict any of that. But we do outline in a very general way the measures that those who hate the industrial system should take in order to prepare the way for a revolution against that form of society. This is not to be a POLITICAL revolution. Its object will be to overthrow not governments but the economic and technological basis of the present society.

Source: http://www.hotwired.com/special/unabom/list.html

Notes

1. The following sections are based on my *New Left Thought: An Introduction* (Homewood, Ill.: Dorsey Press, 1972).

2. For evidence regarding the continuity of American communalism, see Robert S. Fogarty, *All Things New: American Communes and Utopian Movements, 1860–1914* (Chicago: University of Chicago Press, 1990); and Timothy Miller, *American Communes 1860–1960: A Bibliography* (New York: Garland, 1990).